Making the Middle Republic

During the fourth and third centuries BCE, Roman expansion into Italy reshaped the peninsula's Archaic societies and prompted new political relationships, new economic practices, and new sociocultural structures. Rural landscapes and urban spaces throughout Latium saw intensified use amidst novel principles of land management, animal husbandry, and architectural design. This book offers fresh perspectives on these transformations by embracing a wide range of approaches to Middle Republican history. Chapters take up topics and methods ranging from fiscal sociology, bioarchaeology, comparative slaveries, and field surveys to art and architectural history, numismatics, elite mobility, and beyond. An emphasis is placed on how developments in this period reshaped not only Rome, but also other Latin and Italian societies in complex and often multilinear ways. The volume promotes the Middle Republic as a period whose full dynamism is best appreciated at the intersection of diverse lines of inquiry.

SETH BERNARD is Associate Professor of Roman History in the Department of Classics at the University of Toronto. His work focuses on the social and economic history of Rome and Italy, particularly during the Republican period. He is the author of *Building Mid-Republican Rome: Labor, Architecture, and the Urban Economy* (2018).

LISA MARIE MIGNONE is a research affiliate at New York University Institute for the Study of the Ancient World. Her research examines Roman social, cultural, and religious geographies: the ongoing and interactive relationship of historical events, the sites in which they occur, and the people who perform them. She is the author of *The Republican Aventine and Rome's Social Order* (2016).

DAN-EL PADILLA PERALTA is Associate Professor of Classics, and associated faculty in African American Studies, at Princeton University. His main lines of research are Roman Republican religious and cultural history, the history of slavery, and classicisms in the Afro-Atlantic diaspora. He is the author of *Divine Institutions: Religions and Community in the Middle Roman Republic* (2020).

Making the Middle Republic

New Approaches to Rome and Italy,
c.400–200 BCE

Edited by

SETH BERNARD
University of Toronto

LISA MARIE MIGNONE
New York University

DAN-EL PADILLA PERALTA
Princeton University

Shaftesbury Road, Cambridge CB2 8EA, United Kingdom

One Liberty Plaza, 20th Floor, New York, NY 10006, USA

477 Williamstown Road, Port Melbourne, VIC 3207, Australia

314–321, 3rd Floor, Plot 3, Splendor Forum, Jasola District Centre, New Delhi – 110025, India

103 Penang Road, #05–06/07, Visioncrest Commercial, Singapore 238467

Cambridge University Press is part of Cambridge University Press & Assessment, a department of the University of Cambridge.

We share the University's mission to contribute to society through the pursuit of education, learning and research at the highest international levels of excellence.

www.cambridge.org
Information on this title: www.cambridge.org/9781009327992

DOI: 10.1017/9781009327978

© Cambridge University Press & Assessment 2023

This publication is in copyright. Subject to statutory exception and to the provisions of relevant collective licensing agreements, no reproduction of any part may take place without the written permission of Cambridge University Press & Assessment.

First published 2023
First paperback edition 2025

A catalogue record for this publication is available from the British Library

ISBN   978-1-009-32798-5   Hardback
ISBN   978-1-009-32799-2   Paperback

Cambridge University Press & Assessment has no responsibility for the persistence or accuracy of URLs for external or third-party internet websites referred to in this publication and does not guarantee that any content on such websites is, or will remain, accurate or appropriate.

Contents

List of Figures [*page* vii]
List of Tables [ix]
List of Charts [xi]
List of Contributors [xiii]
Acknowledgments [xvi]
Maps [xviii]

1 Introduction: A Middle in the Making [1]
SETH BERNARD, LISA MIGNONE, AND DAN-EL PADILLA PERALTA

PART I HISTORICAL SOURCES [17]

2 Italian Descent in Middle Republican Roman Magistrates: The Flipside of the Conquest [19]
PARRISH WRIGHT AND NICOLA TERRENATO

3 The Long Shadow of *Tributum* in the Long Fourth Century [38]
JAMES TAN

4 Paying for Conquest in the Early Middle Republic [64]
NATHAN ROSENSTEIN

5 Building up Slaveries in Ancient Italy and the Central Sudan [80]
WALTER SCHEIDEL

PART II MATERIAL SOURCES [101]

6 The Strangeness of Rome's Early Heavy Bronze Coinage [103]
LIV MARIAH YARROW

7 Rural Transformations in Middle Republican Central Italy: An Archaeological Perspective [132]
TYMON DE HAAS

8 Towards an Agroecology of the Roman Expansion:
Republican Agriculture and Animal Husbandry in
Context [164]
ANGELA TRENTACOSTE AND LISA LODWICK

PART III   ARCHITECTURE AND ART   [191]

9 No Longer Archaic, Not Yet Hellenistic: Urbanism in
Transition [193]
DOMENICO PALOMBI

10 On Architecture's Agency in Fourth-Century
Rome [210]
PENELOPE J. E. DAVIES

11 Becoming Historical in Oscan Campania [230]
SETH BERNARD

Conclusion [251]

12 Becoming Political: Middle Republican
Quandaries [253]
CHRISTOPHER SMITH

Bibliography [270]
Index [331]

Figures

7.1 The sociopolitical landscape of Central Tyrrhenian Italy in the late fourth century. Drawn by the author. [*page* 133]
7.2 Selected survey areas from the SES, Suburbium Project, and PRP surveys. Areas marked by transparent boxes are additional survey areas of the three projects that are not considered here. For a key to the symbols, see Figure 7.1. Drawn by the author. [140]
7.3 Land-division systems hypothetically ascribed to the fourth and early third centuries BCE. Drawn by the author. [150]
7.4 Reconstruction of the main and secondary canals of the Pontine centuriation in relation to natural streams and rivers. Drawn by the author. [152]
8.1 Map of the study areas. Drawn by the authors. [168]
9.1 Rome, buildings and monuments between fourth and first centuries, after Palombi 2010. [195]
9.2 Signia and Cora after Cifarelli 2017; Palombi 2003. [200]
9.3 The *fora* of Tusculum and Fregellae, after Dupré and Aquilué Abadías 2002; Lackner 2008. [203]
9.4 Ardea and Civita di Artena after Morselli and Tortorici 1982; Quilici 1982. [206]
9.5 Gabii and Norba after Mogetta 2014; Quilici Gigli 2019. [207]
9.6 Greek mythical origins of the cities of the *Latium vetus*, after Palombi 2019b. [208]
10.1 Temple of Castor, phase I, reconstruction c.496 BCE. Drawn by John Burge. [213]
10.2 Forum Romanum and environs, plan, c.337–218 BCE. Drawn by Penelope J. E. Davies and Onur Öztürk. [214]
10.3 Rostra, reconstruction with ships' prows, c. 338 BCE. Drawn by John Burge. [216]
10.4 Map of Rome, c. 337–218 BCE. Drawn by Penelope Davies and Onur Öztürk. [217]

10.5 Cyma reversa molding, Temple C, Largo Argentina, third century BCE, actual state. Photo by the author.   [218]

10.6 Temple plans showing interaxials. Drawn by Penelope Davies and Onur Öztürk.   [218]

10.7 Sarcophagus chest, c.350–300 BCE. Rome, Musei Capitolini, Centrale Montemartini. Photo by the author.   [219]

10.8 Sarcophagus of Scipio Barbatus, c.280 BCE. Vatican Museums. Photo by the author.   [220]

10.9 Temple of Castor, reconstruction c. mid-second century BCE. Drawn by John Burge.   [226]

10.10 Denarii with reverse images of the Temple of Jupiter Optimus Maximus. Left: denarius minted by M. Volteius in 75 BCE. Courtesy of Roma Numismatics Ltd (www.romanumismatics.com). Right: denarius minted by Petillius Capitolinus in 41 BCE. Courtesy of the Classical Numismatic Group (www.cngcoins.com).   [227]

11.1 Andriuolo necropolis, Paestum, Tomb 12A. The return of the warrior, 380–370 BCE. Image © Parco Archeologico di Paestum e Velia/Ministero della Cultura.   [237]

11.2 Cumae, painted slab from a tomb, Benassai 2001 no. Cu.13, c.300 BCE. Drawing by author modified from Benassai 2001.   [238]

11.3 Andriuolo necropolis, Paestum, Tomb 114, north wall. Battle scene, 330–320 BCE. Image © Parco Archeologico di Paestum e Velia/Ministero della Cultura.   [241]

11.4 Spinazzo necropolis, Paestum, Tomb 1, back wall. Older male individual, c.320–300 BCE. Image © Parco Archeologico di Paestum e Velia/Ministero della Cultura.   [246]

Tables

2.1 Grouping of consular families. [*page* 29]
2.2 Patrician families of presumed foreign origin, after Bourdin 2012: 543–4. [30]
4.1 Distribution by age of Roman males, Model West 3 Female, in 340 BCE. Prepared by the author. [68]
6.1 Overview of denominations and types. [108]
6.2 Comparison of *CRRO* and Haeberlin weights for *RRC* 14/1 by denomination. [113]
6.3 Comparison of *CRRO* and Haeberlin mean and median weights for *RRC* 14/1 by denomination, standardized by denomination. [119]
6.4 Summary of typical weight ranges of *RRC* 14 denominations as observed using histograms (Charts 6.3–4). [120]
6.5 Summary of possible typical full unit weight ranges for *RRC* 14/1 and the fit with each denomination. [120]
6.6 Comparison of *CRRO* and Haeberlin weights for *RRC* 18/1 by denomination. [122]
6.7 Comparison of *CRRO* and Haeberlin mean and median weights for *RRC* 18/1 by denomination, standardized by denomination. [123]
6.8 Summary of typical weight ranges of *RRC* 18 denominations as observed using histograms (cf. Chart 6.8). [125]
6.9 Summary of typical weight ranges of *RRC* 14 and 18 denominations compared (cf. Tables 6.4 and 6.8). [128]
7.1 Summary of published settlement data from the Suburbium Project, the Tiber Valley Project, and the Pontine Region Project. [138]
7.2 Land-division systems ascribed to the later fourth/early third centuries. [149]
7.3 Quantification of the volume of main and secondary canals within the Pontine centuriation. [153]

7.4 Minimum labor-cost estimates, assuming 1.5 person-hour per excavated m^3 of soil, 10-hour workdays, and 220 workdays per year (cf. Turner 2018). [154]

7.5 Maximum labor-cost estimates, assuming 2.2 person-hour per excavated m^3 of soil, 10-hour workdays, and 220 workdays per year (cf. Turner 2018). [155]

8.1 Regional and chronological distribution of assemblages/site phases considered in this study. [170]

Charts

2.1 Consulships held by *gens* (366–265 BCE). Based on data from the Digital Prosopography of the Roman Republic. [*page* 27]
2.2 Chronological distribution of new clans attaining high office, after Forsythe 2005: 164. [27]
2.3 Number of families per mobility type. [34]
2.4 Number of consulships held per mobility type. [35]
4.1 Duration of campaigns resulting in triumphs, 370–290 BCE. [70]
6.1 A–B: Relative standard deviations (A) and relative interquartile ranges (B) of *RRC* 14 weights as reported in *CRRO* and Haeberlin. [115]
6.2 Relative mean absolute deviations of *RRC* 14 weights as reported in *CRRO* and Haeberlin. [115]
6.3 Ten-bin (A) and twenty-bin (B) histograms of the *RRC* 14 as based on Haeberlin. [116]
6.4 Histograms of *semis* through *uncia* for *RRC* 14 based on Haeberlin. [118]
6.5 Comparisons of *RRC* 14 and 18 as reported in *CRRO* and Haeberlin showing (A) relative standard deviations and (B) relative interquartile ranges. [124]
6.6 Comparison of *RRC* 14 and 18 as reported in *CRRO* and Haeberlin showing relative mean absolute deviations. [125]
6.7 Mean weights by denomination as reported by Haeberlin (A) and *CRRO* (B). [126]
6.8 Histograms of *as* through *uncia* for *RRC* 18 based on Haeberlin. [127]
6.9 Box and whisker chart showing Haeberlin weights for *RRC* 18 and *RRC* 14 with fractional denominations given as their full pound equivalents. [130]
7.1 Settlement trends in different parts of Central Tyrrhenian Italy. [141]

7.2 Size of late fourth-/third-century farm sites in the lower Pontine plain. [145]
8.1 Frequency of cereals, pulses, fruits, and wild plant foods throughout first-millennium-BCE Italy, by subperiod. [174]
8.2 Frequency of cereals, pulses, fruits, and wild plant foods throughout first-millennium-BCE Italy, by major region. [175]
8.3 Livestock representation on sites in Central Italy. Figures show the relative percentages of the main types of livestock (cattle, sheep/goat, pig) for different sites. [179]
8.4 Relative percentages of pig bones from sites in Central Tyrrhenian Italy. Ordered chronologically from the tenth to second centuries BCE. Numerals indicate century BCE. [181]
8.5 Livestock representation on sites in Southern Italy. Figures show the relative percentages of the main types of livestock (cattle, sheep/goat, pig) for different sites. [182]
8.6 Livestock representation on sites in Northern Italy. Figures show the relative percentages of the main types of livestock (cattle, sheep/goat, pig) for different sites. [184]

Contributors

Seth Bernard is Associate Professor of Roman History in the Department of Classics at the University of Toronto. His work focuses on the social and economic history of Rome and Italy, particularly during the Republican period.

Penelope J. E. Davies is Professor of Art History at the University of Texas at Austin, and Hedda Andersson Professor in Classical Archaeology at Lund University. Specializing in Roman architectural history, she is author of *Death and the Emperor* (Cambridge University Press, 2000) and *Architecture and Politics in Republican Rome* (Cambridge University Press, 2017).

Tymon de Haas is Assistant Professor in Classical and Mediterranean Archaeology at the University of Groningen and guest researcher at Leiden University. His research concerns the landscape, environment, and economy of the Italian peninsula, with a focus on Early Roman Central Italy. He is codirector of the Pontine Region Project.

Lisa Lodwick (1988–2022) was a postdoctoral research fellow at All Souls College, University of Oxford, and was recently appointed to the University Lecturership in Environmental Archaeology at Cambridge. Her publications include the coauthored volume *The Rural Economy of Roman Britain* (Society for the Promotion of Roman Studies, 2017). Her research focused on agricultural practices in the later prehistoric and Roman period and the utilization of archaeobotanical data to investigate human–plant relationships.Lisa was also an energetic supporter of women and of diversity in academia, of early career researchers, and of the importance of the open access agenda.

Lisa Marie Mignone is a research affiliate at New York University's Institute for the Study of the Ancient World. Her research examines Roman social, cultural, and religious geography: the ongoing and interactive relationship of historical events, the sites in which they occur, and the people who perform them.

Dan-el Padilla Peralta is Associate Professor of Classics, and associated faculty in African American Studies, at Princeton University. His main lines of research are Roman Republican religious and cultural history, the history of slavery, and classicisms in the Afro-Atlantic diaspora.

Domenico Palombi is Associate Professor of Classical Archaeology at the Department of Sciences of Antiquity of Sapienza – University of Rome. He studies the urban history of ancient Rome, the architecture and urbanism of *Latium vetus*, the memory of the Antique and the history of Roman archaeology between Roma Capitale and the Fascist regime.

Nathan Rosenstein is Emeritus Professor of History at The Ohio State University. He is the author or coeditor of a number of books, most recently *Rome and the Mediterranean, 290–146 BC: The Imperial Republic* (Edinburgh University Press, 2012). He is currently editor of the Republic volumes of the Oxford History of the Roman World.

Walter Scheidel is Dickason Professor in the Humanities and Professor of Classics and History at Stanford University. His work ranges from ancient social and economic history and premodern historical demography to the comparative and transdisciplinary world history of labor, inequality, state formation, and human welfare.

Christopher Smith is Professor of Ancient History at the University of St Andrews. From 2009 to 2017 he was Director of the British School at Rome. His publications include *Roma medio repubblicana: Dalla conquista di Veio alla battaglia di Zama* (Edizioni Quasar, 2020, coedited with R. Volpe, A. D'Alessio, and M. Serlorenzi).

James Tan is a Lecturer in Classics and Ancient History at the University of Sydney. He is the author of *Power and Public Finance at Rome (264–49 BCE)* (Oxford University Press, 2017).

Nicola Terrenato is the Van Deman Collegiate Professor of Roman Studies and the director of the Kelsey Museum at the University of Michigan. His research focuses on Early Rome, the Roman conquest, and the formation of states and empires. He recently published *Early Roman Expansion* (Cambridge University Press, 2019; winner, 2021 Wiseman Book Award).

Angela Trentacoste is a postdoctoral researcher at the University of Oxford and Humboldt Fellow at the Christian-Albrecht University of Kiel. Her research focuses on animal economies and social change in the late prehistoric and Roman Mediterranean. Her recent publications include the coedited volume *The Economy of Roman Religion* (Oxford University Press, 2023).

Parrish Elizabeth Wright is an Assistant Professor of Classics at the University of South Carolina. Her research centers on the history and archaeology of pre-Roman and Roman Italy. Using both textual and material evidence, she studies how groups use myth to articulate identity and build connections throughout the Mediterranean.

Liv Mariah Yarrow is Professor at the City University of New York, in Classics at Brooklyn College, and in Classics and History at the Graduate Center. Her books include *Historiography at the End of the Republic: Provincial Perspectives on Roman Rule* (Oxford, 2006) and *The Republic to 49 BCE: Using Coins as Sources* (Cambridge, 2021).

Acknowledgments

This volume roared to life at a conference held at Princeton University in May 2019, "The Roman Republic in the Long Fourth Century." We thank the sponsors, whose lavish generosity supported several days and evenings of animated discussion: the Princeton University Department of Classics, the Humanities Council, the Department of Art and Archaeology, the Program in the Ancient World, the Seeger Center for Hellenic Studies, the Princeton Institute for International and Regional Studies, the Center for Collaborative History, the Princeton Environmental Institute, and the University Center for Human Values. University of Toronto participants were additionally supported by a Social Sciences and Humanities Research Council Insight Development Grant from the Government of Canada.

The conference generated convivial debate and disagreement, thanks in no small part to presentations that do not appear in this volume. We are delighted to express our gratitude to the participants in our graduate student poster session: Drew Davis ("Ex pequnia publica: Municipal finances and public building, 200 BCE–14 CE"), Jordan Rogers ("Making neighborhoods, making places: The case of the Vicus Tuscus"), Rebecca Salem ("6th and 5th century sacred architectural foundations: Norba, Pyrgi, Rome, Satricum, and Segni"), Scarlett Strauss ("Depictions of painted pottery in Tarquinian tomb frescoes"), and Keegan Valbuena ("A Roman water world: Temples vowed to water deities, 260–231 BCE"). We are also grateful to those participants who delivered papers, either in person or in absentia, that are not published in these pages: Jackie Elliott ("Person and perspective: Cato's *Origines* and earlier traditions of self-representation and -commemoration at Rome"), Tim Cornell ("Timaeus and the Romans"), Kristina Killgrove ("Bioarchaeology of the Roman Republic"), Saskia Roselaar ("The spoils of war? Changes in patterns of land tenure in the 4th and 3rd centuries"), Francesco de Angelis ("Rome and the visual cultures of central Italy: For an aesthetic history of the 4th century"), Kathryn Lomas ("Coinages in 4th-century SE Italy: Strategies for representing cultural identity between Greek, Roman and Italian"), and

Carlos Noreña ("Legislation, sovereignty, and territoriality in the early Roman Republic").

Our session presiders were instrumental in facilitating the flow of conversation: Many thanks to Harriet Flower, John North Hopkins, Caroline Cheung, and Denis Feeney. Sarah Johnson's live-tweeting of the proceedings under the #C4Rome hashtag preserved a *monumentum aere perennius* of the papers themselves and the lively back-and-forth that ensued. Certainly, the conference could not have unfolded as smoothly as it did without the logistical and budgeting wizardry of Nancy Blaustein and Eileen Robinson, who ensured that we were all lodged and fed.

Moving a volume to publication in the pandemic end-times – and in the midst of a global paper shortage – has been nothing short of a herculean effort. We thank Michael Sharp for welcoming our manuscript, and Cambridge University Press's two anonymous readers for their perceptive reports. Claudia Paparella ably took up the task of formatting the manuscript and preparing the index.

The coeditors would like to dedicate this volume to their children, four of whom were not yet in this world when the idea to organize a conference first sank its teeth into us. (Email subject line, March 13, 2018: "Why are we not doing a conference?")

Maps

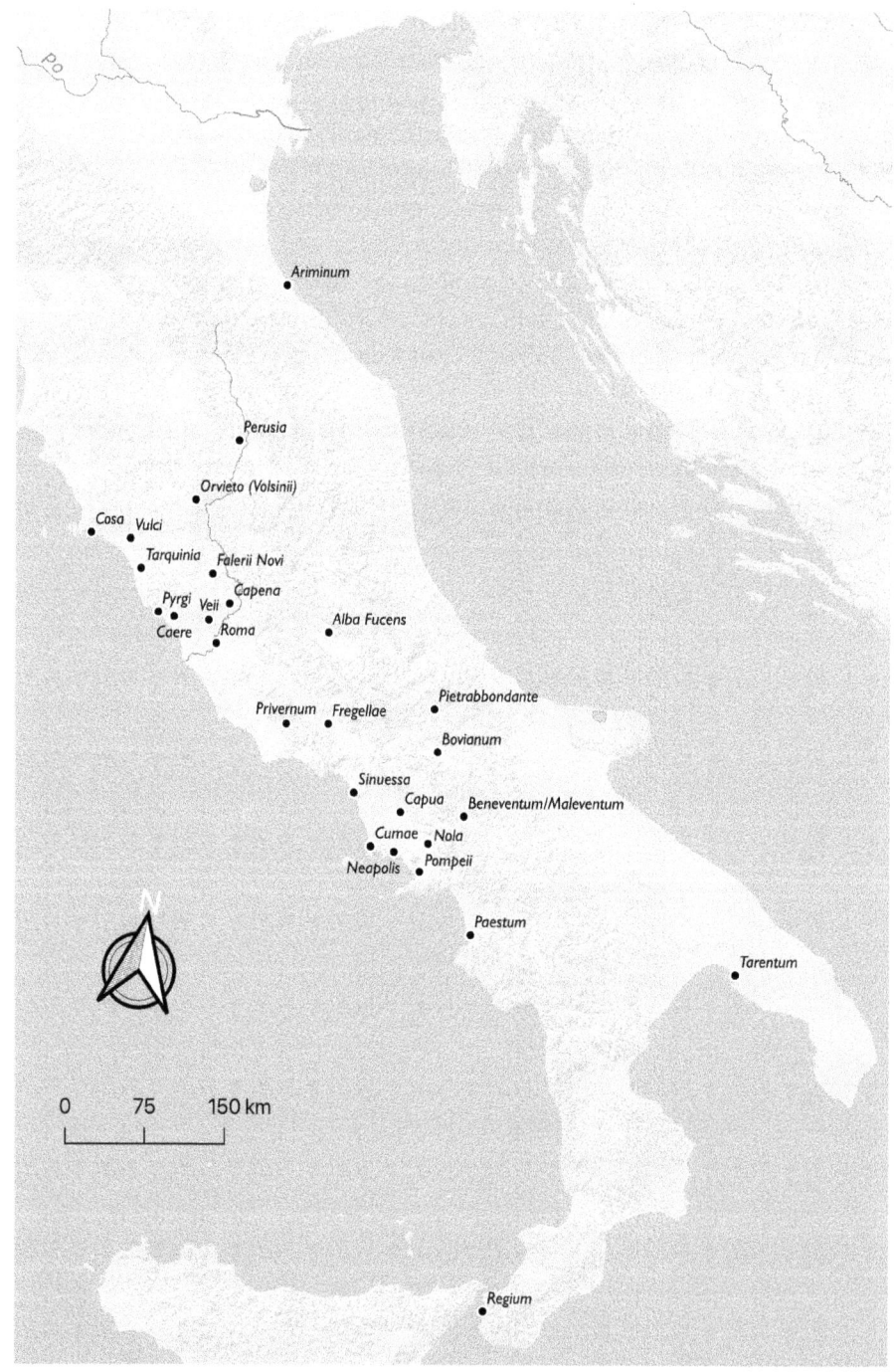

1 Italy, with location of sites named in the text. Drawn by Seth Bernard.

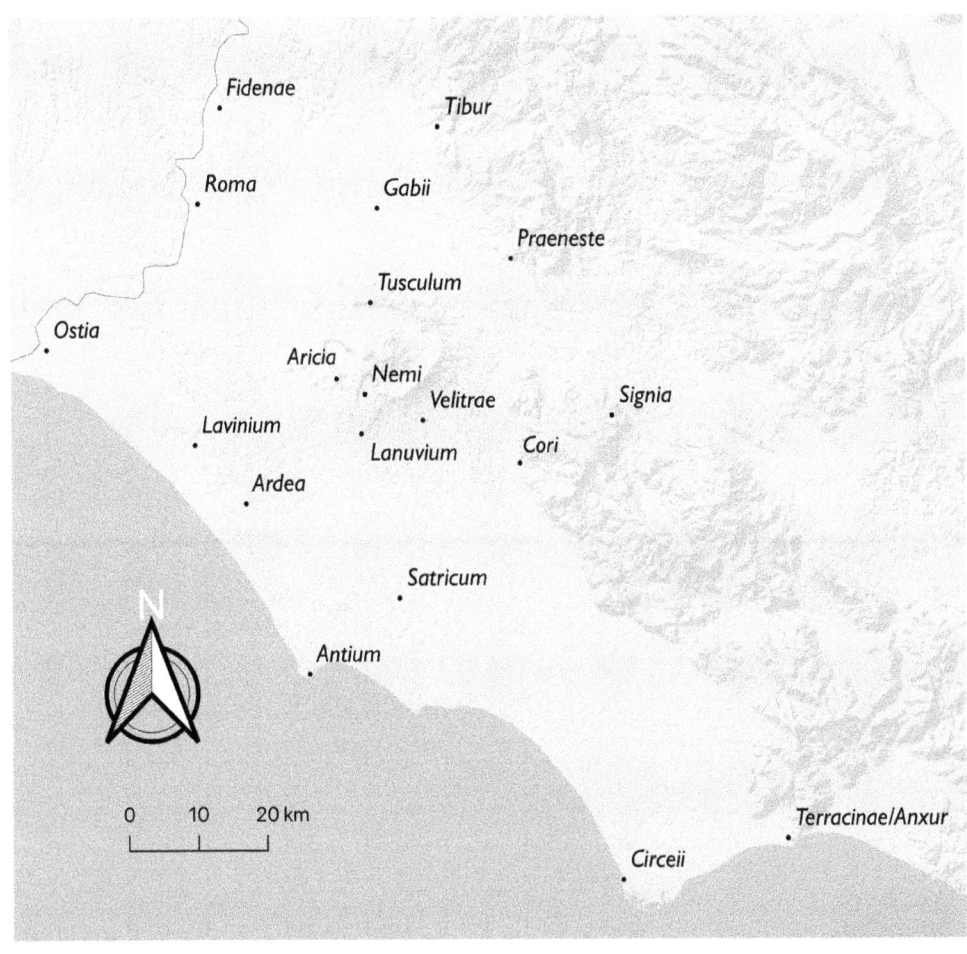

2 Latium, with location of sites named in the text. Drawn by Seth Bernard.

1 | Introduction

A Middle in the Making

SETH BERNARD, LISA MIGNONE, AND DAN-EL PADILLA PERALTA

The word "making" in this book's title embraces two meanings. On the one hand, the essays in this volume hold to the conviction that many of the characteristic structures and institutions of later Roman Republican society emerged in some form during the fourth and third centuries BCE. This was a consequential period for Rome's imperial relationship to Italy, as well as for its own internal political structures: as the "struggle of the orders," which dominates our record of Roman politics in the previous century, began to resolve, the newly emergent patricio-plebeian leadership would direct its energies to the conquest of Latium, Campania, and then other regions further afield.[1] In turn, these transformations in some cases sparked, and in other cases accelerated, developments of great importance to the subsequent construction of later Republican society and the formation of its wider Mediterranean Empire. Yet our title also flags the fact that the tripartite terminology frequently employed to frame this period as "Middle" Republican Roman history – following the end of the monarchy and the Early Republic, and preceding the overseas expansion and civil war of the Late Republic – is an entirely modern convention. The retrospective nature of this division is true both in the specific sense that a "Middle" Republican period never appears as such in ancient sources and in the more generic sense that periodization is always to some extent "intrinsically and inevitably anachronistic."[2] As a means of organizing and informing the study of the Roman past, the Middle Republic is quite literally what we make (of) it.

How does this volume understand the Middle Republican period? In current scholarly parlance, the epoch appears commonly enough as a sort of objectively bounded (if not always uniformly defined) chronological period, normally comprising the fourth and third centuries BCE.[3]

---

[1] The contributions in Raaflaub 2005 [1986] on the Archaic social struggles that have come to be known in modern scholarship as the Struggle of the Orders remain essential.
[2] Flower 2010: 6.
[3] The next few paragraphs condense an argument for conceiving of the period as an internal unity that is set out in greater length in Padilla Peralta and Bernard 2022.

From ceramic typologies to lists of magisterial colleges, various classes of evidence are anchored in time with shorthand reference to the "Middle Republic." Like all epistemological systems, however, this periodization has its own history, and we start by considering some dimensions of its modern use.

Though already making the rounds in the nineteenth century, the idea of a distinct "Middle Republican" Rome took off following its appearance in the title of an epoch-making 1973 exhibition, "Roma medio repubblicana." In the preface to the exhibition's catalog, reprinted for wider circulation in 1977, Coarelli argued that Roman developments between the Late Archaic period and the Late Republic formed a discrete unit of inquiry. For him, the key to distinguishing this period lay in the acknowledgment of considerable originality, visible above all in the period's material culture, which the exhibition sought to assemble and present. This insight stood in contrast to previous opinion, which had tended to see Roman art and culture in this period as underdeveloped in contrast to the contemporary world of Greece. Indeed, the move to promote a "Middle Republican" period at that time may be connected to coeval debates about whether concepts of Hellenization in particular could be appropriately applied to the Italian situation. Just one year before the appearance of the catalog to *Roma medio repubblicana*, Zanker's *Hellenismus in Mittelitalien* (1976) initiated vigorous debate over the relevance to Rome and Italy of the concept of "Hellenism" and the cognate periodization of "Hellenistic" with its own complex and ambiguous history. The conclusions of a recent edited volume on the "Hellenistic West" seem relevant here: While the Western and Central Mediterranean in the fourth and third centuries BCE proffer a seemingly unified appearance to historical inquiry, any uniformity is not because these regions had much to do in a direct manner with the exploits of Alexander and his successors; something distinct was taking place within them. It is not heuristically helpful simply to invoke "Hellenization."[4]

The contributors to the 1977 exhibition catalog were very much interested in using the "Middle Republic" to bracket a turn in Central Italy's material culture. In the wake of the volume, however, its more general sense that the "Middle Republic" was a dynamic period came to inform other lines of inquiry into Middle Republican history, from internal politics and external relations to the parameters of central Italian urbanism and beyond.[5] We strongly agree with Coarelli's insistence that the Roman

---

[4] Prag and Crawley Quinn eds. 2013: 13.

[5] See, for example, Eckstein 1987 on foreign relations (the title of which drops the "Middle Republic" that appeared in the dissertation on which the book is based); the essays in *Roma tra*

Middle Republic was not simply a period of time, but a discrete epoch in the development of Roman Italy that deserves study as such. The question that follows is one of definition: How do we delineate the limits, and specify the contents, of this period of inquiry?

One promising path forward is to rely on chronological boundaries for Roman political and military events. Contrary to the belief in some circles that this path yields "unobjectionable" periods that are organized around "apparently simple criteria,"[6] matters are by no means so straightforward. Coarelli staked the beginning of his Middle Republic to the capture of Veii in 396 BCE, or perhaps the Licinio-Sextian Laws of 367 BCE. But already in antiquity, attempts to divide Republican history according to major turning points proliferated; as start-points for the Middle Republic, the Decemvirate or the Gallic Sack come readily to mind, and many more could be added. At the other end, Polybius' idea that the First Punic war marked a sea change (literally) in the nature of Roman imperialism has anchored the use of 264 BCE as the end of "the beginning of Rome" in modern scholarship from Beloch to Cornell and Leigh.[7] The tools of modern historical research only complicate and blur these dividing lines. Take the Gallic Sack as one example: According to the annalists, the sudden incursion of Gauls over the Apennines overwhelmed the Romans at the Allia and subsequently resulted in the city itself being set ablaze. These were epochal events in the eyes of our historical sources.[8] Yet recent genetic work on Celtic burial sites in the Po Valley suggests that the arrival of transalpine Gauls into Italy was continuous, with Gallic populations arriving for different reasons at different times, and even sometimes intermarrying or otherwise adopting local Italian cultural practices.[9] It is not impossible to reconcile this slower spread with the sudden invasion of Latium reported by our sources, but their history of events conceals (if it does not actively distort) a considerably more complex and multifaceted process.

---

oligarchia e democrazia 1988; Ziolkowski 1992; Feig Vishnia 1996; the essays in Bruun ed. 2000; Valentini 2012.

[6] We quote Toohey 2005: 15, in a discussion of literary periodization.
[7] Polyb. 1.6.1; Beloch 1926; Cornell 1995 and Leigh 2010.
[8] Livy 6.1.2 calls Rome's rebuilding after the Gallic Sack Rome's second origin. The original display of the *Fasti Capitolini* may have centered the two tablets that encompass the years 390 to 154: see the discussion of Elisabeth Nedergaard's reconstruction in Russell 2019: 169–70. For the event and its archaeology, see already Williams 2001; archaeological work at the oppidum of Monte Bibele and nearby sites (see next note) has revealed considerable detail about the Gauls in Italy over the two decades since that book's publication.
[9] Scheeres et al. 2013; Sorrentino et al. 2018. This process had implications for, inter alia, shifts in Roman weaponry: see now Taylor 2020a. For Celtic-Etruscan interactions note also Lejars 2020.

Armed with information of this sort, we may critique particular turning points as only imperfectly registering trajectories of historical change; and we may pivot to the many other possibilities for marking the boundaries of our Middle Republic. Instead, however, we wish to make the broader point that the very multiplicity and blurriness of plausible divisions and periodizations hold meaning in themselves. The inconsistencies that accompany efforts to mark the temporal, political, and social edges of the Roman Middle Republic arise ultimately from the sorts of history (or histories) that scholarship has tended to exemplify and showcase. It is a testament to the period's generativity of boundary markers that this volume's chapters employ a variety of temporal rubrics, in some cases reaching back as far as the Twelve Tables, in other instances encompassing events or evidence up to the outbreak of the Second Punic War against Hannibal. This variety in and of itself should be seen as intentional.[10] Although this volume as a whole argues for a Middle Republican period that forms a coherent unit of historical inquiry, this unit is not necessarily one that can be neatly encapsulated between two major political or military events, much less tidy dates. What we envision instead is a rich and complex period whose most important developments ranged across various timescales and time spans, and throughout all precincts of Roman and Italian life.

In this regard, a primary motivation for the initial 2019 conference at which this volume began to take shape was the identification of those multiple axes along which the changes of the Middle Republican period could be best tracked. Taking the rubric of the "long fourth century" as one of our organizing principles,[11] we had observed at the time that research in a host of different fields, not all necessarily concerned with the Middle Republic per se, was prompting scholars to engage with the period, with the result that they were pointing out a startling variety of significant and arguably convergent processes. At the regional and peninsular level, it is becoming increasingly clear that the stabilization of Rome's *nobilitas* in the aftermath of the Licinio-Sextian Laws moved in tandem both with changes

---

[10] Not in the sense of Foxhall, Gehrke, and Luraghi eds. 2010, although Purcell 2003b's sketch – an inspiration for the chapters of both Bernard and Smith in this volume (Chapters 11 and 12) – of the coming-together of political self-consciousness and temporal conceptualization during our period has suggestive affinities with the "intentional history" paradigm.

[11] The notion of a "long fourth century" has gained momentum in the years since the conference: one panel of the 2021 annual meeting of the European Association of Archaeologists applied the notion to South Italy (with its call for papers crediting Purcell 1994 for inspiration); now Helm 2021 unrolls its account of the Roman expansion "im langen 4. Jahrhundert v. Chr." The "long" century as a historiographical building block: Padilla Peralta and Bernard 2022: 7–8; on polemics for and against centuries and decades as rubrics note Schulman 2021.

to other Italian aristocratic groups and with the role that Italy's elites played at Rome itself.[12] Shifts in settlement patterns in Central Italy become all the more compelling when set against trends in regional ecology and the bioarchaeological data; the vicissitudes of urban development in Latium and Tyrrhenian Italy help illuminate the growth of Rome itself as an urban center; the rising demand for enslaved persons in Roman society interacts with and amplifies structural alterations in the nature and complexion of war-making over the course of the period; and so forth. By placing our Middle Republican period at the intersection of these and other various axes, we seek to promote a big-tent approach to Middle Republican history. Attention to that intersection's properties will, it is hoped, lead to new avenues of inquiry even beyond those collected in this volume. Therefore, one of our core aims is to encourage further work that moves from recognition of the Middle Republic's importance to growing confidence in the application of wide-ranging tools to its study.

Since this volume is committed to exploring the value of innovative methodologies to Middle Republican Rome and Italy, it is worth reflecting briefly on what work has so far been done and what material exists to support the application of new approaches. In both directions, our sounding of current scholarship returns encouraging results. As signaled above, the use of "Middle Republic" in the study of Roman antiquity was popularized by the 1973 Italian exhibition on "Roma medio repubblicana" and the subsequent 1977 catalog, which advanced a new assessment of the period's material culture. This focus on material culture has sharpened considerably in recent years with a number of important new publications of archaeological finds from fourth- and third-century Central Italy. To mark the fortieth anniversary of the exhibition catalog, a conference was held in Rome in 2017. The two resulting volumes offer an enormous amount of new material for subsequent study.[13] Additionally, there has been a proliferation of interest within Italian archaeology in regional studies, accompanied by a burgeoning bibliography.[14]

---

[12] This synchronized movement is coming to the forefront in studies of Italic political structures: see Lanfranchi 2021 on magistracies.

[13] Cifarelli, Gatti, and Palombi eds. 2019; D'Alessio, Smith and Volpe eds. 2021; see also Acconcia ed. 2020.

[14] For example Bradley 2001 and Sisani 2007 on Umbria; Isayev 2007 on Lucania; Colivicchi ed. 2011 and Neudecker ed. 2011 on Southern Italy; Carpenter, Lynch, and Robinson eds. 2014 on Apulia; Scopacasa 2015 on Samnium; Govi ed. 2014 and Pulcinelli 2016 on North and South Etruria, respectively; Vermeulen 2017 on Picenum; Roncaglia 2018 on the Po Valley; Di Fazio 2020 on the Volsci.

With respect to more traditionally historical approaches, the lion's share of work on Middle Republican Rome continues to focus on political history and the idea of political culture.[15] This is understandable enough, as the Licinio-Sextian Laws have long been conceived of as ushering in a period of major political transformation at Rome, in which the previous "struggle of the orders" yielded to new patricio-plebeian leadership over successive generations down through the time of Appius Claudius Caecus.[16] Research into the structures of this Middle Republican ruling class continues with great energy, including both empirical work on magistracies such as the praetorship, consulship, the plebeian tribuneship, and quaestorship,[17] and more theoretical work that situates the Roman *nobilitas* within research on the typologies and attributes of sociopolitical elites.[18] As this latter research (under the guidance of Hölkeskamp and others) now starts to focus on the symbolic systems by which the *nobilitas* constructed their political power, material culture has moved to the forefront.[19] Thus, we find efforts underway to align some of the long-standing historical approaches within the field with the outpouring of new archaeological evidence. If previous collections of volumes on Middle Republican history might be criticized for giving only a passing glance to the material record, in more recent work this is less and less true.[20]

The turn to material culture is especially welcome because the field of Middle Republican political history has traditionally relied on a charitable assessment of the ancient literary sources. This reliance, often trailed by serious anxieties about the non-contemporary literary record's authenticity, has opened up both specific events and the arena of Middle

---

[15] Hölkeskamp 2011 [1987]; 2010; and now 2020. Hölkeskamp 2019's review essay is a first-rate orientation to the field's most recent trends. For trenchant discussion of the limitations of Hölkeskamp's approach, see Richlin 2021.

[16] Accessible and well-resourced introduction: Cornell 1995; for Appius Claudius' role, see Humm 2005. Here we note too that the ancient historical record itself prioritizes these political themes, alongside military ones, and thus has framed and privileged this sort of inquiry.

[17] Praetorship: Brennan 2000. Consulship: Pina Polo 2011; Beck et al. 2011. Plebeian tribuneship: Smith 2012; Meunier 2011 and 2014; Russell 2015; Lanfranchi 2015 and 2021; for other components of plebeian political organization note Taylor 2018 on centurions. Quaestorship: Pina Polo and Díaz Fernández 2019. But a "souveräne Gesamtdarstellung" of the political-institutional order has yet to be written: Hölkeskamp 2019: 25.

[18] Beck 2005; Fisher and van Wees eds. 2015; Stein-Hölkeskamp and Hölkeskamp 2018; Hölkeskamp 2020. For comparatively premised research into the emergence of Rome's patrician–plebeian elite, note for example Rosenstein 2010a.

[19] Hölkeskamp 2010 and 2020.

[20] Thus, archaeology plays only a minimal role in Raaflaub 2005 [1986], Eder 1990, or Mineo and Piel eds. 2014, but starts to find more room in Bruun 2000. Most recently, Cifarelli, Gatti, and Palombi eds. 2019 and D'Alessio, Smith, and Volpe eds. 2021 reverse course entirely by incorporating select historical contributions into otherwise archaeological discussions.

Republican politics as a whole to source-critical attacks.[21] At times, debates about the veracity of the tradition, or about its literary qualities, have dominated discussion and inhibited thinking about historical structures and processes. The authors in this volume make no claim to unravel this Gordian knot. Perhaps we might note optimistically that the Middle Republic was closer to the living memory of Fabius Pictor and his contemporaries, and that recent efforts have shed considerable light on those mechanisms by which Romans transmitted their past outside of historiographical channels.[22] Nevertheless, the issue often continues to resemble one of faith: The contributors to this volume approach the record of Middle Republican Rome with varying degrees of fidelity.

Long-standing dilemmas about the sources for this period and their interpretation are unlikely ever to be definitively resolved by new material. Instead, what the situation calls for is expansion and inclusion, both in terms of the evidence and methods we employ and in terms of the questions we ask. When applied to source narratives, theoretical or comparative frameworks help refine our expectations and identify the limits of the possible. We are encouraged, following Gabba's advice, not to use the increasingly copious archaeological data simply to verify or falsify the narrative of the sources, since a more rigorous application of this material to our histories of the period will require adopting archaeology's own intrinsic methodologies.[23] There is no question that continuing engagement with these methodologies will force the refinement and, in some cases perhaps, even the overhaul of some of this volume's conclusions. But as new approaches open up novel and unexpected directions, we remain convinced that these contributions will stand up as demonstrations of the Middle Republic's broad-ranging import and of its merits as a standalone unit of historical analysis.

This volume maps out this expansion in our making of the Middle Republic with ten contributions divided into three sections. The first suite of chapters concentrates on approaches employing, and in some cases rereading, the **Historical Sources (Part I)**. The aim of these chapters is to reinvigorate traditional subjects of historical inquiry, such as the composition of the Middle Republican ruling elite and their social and economic foundations, with the aid of fresh approaches.

---

[21] For example, Millar 1989; Forsythe 2005: ch. 3.
[22] Thus, the situation with regard to the sources seems different from Early Rome, as see Wiseman 2008: 15; otherwise, note the important exposition of the sources of annalist history in the opening volume of Oakley 1997–2005; Sandberg and Smith eds. 2018; there is much valuable thinking on this theme in Purcell 2003b.
[23] Gabba 1993: 22; see now Padilla Peralta and Bernard 2022: 9–11 and *passim*.

In the first chapter in this Part (Chapter 2), Parrish Wright and Nicola Terrenato argue for a greater presence of Italian elites among the Roman *nobilitas* than previously assumed. Although elite horizontal mobility has long been considered a defining feature of Archaic Central Italian society, their study suggests it continued into the Middle Republic, as prominent Italian families strove to obtain Rome's highest political office. In Chapter 3, James Tan then turns from the identities of office-holders to the nature of state power, and in particular to the topic of Republican fiscality, largely overlooked since Nicolet's work a half-century ago.[24] As Tan notes, one of the most regular actions taken by Roman citizens in this early period was likely to have been that of paying taxes. It is possible, however, that the arch importance of early fiscal institutions like *tributum* and *stipendium* has been obscured by their unfamiliarity to later sources that were better versed in an entirely different fiscal system. The narrative that Tan reconstructs thus reads against the familiar, Livian grain and offers a hypothetical, if plausible and necessary, reconstruction of Middle Republican fiscality. Tan draws inspiration from theories of fiscal sociology in rereading our sources and restores taxation to its central place in Middle Republican history. Next, Nathan Rosenstein's chapter (Chapter 4) continues this exploration of fiscal history with particular regard to warmaking, a fixture of the period. The transformation of Roman fighting technologies around this time was enormously consequential, even if many of the finer details of such changes are ultimately irrecoverable. Instead of tackling old and probably insoluble questions about the timing of manipular warfare's emergence,[25] Rosenstein focuses on logistics, beginning with the Roman army's ever-expanding theater of operations in Central Italy. The longer and more distant campaigning upon which Rome embarked starting in the late 340s BCE posed all sorts of new problems in terms of resource provision. The old system by which the army largely paid for its own activities through raiding no longer sufficed, and transformations were needed across the entire supply chain.

It seems reasonable to connect the pressures of changing warfare to changes in those systems of *tributum* and *stipendium* – those state-level institutions of income and expenditure that sustained Rome's early drive to empire – at the core of Chapter 3. Another theme related to this cluster of changes in the period was slavery. The human spoils of war, combined with the increasing need to ramp up production to feed the army, shaped both the supply and demand for enslaved labor. Walter Scheidel's chapter

---

[24] Nicolet 1976. [25] The newest entrant in the conversation: Taylor 2020b.

(Chapter 5) takes up this topic, which still remains undervalued in assessments of the period's historical importance. This underappreciation stems partly from the nature of the evidence, which gestures to the numbers of enslaved persons in Roman hands by our period's end but inhibits any sort of quantified or otherwise detailed understanding of how this came to be. Much of the archaeological evidence, and particularly those signs of large slave-staffed villas in Tyrrhenian Italy that correspond directly to Rome's slave economy, are later in date.[26] Scheidel probes this disconnect between signs of an enormous, if unquantifiable, ramping up of slaveholding and a somewhat delayed increase in the evidence of agricultural estates. From where did all of these slaves come and, most importantly, where did they go? To answer these questions, he pursues a comparison between the emergence of the Middle Republican Roman state and the rise of the Sokoto Caliphate in sub-Saharan Africa in the early years of the nineteenth century, building on a proposal first floated in 2012.[27] While mass enslavement through war played a fundamental part in the political economy of this West African state, whose rapid rise went hand in hand with the capture and trafficking of hundreds of thousands of individuals, it is the nature of their exploitation that invites comparison to Middle Republican Central Italy: large numbers of enslaved people were sold domestically and, in due course, came to form an important social class.

The implications of this group of papers for the period's history do not always run in the same direction – and that is to be welcomed. It is the aim of this volume to present a plurality of approaches and considerations rather than to write a single, systematized historical narrative. Thus none of the papers pretends to be the final word. For Tan and Rosenstein (Chapters 3 and 4), taxation becomes a driver of socioeconomic transformation, first helping to integrate the Roman political community and then serving to spur development; the need to pay for ever more costly warfare will have motivated the intensification of agricultural production, sometimes with the very persons enslaved through Roman war-making, producing a sort of positive feedback loop. By contrast, Scheidel suggests that taxation rates in this period were low, at least in a broad historical perspective, and that demand for domestic slaves initially drove Roman slave-taking. Only at a later date, after the slave supply had increased

---

[26] The evidence for the late development of villas in Italy is set out in Terrenato 2012 and 2019; but there is at least indirect evidence from our period for intensification of the production of wine and oil in bulk, associated with later slave villas, as see Panella 2010.

[27] Scheidel 2012. See Roth 2013a for application of a model first developed for the study of sub-Saharan Africa (Igor Kopytoff's "internal frontier") to Hellenistic South Central Italy.

significantly, did enslaved labor become a factor in the intensification of agricultural production. As he notes, the state of the evidence means that we suffer from "profound ignorance" in assessing the Roman tax on income rate in this period in any direct manner, and for us this is a more important point than choosing between these different scenarios. In any case, faced with the evidence in its current form, we are unlikely to reach a point of consensus by operating in an empirical or positivistic way. Instead, the problem is best approached as all of these authors do, by thinking about the wider implications of various scenarios and testing different models for their interpretation. In this respect, this cluster of chapters represents a start and (we hope) an invitation.

The second suite of chapters turns to **Material Sources (Part II)**. Here, three contributions treat evidence that has so far played less of a role in mainstream historical reconstructions. Contributors also draw from fields that are not necessarily concerned with the Middle Republican period but whose findings bear on transformations to facets of Roman society during that time. This is not to say that this group of chapters discloses few connections with those of the previous section – quite the contrary. As Liv Yarrow's chapter on Roman heavy bronze coinage (Chapter 6) stresses, the creation of coined money at Rome stands as one of the greater novelties of the Middle Republican period. The shifting use of currency for various state needs is of vital relevance to preceding discussions of fiscal institutions like *stipendium* or *tributum*. As she points out, the heavy bronze issues of the early third century remain far more difficult to understand from an economic standpoint than the better-studied contemporary precious metal coinage. She looks in detail at aspects of these heavy bronze issues' production and weight, wielding a number of statistical methods not previously applied to these coins. Grounded in technical discussion of the material at hand, the results have wide-reaching implications. Yarrow emphasizes the irregularity and "strangeness" of this cast coinage, at least insofar as it imperfectly matches our expectations of what coined money does, or the complexities such irregularity implies in terms of the standardization of economic exchange. On her reading, Rome's early coins were more fluid conveyors of value than has traditionally been supposed. This conclusion significantly complicates modern ideas of standardized exchange or Middle Republican notions of value and wealth.[28]

Tymon de Haas' chapter (Chapter 7) turns to landscape archaeology, which has made enormous gains over the last decade on account of recent

---

[28] The tension between the two has sharpened of late: see Rosenstein 2017's review of Coffee 2017.

publications as well as the ongoing work of integrating various datasets in order to build up a larger picture of changing Italian settlement. The question is not only how to read the results, which in de Haas' view suggest a highly dynamic Middle Republican period for the human landscape of Central Tyrrhenian Italy, but how to endow this reading with historical meaning. How do we interpret period-specific trends such as the rural infilling of diversified settlements in ways that remain alert to our sources without being beholden to them? De Haas suggests one path forward: reflection on the investments of human labor that are implied by those changes to the landscape visible in the record of survey archaeology. Employing the tools of recent energetics work in both archaeology and anthropology, he forms quantitative estimates of the fourth- and third-century efforts to reclaim marginal land in the Pontine region for human settlement and use. The results serve to repopulate, so to speak, the countryside of Latium, by bringing to light (through a cross-cultural methodology) the human labor expenditures entailed by those changes in landscape that are observable in the period's archaeology.

In the last chapter in this Part (Chapter 8) Angela Trentacoste and Lisa Lodwick synthesize recent results from bioarchaeology, a field that has so far made precious few inroads into Middle Republican history. As they suggest, the considerable quantity of data now available from Iron Age sites around the peninsula offers exciting opportunities for understanding developments in farming and animal husbandry over time. Integrating this material with standard historical accounts will require work, especially as this field tends to operate on temporal rhythms of wider amplitude than traditional historiographical or agronomic literature. Nonetheless, the evidence brought forward by Trentacoste and Lodwick is sufficient to draw attention to the Middle Republic in Central Italy as a turning point in crop and animal-husbandry strategies. Their chapter suggests a significant acceleration of animal-husbandry practices in place since the Bronze Age, both in terms of the types of animals raised for food (more pigs and chickens; larger cows) and in the mobility of pastured animals. This pattern of change contrasts with stability in crop selection and in the variability of agricultural practices, trends which again start to appear much earlier and, in this case, endure until the very Late Republic. Taken together, these insights represent a powerful empirical contribution to future historical work. Previous discussions of Roman Republican farming and pasturage, reliant as they have been on archaeological and literary evidence for villa-agriculture, have tended to focus upon the singular if perhaps exceptional question of the emergence of large estates geared toward export production of oil and wine. The lift-off of this phenomenon is sometimes dated to later periods of Republican history.[29] In the aggregate, changes detectable in the record for arable cultivation are much less pronounced; it is instead in livestock practices that we perhaps see more dramatic shifts. As economic historians increasingly point to a "revolution" of productivity in Rome and Italy during the Republic, the pace and timing of these dynamics and their relationship to longer-term factors, ecological as much as sociopolitical in nature, will only grow in salience.[30]

Each in their own way, Chapters 6–8 employ material culture to draw new groups of Romans and Italians into our conversation of the period. The small value represented by cast bronze coin indicates that these coins must in part have pertained to the world of daily economic transactions as much as to state payments; but Yarrow's discussion in Chapter 6 also destabilizes this sort of thinking, by raising the idea that cast bronze fulfilled a wider array of social and cultural (and not merely economic) functions relevant to the lives of elites and nonelites alike. Meanwhile, the application of landscape or bioarchaeological data allows us to capture historical trends among smallholders or peasants that are simply not visible in our traditional sources of evidence. All three chapters share a commitment to the application of methods that, originally developed or refined in disciplinary communities beyond classics and ancient history, yield remarkable rewards when brought into conversation with the heterogeneity of the Middle Republic's material culture. Through these methods, which enable us to mine available evidence for new information or to expand the range and interpretive affordances of the evidence already at our disposal, we arrive at a far richer and more inclusive picture of cultural dynamics during the Middle Republic.

The third and final suite of chapters concentrates on **Architecture and Art (Part III)**, extending the previous Part's conclusions about material culture's usefulness to historical inquiry by prioritizing other sets of evidence and approaches. In its fresh appraisal of categories of material evidence that are frequently interpreted as political in nature, this group of chapters identifies and builds bridges between the preceding two. Domenico Palombi's chapter (Chapter 9) starts off this discussion by looking at urban planning in Latium. There has been much discussion lately about the urban types or models generated by Rome in this period and then propagated through colonization and other imperialist processes

---

[29] See above n. 26.   [30] Economic "revolution" as described by Kay 2014; Roselaar 2019.

around the peninsula. That cities and their physical organization could be read so directly to reflect Roman political power is an old idea, traceable as far back as Haverfield's development of the concept of "Romanization."[31] More recently, however, this idea has been challenged from two directions, first by the archaeological discovery that town planning, often associated with Roman Middle Republican colonial settlements, was in fact highly diffuse in Italy in both Roman and non-Roman settlements;[32] and second, in the closer look at the layouts of colonies and Roman-influenced towns in the later Republic, which reveal their considerable variability of form, especially as they seem everywhere to reflect local contingencies.[33] Palombi's innovative discussion sits at the intersection of these two lines of scholarship in that it juxtaposes trends at urban sites in Latium, including Rome. As he notes, the last few decades of archaeological research have demonstrated that the fourth and third centuries comprise one of the more important moments in the urban design of the region, with a variety of Archaic settlements undergoing considerable monumentalization and transformation.[34] From what we can tell of these trends (and our perspective is everywhere limited), a common kit of infrastructure and monument types seems to be emerging in the Latin cities, but one which was everywhere deployed within its specific historical and topographical contexts. In light of these changes, Palombi proposes a radical rethinking of the diffusion of urban forms in Italy in this period, not as Romanization in the Haverfieldian sense, or as Hellenization as sometimes held, but as Latinization. After the political integration of Latium under Rome, it was these trends in Latin urbanization, broadly coherent but locally deployed, which established templates for urban developments elsewhere in the peninsula in the wake of Rome's subsequent expansion.

In Chapter 10, Penelope E. J. Davies moves from the cities of Latium to Rome itself. The capital saw intense architectural expansion in this period, starting with the construction of massive new circuit walls in Grotta Oscura tuff following the Gallic Sack, and followed by the building of a large number of temples and other public monuments. This wave of Middle Republican architecture has attracted significant recent scholarly attention for various aspects, from the religious importance of temple-building to the

---

[31] Haverfield 1906 and 1913, with Dench 2018: ch. 1 for a fresh critical reassessment.
[32] Mogetta 2014; Johnston and Mogetta 2020.   [33] Bolder-Boos 2019.
[34] For a recent presentation of this work, see, along with the multiple volumes of *Lazio e Sabina*, Cifarelli, Gatti, and Palombi eds. 2019, including Palombi's contribution there on similar themes.

political and economic impact on urban society.[35] In general, these studies tend to employ Rome's architecture as a path to accessing various aspects of Roman society, but the city remains in this case a mostly passive backdrop of various historical trends, which (on the standard interpretation) it does not directly create or mold. Davies inverts this line of reasoning by drawing from current theoretical discussions of entanglements between object and humans in art history and archaeology to grant greater agency to the Middle Republican city's "object-scape." With this phrase, Davies innovatively applies posthumanist theory to architecture, treating Middle Republican Rome's buildings both individually and in their ensemble as objects, which, once produced, took on lives of their own and drove consequent material choices. In this provocative view, temples and other monuments were not merely indices of social and political change but helped stabilize and at times spur them.

Moving out to the peninsula, Seth Bernard's paper (Chapter 11) explores the idea that material culture forms an important conveyor of sociopolitical meaning with a case study on visual narratives for Campanian history. A number of painted tombs from Oscan Campania in the fourth and third centuries BCE display features that justify understanding them as historical in nature, even if we are rarely able to identify the specific episodes or events that they intend to describe. Bernard investigates how these paintings speak to commemorative practices among these Oscan communities, locating in their recourse to past events a potent source of legitimacy for new elite groups in this period. Far from being another reflective byproduct, historical painting is central to those expansive territorial state-formation processes that Terrenato has characterized as unfolding across the length of the peninsula.[36] This argument is not dissimilar to what others, especially Flower and Purcell, have proposed for Rome, where nonwritten forms of historical information, including painting, supported elite self-fashioning well before the advent of written history around the time of the Second Punic War.[37] As Bernard points out, whereas the Roman process of "becoming historical" is well studied for this period, the Italian version garners much less attention. Accordingly, his chapter closes with an appeal to restore to mainstream study Italians' own intellectual history, as it interacted with Roman practice, but most importantly on its own terms.

---

[35] In the first category, see now Padilla Peralta 2020a; earlier scholarship includes Ziolkowski 1992; Orlin 1997; for politics, Davies 2017a; economics, Bernard 2018a. Several new discoveries from Rome's Middle Republican phases are presented in D'Alessio, Smith, and Volpe eds. 2021.
[36] Terrenato 2019.   [37] Flower 1996; Purcell 2003a.

These three chapters all insist that material culture forms a vital way of understanding the history of elite behavior both in Rome and in the various Italian communities with which it interacted in the Middle Republic. As we reach the limits of what can be extracted dependably from traditional historiographical sources, there is encouraging material in these chapters for extending our awareness beyond this interpretive threshold, both at Rome and elsewhere in Italy.

***

As we have already stressed, this volume's collective chapters seek not so much to offer an authoritative account of Middle Republican Rome as to chart some of the different and exciting roads to such an account's realization. At the same time, our volume does not shy away from tallying the tangencies and gains of our contributions. Smith's concluding chapter (Chapter 12) rounds off the discussion by proposing one way of weaving all of these chapters together into a coherent narrative, one that centers the Middle Republic as a time when the Roman community "becomes political" and that underlines the degree to which the radical changes of our period built upon developments of the preceding centuries. The major through-line for Smith is legal history, and specifically the evolving relationship of conceptions of property to state formation. It is here, his envoi suggests, that we can see a political community attaining self-consciousness in the Middle Republican period; the signs of that surging awareness are apparent in all of the domains of interest to our contributors.

Awareness of this kind will inevitably return us to where we began: chronological horizons and contestable habits of periodization. Having opened this introduction by flagging the Middle Republic as a crucial period from the vantage point of what follows – the full-throated articulation of a "Roman dialect of empire"[38] – we want to stress, in the spirit of Smith and other contributors, that changes unfolding at this time were grounded in the earlier Roman and Italian past. Especially as historians engage increasingly with fields such as landscape survey or bioarchaeology, which operate at far different scales of chronological resolution than the annual rhythms of the consular *fasti*, we will need to reckon with the various temporalities of those forces at play in making Middle Republican society. In this sense, as Smith's conclusion also ably reminds us, the Middle Republic was and remains an era in which the collision of multiple developmental processes in Italy, not all of them necessarily or strictly connected at first, produced new and enduring social forms.

[38] Dench 2018.

Ultimately, then, this volume makes the Middle Republic into a period of significantly widened horizons. The individual chapters work both as expositions of particular topics and as invitations to expand inquiry. Of course, the breadth of historical inquiry to which we aspire should not only be understood as topical or empirical in form or aspiration. It is our expectation that our volume will stimulate research into the Middle Republic that is more robustly egalitarian, attentive to the identities and practices of nonelites or non-Romans while not losing sight of Rome's ruling classes and their application of the hegemonic arts. This egalitarian emphasis is already, and will in the long run remain, inseparable from a commitment to diversity and equity in the representation of scholarly voices. To mention only one gauge of this commitment, five of our twelve chapters are authored or coauthored by women scholars, a move toward gender parity in scholarship that is without precedent in previous collected volumes on the period. Our commitment to diversity is what underwrites this volume's methodological versatility and historical rigor. We strive with this collection to model the kind of expansiveness and inclusion that will make the Middle Republic into an ever-more-welcoming space for social-scientific, statistical, archaeological, and art-historical practitioners of all backgrounds, interests, and tastes.

PART I

Historical Sources

2 | Italian Descent in Middle Republican Roman Magistrates

The Flipside of the Conquest

PARRISH WRIGHT AND NICOLA TERRENATO

2.1 Introduction

Recent research on Iron Age and Archaic Italy has demonstrated the widespread nature of human mobility across the Italian peninsula (and even the Mediterranean), with a focus on the exchange of goods and ideas, the creation of networks, and the formation of cultural identities. There is no reason to assume this trend would have changed in the Roman Republican period. From a close look at our evidence for who constituted the highest elite at Rome in the Middle Republic (i.e. the *Fasti Consulares* and our ancient literary sources), it becomes increasingly clear that many of these powerful individuals and families had origins outside the city of Rome. Understanding who constituted the upper levels of the Roman aristocracy – those responsible for driving decision-making at home and foreign policy abroad – is critical if we are to make sense of the sometimes-garbled accounts of this period in our ancient sources. In contrast to the constant debate on the primary goals of the plebeians in the class struggles of the Early and Middle Republic, our approach centers on the fact that many of the leaders of the plebeian cause were members of elite families who had immigrated to Rome, and who were not necessarily from a humbler background than the patricians themselves. This allows us to reconsider their motivations: Many were (as our sources note) motivated by "typical" plebeian concerns, such as *nexum* or land distribution; others, however, were seeking more political power in Rome in order to promote their own families' agendas or even those of their city or region of origin. The evidence supports a reconsideration of the Struggle of the Orders not only in social terms but also along the tension between old and newly-settled noble families.

2.2 Historical Background

Our primary dataset is the list of Roman consuls, as preserved through both the inscribed *Fasti Consulares* and the historical tradition. The lists of Roman consuls represent a precious source of information about office-holding and power-sharing in one of the many states that thrived in first-millennium-BCE Italy before its unification. We should consider ourselves extremely lucky to have it, especially considering the dearth of anything quantitatively comparable for neighboring political systems, Greek-speaking ones included. Containing many hundreds of names, the consular lists are not only a rich source of data but also, essentially, a complete and unbiased one, which has few parallels across the ancient Mediterranean.[1] As a result, they possess a statistical representativity that few other ancient historical documents can claim. The consulship represents the pinnacle of political achievement at Rome, and being annual and shared, the list constitutes a large enough dataset to be a (imperfect) proxy for the nobility as a whole. Furthermore, recent scholarship has moved toward considering the lists as generally accurate, despite a moderate amount of wobbliness on first names and *cognomina*.[2] Such reliability is particularly valuable for the fifth and the fourth centuries, for which the literary record is scantier and relevant epigraphic evidence almost nonexistent. Despite this scantiness, it does not follow that writing itself was rare in the Archaic and Early Republican periods. The evidence we have, such as the Forum *cippus* and other inscriptions such as the *Lapis Satricanus* – along with references in literary sources to written documents, such as the treaty between Rome and Carthage or the *Foedus Cassianum* – indicate that by 500 BCE writing was part of public life in Latium, underscoring the likelihood that an original list of magistrates existed at Rome.[3]

Ultimately, arguments for the existence of two annual magistrates who simply had differing titles (*praetores*, an annual *dictator*, and *magister*

---

[1] At Rome, the only exception would be the dictatorship and the mastership of the horses, for which we also have mostly complete records, but which was not a yearly office like the consulship. The Roman lists are easily the most complete of city-states in Italy, and even compared to lists of eponymous magistrates from Greek *poleis* such as Athens, or Miletus, the scale of the Roman lists of magistrates, from both literary and epigraphic sources, is impressive. See Sherk 1990 for a catalog and comparison of various eponymous magistrate lists; for the reliability of the Athenian archon list see Cadoux 1948.

[2] The modern debate is summarized in Ridley 1980 and updated in Smith 2011. *Cognomina* before their first attestation in the early third century BCE especially indicate that the list has been revised – but the addition of information does not necessarily negate the overall value of the *fasti*, nor the historicity of the gentilical *nomina*. Later epigraphic evidence, for example an inscribed breastplate from Falerii, has similar types of discrepancies in the filiation rather than the *nomen*; see Flower 1998. The relatively widespread use of the binomial system in central Italy by approximately 650 BCE underscores the idea of a horizontally mobile aristocracy and that these naming systems had cultural power in various communities, see Salway 1994.

[3] Cornell 1995: 24–32, Bradley 2020: 8–10, 133. The eponymous nature of the consulship also in some ways necessitates an authoritative list early on, since it was the typical way to structure understanding of the past. See Feeney 2007 and Clarke 2008 for the mentality of eponymous magistrates in Mediterranean city-states.

equitum, etc.) do not necessarily call into question the *nomina* themselves – which should be considered the historical kernel of the document.[4] The fact that the list of names also contains discrepancies with the Roman conception of their own past (i.e. plebeian names before the Licinio-Sextian laws), as others have argued, attests to the historicity of these names rather than the opposite.[5] If they had not been firmly embedded in the historical record, they would have been deleted for the sake of consistency. Other arguments against the historicity of the *fasti* include our own Roman authors and historians, who blame predecessors or family histories for aggrandizing their ancestors or inserting relatives into the list. This is more likely for the offices and years where there is clear confusion, especially the years of consular tribunes. The pride which families would take in their ancestral achievements, however, should also be considered as a preventive measure against the insertion of names, which would have necessitated the deletion of others, whose descendants would not have allowed this to happen.[6]

To state the obvious, the main informative element the list offers is the sequence of names, since no other information is given about the office-holders.[7] Similar evidence is, of course, provided by Livy and other later historians, but it has a completely different epistemological value. The value of this list is, consequently, primarily limited to the study of prosopography and of family politics, and it is especially to the latter that our study will turn. A preliminary observation is that, for the period in question, the potential of the lists has not been exploited in full. This is arguably connected with how recent historiography saw the role of elite kinship groups in the Middle Republican period.[8] Perhaps influenced by later Roman ideas, there has often been a sense that it did not make a big difference which *gens* a specific consul belonged to, since they all more or

---

[4] It is much easier to understand how the list could be the result of genuine record-keeping with some later modifications, especially in the case of *cognomina*, than how it could have been fabricated wholesale.

[5] Bradley 2020: 245.

[6] Cornell 1995: 12–16, 218–23. Oakley 1997–2005: 31, 38–41. A recent argument against this optimism is Richardson 2017, who argues that this line of reasoning uses "modern assumptions and standards" which the ancient Romans might not have held.

[7] An exception would be the record for years with multiple consular tribunes, which seem to indicate a change in the constitutional system. The interpretation of those years, however, is controversial and falls before the period in question here.

[8] For the study of the *gens*, see Smith 2006, reconsidered and updated in Smith 2019. While recognizing that the term refers to a dynamic institution with a particularly Roman emphasis, we will generally use terms such as family to indicate similar (but not identical) kinship structures throughout Italy.

less single-mindedly pursued the same goal: the ruthless expansion of the empire's borders.[9] Considering the emphasis on collective, "ethnic" action that characterizes Romantic-era scholarship, perhaps this is not surprising.[10]

A turning point in the study of family politics came with Münzer's 1920 *Römische Adelsparteien und Adelsfamilien*.[11] While he was working on individual Republican entries for the *Paulys Realencyclopädie*, Münzer started to see patterns and recurrences in the names of the consuls and had the innovative idea of analyzing them as a body of evidence. Despite its brilliance, this revolutionary book has had a mixed fortune: Some hailed it as crucial to understanding Roman politics;[12] others were critical of its overall framework.[13] In part, this must be due to the recoiling reaction that we reserve – probably with good reason – for any distorting modernizing analogies, in this case with political parties, which certainly did not exist before the Gracchi. A large part of the problem is in the very title: the mention of *Adelsparteien* caused immediate skepticism in many later readers (and especially English-speaking ones). Conversely, inveterate modernists like Càssola, in line with Italian and French Marxist scholarship, wanted Roman political life to be similar to ours, and so they read Münzer in a presentist perspective that was not in the original. We know that there were no entities that it is useful to describe as political parties in the Roman Republic (and certainly none in the period at hand). Yet a close reading of Münzer reveals an implicit definition of *partei* that has more to do with Italian *parte* (whence English partisan), which is much closer to a faction than to a political party. In simple operational terms, we can define the difference to be that parties push for diverging political goals while factions compete over the same political objective, that is, power.

Even in such a cursory literature review, it should be noted that several later historians have shown a sustained interest in personal power networks, but primarily for the Late Republican and early Imperial periods.[14] The earlier and Middle Republic continued to be seen as a monolith of state

---

[9] For example Beck et al. eds. 2011: 5: "From the second half of the fourth century BCE, once the direct patrician–plebeian confrontation was over and as the integration of the plebeian elite within the new Roman aristocracy was in progress, the central feature of the history of Rome is external expansion."

[10] Overview in Holzer 2013.   [11] Münzer 1920; Münzer 1999.

[12] Ridley 1986, and especially the largely positive new introduction by Ridley in the 1999 edition.

[13] Hölkeskamp 2001, Develin 1985. See most recently the contributions in Haake and Harders 2017 for both positive and critical evaluations of Münzer's scholarship and its legacy. Zanin 2021, a reconsideration of Münzer 100 years after the publication of *Römische Adelsparteien und Adelsfamilien*, attempts to highlight the important broader historical arguments of the book, and is much more than simple, uncritical, prosopography.

[14] Such as Wiseman 1971 and many others.

agency, as it had been found in Livy and in many of those nineteenth-century readers of Livy.[15] Evidently, in this view, the great conquering machinery of Rome could not be factional and successful at the same time. It is only in some works of the last decade or two that attempts have been made at reconstructing the connections and interactions among Middle Republican politicians.[16] These have tended to focus primarily on individual families or specific events, like the First Punic War. Such important, if as yet unsystematic work, is finally opening the way for a deconstruction of traditional views about decision-making at the time of the conquest of Italy.

An important element of Münzer's multilayered analysis focused on highlighting the exogenous provenance of some of the new noble clans in Rome. Despite being central to the overall argument of the book, the chapter devoted to the "foreign princes" who become Roman citizens has had much less impact than other parts of his work.[17] Scholars have tended instead to get worked up over whether political alliances and parties were truly recognizable in the record or not. Surprisingly little systematic research, on the other hand, has pursued Münzer's insight about elite movement between different central Italian states. Scholars like Torelli, for instance, who are just as conversant with the record as Münzer was, have tended to focus their attention on the relationship between the families on the consular list and the later epigraphic record, only occasionally considering the broader implications. Their primary goal has been centered on the fine-grained work of attaching later senatorial families to specific Italian cities, as well as reconstructing their family trees, a pursuit that is almost always impossible for the Middle Republican period.[18] This approach is not being criticized here, since it has produced some fascinating and insightful results; the point is rather that there is another possible level of analysis, in which the influx of outsiders to the consulship is considered holistically and in its larger, long-term scope.

On the whole (and with some exceptions), the phenomenon of the appearance of a number of new family names in Rome in the late fifth, fourth, and third centuries has not been fully considered, especially within the context of Roman internal politics. For the part that happened after 367,

---

[15] Overview in Terrenato 2019: 10–24.
[16] For example Massa-Pairault 2001, Bleckmann 2002, Humm 2005. Loreto 1993 is an early exception.
[17] The legal status of these newcomers is an interesting question, and how they were legally integrated into the Roman state depends on the time period at hand. Elites from neighboring communities had several "pathways to citizenship" of Rome, such as intermarriage, adoption, or simply moving to Rome.
[18] Torelli 1982; see also Cébeillac-Gervasoni ed. 1983, Farney 2007.

the main historical framework that has been evoked is that of the Struggle of the Orders, with the often-untested assumption that, aside from a few blatant exceptions, the new clans were mostly up-and-coming families that originated from Rome, constituting the new patrician–plebeian *nobilitas*. In light of this, the research question posed here is simply the following: How big was the influx of new families reaching the consulate and where were they from? This fundamental issue is only partially resolvable at present, but it needs to be investigated to test the hypothesis described in this chapter. The importance of such a distinction should be self-evident; vertical mobility of formerly subordinate families from Rome and horizontal mobility of families from other cities are two different historical processes that should not be confused. Both certainly took place, and once horizontal, families could, of course, later have increasing vertical success at Rome, but any step toward quantifying their relative importance is essential to understanding a key mechanism of the Roman conquest in Central Italy, as well as internal politics in Rome itself.

The mobility of people and especially of elites within Italy in the Iron Age and Archaic periods is generally accepted in scholarship on the period.[19] The same can be said of the Late Republic, where the predominance of "new men" and their acceptance into the Roman political system have been studied intensively.[20] This evidently leaves out the Middle Republican period. Are we to trust our sources who point to this period as a golden era of quintessential Romans?[21] The concept of the "closing of the patriciate," which supposedly occurred at the beginning of the Republic, has contributed to this idea of a stable Roman aristocracy, at least on the level of those achieving the consulate.[22] The aristocratic mythmaking and embellishment which Cicero famously maligns in the Late Republic also demonstrate some of the ways in which families would have invented legends that established them as Roman, likely often obscuring their origins outside the city.[23] This makes the stories of foreign origin that have remained, and our epigraphic evidence of mobile families, even more remarkable and valuable.

---

[19] Originally Ampolo 1976–7, and more recently see, for example, Moatti 2004; Bourdin 2012; Bradley 2015; Armstrong 2016; Isayev 2017; Bradley 2020.

[20] Most prominently in Wiseman 1971, but studies of *novitas* in the Late Republic continue; see van der Blom 2010. Beck 2005 begins at 290 BCE.

[21] Ironically, the exemplars of *romanitas*, such as M.' Curius Dentatus or Cato the Elder, are known to belong to *gentes* which migrated to Rome.

[22] De Sanctis 1965 coined the term "la serrata del patriziato." Raaflaub 2005 [1986] contains more recent approaches.

[23] Bradley 2015: 95 argues that "this sort of primordialism can be seen as a response to rapid social change."

This approach allows us to ask (if not answer) questions about identity in the Early and Middle Republic. While the question of what it means to be Roman (or how we could even understand that question in relation to an individual from our sources) is too broad for this chapter, we can start to see how nesting layers of identity were part of Roman self-consciousness at this time. We are dealing with approximately three of these layers: first that of a family, a *gens* at Rome (though again, the relevance of this term outside of Rome is unclear), which is preserved for us in the *nomen* or what we can determine is a family name in other traditions.[24] The next level is that of a city – the citizenship, locality of origin, or the place of residence of a given person. Next, the fraught idea of ethnicity, a Greek borrowing used in Italy to describe groups such as the Latins, Sabines, Etruscans, and Volscians – terms and groupings which we use in this chapter with the recognition that these names may not have truly mapped on to any actual community, or even have represented a self-identification, but rather a Roman perception of otherness.[25] In reality, Italy during the Early and Middle Republic was a heterogeneous peninsula, with many more gradations in identity (including, of course, status, class, profession, gender) than are preserved for us, and certainly more than our simple categories can convey.

In the Middle Republic of the fourth and third centuries BCE, the Roman state was still grappling with the questions of how it would function and who constituted the ruling elite, as well as with increasing threats from abroad. Rome was famously open with its citizenship, and while "Romulus' Asylum" is not an accurate depiction of the Middle Republic, this mentality, embedded in Roman foundation stories, demonstrates the extent to which the Roman elite was characterized by fluidity and social mobility.[26]

2.3 A Quantitative Analysis of Consular Lists

In an attempt to understand the different processes through which new families could gain power in Rome, we have analyzed the evidence for the families in the consular *fasti* from 366 to 264. The 205 (or so) consulships were

---

[24] For recent work on *società gentilizia* within and outside of Rome, see the contributions in Di Fazio and Paltineri 2019.

[25] The increasing focus on mobility and permeability in early Italian city-states calls for a reconsideration of the terminologies typically employed by ancient historians and archaeologists. A recent trend is toward "peoples" (Farney and Bradley eds. 2017, Bourdin 2012), rather than "ethnicity," "ethnic group," "cultural identity," or "race," all of which perhaps indicate more group solidarity than existed. For race as a useful term for the ancient world (in comparison to ethnicity or cultural identity) see McCoskey 2012, esp. 27–34, and 68–75 for this period of Roman history.

[26] Dench 2005.

held by 132 unique individuals in 46 different *gentes* during this period; this information represents the dataset for our chapter. The new Digital Prosopography of the Roman Republic, a database created by a team led by Henrik Mouritsen and Maggie Robb and containing Broughton's *Magistrates of the Roman Republic* (*MRR*) along with other lists of priests, family relationships, defeated candidates, and senators in a searchable form, has been our main tool for investigating patterns in office-holding in general and within families.[27] The database allows us to search by year, mimicking the style of *MRR*, but also by *nomen*, allowing us to easily see all of the available evidence for office-holding within a particular family as well as a full *cursus* for any specific individual. While it would be ideal to see whether similar patterns emerge in magistracies other than the consulate, the data is simply too fragmentary to carry out these analyses. For example, from 509 to 264, we have the names of only nineteen quaestors. A recent study of the tribune of the plebs by Lanfranchi estimates that we have names for only around 6 percent of the tribunes from 493 to 287. He does argue, even with this scanty evidence, that many of these early tribunes had non-Roman origins, which would be expected for this lower position in a time of high lateral mobility around Italy.[28]

Chart 2.1 shows the *gentes* who held the consulship during the crucial period from the Licinio-Sextian laws down to the start of the First Punic War. The top five, the Cornelii, Fabii, Valerii, Aemilii, and Sulpicii, account for a quarter of the total consulships. However, there are many new *gentes* who, while far from being numerically dominant, are reaching high office at Rome in significant numbers. This phenomenon can be seen clearly in the data put forth by Gary Forsythe in his 2005 book. Here, he took a similar approach to this question (Chart 2.2), seeking to quantify the number of new families in the *fasti* for every ten-year period.

While the first three decades of the Republic obviously see an abundance of new names in correspondence with the newly established governmental system, Forsythe shows that, on average, 20 percent of consuls in the *fasti*

[27] http://romanrepublic.ac.uk. According to the authors:

> The project incorporates directly into its database the information on office holders presented in Broughton's *Magistrates of the Roman Republic*, which forms the backbone of the database, Rüpke's inventory of Roman priests in the *Fasti Sacerdotum*, the collection of information about family relations found in Zmeskal's *Adfinitas*, and Pina Polo's work on *repulsae*, defeated candidates. In addition, the team has drawn extensively on Brennan's work on the praetorship, Nicolet's on the equestrian order, Shackleton Bailey's onomastica to the works of Cicero, Rich's consolidated list of triumphs, and Hinard's study of proscriptions.

[28] Lanfranchi 2015, especially chapter 2.

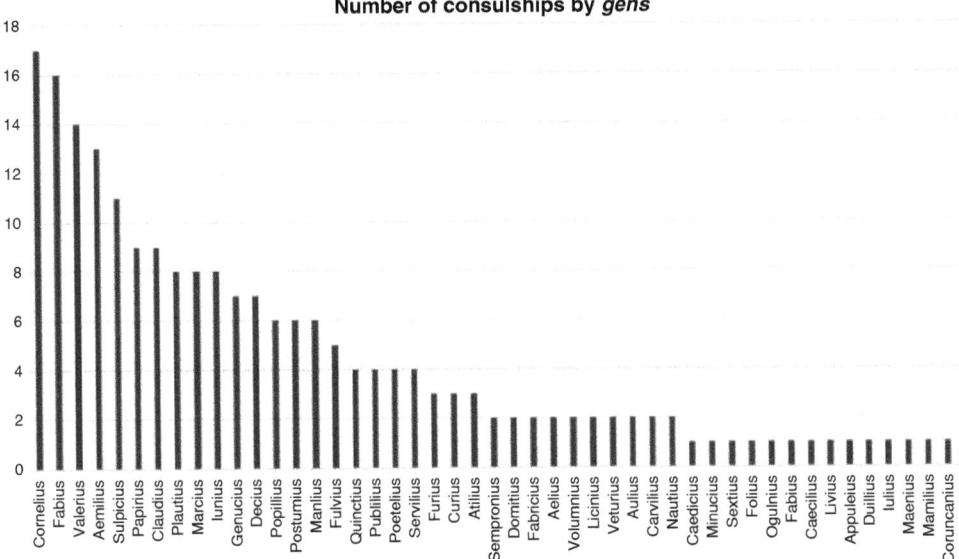

Chart 2.1 Consulships held by *gens* (366–265 BCE). Based on data from the Digital Prosopography of the Roman Republic.
Prepared by the authors.

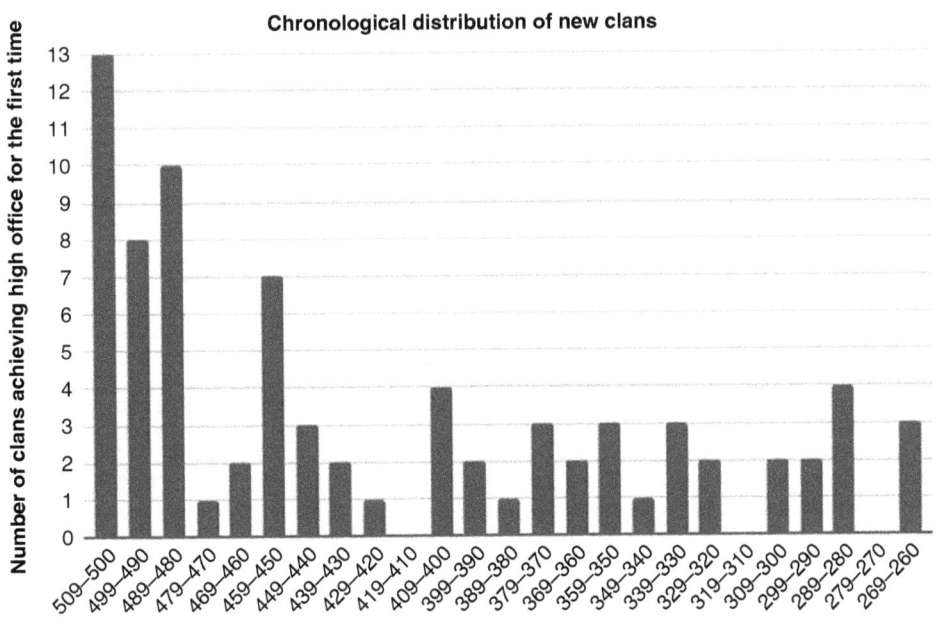

Chart 2.2 Chronological distribution of new clans attaining high office, after Forsythe 2005: 164.
Prepared by the authors.

are from new families, particularly in the years 359–260.[29] His results provide another way of grouping the evidence and demonstrate that the Roman aristocracy was fluid and open to the inclusion of new members. Our question is whether or not these new families were all upwardly mobile Romans, as it is typically assumed. To understand and quantify these new magistrates and where they came from, we have attempted to categorize families into various types of mobility. For our classification, we came up with five main categories:

1. **Established** for those who already held consulships prior to 367
2. **Pre-367 Horizontal** for families who are present in the *fasti* before 367 but are known to have origins outside of Rome
3. **Horizontal** for families whom we can reasonably assert moved to Rome and entered high office during the period of 367–260
4. **Vertical** for families already established within the city who rise through the political ranks at Rome
5. **Unknown** for families whom we cannot tie to Rome or to any other polity.

To compensate for some of the ambiguities in the records of office-holding, we combined our data-driven analysis with a holistic assessment of our knowledge of particular *gentes*, such as literary evidence for the migration of a family or epigraphic and onomastic evidence which points toward an origin outside of Rome. This can help us determine whether we are looking at a family that rose up the ranks within Roman society, migrated horizontally during the Middle Republic, or perhaps moved to Rome and entered into the upper echelons of power even earlier, with roles in high offices such as the Decemvirate or as military tribunes with consular power. This methodology is imperfect, as the evidence locating the origin of a certain *gens* as from outside of Rome is often late or is based on scanty literary evidence or linguistic roots of the gentilic name. For this reason, there are several *gentes* in our study who can only be classified as "unknown."

Table 2.1 demonstrates our classifications and the families that fall into each category. It is also important to note that these categories should not be considered as static: it is possible that a family that was new to Rome

---

[29] Forsythe 2005: 164–5. However, he seems to automatically attribute these new names to a form of vertical mobility: "the Roman political system was conducive to the upward social mobility of individuals or families of means who had political and military abilities and aspirations" (276). Elites from "outlying communities" are also mentioned, but how he sees their role in the government and foreign policy at Rome is unclear, other than his suggestion that their inclusion may have been a tool that won over the "hearts and minds" of Rome's adversaries.

Table 2.1 *Grouping of consular families*

Established	Pre-376 Horizontal	Horizontal	Vertical	Unknown
Aemilius	Aelius	Curius	Appuleius	Domitius
Claudius	Atilius	Fabricius	Carvilius	Folius
Cornelius	Caecilius	Fulvius	Sextius	Maenius
Fabius	Caedicius	Livius		Poetelius
Genucius	Decius	Mamilius		Popilius
Iulius	Duillius	Ogulnius		
Iunius	Furius	Plautius		
Manlius	Licinius	Coruncanius		
Marcius	Volumnius	Aulius		
Minucius				
Nautius				
Papirius				
Postumius				
Quinctius				
Sempronius				
Servilius				
Sulpicius				
Valerius				
Veturius				

Prepared by the authors.

could increase their status once they were in the city, which was likely a key motivation for moving to Rome throughout this period.

In his recent book on the people of pre-Roman Italy, Stephane Bourdin produced this table (Table 2.2) presenting the alleged non-Roman origins of many of the patrician *gentes* which we categorized as "established," including the Postumii, Valerii, even the Sulpicii, and, of course, the Claudii, with their thousands of followers.[30] We certainly do not suggest that these early and probably fictitious stories should be lumped together with the better attested later ones, but rather that these narratives were part of a local cultural discourse that characterized Roman society as distinctively open (for instance in contrast with Greek cities), within the context of an intense horizontal mobility that characterized archaic Central Italy more broadly, and not only in the direction of Rome. Evidence for Romans and Latins outside of Rome is abundant in Etruscan necropoleis, where there are often names indicating origins in Latium or Rome.[31]

[30] Bourdin 2012: 543–4.   [31] See Bradley 2015 for a clear summary.

This table also demonstrates the bias in our sources toward Etruscan origins, owing to the respective wealth of information on Etruscan onomastics from necropoleis, whereas we are much less informed for other areas of Italy.

Those families, almost all patrician, with a long record of holding high offices from the earliest days of the Republic, are considered established; these are the Aemilii, Cornelii, Fabii, and so on, in the furthest left column of Table 2.1. While these families undoubtedly represented an element of political continuity in the period in question, it should be remembered that for many of them there were also narratives involving foreign origin at various times in Roman history, as noted in Bourdin's table. Despite these attributions to other Italian cities, we have considered these families established at Rome because of their prominence in the *fasti* in high offices early in the history of the Republic.

Table 2.2 *Patrician families of presumed foreign origin, after Bourdin 2012: 543–4*

Gens	Date of first consulship	Presumed origin
Tarquinii	509	Etruscan
Horatii	509	Etruscan
Valerii	508	Sabine
Lucretii	508	Etruscan
Larcii	506	Etruscan
Herminii	506	Etruscan
Postumii	505	Sabine
Menenii	503	Etruscan?
Verginii	502	Etruscan
Cominii	501	Etruscan
Aebutii	499	Etruscan
Veturii	499	Etruscan, Sabine
Claudii	495	Sabine
Nautii	488	Etruscan, Latin?
Siccii	487	Etruscan
Aquilii	487	Volscian
Manlii	480	Etruscan
Volumnii	461	Etruscan
Romilii	455	Etruscan?
Tarpeii	454	Etruscan?
Aternii	454	Etruscan?
Folii	433	Sabine, Volscian?

Prepared by the authors.

Narratives about the Sabine and Etruscan origins of mythical kings further reinforced ideas about strangers attaining supreme power at Rome in the early years of its history as a city. The *gens Mamilia*, one of our "horizontal" families and a leading family in Tusculum in the fifth century BCE, was allegedly given Roman citizenship in 458 after Lucius Mamilius rescued the city from the attack by Appius Herdonius. Despite this heroic act and his place as the ruler of Tusculum, no Mamilii appear in the *fasti* until 265 BCE.[32] This is to say that there is some ambiguity between what constitutes an "established" family and the next category, pre-367 horizontal.

2.4 A Quantitative Analysis of Consular Lists: Various Mobilities

The families which we have designated pre-367 horizontal (see Table 2.1) appear with various magistracies in the early *fasti*; however, there is more secure evidence linking them to cities outside of Rome. Some of these families seem to have claimed a foreign origin story, while others appear to have originated from outside Rome based on the epigraphic record. Many individuals from these *gentes* which we consider horizontal played key roles in the narrative of early Roman politics. For example, the *gens Licinia* has a member as tribune of the plebs in 493 as well as fifth-century military tribunes with consular power, indicating their early presence in the Roman ruling class. There is, however, evidence that the Licinii were originally Etruscan, with epigraphic evidence for the gens *Lecnie* (or *Leceniie*) in the area around Adria as early as the fifth century BCE.[33] Morandi Tarabella also connects this *gens* to the *Lence/Lecni* family attested in the area around Siena.[34]

There are also attestations of *Leceniies* in the area around Orvieto, dating to approximately 300–100 BCE. Another second-century BCE inscription distinctly connects the *Lecne* to the Licinii.[35] Cumulatively, this evidence

---

[32] Livy 3.29.5; Cornell ed. 2013: s.v. Cato F25; the Mamilii were allegedly enrolled as a plebeian *gens*, which could account for their absence from the *fasti* as we have them. They advertised their status as Tusculans through their supposed descent from Telegonos, the reputed founder of the city and son of Odysseus and Circe. See Münzer 1999: 64.

[33] Morandi Tarabella 2004: 277, citing *ET* Vs 2.48, an inscription with *mi Venelus Leceniies*, with the possibility of an earlier example (*ET* Ta 7.21, ca. 520 BCE) from a tomb in Tarquinia, though the reading in that case is uncertain (*Recieneies* or *Lecieneies*).

[34] Morandi Tarabella 2004: 277 (*ET* AS 1.318–33, 1.489 for the inscriptions around Siena).

[35] Benelli #5 = TLE 45: *C. Licini C.f. Nigri/v. lecne v. hapirnal*, interpreted as a bilingual inscription of the Licinii/Lecne family.

indicates that we have an early Etruscan family group which likely had a branch that immigrated to Rome early in the city's history.[36] The widespread nature of the attestations of the family show that this mobility was not unidirectional toward Rome, nor is it necessary to imagine that all of these individuals were blood relations, but rather that they considered the name Licinius (in whichever spelling, language, iteration), as a signifier of their identity and the larger network to which they belonged.[37]

The next category is horizontal mobility: those families who have a member achieve the consulship for the first time in the long fourth century and are more securely attested as having elite non-Roman origins. A complementary indication for this category is a lack of holding some of the lower offices on the *cursus honorum*, although this can also be an artifact of the lack of systematic records for lower-office-holding. An example of this category is Lucius Fulvius Curvus, who famously went over to the Roman side while holding the highest office in his native Tusculum.[38] Most of these new families in both of the horizontal categories were from other cities in Latium, such as the Caecilii, who claim to be from Praeneste; the Fabricii, another family from Praeneste; the Furii, attested epigraphically at Tusculum; the Coruncanii, also from Tusculum; the Plautii from Praeneste; as well as several from Etruria, the Licinii, Volumnii, and Ogulnii; and from Campania, the Atilii and Caedicii.[39] Some of these examples will be explored in detail later in this chapter.

We identify as "vertical" families those which held several lower offices in the years leading up to 376 and for which there is evidence of long residence in Rome. For example, the *gens Sextia*, which had a member become tribune of the plebs in the fifth century before their string of tribunates in the fourth century and their first consulship in 366 BCE.[40] There can have been overlap between our categories of vertical and

[36] Farney 2007: 151.
[37] For an example of this expanded model of the *gens* and kinship relationships see Naglak and Terrenato 2019, which uses the Lévi-Straussian idea of a House to understand these networks.
[38] Pliny, *Natural History* 7.44; in 323, Fulvius was a consul in Tusculum, who led his city in a harsh confrontation with Rome. Diplomacy prevailed, however, and Fulvius was a consul in Rome the following year; see Terrenato 2019: 185–9 for an analysis of this episode.
[39] Caecilii: Licordari 1982, 52, Furii: *CIL* I² 166–72 = XIV 2701–07 as the Furii, see Licordari 1982: 49; Plautii: Terrenato 2014, Licinii: see n. 35, Volumnii: Etruscan based on the family tomb of the Velimnas in Perugia, dating to the third century BCE, although the inscription connecting the Etruscan and Latin versions of the name is from the early imperial period, see Nielsen 2013: 181–2; Ogulnii: see later in this section, Atilii: likely from Cales of Calatia, see Licordari 1982: 53, Münzer 1999: 58. Caedicii: Campanian, see Licordari 1982: 52.
[40] Likely an economically upwardly mobile family with wealth coming from the ceramics industry, as indicated by the name of a slave of the Sextii on kiln-wasters from the Esquiline, see Coarelli 1996: 40–1. We thank the editors for bringing this connection to our attention.

horizontal, but its impact cannot be measured here; there must have been families who both immigrated to Rome and then later rose up through the ranks, although their original entry into Rome is invisible to us.

Within these categories there is, of course, variation in the *cursus* taken by individuals. An interesting example is the Ogulnii, two brothers from Etruria whose first appearance in Roman politics is as tribunes of the plebs in 300. Thirty years later one brother, Quintus, becomes consul.[41] Onomastic and linguistic evidence points to a family origin in Etruria, most likely Caere, if we can connect them with the legendary king named in the *Elogia Tarquiniensia*, Orgolnius Velthume.[42] Other evidence for Etruscan origins includes an inscription from Perusia with the family name *uclona* and, according to Torelli, an inscription from Bolsena indicates a connection between the family and a powerful family in Volsinii known in Etruscan as *hescanas*.[43] Their path into power at Rome is probably fairly typical, as they are associated in the tradition with the Fabii and likely enjoyed their patronage.[44] The Ogulnii thus represent a family that blends the line between vertical and horizontal mobility. Entering at the level of tribunes of the plebs, they are very effective in that role, responsible for the eponymous *lex Ogulnia*, and famously commissioning the statue of Romulus and Remus and the wolf at the *Ficus Ruminalis*.[45] The *lex Ogulnia*, which opened up several important priesthoods to the plebeians, is traditionally considered a key win for the plebeians in the Struggle of the Orders. Considering the framers of the law as newcomers to Rome rather than as an abstract idea of a plebeian gives us some insight into their goal – access to power within the Roman system.[46] A descendant of these Ogulnii also shows the benefit the Italians bring to the Roman state as agents of diplomacy within Italy; a Marcus Ogulnius served as a legate to Etruria in 210 BCE to acquire grain for the Roman garrison in Tarentum.[47] It is likely his linguistic skills or existing relationships with local elites were the prerequisite for this appointment.

---

[41] Livy 10.6–9.2 for their tribunate. [42] Torelli 1975: 39. [43] Torelli 1995: 43–4.
[44] Torelli 1995: 44.
[45] Orlin 2010: 67 suggests that the statue, combined with their "Hellenizing" action of the introduction of the Asclepius cult at Rome, should "be seen as part of an effort to present the Romans as open to the involvement of outsiders while continuing to stress their own unique sense of identity." Our view of the Ogulnii reinforces this idea – they are outsiders to Rome, but ones that benefit from ideals of Romulus' asylum expressed in the mythology of Early Rome.
[46] Livy 10.6 clearly states that the intended beneficiaries of the *lex Ogulnia* were not the typical urban poor, but the leaders of the plebeians: *eam actionem susceperunt qua non infimam plebem accenderent sed ipsa capita plebis* (They undertook this action, not to rouse up the plebeian base, but the leaders of the plebs themselves).
[47] Livy 27.3.9.

Another example of horizontal mobility where the individual rose up the ranks much more quickly is that of Gaius Fabricius Luscinus. Of Latin origin, after a year as a legate in southern Italy he was elected consul and celebrated a triumph in 282 BCE. Münzer attributes his success at Rome to a family alliance with the Aemilii, with whom they hold office repeatedly.[48] These two examples demonstrate that the path to power in Rome was dependent on many factors, such as the person's family circumstances in the city of origin, their reason for migrating to Rome, and the power of their allies already in Rome, as well as many others less visible to us.

Chart 2.3 demonstrates that we have almost as many horizontally mobile families as established ones if we consider both horizontal categories together, and that, despite the rhetoric surrounding the so-called Struggle of the Orders, the new laws do not seem to have helped many vertically mobile families from Rome itself reach the highest office. This chart flattens out our families, but in Chart 2.4 the bars represent numbers of consulships rather than each family as one unit, which demonstrates the dominance that established families still exerted on the consulship even after the Licinio-Sextian laws.

A better understanding of who made up the Middle Republican nobility and where they came from can help us make sense of the internal politics at Rome. Thinking about the Licinii as Etruscans who have broken into the

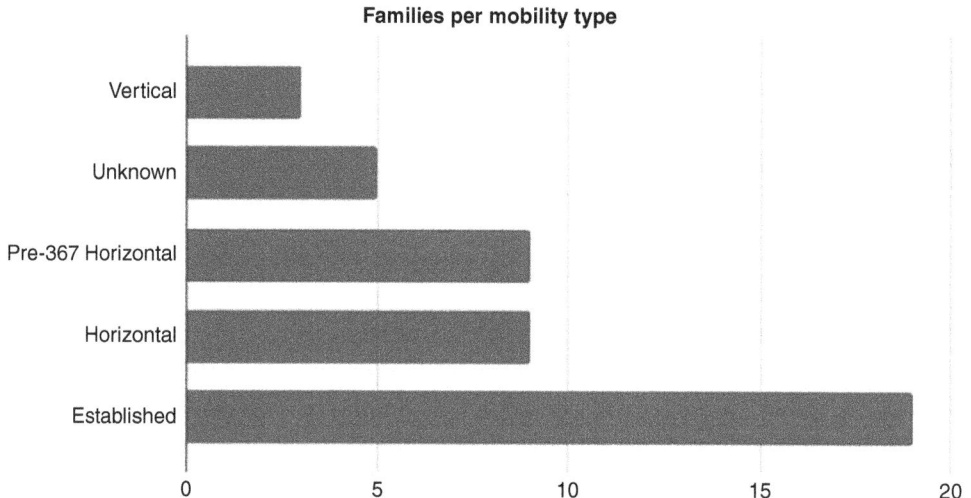

Chart 2.3 Number of families per mobility type.
Prepared by the authors.

[48] Münzer 1999: 61.

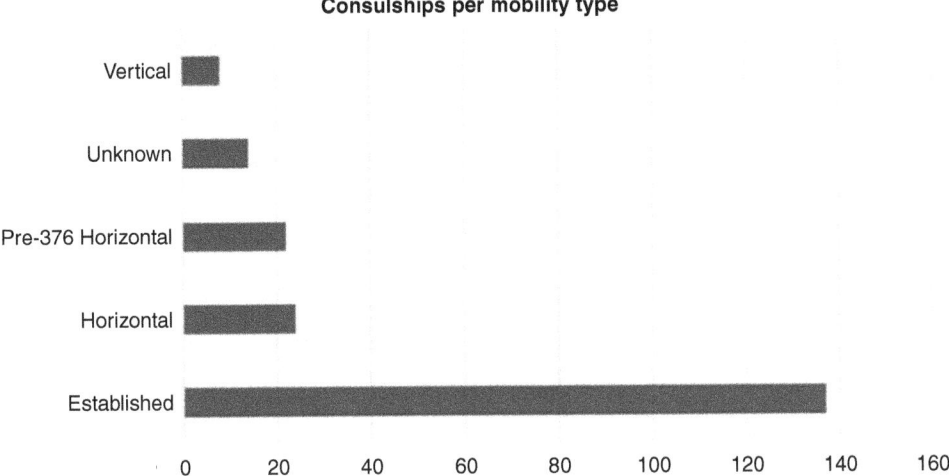

Chart 2.4 Number of consulships held per mobility type.
Prepared by the authors.

political world of Rome can help us understand the goals of the Licinio-Sextian laws, which might have been more aimed at opening up the consulship to people like the Licinii, rather than your average (if wealthy) Roman, as argued above for the *lex Ogulnia*. We can continue to extrapolate in this way for other office-holders who appear to be horizontally mobile, such as Tiberius Coruncanius, a native of Tusculum who first achieved the consulship in 280. He later became the first plebeian Pontifex Maximus and is credited with being the first to publicly practice and teach Roman law.[49] In this act, perhaps Coruncanius was pioneering another way to facilitate openness and access into the Roman system. This line of thinking points to the need to reconceptualize the Struggle of the Orders as a complex phenomenon in which the aspirations of newly arrived elite foreigners were more or equally as important than those of upwardly mobile established Romans.

2.5 Conclusions

A quantitative review of the consular lists has the potential to produce results that throw valuable light on the political process in Rome at the time of its expansion in Central and Southern Italy. While there are many uncertainties (and a few pitfalls) in determining the regional provenance

---

[49] Livy *Per.* 18, Livy 25.6.3.

of new consuls, globally it is hard to deny the significance of the influx of new families coming from a broad variety of ethnic backgrounds. Once the pervasive assumption that most of the *homines novi* were upwardly mobile Roman families is called into question, a pattern becomes discernible, at least in part. It is worth repeating that what can be ascertained or reconstructed necessarily underestimates the phenomenon, given the presence of many names for whom the judgment must be suspended due to lack of evidence. Analogously, the lower magistracies, for which only a fraction of the names survives, must have seen similar processes (if not even greater participation of newcomers), but the fragmentary nature of this data, in comparison with the consulship, would make a similar statistical approach misleading.

The influx of outsiders into the Roman consular ranks has significant implications on several levels. In terms of internal politics, it offers a counterpoint to the widely held view that the outcome of the Struggle of the Orders primarily favored up-and-coming local families of plebeian rank. These no doubt existed and had a role in the process, but at least as many plebeian newcomers were Münzer's "foreign princes"-aristocrats (sometimes even of royal rank!) from other polities who were classified as plebeians because there was simply no path for them that led into the patriciate.[50] This opens up another dimension of the struggle that has been typically seen in social terms, that is, the tension between old Roman families and their peers elsewhere in Italy who were lobbying for more power in what was becoming the capital of a new territorial state. A next step in this analysis would be to reconsider our known political alliances and platforms from this period. One key example would be the alliance between C. Licinius Stolo and L. Sextius Lateranus, who were classified as horizontal and vertical respectively, and who clearly recognized that gaining access to higher political power at Rome would allow them to pursue their own agendas.[51]

At the level of Italy-wide politics, what was happening in the government at Rome arguably shaped the future of the whole alliance. Originally conceived to run a city-state a few tens of miles in radius, the Roman political system necessarily had to adapt to its new function as the core of an expanding regional power. As it is often the case in many empires, a fundamental decision had to be made concerning what opportunities to afford to elites in incorporated communities. As has been recognized by several scholars, Rome always maintained very inclusive policies, which

---

[50] The Claudii were somehow an exception, having been admitted in the patriciate upon their arrival in Rome. Wiseman 1979: 57–70.

[51] The impetus for this political action given in Livy (6.34), the jealousy of a young Fabia, makes for a good story, but ultimately requires more explanation.

built on a tradition of accepting elite newcomers that went as far as the city itself.[52] More recently, the access that central Italian families had to the control room of the Roman state and of its army has been seen as a crucial part of a global mechanism that led to the unification of Central Italy.[53]

What has been reviewed here is arguably only the tip of an iceberg of considerable import, since many other families that we do not know about probably followed the same horizontal path but did not enjoy the same, highly visible political success. The role of women and intermarriage in the movement of peoples and families across the peninsula must have been substantial, if mostly irrecoverable in our sources. In addition, mobile craftsmen, merchants, and mercenaries are also known throughout this period and must have been moving across the Mediterranean in large numbers.[54] It should also be considered that the phenomenon continued unabated after the period in question (as shown by scholars like Syme, Wiseman, and Torelli for other periods), remaining a constant of the way in which new participants in the expanding empire were integrated. Their ability to move to Rome and become an active part of an elite that steered the political and military machinery must have been instrumental in making the unification centered on Rome an interesting option for well-connected non-Roman aristocrats.

The net result of Roman inclusive policies was to constantly broaden the base of elite stakeholders. Once inside, the newcomers made sure that the door did not close behind them, acting as political brokers toward their communities of origin (where they often maintained a foothold). It is essential to stress that this process was not a result of any ethically inspired moderation on the part of Roman leadership; it can instead be seen as instrumental (if not actually indispensable) to the success of the entire expansionist movement in Italy, whether it was calculated or not. In a fourth-century central Mediterranean characterized by several imperialist bids, it was essential to coagulate consensus around a specific core area, making it more competitive than any of its rivals. Since independence was no longer among the realistic options open to small Middle Republican polities, there might have been an attraction toward an expanding empire that could boast a track record of centuries of horizontal integration of elites at the highest political level. Read in this light, the consular lists of Rome would contain a precious trace of the phenomenon that made the unification of Italy so successful and long-lived.

[52] Overview in Dench 2005.   [53] Terrenato 2019: 158–74.
[54] See Bernard 2018a: 173–4 for examples of nonelite mobility in the case of Latin authors and other skilled professions such as architects and artisans; see 187–91 for supporting epigraphic evidence.

3 | The Long Shadow of *Tributum* in the Long Fourth Century

JAMES TAN

A sketch of the Roman citizen in action will produce certain familiar motifs. The *civis* fighting in the legions will be a common scene. The *civis* voting, or attending a *contio* (public speech) or participating in this or that religious ceremony – all will be likely candidates. Yet in sheer number of participants, none of those could match the paying of *tributum* (a property levy to fund soldier pay) and the receiving of *stipendium* (soldier pay). Unless he was under arms, every landowning *pater familias* paid *tributum*, while every soldier received *stipendium*. And given Rosenstein's demonstration of how many Romans were paying *tributum*, it is no exaggeration to declare that paying tax was the single most ubiquitous – the single most normal – thing that a Roman citizen did in a year of civic participation.[1] A sketch of the Roman citizen in action really should feature a farmer paying *tributum* to a *tribunus aerarius*.

Once the prevalence of taxation is incorporated into our understanding of Roman civic life, things start to change. When patricians and plebeians engaged in political battle, who precisely was involved? And where? Take this instance from the year 401, in which Livy nonchalantly discusses "tribunes":

> Incited by these speeches, the *plebs* condemned the accused to pay each a fine of 10,000 pounds of bronze. It was in vain that Sergius blamed Fortune and the common chance of war, while Verginius begged that he might not be more unlucky at home than he had been in the campaign. On them the wrath of the people was poured out ...
>
> The victorious *tribuni*, so that the plebs might have an immediate reward for its judgment, proposed a land-law and forbade the gathering of *tributum*, notwithstanding that pay was needed for so many armies, whose campaigning, though successful, yet failed to realize the desired end in any war.[2]

---

[1] See Rosenstein (Chapter 4) in this volume for discussion of how many citizens were paying *tributum* and receiving *stipendium*. This is not to say that citizens invested less time or energy in war or religion, on which see Padilla Peralta 2020a: 244.

[2] Livy 5.12.1–4 (after Loeb trans.): *His orationibus incitata plebs denis milibus aeris gravis reos condemnat, nequiquam Sergio Martem communem belli fortunamque accusante, Verginio deprecante ne infelicior domi quam militiae esset. In hos versa ira populi cooptationis tribunorum*

3 Tributum in the Long Fourth Century

Livy and his sources presumably had very little idea of who did what in 401. The emergence of four plebeian consular tribunes in the following year suggests that there was indeed a clash of some kind, and the record insists that *tributum* was wielded as a political weapon in this period – as discussed in this chapter, it recurs in accounts of the succeeding years. But it was left to later writers like Livy to create a narrative. They assumed that the plebeians were led by men called tribunes and that all the tribunes in question here were the *tribuni plebis* (tribunes of the *plebs*) conducting politics on the familiar stage of the Forum. And so we read that *tribuni plebis* prevented the collection of *tributum*. The reality, however, was likely more complicated. Yes, it must have been tribunes of the *plebs* who ran the trials and who agitated for this or that law, but it is not obvious how ten leaders, who were confined to the city and who relied on physical interposition for their obstruction, could have blocked thousands of payments of *tributum* in each *pagus* of the countryside.[3] It was the *tribuni aerarii* (those who collected *tributum* and who paid out *stipendium*) who could do that.[4] If we accept that disrupting *tributum* really was a political tactic – and I will argue throughout that it indeed was – then it is best to envision two sets of tribunes operating in cahoots: The *tribuni plebis* were the plebeian agents in matters of justice and legislation, but the *tribuni aerarii* were turning the screws on the fiscal front. The *tribuni plebis* were the face of plebeian politics in the city; the *tribuni aerarii* were the strong arm in the countryside.

That these *tribuni aerarii* do not feature in Livy's history should not be surprising. Their fiscal function had been extinct for over a century by the time that Livy was born, and while he himself witnessed the heavy exactions of the triumviral period, these were nothing like *tributum* in their mechanics; they were not collected on the same basis in the same ways by the same people, and their context was more centralized, monetized, and menacing. The world of early *tributum* was thus an entirely foreign process to Livy and to those of his sources that postdated its suspension in 167. Among the

---

fraudisque contra legem Treboniam factae memoriam obscuram fecit. Victores tribuni, ut praesentem mercedem iudicii plebes haberet, legem agrariam promulgant tributumque conferri prohibent, cum tot exercitibus stipendio opus esset resque militiae ita prospere gererentur ut nullo bello veniretur ad exitum spei.

[3] Bleicken 1955: 5–9.
[4] There is no way of knowing whether the label *tribunus aerarius* applied from the beginning, but it will be adopted throughout in lieu of a better alternative. It is possible that they were originally called something else or that they had no term at all, and that, as bronze became a ubiquitous medium of payment, the label *aerarius* (of or concerning bronze) came to apply. The evidence, unfortunately, does not allow any firm claim on this front.

poorly preserved earlier sources, it is not clear that *tributum* and the *tribuni aerarii* were so invisible. Cato is the best example. Very familiar with *tributum*, he showed lexicographical interest in "*pignoriscapio*, resorted to because of military pay which a soldier ought to receive from the *tribunus aerarius*."[5] In the *Origines*, he was also aware that high levels of *tributum* threatened the economic interests of landowners: Although the context is a mystery, he noted that a decision was made "so that estates would not be put in danger when *tributum* was exacted."[6] If later authors showed less interest, it is far from inexplicable. They knew nothing of that taxpayers' world. Furthermore, the elite authors of Republican history showed little inclination to highlight the agency of nonsenators and their neglect of the grubby world of money and rural politicking should surprise no one. But absence of evidence is clearly not evidence of absence here. It has to be emphasized that the central fact of this story – that Romans paid and collected *tributum* – cannot be dismissed simply because our sources rarely mention it. Even if it were true that Livy preserved nothing of fiscal history, it would be absurd to conclude from this that Romans never paid tax. Of course they did. And both Cato and Livy knew it; in fact, anyone who reads Livy with an eye to fiscal matters will be surprised at just how much interesting material even he has transmitted from his earlier sources. Given all of this, the historian's task is to convert our scraps of evidence into the most sensible fiscal model manageable, and to think through the ramifications of that reconstruction for our understanding of the period.

At the same time, however, there is obviously a great deal in Livy that cannot be trusted. How to proceed? I accept aspects of Livy's account on two main grounds. The first is that I take the *fasti* to be a more or less accurate source for the period. This list of annual office-holders has come under sustained assault over the years, but my own view is that it has survived these trials with its authority intact.[7] No critique has overcome Broughton's characteristically sensible assertion that it is easier to explain how an accurate record of office-holding survived than it is "to find a period

---

[5] Gellius, *NA* 6.10.2–3: *Pignoriscapio ob aes militare, quod aes a tribuno aerario miles accipere debebat.*

[6] Cornell 2013: Cato F118: *ne praedia in lubricum derigerentur, cum tributus exigeretur.* It is possible that this refers to overseas *tributum* levied on provincials, but there is little reason to think that. See the commentaries at Beck and Walter 2001 and Cornell 2013. My thanks to Dan-el Padilla Peralta for highlighting the importance of this fragment.

[7] Inter alia, Hanell 1946, Ridley 1983, Mora 1999, Holloway 2008, Richardson 2017, with the surveys at Ridley 1980 and Smith 2011. Hölkeskamp 2011 [1987]: 21–2 correctly notes that skepticism towards the first decades of the *fasti* should not negate study of the fourth century.

when the list as we have it could have been invented."[8] The second principle for reading Livy is to focus on issues that were entirely foreign to his or his sources' experiences and that flew in the face of his own narrative or thematic priorities. This method, akin to the (not uncontroversial) "criterion of dissimilarity" in New Testament Studies, is particularly useful when focusing on disputes about *tributum*.[9] Most Roman authors only knew a post-*tributum* world – even fewer had witnessed a refusal to pay – and so this cannot be a case of anachronism. There was no great reason for first-century writers to think of Roman taxes at all, and to the extent that some did, there were few incentives to embed them in the narrative of early Rome. Pro-patrician traditions had no reason to embellish the financial travails of the plebeians, and pro-plebeian authors would not necessarily revel in images of plebeians bickering about money when they could be railing against such travesties as *nexum*, rape, or corporal punishment. Later Romans, after all, were heavily invested in a portrait of their ancestors as uninterested in finances and profits. What Roman agenda, for example, was served by the story of greedy, mutinous troops stoning a duplicitous consular tribune in 414 when he reneged on promises to distribute booty?[10] Nobody emerges well from that vignette. So when Livy does discuss protests or controversy surrounding public finance, the criterion of dissimilarity suggests that we should at least take such instances seriously as real historical events, because it is difficult to see what incentive might have led someone to invent them.

How far should we take this? When it comes to combining the *fasti* with reports of fiscal politics, there is a weak reading and a strong reading available. The weak reading would insist that no individual episode discussed by Livy is in itself reliable, but that each fabricated event had to be concocted according to certain expectations about how society operated. And so, if a political event is driven by something like a refusal to pay *tributum*, we should accept that in some years – even if not in the years Livy claims – politics really did operate like this; otherwise we might expect authors to have concocted stories based on other mechanisms (like debt, land shortage, or sexual assault) that they believed to have affected the Struggle of the Orders. In the absence of any Late Republican inspirations for fiscal politics, the only reason why authors would construct narratives featuring taxation is that *tributum* really was preserved in the inherited

---

[8] Broughton 1951–86: I.xi. For recent and concise discussion of the record of magistrates, see Smith 2011.
[9] For a concise introduction, see Ehrman 2011: 204–6 and (with more context and history) Holmén 2014.
[10] Livy 4.49.9–50.6.

explanations for how this family's first consulship was won or that reformer's debt law was passed. The goal in this case would be to produce a broad sketch of political sociology that describes the overall period, even if the year-by-year account is unreliable. A strong reading would insist that a political dispute in Livy really is trustworthy as a discrete episode in this or that year, and that a record of such annual events was available to later writers. In what follows, the strong reading will be adopted, partly because it delivers clearer explication, and partly because it makes greater sense of the *fasti* and of fluctuations in the success of plebeians and patricians.

Whether one takes a strong or weak reading, it is important to note that evidence for the *tributum–stipendium* system is indeed fraught. Thankfully, there is a much clearer theoretical approach to political change. The rise of the *tribuni aerarii* was part of a change in "regime," or a change in the configuration of stakeholders and principals within the community.[11] By occasioning thousands of new interactions between leaders and citizens – and by instituting the *tribuni aerarii* to manage them all – the institution of *tributum* altered the Roman regime, and the purpose of this chapter is to examine how that alteration affected Roman politics. The approach will be one that is familiar to students of the conflict perspective of sociology. Regimes are of fundamental importance here because it is their strengths and weaknesses that deter or incentivize certain types of political action. An industrial regime, for instance, is prone to workers' strikes, while a feudal regime is vulnerable to a peasant rebellion. A theocratic regime might fear reinterpretations of weather or other natural events.[12] All of this is because each regime is vulnerable wherever it relies on certain resources and on certain types of participation to survive. Those various vulnerabilities represent that regime's specific "political opportunity structure"; that is, they represent how opponents can fruitfully attack the regime or force it into concessions. To take advantage of this structure, political opponents tailor new and specific "repertoires" of action. Prior to *tributum*, Rome's political opportunity structure might have incentivized a repertoire of secession to a foreign city, refusal to serve in the army, or sabotage or theft of agricultural production. After *tributum*, the opportunity structure included resistance to taxation as well. That is why the institution of *tributum* is so important. *Tributum* created a set of tasks that needed to be completed; it then instituted a new set of roles to complete those tasks; then it elevated a set of

---

[11] For this and the exegesis that follows, the standard account remains Tilly 2010, or more briefly at Tilly and Tarrow 2015: ch. 3.

[12] Of course such reinterpretation only occurs retrospectively in the work of later writers who know that the regime has fallen (e.g. Bielenstein 1986: 223–4 on Wang Mang's loss of the mandate of heaven in Han Dynasty China).

people in order to fill those roles; and finally those people developed new tactics to derive maximum benefit from their new functions. By the end of this process, the ways in which leaders and citizens interacted were different. Soldiers relied on the *tribuni aerarii* to pay up when *stipendium* was due. *Tribuni aerarii* relied on farmers to pay, while plenty of farmers must have relied on *tribuni aerarii* to cut them some slack or to be flexible in how or when to hand over *tributum*. Most of all, patrician leaders relied on *assidui* and *tribuni aerarii* to move all of these resources in order to keep the war machine rolling on. Thus, the commitment to pay troops from dedicated revenues – a system that will be referred to here as *tributum–stipendium* – demanded thousands of interpersonal transactions, comprising a network of resource movement, that made the annual routine of war and politics work differently.

To show that the institution of *tributum* produced just this cascade of political change requires, however, a preliminary discussion of how *tributum* worked in the first place. The old fifth-century army may well have moved similar resources along gentilicial or other decentralized pathways, but the regularization of such movements within civic institutions was transformative.[13] Such reform altered the nature of status and prestige by embedding it in the *res publica*. More importantly, it funneled the redistributive system into fixed channels that could be more easily controlled by those who were regularized year after year as *tribuni aerarii*. There were of course influential people in the old networks of the Fabii or the Valerii, but now, instead of cooperating with these great clans, farmers and soldiers had to deal with local *tribuni aerarii* to pay and to be paid. The ordering principle became the *tribus* or district, rather than patronage, and while the extent to which these networks overlapped in this period is the source of debate, it is not hard to see how patrician control stood to lose from this transformation. The *tribuni aerarii* now had a centralized, monopolistic control over the army pay, year after year. It would be astonishing if they had not maximized their resulting leverage. The challenge is to find evidence of it.

3.1 Reforming the Regime

Though I will quibble with some details, Nicolet reconstructed the basic mechanics of how *tributum–stipendium* operated.[14] Soldiers returned from campaign and went to a group of wealthy men in each tribe known as

---

[13] Armstrong 2016: chs. 4–5, Terrenato 2019.
[14] Nicolet 1976, Nicolet 1980: ch. 6, Nicolet 2000: ch. 3 and 4, now with France 2021: ch. 2. Most of what we know can be garnered from Dionysius as the main source (*Ant. Rom.* 4.19 and 19.16.3),

tribuni aerarii to collect all pay (*stipendium*, also known as *aes militare*) that they were owed after deductions for food, equipment, and clothing had been calculated.[15] The *tribuni aerarii* provided this pay from their own purses, and reimbursed themselves by collecting *tributum*, a tax or levy paid by the broad population of landowners (*assidui*) as a proportion of each man's overall property.[16] *Tributum–stipendium* created a neat extraction system in which one group of citizens supplied military labor while the rest provided revenue to pay the soldiers. This was no doubt a revolutionary change in military affairs, as soldiers went from being unpaid to paid, but it was even more disruptive on the home front. Wealthy men (*tribuni aerarii*) in each tribe now had to manage a complex fiscal system. They had to mediate between several thousand Romans who were mustered as soldiers needing pay, and even more farmers who were at home that year and had to supply *tributum* payments. It must have been a high-profile, complicated, and difficult job.

What needs to be emphasized for now, however, is that there is no evidence that a central treasury was involved at all.[17] Livy never describes *stipendium* as being paid *ex aerario* or *tributum* being paid *in aerarium* until the age of long, overseas campaigns, when the supply arrangements must have been different. There is a suggestion that the *aerarium* might have had a role in paying rowers in 210, but only to replace *assidui* who were explicitly drained of all capacity to pay more; this is not evidence of how *tributum* was paid, but how it was substituted when it could not be paid.[18] In contrast, even the first *stipendium* is described as having been paid *de publico* instead of *ex aerario*, while loans to fund rowers in 210 were made *in publicum* (to the *triumviri mensarii*) instead of *in aerarium*.[19] And although no source explicates precisely how *tributum* was paid, there is a wealth of evidence that *tribuni aerarii* interacted directly with the troops,

---

    with Plaut. *Aul.* 525, Varro, *LL* 5.181, Livy 4.59–60 and 10.46.5, Gaius 4.26–7 and Gellius, *NA* 6.10.2–3.

[15] On such deductions, see Polyb. 6.39.15.

[16] On the ballpark percentages paid as *tributum*, see Rosenstein 2016b: esp. 92–4, Taylor 2017: 162–6.

[17] Nicolet (see references above n. 14) envisaged a role for the treasury in receiving an advance from the *tribuni aerarii*, but there is neither evidence nor need for this step. This leap derived from a supposed similarity between Roman and Athenian fiscal systems, which appears to be mistaken (Northwood 2008: 268).

[18] Livy 26.35.3–10, 29.16.2.

[19] Livy 4.59.11, 26.36.5–11, 34.6.14. Interestingly, the estates of widows and orphans that funded cavalry were seized during the Hannibalic War and managed by the *aerarium* (Livy 34.6.14, 34.5.10). This was presumably because, having been converted into temporary state property, they were categorically different to private farms paying *tributum* to *tribuni aerarii*.

independent of any treasury role. A scene from Plautus' *Aulularia* features a *miles* approaching a wealthy man – surely a *tribunus aerarius* – for his money (*aes*), but he is thwarted because his payer's bank account is in arrears.[20] Similarly, at *Poenulus* 1286, a veteran can force payment from another character by framing it as *aes militare*. Similar demands *in extremis* were endorsed by Roman law through *pignoriscapio*, which allowed a man to seize the private property of the *tribunus aerarius* who owed him pay.[21] All of this strongly suggests that the soldier received his pay directly from a *tribunus aerarius* and not from the treasury. When it comes to understanding how the Roman "regime" was remade by *tributum*, this is critical. This fiscal system – leaving aside Rome's other revenues – relied almost entirely on the cooperation and management of the *tribuni*, and not on the workings of a treasury under the centralized control of elected leaders.

That system was tailored to the historical realities that its founders knew. Livy and his sources believed that *tributum–stipendium* began in 406.[22] Crawford and Mersing have shown that there is nothing inherently implausible about the date and that the sources show a remarkably consistent pattern of change in its wake; for example, the Romans after this date began to demand that conquered enemies provide pay for the troops who had just defeated them.[23] While there is no need to repeat their thorough treatments of the topic, it is worth noting a few additional points. The resonance of *tributum–stipendium* has left traces not only in the annalistic narrative following 406, but also in that for the preceding years. In 424, there was apparently a proposal to institute military pay from public land rents, in 414 the troops stoned a consular tribune for his stinginess with plunder, in 410 the Volsci supposedly invaded with paid troops instead of volunteers, and in 409, plebeians gained access to the quaestorship to help manage public finance.[24] All of this makes sense in the context of

---

[20] Plaut. *Aul.* 525. Rosivach 1989 unnecessarily argues that this could not be a soldier because there would not be war and luxury (a theme of the play at this point) at the same time. Gabba 1977: 30 suggests that the *miles* was a mercenary looking for pay, which Aen. Tac. 13.4 tells us was possible. Yet there is no positive reason to accept this, and other requirements – like providing accommodation to a mercenary – are missing (Muñiz Coello 2011: 139–40).

[21] Gaius 4.26–7, Gellius, *NA* 6.10.2–3. Lengle 1936 and Hill 1946 each show from tenses that the practice was already in the past by the time Cato the Elder was writing, which was presumably after 167.

[22] Livy 8.8.3, with Diod. Sic. 14.16.5.

[23] Crawford 1985: 22–3, Mersing 2007, with Gabrielli 2003: 84–8.

[24] 424: Livy 4.36.2, with Crawford 1985: 23. 414: Livy 4.49.9–50.6, despite the notion at Holloway 2008: 123–4 and Armstrong 2016: 198 that this must be a war band because real Roman soldiers would not behave this way. It is even harder to see how an army bound to

pressuring or preparing for the institution of military pay. It also has to be emphasized that the Varronian year 406 is – once the dictator years and the Licinio-Sextian anarchy have been taken into account – probably sometime in the early 390s.[25] This was a time of roaring mercenary wars in Sicily, and we know that Italians were being recruited for these armies.[26] In this context, it makes sense that the Romans would take the decision to start paying troops in order to retain manpower.

Yet various scholars have rejected the possibility that military pay as described above could have been implemented as early as 406.[27] Brunt dismissed the date as "transparently anachronistic."[28] The reason for this skepticism is that people have been unable to see how *tributum* and *stipendium* could have operated without the proliferation of coinage. The objection is not without merit. If we insist on the view that the treasury had to receive and issue tens of thousands of precisely quantified payments, then the absence of coinage would indeed be an insurmountable hurdle. But the treasury played no such role, as the system was instead local and interpersonal, and this weakens the skeptical position significantly. The countryside was already buzzing with economic networks of exchange, in which people worked for each other, borrowed from each other, gave dowries to each other, bought from each other, sold to each other, and so much more. Capogrossi Colognesi has argued that the Roman countryside could be characterized as a network of small farms that were legally *in*dependent but economically *inter*dependent.[29] Despite its flaws, Cato's *De Agri Cultura* reinforces this portrait. The world it depicts – a world with constant movement of goods and services from farm to farm in each

---

a (gentilicial) warlord by personal ties would decide to stone its leader. 410: 4.53.1. Whether Etruscan cities were paying soldiers is entirely unknowable (Massa-Pairault 1986: 41). 409: Livy 4.54.2-3, with Mora 1999: 39.

[25] For discussion, see Drummond 1990, Cornell 1995: 399–402, or Oakley 1997–2005, 1: 104–6.

[26] Diod. Sic. 14.8-9, 14.15.3, 14.58.2, 14.61.4-6, with Lomas 2004. On the archaeological evidence, see Tagliamonte 2002 and Sole 2014, and for Carthaginian coinage to fuel this recruitment, see Frey-Kupper 2014: 81 and Visonà 2018: 12–15. Bridgman 2003 has argued the Syracusans might have been hostile to Romans, but the Persian case proves that mercenaries could be recruited from hostile cities, and there is no reason to doubt that the Carthaginians would have welcomed some grizzled Latin infantry. On the relationship between mercenary service and the Romans, see Trundle 2004: 35, Lendon 2007: 508–12, Prag 2010: 107–8 and Sanz 2011.

[27] See, for examples, Nicolet 1966: 35–42; Marchetti 1977; Harris 1990: 507 and 2016: 32, Mitchell 1990: 163, Raaflaub 1996: 290, Humm 2005: ch. 7, Rich 2007: 18, MacMullen 2011: 105, Ñaco del Hoyo 2011: 382.

[28] Brunt 1971: 641.

[29] Capogrossi Colognesi 1990: 245–8, Cornell 1995: 269–71, Smith 2006: 244–7, Rich 2008: 562, Cifani 2009: esp. 312–15, Roselaar 2010: 20–4, Capogrossi Colognesi 2012: 95–121, Bernard 2016: 322–4, Lanfranchi 2015: 410–13, Smith 2017: 20–1.

locale – also resembles other well-studied preindustrial rural contexts.[30] Even in an undermonetized world, and even without the notaries of Southern Europe, medieval English villages were still thriving debtscapes of deferred payments, loans, community contributions, and so on: "In some [fourteenth-century] villages, lending, and indeed borrowing, was so widely disseminated that almost everyone must have been involved in it."[31] This was all part of "a necessary collaboration," in which capital and labor had to circulate in ways that "mirrored economic interdependence."[32] These people were not economically paralyzed. The problem with insisting that Romans could not pay *tributum* and *stipendium* without coinage is that it insists that fiscal payments were substantially different from all the other transactions that occurred in rural areas throughout the premodern world. Long before coinage, Romans were well versed in moving resources into and out of each other's estates. Even in the Late Republic, as Hollander shows, rural Italy was managing a thriving economy with limited reliance on coinage.[33]

Moreover, insisting that *tributum* must have been paid in coin is not as simple as waiting for the first Roman minting. In Chapter 6 in this volume, Yarrow shows that even as late as the First Punic War, Roman coinage was nowhere near capable of sustaining the quantity of payments or range of denominations required by *tributum–stipendium*. It is ludicrous to think that Rome's first emissions could instantly find their way to taxpayers' purses and then on to the *tribuni aerarii* and the troops. Nor can the irregularity of early coinage emissions be reconciled with the regularity of Roman warfare, and it would take years – decades – for emissions to be copious enough to sustain a coin-based *stipendium* system.[34] To delay military pay until every corner of the rural economy was monetized enough to sustain *tributum–stipendium* would be to delay it much later than is plausible, perhaps as late as the Hannibalic War.[35]

Instead of fixating on what the Romans did not have (i.e. coinage), we should be examining the roles played by Rome's existing socioeconomic networks. It is pointless to ask how they could have tax without the institutions that sustained it in later periods; the real question is how the tax that emerges in our evidence was crafted to fit the context that they did have in their own period. Central to this enterprise will be the *tribuni aerarii*. To

---

[30] For example Cat. *De Ag.* 4.1 and 5.3. On its flaws, see Terrenato 2012. [31] Briggs 2009: 146.
[32] Clark 1981: 261. [33] Hollander 2007: 122–35 on "the rural monetary zone."
[34] Cornell 1995: 396–7. On the ill-fit of minting and warfare, see Bernard 2018b: 4–6.
[35] I benefitted greatly from an email exchange with Liv Yarrow about the restricted scale of issues before the quadrigatus, on which see also Bernard 2018b.

establish their role – and to understand why *tributum–stipendium* was placed in their hands to manage – it is worth returning to studies of fourteenth-century England. While there are no detailed sources on the sociology of rural Rome in this period, the English case shows how pervasive and entrenched credit networks could be, and reveals what was possible within the portrait of interdependent farms sketched by Capogrossi Colognesi and others.[36] This is all the more apt because neither Rome nor medieval England had specialized moneylenders or high volumes of coinage.[37] While most English lending occurred "horizontally" within classes, leading to a great deal of mutual indebtedness, there were nevertheless also a few disproportionately well-represented heavy lenders; this wealthy minority comprised around 10 percent of loans in the village of Writtle, and tended to engage in long-term relationships across multiple loans.[38] Their superior wealth led to more transactions with more people; they became more embedded in these exchange networks. They were more active in hiring labor, more likely to control necessary equipment and capital, and more able to help those in need, and they had more surplus to trade with more people. They were also more prominent in managing contributions to local religious and civic organizations. All of this could be expected of *tribuni aerarii*, too.[39] They were more likely to hire workers for their land, more likely to control capital equipment, and more likely to manage the resources of cults and other communal organizations. Their greater resources meant that they were already the most active nodes in these exchange and credit networks. They had disproportionate knowledge of who owed what.[40] Furthermore, they had to know how to manage those debts in socially sustainable ways.[41] In 406, amid all of these interactions, they were asked to factor extra transfers of *tributum* and *stipendium* into the already dynamic

---

[36] Hölkeskamp 2011 [1987]: *passim* on Roman debt, and above n. 29 for rural communities.

[37] Briggs 2009: ch. 4 on English lenders. Clark 1981: 255 notes that some of these credit transactions were eminently productive. English growers would advance malt to brewers, for example, knowing that they would not be paid until the beer was sold. Dairy farmers advanced milk to cheese makers.

[38] Clark 1981: 262–5; Briggs 2009: 147. Established elites have every reason to be less vampiric and to prioritize enduring relationships; see, for example, the contrast between the low interest rates of old nobility and the aggressive profits of "emerging households" in prerevolutionary Jiangxi (Averill 1990).

[39] On their wealth, see Nicolet 1966: 598–606. De Haas in Chapter 7 surveys the evidence for estates of different sizes.

[40] Platteau 1995: 637 notes that the economic health of many debtors is understood in an area because its causes are common knowledge. Drought, locusts, a patriarch's death, or various other reasons for struggles were obvious to outsiders.

[41] Clark 1981: 270–1: English "villagers readily balanced demands for payment against the personal benefits and trust involved in maintaining long-term relationships."

networks of each neighborhood. In the debt-riddled community of fourth-century Rome, there is even a good chance that the *tribunus aerarius* was the creditor of the soldier to whom he owed *stipendium* or the seasonal employer of the sons of *assidui* owing *tributum*. *Tributum–stipendium* piggybacked on these local economic networks. The system was attached to the estates of the *tribuni aerarii* precisely because they were so used to managing such flows in a precoinage context.[42]

All of this fiscal change looks quite different once *tributum* and *stipendium* are situated in the socioeconomic networks of rural communities. Larger landowners, who must always have been influential anyway, now had an extra set of payments – coerced payments – to use in exercising their dominance and patronage over their neighbors. To gain some clearer sense of this group of *tribuni aerarii*, there needs to be some sense of how many there were of them relative to the rest of the population. A small number would create a portrait in which a handful from the upper elite of Roman society managed the public revenues of large areas of farmland, while a larger number would create a larger number of smaller "fiefdoms" run by men who often would have no ambitions to win elections or lead armies. Again, there is no direct data on this. There are, however, guardrails that provide some limitations, or that at least reveal a scholar's assumptions and preferences.

The first step is to establish basically how many *tribuni aerarii* there were. According to Rosenstein's reconstruction in Chapter 4, the number of Roman citizen men in 341 would have been around 40,000 (following Afzelius), of whom only around 30,000 would be *sui iuris*. Rosenstein estimates that, of those 30,000, something like 25,800 would be landowning *assidui* and hence eligible to pay *tributum*. In any given year, however, those who were conscripted would not have to pay *tributum*, since, as contributors of military labor instead, they were eligible to receive *stipendium*. Removing those soldiers would leave something like 17,000 citizens paying *tributum* in each year of warfare. As Rosenstein notes, that is quite a small number, yet it still provides some sense of the daunting coordination needed to keep the troops paid. To envision 17,000 taxpayers is to envision something like 17,000 tax payments. How many *tribuni aerarii* would be required to process all of this? That depends on how many taxpayers each *tribunus* can be

---

[42] The lack of coinage raises the question of why they were named *tribuni aerarii* ("bronze-dealing tribunes") and why military pay seems so often to have been dubbed *aes militare* ("military bronze"). These terms imply an assumption of bronze payments, but whether these labels and a bronze medium were there from the beginning is unknowable (see above, n. 4). On the early use of bronze in the Twelve Tables and in procedures such as *mancipatio*, see Mersing 2007: 232 and Bernard 2018b: 6–7.

expected to have "managed." If each *tribunus aerarius* had to collect the *tributum* of 20 farmers, then there would have to be around 850 *tribuni aerarii*; if each *tribunus* was responsible for 100 taxpayers, then there would be 170 *tribuni aerarii*. Something between those two seems the right order of magnitude, and I would be inclined – though there is no evidence either way – toward the upper end of that 170–850 range. The higher number seems more plausible to me for three main reasons. The first is that the administrative work must have been demanding, and so requiring a *tribunus aerarius* to collect *tributum* from more than a few dozen *assidui* asked too much of the time and skills of the leaders involved. The second is that *tribuni aerarii* had to have sufficient capital to cover the pay of troops within their jurisdiction – the assumption of the aforementioned *pignoriscapio*, after all, was that a stingy *tribunus aerarius* would have distrainable property for each soldier[43] – and hence too few *tribuni aerarii* would have forced each tribune's estate to be responsible for too many soldiers. The final reason is that the movement of resources in the precoinage era would have occurred most easily on a very local level between people with some familiarity, and so *tribuni aerarii* would likely have been closely spaced to keep networks small – one reason why *tributum* was based in tribes was presumably to make sure that collectors were not dealing with unknown payers across significant distances. Thus, for a population of roughly 40,000 adult males in 341, a roster of more than 300 or 400 *tribuni aerarii* does not strike me as implausible. For comparison, the two legions of the mid-fourth century would have required 600 cavalrymen each year; these wealthy young men must have come from the same high-placed families that provided the *tribuni aerarii*.[44] Rosenstein's age distribution table suggests that there should be something like 1.6 times as many fatherless *patres familias* aged over thirty as there should be total males in a cohort aged seventeen to thirty.[45] It seems more than plausible, therefore, that a society that could field 600 rich young men annually in the cavalry could empower at least that many rich older men as *tribuni aerarii*. I see little reason, therefore, to dismiss a number in the hundreds for a year like 341. On the contrary, insisting on a lower number would require unconvincing arguments. One would have to rework Rosenstein's numbers in less plausible ways, reject the reconstruction of *tributum*

---

[43] Nicolet 1966: 608; Bleicken 1995: 12. By the Late Republic, the *tribuni aerarii* were drawn *amplissimo ex censu* (Asc. 17C, with Wiseman 1970: 80).
[44] Using Polybius' (6.20.9) numbers for cavalry per legion.
[45] Rosenstein, Chapter 4 in this volume.

collection we have just outlined, or assume that *tribuni aerarii* each managed payments of a huge number of estates and soldiers.[46]

The sheer number of *tribuni aerarii* envisaged here means that, even if every patrician *pater familias* were enrolled among them, the vast majority still had to be plebeian. Whether one conceives of fifth-century warfare as a gentilicial phenomenon or as one conducted through more centralized, civic institutions, the embedding of wealthy plebeians in the heart of military administration must have disrupted a society in which patrician names enjoyed an all-but-monopolistic hold on the *fasti*.[47] The *res publica* had never before permitted such institutionalized plebeian influence in military matters. These plebeians thus became central to the community and to the state in new ways.[48] The army obviously depended on their efficacy for its pay, but their importance must have been even deeper, because they now decided how, when, where, and even whether a farmer paid his taxes. Every act of taxation, after all, is a political act.[49] Every act of taxation signals consent and the acceptance of the status quo; or it is the result of resistance, coercion, and bargaining. Plebeian *tribuni aerarii* were central to this political realm almost every year. They could be tough on farmers who struggled to pay, or they could dole out favors. They could accept delays, they could grant discounts in light of known hardships, or they could negotiate and haggle over the form of payment. A *tribunus aerarius* might go easy on a few farmers on the understanding that the farmers' sons would feel obliged to dig out a drain or remove a fallen tree. Or he might go easy on them because, in a year when his son was running for military tribune, he was campaigning for votes. *Assidui* and *tribuni aerarii* were left no choice but to interact, to bargain, and to do deals. Once the state created a compulsory payment, it empowered the *tribuni aerarii* to dispense favors and punishments, and it is unrealistic to think that the potential of this new dynamic was lost on contemporaries.

---

[46] One could claim that the system was coordinated by a small number of *tribuni aerarii* in each tribe, but that the collection was done by other figures on a local level; this is possible, but it is more a matter of shifting the titles of the actors than of reimagining the number of people involved. My thanks to Jeremy Armstrong for noting this possibility.

[47] Armstrong 2016: ch. 4–5, Terrenato 2019.

[48] Martin (1990: 228–9) and Eder (1990: 27) have noted that a "state" is even more problematic in this period than in other periods of ancient history because of the cleavage between plebeians and patricians. The cooperation of plebeians who funded wars led by patricians is not only illustrative of that observation but also offers an insight into how the cleavage was mended.

[49] For theoretical discussion, see Martin, Mehrotra, and Prasad 2009.

3.2 Reforming the Repertoires

The remainder of this paper will explore how the plebeians and patricians could adopt new repertoires of political action in response to this new regime. The starting point will be to re-examine fourth-century Rome in light of a simple assumption: that instituting military pay and the *tributum* needed to pay it must have had social and political consequences. If that premise is accepted, then it is worth testing hypotheses that follow from it. Those hypotheses must in turn possess two basic characteristics. They need to be logically coherent expectations of cause and effect, and they also need to be identifiable in the types of sources that dominate the surviving evidence. There is no point, in other words, in positing a precise cliometric hypothesis that can never be demonstrated by extant data, or in wading into the cultural and psychological effects on the almost entirely unattested "everyday Roman." It is, however, possible to expect evidence of – and thus to test – the following four claims:

1. Demanding new revenue (*tributum*) provided those who paid it with a potential grievance that could produce political contention.
2. Not all payers had the payment on hand when it was needed, and thus some must have been forced into debt. This too could lead to political contention.
3. Those on whom *tributum* was most reliant could make the most consequential claims in this contention, since payments would collapse at once without their participation.
4. Leaders' dependence on revenue and on those who paid it affected the decisions they made.

Each of those claims can be taken a priori as reasonable. Whether they are useful will depend on whether they can make better sense of the evidence as we have it than previous claims, and that can only be ascertained with more detailed examination of the historical record.

3.2.1 Demanding New Revenue (Tributum) Provided Those Who Paid It with a Potential Grievance that Could Produce Political Contention

According to Livy, *tributum* elicited protests in 406, 401, 397, 385, 380, 378, 377, and 348. Not all of these attestations are as reliable as others, but it is certainly a consistent theme. Immediately striking is the way in which the *dilectus* (the levy of soldiers) became the focal point of this new fiscal politics. Protested levies were not in themselves a novelty, but the issue now was less a refusal to serve than a refusal to pay troops. This raises methodological difficulties. The raising of the army was also the first step in occasioning *tributum*, since there was no military pay without troops, and thus preventing conscription was a way to prevent *tributum*. So, if Livy reports a disrupted *dilectus*, it is not immediately obvious whether the community was refusing military service or refusing to allow the army to be raised. Yet, perhaps surprisingly, the evidence is often specific that the financial concerns were the more pressing ones.

In this regard, two revealing cases date to 378 and 348. In the first, the Romans were facing war with the Latins, and with Praeneste in particular. It is worth following Livy's chain of causation. According to his version, in 380, debt problems were so severe that tribunes of the *plebs* blocked the levy; no army could be raised until the Praenestini were approaching the city, at which point a dictator was appointed and everyone, out of fear of his powers, obediently submitted to the levy.[50] The plebeian obstruction returned in 378, so that no levy could be held until the patricians finally acceded to demands that reveal what the fight was really about: "that, until the end of the war, neither anyone pay *tributum* nor any legal proceedings take place with respect to debt."[51] When crafting a narrative that explained the events as he understood them, Livy at first fell back on the easy trope of the fearsome dictator; people did not want to fight, but then the war happened because they were cowed into serving. Yet his record of troubled levies persisted. Instead of returning to one of these tropes of awe-inspiring ancestors, however, this time he claimed that problems were resolved by fiscal and financial measures. We cannot know what his sources were, but they convinced him that the point of blocking the levy was not to earn a reprieve from military service, but to earn a reprieve from *tributum*.

Then, in 377, we are also told that *tributum* was raised for the building of the city wall.[52] There are problems with the notion that *tributum*, a levy attached specifically to *stipendium*, was used to pay for public works, but what is of greatest interest here is the way in which Livy assumes that people disrupted the *dilectus* to gain tax relief.[53] According to his account, the *plebs* was compelled (*coacta*) to pay *tributum* because there was no army needed that summer, and hence there was no *dilectus* to impede and hold for ransom. This comment is especially revealing of Livy's thinking

---

[50] Livy 6.27.8–28.4. See Section 3.2.2 for a different reconstruction. [51] Livy 6.31.4.
[52] Livy 6.32.1–2. [53] Bernard 2018a: 112–13 on labor and *tributum*.

because, just lines later, we are informed that the levy for a Latin–Volscian war went smoothly.[54] The contradictions here – that there was no *dilectus* but then there was a *dilectus* – reveal Livy's thinking as he wrote. Aware that the year had yet to produce an army, Livy assumed that the reason harsh taxation was possible was that there was no *dilectus* to impede. The fact that an army would then be enrolled without a hitch reveals that he had simply assumed that people would (a) resent taxation and (b) make that known when it came time to enroll the two legions. It seems likely that his comment arose not from the historical record, but from Livy's own conception of how fourth-century fiscal politics operated. He was convinced by his own reading – not by his own experiences – that demands for *tributum* could be resisted if there was a levy to disrupt.

Following what may have been an enlarged draft in 350 and a refusal of the Latins to supply troops in 349, the Romans of 347 faced a continuation of a prolonged debt crisis.[55] Their response comprised two parts. The first was the thoroughly financial measure of lowering interest rates, but the second, which Livy believed was the greatest source of aid (*levatae maxime res*), was to avoid a new *dilectus* and forego the related *tributum* in 347.[56] It is entirely possible, given the quietude of 348, that this was actually a policy over two years instead of one (see the next section). In any case, Livy is explicit that foregoing *tributum* produced domestic *otium* (peace). The patricians had apparently learned their lessons. In 348–347, just as in 378, it was not resistance to military service so much as resistance to *tributum* that caused disruptions of the levy. The patricians avoided trouble by simply not holding the *dilectus* and hence not demanding *tributum*.

There is, therefore, a recurring insistence that *tributum* was a potent political problem and that its presence or absence was a motivation for political behavior. Why, however, would the community remember such a theme? How would it be embedded into the stories and narratives that preserved the past? One reason may have been that it was so tightly bound with an issue of undoubted importance to legislation and to the ideology of an unoppressed people: debt.

---

[54] Livy 6.32.4.
[55] Livy 7.27.3–4. Hölkeskamp 2011 [1987]: 101 situates the episode within a larger context of debt problems.
[56] Livy 7.27.3–4.

3.2.2 Not All Payers Had the Payment on Hand When It Was Needed, and Thus Some Must Have Been Forced into Debt: This Too Could Lead to Political Contention

It would frankly be bizarre if *tributum* did not exacerbate debt problems. Although military pay was a boon to those who served in the legions in any given year, it is self-evident that those farmers who had to make one more payment each year suffered financially. If they were already struggling to pay off debts, *tributum* cannot have helped. This is not to argue that every mention of *tributum* is accurate – or that all debt was caused by taxation – but it is to argue that, in the engine that powered fourth-century Roman history, *tributum* was an integral moving part, and it was remembered as such.[57]

Livy's first mention of someone being impoverished and indebted due to *tributum* took the form of a veteran in his thoroughly anachronistic account of the year 495. This cannot have been historical, but the episode testifies to the Romans' assumption that *tributum* and debt were interwoven in "the old days."[58] That link is difficult to avoid in the record as it stands. I have already noted that, at least according to Livy, the tribunes of 378 and 347 believed that a reprieve from *tributum* would be central to alleviating the problem of debt.[59] In the former instance, the tribunes managed to extract a concession from the *patres* that *tributum* would be suspended as a way of alleviating the debt problem. Debtors would obviously be helped if they could avoid paying the state in addition to servicing their loans, but the focus may also have been on preventing payers from having to take on new debts to meet *tributum*. Importantly, events of 378 are coupled with debt reform, this time the halving of interest from 1/12 to 1/24, presumably per month.[60] Livy also believed, as just discussed, that *tributum* to fund construction of the city wall exacerbated debt problems in 377, and Bernard has shown how much strain households must have been under to meet the resource requirements of that immense project.[61] There were also intense debt problems in the early 280s. Higher than usual *tributum* in the Third Samnite Wars must have made the financial pressures greater, and it is entirely plausible that debts inflating in the 290s were bursting a few years later.[62] Even in 306, with a much cheaper campaign, the people had felt burdened enough that they dedicated a statue to Q. Marcius

---

[57] On the problem of anachronism and a chronic issue like debt in the ancient world, see Cornell 1995: 327–8. The nexus of taxation and indebtedness may well have been a recurring part of Roman expansion in the provinces as well; see, for example, Woolf 1998: 40–5.
[58] Livy 2.23.3, with Dion. Hal. 6.26.1.   [59] See above nn. 51 and 55.
[60] Livy 7.27.3–4, Hölkeskamp 2011 [1987]: 99.   [61] Livy 6.32.1–2, Bernard 2018a: ch. 4.
[62] Maddox 1983: 278–86.

Tremulus for canceling one year's *tributum*; obviously the years 296 and 295 were even more onerous.[63] It is not difficult to see how they would have led to debt, and to the explosive debt politics of the so-called secession.[64]

Nor was the link between *tributum* and debt unidirectional. Take, for instance, the repeated calls for censuses.[65] As debtors handed over property to creditors, new censuses were important because they allowed estates to be revalued on the rolls. In a timocratic system, in which wealth brought political privileges, there was only one incentive for debtors to call for a diminishing of their census ratings: It reduced the amount of *tributum* they would have to pay in future.[66] A citizen who lost half his estate to a creditor would only have to pay half his old *tributum*, since he was now being assessed on half the old property valuation. This would explain the repeated calls for censuses. In 380, as noted earlier, a census reportedly failed due to the death of a censor and then a flaw in the election of replacements.[67] The *plebs* was outraged. Yet censors in 378, still embroiled in the same debt strife and disputed levy, also apparently failed to conduct a census because of war with the Volsci.[68] The link between debt and *tributum* might be most meaningful in the case of the census of 351.[69] This year's censors followed the debt resolutions of the year before, when a board of five used public money to resolve as much of the debt problem as possible.[70] Livy claims that, with the recalibration of people's finances and the transfer of property that resulted, it was time to rerecord the estate of each citizen. It was surely understood by all that, by reducing the declared valuation of so many who had forfeited property to creditors, the censors would as a result be recalculating how *tributum* would be levied. No doubt former debtors, who had parted with assets in order to pay off their debts, were eager to have their obligations reduced.

3.2.3 *Those on Whom* Tributum *Was Most Reliant Could Make the Most Consequential Claims in This Contention, Since Payments Would Collapse At Once Without Their Participation*

Although thousands of citizens had to pay *tributum*, it was upon the *tribuni aerarii* that the system relied most heavily. Not only did these rich citizens pay the most, they managed all the payments and determined whether the system

---

[63] Pliny, *Natural History* 34.23. On the number of legions, see Cornell 1995: 361 and Oakley 1997–2005, vol. 4: 282–3.

[64] Cass. Dio 8.37.2–4, Zon. 8.2, Livy, *Per.* 11. [65] Oakley 2002: 20, Humm 2006: 47–8.

[66] On the impoverishment and demotion of those who forfeited property to clear debts, Hölkeskamp [1987] 2011: 100–1.

[67] Livy 6.27.3–8. [68] Livy 6.31.2–3. [69] Livy 7.22.6–10. [70] Livy 7.21.5–8.

ran at all. If they declared that there would be no *tributum* or *stipendium*, then there would be no *tributum* or *stipendium*. As already noted, the majority of these *tribuni* must have been plebeians, and there is good reason to believe here that the *tributum* system could be wielded as a weapon to secure their political goals in the Conflict of the Orders.[71] The link between *tributum* and the *fasti* provides the most illustrative evidence here.

The protests about *tributum* in 380–378 have already been discussed in this chapter. What is worth noting here is that, in the same year as the refusal to raise and fund an army in 380, elections returned the anomalous college of three patrician and either three or five plebeian consular tribunes.[72] It is possible that, far from crumbling in the face of a dictator, as Livy claims, protests of *tributum* were relaxed after plebeian leaders had extracted a year of high office. That impression is even more likely given patterns in the *fasti* after 401. In the episode that began this chapter, "tribunes" promised to cancel *tributum* and that boycott was not overturned until the elections returned a college for 400 of 2 patrician and 4 plebeian consular tribunes. In 399, that was expanded to five plebeians and one patrician, and this was repeated in 396. These plebeian years are entirely at odds with the norm: Only patricians had held the consular tribunate since Q. Antonius had done so as a plebeian in 422, and, before him, L. Atilius as a plebeian in 444. The years 400, 399, and 396 are pure aberrations.[73]

What can explain this discontinuity? The rise of *tributum* had left the regime vulnerable to a new repertoire of fiscal protest. *Tribuni aerarii* could now squeeze patrician leaders in ways that they could not before. As already noted, 401 saw tribunes refuse to allow the collection of *tributum*. A refusal to pay the troops meant that no army could be raised – the war with Veii was ongoing in these years – and the foot was not taken off the fiscal throat until the plebeians got what they wanted: consular tribunates. Livy is explicit: "Overjoyed at their victory in this election, the tribunes of

---

[71] Jerome France (2021: 25–7) has raised doubts as to whether taxation really did generate political leverage in antiquity, as envisioned by Tilly (1993) for the early modern period, or whether that is all too redolent of a modern representative democracy and a taxation–representation axis; without that context, he suggests, there are many other reasons why people act politically. This is a valid point. At issue here, however, is simple bargaining power. Once plebeians could withhold something that the patricians needed, that could be leveraged for bargaining; the same dynamic would apply in any society or political system. Early modern taxpayers happened to desire greater representation and state services, and the so-called Struggle of the Orders shows that plebeians desired economic relief and political reform. The bargaining power will follow the dynamics of the society in which it is found.

[72] Livy 6.30.2 lists three plebeians, while Diod. Sic. 15.51.1 adds two extra.

[73] Brennan 2000: 50: "Impossible to explain." Smith 2006: 271: "no obvious explanation."

the plebs withdrew that opposition to the tax which was the greatest obstacle to the business of the state."[74] Once the consular tribunate was won, *tributum* flowed again. The plebeian leaders in the next year again won the elections, and so there was no need for disruption of the *dilectus*.

In this case, the sources for political events correspond perfectly with the testimony of the *fasti*, and the importance of that alignment needs to be appreciated. A strong reading would argue that the alignment reflects actual events. Even a weak reading, however, would have to ask why this fiscal story was concocted. On what grounds did a historian decide to invent the notion that plebeians held *tributum* hostage to win elections? Given that the *fasti* must surely predate the first written histories, it might be supposed that a second-century historian noticed the sudden flurry of plebeian names in the *fasti*, and, tasked with inventing a plausible explanation for this anomaly, he chose a narrative of taxation as his best option. Later sources then found this compelling enough to transmit. And so, even if it rejects the precise historicity of Livy's account for the year, that conspiratorial reconstruction still has to acknowledge that the exploitation of *tributum* was deemed the best explanation for the patricians' thwarted hold on military command. Something in the fabricator's mindset left him convinced that a fiscal explanation really was best able to explain the political affairs of his ancestors. Furthermore, as scholars have pointed out before, he showed an impressive awareness of 406 as a turning point.[75] As already noted, the sources mentioned tumultuous levies in earlier years, but they were certainly never this successful; the addition of *tributum* and the elevation of the *tribuni aerarii* explains why the tactic was so effective now.[76] Whether in real history or in a fabricator's narrative, the tax boycott was a new and potent part of the plebeian repertoire.

For the patricians, this was a nightmare. After two years of failed elections, they dialed up the religious pressure. Livy, who may well be reflecting what the patrician *pontifex maximus* chose to record in his *Annales*, suddenly begins to report the weather.[77] It was not pretty. The

---

[74] Livy 5.12.13: *Hac victoria comitiorum exsultantes tribuni plebis, quod maxime rem publicam impediebat de tributo remiserunt.*

[75] Above n. 23.

[76] The last disrupted levy was as recent as 409, but failed: Livy 4.53. Although the logic was strong (Raaflaub 1996: 290–5; Drogula 2017: 112), such boycotts usually failed (Rosenstein 1999: 198). On the unexpected appearance of plebeians in the *fasti* here, see Cornell 1983: 113, Brennan 2001: 50, Smith 2006: 271. On the families involved, see Ranouil 1975: 190–210.

[77] Livy 5.13.4. The ultimate origin of the information is unknowable. However, the meteorological displays of divine displeasure and the religious innovation that followed both suggest the *pontifex maximus* as a plausible source; portents and a new festival are likely candidates for his record. The probable mention of an eclipse in June of 400 BCE is, moreover, evidence that these

plebeian college of 400 was greeted by a harsh winter, while the second in 399 held office amid a sweltering, pestilential summer. To demonstrate the gravity of divine displeasure, patricians closed the courts, consulted the Sibylline Books, marshaled every home to partake in banquets and, in a spectacular tour de force of religious authority, instituted the first ever *lectisternium*.[78] Overawed voters granted them a purely patrician college for 398. Patricians retained their monopoly for the following year (see the next section for their tactics of alternative fundraising), but plebeians again blocked the levy in 397.[79] In the elections of that year, five out of six victors were plebeian. It is clear enough that, in these years 401–396, the plebeians could bring the patricians to their knees whenever they could shut off *tributum*, and through this they could extort consular tribunates.

Refusing to pay the troops was a risky gambit, and it was not something that could happen every year. It should, however, be clear that the instituting of *tributum* in 406 made this sort of politics possible, and that the first generation of leaders exploited it. That is clear from the *fasti* of the 390's and 370's. It was a gamechanger, and the patricians needed an answer.

3.2.4 Leaders' Dependence on Revenue and on Those Who Paid It Affected the Decisions They Made

Patricians could neutralize their weakness by appeals to traditional or religious authority – this was their tactic when they first instituted the *lectisternium* in the year 399 – but they could also attack the problem financially, whether on the revenue side or the expenditure side. The most obvious way for the patricians to respond was to source revenue from elsewhere so that there would simply be no need for *tributum*. Livy emphasizes the efforts of patrician commanders to raise money in war in 398, 394, 391, and 389.[80] It would take some bravery to accept every such

---

years were indeed addressed in the *Annales Maximi*. For discussion, see Cornell 2013, vol. 1: 148–9 and *Annales Maximi* F5.

[78] Livy 5.13.6–8.

[79] Livy 5.16.5. The consular tribunes resorted to volunteers in lieu of a paid army. It is worth asking why plebeian intransigence returns in 397 but not 398. One answer might be the raging success of the patricians' religious offensive, but another might be more pragmatically financial. Livy (5.14.6–7) disparages the leaders of 398 as achieving nothing but pillage, and it is possible that their aim was to raise enough money to pay *stipendium* without having to ask the *tribuni aerarii* for *tributum*.

[80] Livy 5.14.6, 5.27.15 (*stipendium militum eius anni, ut populus Romanus tributo vacaret, pecunia imperata*), 5.32.5, 6.4.2, 7–11. The campaign of 389 was, by Livy's own admission, militarily unnecessary but economically lucrative; the booty promptly made it into the soldiers' hands. See also Oakley 2002: 14 on the phenomenon in this period of campaigns for plunder.

detail in Livy's account, but the pattern he provides is a reminder of a definite fiscal logic: So long as *stipendium* could be funded via plunder, patricians would not be dependent on *tributum*. The case of 398 illustrates the dynamic well. As already noted, a refusal to pay *tributum* had led to a majority-plebeian college in 400, and then there was another plebeian college in 399. Deploying all of their religious authority, the patricians returned to power in 398, but their accomplishments did not impress Livy: "nothing memorable was done at Veii; all their energy was dedicated to pillaging." Yet, despite Livy's disdain, patricians were nonetheless successful in the elections for 397. That year's *comitia* then saw another boycott, and the plebeians dominated the consular tribunate of 396. The puzzle, therefore, is why the plebeians – so willing to flex their fiscal muscles in the elections of 401, 400, and 397 – did not protest in 398, despite what was apparently an underperforming college? At least within the logic of Livy's narrative, the obvious answer is that the patricians raised funding on campaign and never needed *tributum*. This neutralized the ability of the *tribuni aerarii* to withhold revenue. The plebeians could not hold for ransom what the patricians never asked for.

Another possibility was to escape *tributum* on the expenditure side. *Tributum* was an ad hoc revenue demanded for military campaigns, but this meant that, if the Romans could avoid war altogether, then they could avoid having to collect *tributum*. War was already a regular activity in the fifth century, and in the twenty-six years from 415 to 391, there were just two years without campaigns (8 percent). In the fourteen years from 389 to the beginning of anarchy in 375, however, there were also two peaceful years in Livy's narrative (14 percent).[81] Between plunder and a judicious avoidance of campaigning, therefore, leaders successfully reduced dependence on *tributum*. Though historiographically risky, a year-by-year account reveals this. In 394, *stipendium* was funded by the enemy, and this happened again in 391. Then in 387 there was no war, and again in 384, before *tributum* was canceled in 377. That is – if Livy's evidence can be trusted for this fraught period – there were five years out of nineteen in which the taxpayers had zero obligations. The account is surely not accurate in every detail, but the emergence of this odd pattern is at least suggestive of possible patrician tactics.

More enlightening than the statistics, however, is a focused study of the years 348 and 347.[82]

---

[81] Oakley 2002: 15; Harris 1990: 495.
[82] Livy 7.25.3–26.15. Rosenstein in Chapter 4 of this volume.

350: Large campaign against the Gauls.
349: Large campaign against Latins.
348: Little if any campaigning.
347: No campaigning.

Debt reform in 352 and 351 seems to have facilitated an enlarged levy and prolonged campaigns in 350 and 349. But, especially in light of hostility in Latium and at sea, the exertion of these two years appears to have been more than the community could sustain.[83] There is a rupture in the pattern of the preceding period: Plebeians held consecutive consulships for the first time in nearly a decade and there was little if any campaigning. In 347, we are told, interest rates were reregulated and repayments were restructured, but, as discussed earlier, "matters were most of all improved" (*levatae maxime res*) because of the decision not to fight wars, and hence not to demand *tributum*.[84] There were certainly other factors in play – plague, hostility from the Latins, and a mysterious fleet off the coast, for example – but contemporaries must have known that two years without *tributum* was an effective way to relieve both political and financial pressure. To relieve tensions, and to prevent a more explosive protest about *tributum* and debt, it was agreed that no armies would be enlisted for a couple of years. *Tributum* was avoided.

Finally, expenditures could be reduced by shifting manpower from the citizen category to the unpaid Latin category, and this might have something to do with the uptick in colonization after the institution of *tributum* in 406.[85] In the eighty-nine years from 491 to 402, there were just three colonies: Antium in 467, Ardea in 442, and Labici in 418.[86] Then, however, there was Velitrae (refounded) in 403 and Circeii in 393.[87] Vitellia was also a colony by 393, though the exact date of founding is unclear.[88] The same period seems to have seen colonies founded at Nepet, Sutrium, Satricum, and Setia, though again the chronology is vexed.[89] They also apparently attempted a Sardinian colony, which Diodorus explicitly notes was not to

---

[83] Livy 7.25.4, 25.12–13, 26.12–13.
[84] Livy 7.27.4. A similar dynamic can be found at Livy 6.18.2 during the Manlius Capitolinus affair. On interest rates, see still Billeter 1898: 115–57 and Appleton 1919, with Zehnacker 1980 and Savunen 1993.
[85] For the context of colonization, see Armstrong 2016: 219–31.   [86] Cornell 1995: 303.
[87] Diod. Sic. 14.34.7, 14.102.4. For convenient presentations, see Cornell 1995: 303, 383, de Haas 2011: 17, Scopacasa 2015: 38. I have very tentatively suggested elsewhere that Velitrae might have been refounded as a citizen colony at this point or in 380 (Tan 2020: 56–7).
[88] Livy 5.29.3. A date of 395 is given at Oakley 1997–2005, 1: 342 and Cornell 1995: 303.
[89] Livy 6.16.6, 21.5, 30.9, Vell. Pat. 1.14.2, with Oakley 1997–2005, 1: 571.

be part of the fiscal system.⁹⁰ There were of course various advantages to colonization, and scholarship has long noted the strategic purposes and the benefits in terms of land distribution. All of this explains why there was a Roman presence, but not why these settlements were categorized as colonies. Underappreciated, however, has been the fact that Latins did not earn *stipendium*, and thus did not need to be paid.⁹¹ This meant that, because the colonists were serving without pay, Latin colonization allowed an army of the same size to be fielded for less money, and it alleviated the problem of how to raise *tributum*.

3.3 Conclusion

From small farmers to the wealthy elite, Roman landowners interacted differently after the institution of military pay in 406. It initiated an immense increase in the number of civic interactions – potentially coercive and contentious interactions – once thousands of farmers had to provide revenues to *tribuni aerarii*, who in turn had to provide *stipendium* to the soldiers. All of this back and forth must have been intensely political – this is what fiscal sociology would predict, and it is something that the Roman evidence appears to confirm. More than anything, a class of wealthy plebeians was elevated to a position of prominence and influence. Those with ambitions of leading an army required payers to supply *tributum*, but they especially relied on the *tribuni aerarii* to participate as the critical mediators of the new fiscal system. The patricians, in ways that had never been true before, were bound to the consent of the nonpatricians. *Tributum* altered Rome's regime by reconfiguring the ways in which different stakeholders held power over each, and it did not take long for the newly empowered to reform their political repertoires to leverage their gains.

And so, as the fiscal system asked more of them across the fourth century, the *tribuni aerarii* became responsible for more of civic life. This gave them leverage and bargaining power, which I have explored in this chapter, but it also created a much more cohesive, much more dynamic, much more concretized body politic. It turned out that, by the third century, it was not only the priests, magistrates, and ex-magistrates who held prestigious positions of leadership. Public service descended in typically Roman gradations of service and status, of hierarchy and

---

⁹⁰ Diod. Sic. 15.27.4: *epi ateleia*. That they did not pay tax suggests that, like other colonists, they did not receive *stipendium*.
⁹¹ Tan 2020.

exclusivity.[92] The consuls at the top led the army, but there were roles for the population as well. As young men, the mass of landowners filled the legions, and the wealthier ones served in the cavalry. Once their years of fighting were over, the old legionaries contributed by paying *tributum*, while many of the old *equites* retained their hierarchical edge by becoming *tribuni aerarii*. Everyone performed a role, and so everyone occupied a rung on the ladder. Sure, it was great to win elections, but only so many people could do that. Many more could be the big man in the village, or a leader in this or that tribe. *Tributum–stipendium* thus helped to create the functions and duties that located all citizens within a more institutionalized civic hierarchy. Creating a single revenue stream for Rome's pursuit of warfare must have streamlined the community's various projections of force and left the centralized army by far the most effective and prestigious purveyor of violence. Every landowner, across ages and classes, became formally tied to it and its need for manpower and revenue.

By forcing people to exchange resources to keep the army running, *tributum* encouraged demands and bargaining. Taxpayers could refuse to pay unless they earned this or that reprieve, while *tribuni aerarii* could refuse to operate the system unless this or that ambition was fulfilled. It is clear enough that the patricians saw military advantages to a paid force, but they got much more than they bargained for. Gentilicial warfare had suited them because they had controlled the networks of resource mobilization. Once *tributum–stipendium* made them dependent on plebeian resources and participation, however, their monopoly on political and military power was doomed. There was simply no way that they could make themselves so dependent on the wider community without having to grant concessions as well. The plebeians were destined to win their prize of political equality.

---

[92] Gabba 1977: 15.

4 | Paying for Conquest in the Early Middle Republic

NATHAN ROSENSTEIN

The army that won Rome its empire was forged over the course of the Middle Republic, and especially the fourth and third centuries. The years between the mid-300s and the late 270s saw the gradual standardization of its weaponry and armor – short sword and heavy *pilum*; open-faced Montefortino helmet, pectoral, and *scutum* – in a process of adoption, adaption, and interchange among the various peoples of Central and Southern Italy. Allied with this development and likely coevolving with it was the creation of the manipular tactical system. Growing out of the war bands of early gentilician Rome and reflecting increasing state control over war-making, maniples were units of a standard size of heavily armed combatants grouped according to age and marshaled in three lines of ten maniples each – the *hastati*, *principes*, and *triarii*. Together, they along with a complement of light-armed skirmishers and cavalry constituted a Roman legion. In battle, lines of maniples advanced together to engage with the enemy or retired from the fighting as the next line moved up to replace it. Within the individual maniples legionaries likewise moved to the front ranks and direct combat with opponents or, when exhausted, fell back along their files while men behind them stepped forward to take their places, thus ensuring that a line of fresh fighters continuously faced the enemy's troops. The years between the mid-300s and the late 270s also saw the emergence of the legions' characteristic marching camps. These, too, were standardized, laid out ideally in a rectilinear square with each class of legionary infantry encamped in their maniples (or *termae* for cavalrymen) along designated streets, the whole surrounded by a trench and palisade of stakes. Procedures for mounting night watches, for making and breaking camp, and for the army's order of march all developed consistent forms. Finally, military command was regularized, as two annually elected consuls replaced the variable numbers of generals, the military tribunes with consular power, selected annually prior to 367. Each consul now led a force comprised at first of a single legion and then, shortly before 311, increased to two legions accompanied by a large force of allied troops.[1]

---

[1] On the military developments, see: Burns 2003; Armstrong 2016: 260–9; Rosenstein 2012: 94–8; Dobson 2008, Rawlings 2007: 55–8. The regular election of consuls beginning in 367: Cornell 1995: 334–40; Drogula 2015: 33–45; Armstrong 2016: 241, 272–7.

Unfortunately, the chronology of these developments is largely beyond recovery.[2] Apart from the two dates just noted, all that can be said with some certainty is that the army's manipular structure was mostly in place by the 280s, when Rome confronted Pyrrhus in Southern Italy. Ancient accounts of those battles, which very probably draw on Greek sources contemporary with the events, highlight key components of the manipular system. Thus, a fragment of Dionysius of Halicarnassus' account of what seems to be the battle at Maleventum in 275 mentions the second line of maniples: "those ... who usually save the day in battle are called *principes* by the Romans."[3] Plutarch's account of the battle at Asculum in 280 likewise reports that the Romans fought fiercely with their swords against Pyrrhus's soldiers' *sarissas*. The same author also mentions the Roman army's "parallel retreats and advances," which seems to be a description of the advances and withdrawals of lines of maniples during combat, and that Pyrrhus himself was wounded by what appears to have been a *pilum*.[4]

What is clear, however, is that fundamental to all of these developments was the creation of a means of providing long-term logistical support for the army in the field. Training, discipline, and transmission of know-how were essential to turning recruits into legionaries capable of making the manipular system work, not simply from day to day but most importantly in the crucible of life-or-death, hand-to-hand combat. That process required time – months of working and living together – which not only instilled in the soldiers the conditioning, skills, and knowledge they needed but, as importantly, forged the unit cohesion essential to enabling a maniple to withstand the pressures of battle. Time was also critical for the operational effectiveness of the army as a whole. The ability to remain in the field for months or eventually even years at a time enabled Roman forces to travel to and conduct operations against distant foes. Once there, an army could carry out extensive devastation of the enemy's crops, houses, and agricultural infrastructure, forcing upon them a choice between leaving the protection of their fortifications to face the Romans in battle – where the odds favored the better-trained legions – or surrender.

Sometime in the fourth century, therefore, the Republic organized a system of regular distributions to support its legionaries, the *stipendium*, furnished by

---

[2] Evidence for the development of Roman castrametation is particularly vexed: Plut. *Pyrrh.* 16.5 seems to indicate that the process was well along by the early third century, when Pyrrhus reportedly admired the organization of a Roman encampment, but Livy 35.14.8 and Front. *Strat.* 4.1.14 claim that the Romans adopted the layout of their camps from Pyrrhus'. On the increase in the consuls' armies from a single legion to two each: Livy 9.30.3 with Oakley 1997–2005: 3.390–1.
[3] Dion. Hal. 20.11.2 (trans. Cary); Rawson 1971: 24–5.
[4] Plut. *Pyrrh.* 21.6.9, cf. Rosenstein 2010b: 302–3.

an impost on citizens not serving in the legions that year, the *tributum*. (Roman sources record the establishment of *stipendium* in connection with the siege of Veii at the close of the fifth century. Even if this information is correct, it is not clear that payment became regular for soldiers before the mid-fourth century.) Eventually, the *stipendium* would take the form of payments in coin, out of which the cost of a soldier's wheat rations as well as any other expenses were deducted, but initially and probably down to the age of the Pyrrhic Wars, the *stipendium* was probably disbursed as grain, a practice that survived in the wheat Rome continued to provide to allied troops after the legions began to be paid in cash.[5] Much about *tributum*, on the other hand, remains uncertain, especially how it was apportioned among the *assidui* (those Roman citizens liable for payment of *tributum* or service in the legions), how it was collected by the *tribuni aerarii*, and how it got from them to the troops.[6] One feature that is clear, however, is that it could be repaid out of the spoils of victory, which has led to its characterization as akin to a "loan." Yet if at some stage repayment had occurred frequently, by the early years of the fourth century that prospect had become increasingly rare, which raised implications that policymakers in Rome could not ignore.

Between 367 and the outbreak of the Latin War in 341, the Republic fielded two armies annually. Of these, thirteen won victories and returned to celebrate triumphs, bringing with them the spoils from those victories. As I have shown elsewhere, during the first decades of the second century, when we have Livy's reports of armies returning to Rome in triumph, the booty displayed in those processions and conveyed into the treasury typically did not equal the cost of the *stipendium* paid to the soldiers who won it, to say nothing of all the other expenses these wars entailed. In other words, Roman warfare in these years did not ordinarily pay for itself apart from a few spectacularly rich conquests.[7] The same was likely true of the First Punic War and certainly the case in the Second. Thus, we cannot automatically assume that in the fourth century the booty from the victories Roman armies won normally equaled or exceeded their costs to the treasury and ultimately to the *tributum*-paying *assidui* who funded them. But more importantly, the thirty-nine other armies dispatched annually in these years did not win victories meriting the award of a triumph, three times

---

[5] Harris 1990: 507 cf. Crawford 1985: 22–3; Armstrong 2016: 211 no. 134. The alternative, payment in uncoined bronze, *aes rude*, is less likely in view of the wheat paid to the *socii*.

[6] Nicolet 1976 is fundamental, cf. Nicolet 1980 and Kondratieff 2004: 21–6. However, see now Tan's important discussion of the *tribuni aerarii* and the mechanics of collection and disbursement in this volume (Chapter 3). I cannot agree with Taylor's (2017) reconstruction of how assessments were calculated. My own view: Rosenstein 2016b.

[7] Rosenstein 2016a cf. 2011.

the number that did. Even assuming that some of these thirty-nine armies returned with spoils, it is far less justified to presume that any of these will have equaled the value of the *tributum* that funded legions' *stipendium*.

Concern over funding the Republic's military operations will have been on the minds of policymakers for two reasons. The first was the ratio of *tributum*-paying *assidui* to those serving in the legions. Secure figures for Rome's citizen population in the mid-fourth century are of course lacking; the best we can do is work from Afzelius' population estimates, which put the number of inhabitants of Roman territory at about 124,600 in 341.[8] About half will have been males, of whom about 40,000 were citizens aged 17 and older (see Table 4.1 below).[9] The total number of potential *tributum* payers will have been no more than about 30,000 citizens who were *sui iuris*, meaning that their fathers had died and so they were no longer in their fathers' *potestas*.[10] We do not have a reliable figure for the size of a Roman legion in this period, but the assumption that its size was similar to those levied a century or so later seems not unreasonable. If so, then the two legions fielded annually will have contained about 4,200 infantry and 300 cavalry each, a total of 9,000 men. Those 9,000 *assidui* were excused from paying *tributum*; otherwise, it would have amounted to levying a double tax on them (or their fathers, since a son *in potestate* could serve in place of his father). *Tributum*, as Nicolet saw, was a payment for the benefit of those who served by those who did not.[11] Thus the actual number of *tributum* payers would have been around 21,000. The ratio of these *tributum* payers to the soldiers their *stipendia* supported was thus about 2.33:1 – or even less if *proletarii* made up a significant portion of the citizenry at this date. In 214, about 14 percent of adult male citizens were *proletarii*, meaning that they were

---

[8] Afzelius 1942: 149–50. Note, however, the sensible cautions expressed by Roselaar 2010: 35, although she agrees that his figures are "at least in the right order of magnitude."

[9] This figure and those in the discussion that follows as well as in Table 4.1 are based on the Coale–Demeny² Model Life Table Model West Level 3 Female. Coale and Demeny's model life tables are mathematically derived presentations of the age structures (by five-year cohorts) of hypothetical populations with a given life expectancy at birth and a given rate of increase or decrease. Scholars of Roman demography conventionally use Coale–Demeny² Model West Level 3 Female to represent the Roman population during the Republic and Empire. In this model the average life expectancy at birth is twenty-five years and the size of the population is neither increasing nor decreasing, represented as $e_0=25$ and $r=0$. For a brief description of the uses and limitations of model life tables, see Morley 2006: 320; fuller discussion in Parkin 1992: 67–90. It should be noted that "female" and "male" in these tables refer only to the hypothetical age structure of a population, not its gender.

[10] These estimates are based on Saller 1994: 48–65, who calculates how many males would have had a living father, in five-year cohorts, based on a model population with the age distribution of Coale–Demeny² Model West Level 3 Female, $e_0=25$ and $r=0$.

[11] Nicolet 1976: 29, 33 on Livy 5.10.5.

Table 4.1 *Distribution by age of Roman males, Model West 3 Female, in 340 BCE*

Age	% at age, r=0	n=63200			% w/ living father	# w/ living father	# w/out living father
0–1	0.0321	2029					
1–4	0.0953	6023					
5–9	0.1053	6655					
10–14	0.1	6320					
15	0.01892	1196					
16	0.01892	1196					
17	0.01892	1196					
18	0.01892	1196					
19	0.01892	1196					
17–19			17–19	3587	0.63	2260	1327
20–24	0.0881	5568	20–24	5568	0.51	2840	2728
25–29	0.081	5119	25–29	5119	0.39	1996	3123
30–34	0.0736	4652	30–34	4652	0.28	1302	3349
35–39	0.0662	4184	35–39	4184	0.17	711	3473
40–44	0.0591	3735	40–44	3735	0.09	336	3399
45–49	0.0522	3299	45–49	3299	0.04	132	3167
50–54	0.0452	2857	50–54	2857	0.01	29	2828
55–59	0.0375	2370	55–59				2370
60–64	0.0291	1839	60–64				1839
65–69	0.0203	1283	65–69				1283
70–74	0.0123	777	70–74				777
75–79	0.0058	367	75–79				367
80–84	0.0019	120	80–84				120
85–90	0.0004	25	85–90				25
		63,200					
All males 17–90		39,782	total potential taxpayers (*sui iuris*)				30,175
			two legions, infantry and cavalry				9000
			taxpayers less two legions				21,175
			taxpayers if *proletarii* = 14 percent of all *sui iuris*				16,950

Prepared by the author.

exempt from both legionary service and payment of *tributum*.[12] If their numbers were similar in 341, only around 25,800 citizens might have been potential *tributum* payers, meaning that actual *tributum* payers could have been as few as 16,950 or only 1.88 for every legionary.

[12] Rosenstein 2002.

Although these figures cannot pretend to be anything more than an approximation of the financial base upon which payment of the mid-fourth-century *stipendium* depended, they do suggest that the comparatively small number of *tributum* payers supporting the Republic's military efforts is quite likely to have constituted an ongoing cause for concern among Rome's leaders. Coupled with a second development, it will have begun to raise alarms for policymakers. That development was the increasing burden that the growing costs of Rome's wars was placing on these few *tributum* payers, itself a consequence of the increasing length of the campaigns that were required to wage them. Chart 4.1 illustrates this development. It plots the duration in numbers of days of all campaigns that eventuated in triumphs between 367 and 291, with each data point representing one triumph. The chart is based on a number of assumptions, the most important of which is the reliability of dates that the *Fasti Triumphales* record for triumphs celebrated in this period. Their historicity has long been a matter of dispute among scholars, with some expressing serious doubt about the veracity of much if not all of the information contained in the *Fasti Triumphales* prior to circa 300.[13] Others, however, defend their general accuracy in the great majority of cases.[14] More important than the authenticity of any particular triumph that the *fasti* record, however, is the overall impression of the data when viewed as a group, which is largely unaffected by the omission of one or even several points from the data set. Secondly, the table assumes that the Roman calendar was generally in accord with seasonal time in this period and that consequently the dates at which triumphs were celebrated were as well. Much is uncertain about the state of the calendar prior to the third century, but the one piece of evidence we have tends to suggest that it had not gotten as far out of sync with solar time as was the case in the early second century. Cicero mentions in the *De republica* (1.25) an eclipse of the sun that occurred on June 5 about 350 years after the foundation of the city: *Nonis Iunis soli luna obstitit et nox*. Scholars are divided as to whether this was an eclipse that took place on June 21, 400 or a few years later on June 12, 391, but in either case, Cicero's testimony would indicate that the Roman calendar was no more than sixteen days behind solar time and thus well within the variation that one would expect of the pre-Julian luni-solar calendar.[15] Finally, establishing the duration of a campaign requires knowing not only its

---

[13] For example Beloch 1926: 86–92; recent skepticism in Beard 2007: 72–80. Cf. Bastien 2007: 85–118 on the falsification of triumphs in the literary sources.
[14] Recently Oakley 1997–2005: 1.56–7, 4.487–9. See now, Tan in Chapter 3 of this volume.
[15] Rosenstein 2004: 180 with references to earlier discussions.

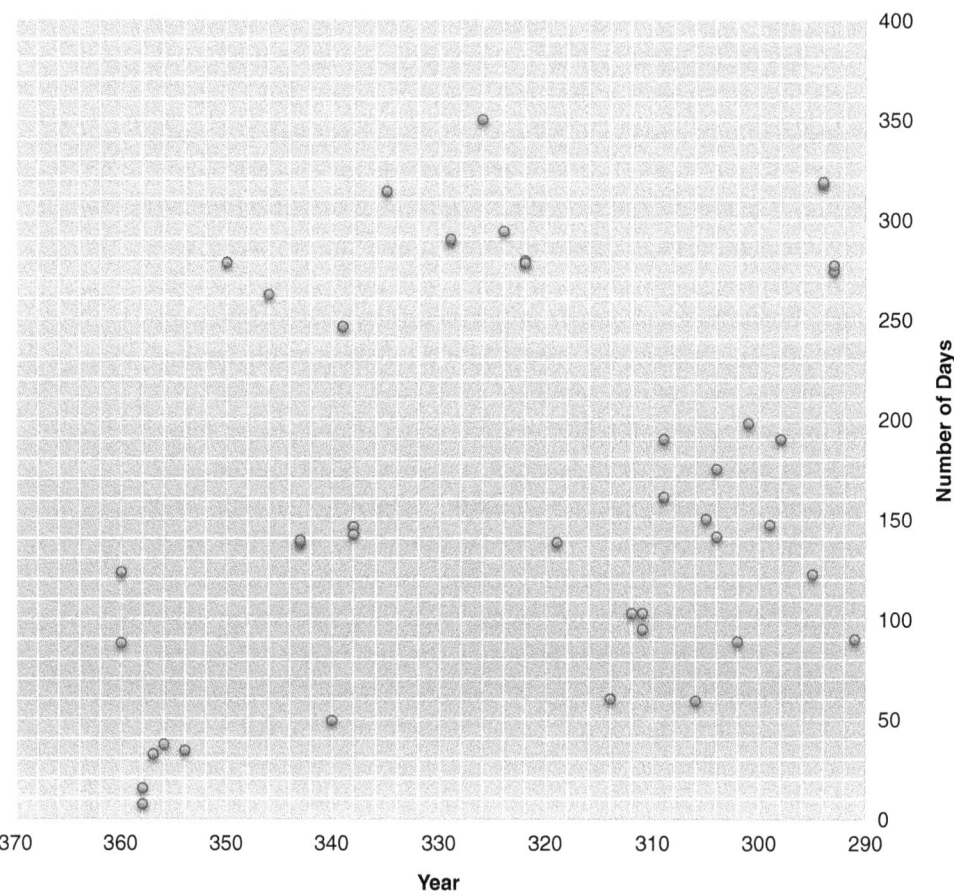

Chart 4.1 Duration of campaigns resulting in triumphs, 370–290 BCE.

end date but when it began, and for this last we have no contemporary evidence whatsoever. Based on the patterns of warfare observable in the later third and early second centuries as well as on the complex of ancient ritual preparations for war that took place in March and April, such as the dance of the Salii, the *Equirria*, and the *Tubilustrium*, I have assumed that Roman armies ordinarily set off for war in the spring and made May 1 the starting point for all campaigns while acknowledging that this date might vary by as many as thirty days one way or the other in any given case.[16]

In view of the several assumptions on which Chart 4.1 has been constructed, it cannot pretend to present anything more than an overall

---

[16] The starting date of the campaigning season is a separate question from the well-known problem of the date at which consuls in this period entered office: see, recently, Pina Polo 2011: 13–15.

impression of a general trend in the durations of Roman military campaigns. However, that impression is important, for it demonstrates that after circa 350 campaigns lasting 100 days or more become common. The wars that ended in these triumphs were regularly requiring the armies that waged them to spend lengthy periods in the field. Even more important is the fact that the chart does not present data on campaigns that did not end with the armies that conducted them returning to Rome in triumph. One must assume that the durations of these campaigns, which between 367 and 341 outnumbered triumphs 3:1, were more or less similar. There should be nothing surprising in this; the increasing length of time Roman armies were spending in the field is of a piece with the Republic's increasing penetration of the Sacco valley and Campania in the 350s and 340s. Marching from the city to these theaters simply took longer, but more was involved in these campaigns than just showing up and fighting. As already discussed, armies engaged in extensive devastation of crops, buildings, and agricultural infrastructure in order to force a confrontation with the enemy's forces while maneuvering, and preliminaries to battle could take additional time. Moreover, in as much as war is always the "continuation of policy with other means" (in Clausewitz's famous dictum), Rome's military operations should be assumed as part of a strategy to win over towns and cities by establishing supporters in power, defending them against challenges from rivals both internal and abroad, and manifesting the reality and proximity of Roman might.[17] Part and parcel of such efforts was the establishment of personal links between aristocratic Roman generals and leading members of the communities they came into contact with.[18] All of these things simply will have taken longer to accomplish as the Republic's armies moved farther and farther afield. The details of these events, even if they could be recovered, are less important than their financial implications, which formed the second major concern occupying policymakers at Rome in the years prior to the Latin War.

An increase in the duration of campaigning correspondingly increased its costs, principally the *stipendium*. Since at this date the *stipendium* was not yet denominated in coins but probably represented a ration of grain, we can consider the daily wheat requirements of 4,500 soldiers, the presumed size of a mid-fourth-century legion. At 850 grams of wheat/day/man this is

---

[17] Fronda 2010: 13–34.
[18] On the role that personal links between Roman and Italian aristocrats played in establishing and shaping the nature of Rome's hegemony in Italy during the early and Middle Republic, see now Terrenato 2019 and Wright and Terrenato in Chapter 2 of this volume. See also Fronda 2010; Kent 2012: 80–1.

the equivalent of about 3.825 metric tons of wheat per day, which would supply about 70 percent of the calories these men required.[19] Thus a campaign like the one that the *fasti* record as resulting in a triumph over the Hernici on May 15, 358 implies that the legion that waged it spent 15 days in the field (assuming it left Rome on May 1), and required about 57.4 tons of wheat, an average contribution of about 2.73 kg from each *tributum* payer. The legion that triumphed over the Tiburti a few years earlier, on June 3, 354, similarly will have consumed about 130 tons of wheat during the 34 days it spent campaigning, requiring on average about 6.19 kg from each *tributum* payer. A little more than a decade later, the expense of campaigning had risen dramatically. The triumph celebrated on September 20, 343 implies a campaign of 138 days and the consumption of 528 tons of wheat, while that celebrated on February 1, 346 will have required 262 days and 1,002 tons of wheat to complete; that is an average *tributum* of roughly 25.1 and 47.7 kg respectively from each *assiduus* not serving in the legions. And since these figures represent the *stipendium* of only one of the two legions operating in each of these years, we might assume that the average *tributum* assessments for these years would have been more or less double those amounts. Moreover, the figures for *stipendia* do not include the various other costs that these and similar operations will have entailed: additional food, transport, and equipment.[20]

Naturally, these numbers cannot pretend to offer anything more than a general sense of the increasingly daunting logistical challenges the Republic would face as its armies waged campaigns against increasingly distant opponents, challenges that were increasing the cost of warfare by a factor of as much as nine or ten with little likelihood that booty would ever recoup those higher costs, particularly since lengthier campaigns did not translate into corresponding increases in booty to offset them. It cannot be doubted, therefore, that the men who sat in the senate and deliberated

---

[19] Roth 2012: 24.

[20] Rosenstein 2016a: 115. While legionaries could expect to feed themselves to some extent through forage and/or pillage, no army could expect to live off the land for any length of time: Erdkamp 1998: 122–40. Short, early summer campaigns during the harvest, in other words, might have alleviated somewhat the financial burdens on *tributum* payers, but operations commencing in the spring before grain ripened and extending well into summer and fall after the crops had been harvested will have required far greater logistical support. And while Livy and Dionysius preserve reports of payments of food and/or *stipendium* (or clothing) by defeated enemies, their veracity is questionable: Oakley 1997–2005: 3.539–41 for a list and discussion. Yet even granting that such payments occurred, these required victories that compelled enemies to sue for peace, a result that only a minority of campaigns will have achieved. Allies might sometimes supply provisions to Roman forces campaigning nearby, for example Livy 9.36.8, but operations in hostile territory will have foreclosed these sources of food.

on Roman foreign policy, many of whom will have had extensive experience at war and in the organization of military operations, saw in a number of the campaigns that the Republic's armies waged in the 340s a foreshadowing of the resources that prolonged warfare in the south would require, warfare that in turn was going to demand a substantial increase in *tributum* from the citizenry.

It is impossible to form even a ballpark estimate of the burdens such an increase might have placed on *assidui*. The variables are far too numerous.[21] As already noted, we have no evidence for how *tributum* might have been assessed and collected in this period. Possibly *assidui* paid in proportion to their wealth, as was the case by the later third century, but the existence of a uniform contribution from each one cannot be ruled out. Yet even if some notion of how much wheat might have been exacted from each *tributum* payer could be established, reckoning what that sacrifice represented involves a host of uncertainties. Although scholars generally assume that individual holdings were typically small in this period – on the order of 7 *iugera* – the productivity of a given piece of land could vary widely.[22] Figures from Latium in the early nineteenth century suggest that yields could range from 1:3 or 1:4 seed to harvest on poor land to as much as 1:10 from the best fields.[23] Consequently, what might have seemed a manageable contribution from one farm would have imposed a serious hardship on another. And of course harvests from any field could vary substantially from year to year. Family configuration, that is the number of members and their ages and genders (since in general the caloric needs of men are greater than those for women), introduces still further complications, since how many mouths a farm has to feed determines whether its productivity is sufficient, more than enough, or falling short. Finally, any family disposed of only a finite amount of labor with which to grow the crops it needed to survive (whether on its own small holdings or by cultivating *ager publicus* in addition). Some families will have had more than enough to meet their needs and so might have been able to use the excess to grow the additional crops an increase in *tributum* would require, while others with little or no surplus will have found the extra burden unsustainable. What seems clear, however, is that throughout the fifth and fourth centuries a continuous demand on the part of the Romans for more

---

[21] On the varied economic and demographic developments in this period, see de Haas in Chapter 7 of this volume.
[22] On the size of farms in this period, see Oakley 1997–2005: 1.676–7 for sources and references to earlier discussions.
[23] Spurr 1986: 87.

farmland played an important role in impelling Republican warfare.²⁴ That demand strongly suggests that a substantial portion of Roman farms were barely adequate to meet the needs of the families they supported and that, if they were burdened with regular demands for greatly increased amounts of *tributum*, many of them would be pushed beyond their capacities to pay.

By the mid-340s, therefore, leaders at Rome faced a dilemma. While occasional lengthy campaigns could be supported, prolonged deployments in Campania and elsewhere year after year would soon outstrip the resources available to sustain these operations. Even assuming that by this date some method existed of distributing the burden of *tributum* according to wealth, as was the case in the later third and second centuries²⁵, that arrangement would only have increased the economic pressure on the marginal members of the wealthier classes. As these *assidui* fell into lower-rated classes, fewer in the higher classes would be left to shoulder their collectively heavier burden of *tributum*. It will have been clear to senators, therefore, that obtaining the amounts of *tributum* that the much longer duration of future warfare would require from the current number of *assidui* was not going to be sustainable in the long run.

The tension at Rome between the logistical demands of warfare in the 340s and the agricultural resources needed to support it does much to clarify the senators' aims as they contemplated the settlement they crafted in the aftermath of Rome's victory in the Latin War.²⁶ As is well known, the settlement incorporated the majority of Rome's defeated former allies into the Republic as citizens. A number of formerly independent Latin communities became citizens *optimo iure*, that is with full civil and political rights, while most of the rest, especially the Campanians and Volscians, had citizenship without the vote, *civitas sine suffragio*, imposed upon them.

Scholars have commonly seen *civitas sine suffragio* as the critical innovation that enabled Rome to accumulate the massive reserves of manpower that would enable it to conquer Italy, withstand Hannibal's onslaught, and go on to conquer the whole of the ancient world.²⁷ To be sure, Roman

---

²⁴ Harris 1979: 60.   ²⁵ Rosenstein 2016b.
²⁶ On causes and course of the war: Cornell 1995: 347–52.
²⁷ For example Sherwin-White 1973: 47, "The Romans ... saw in the Campanians an ample supply of legionary recruits ... "; Forsythe 2005: 292, "[t]his status ... granted Rome access to the community's manpower, which was a vital factor in Rome's ability to wage war continuously ... "; Cornell 1995: 351, "citizens with suffrage were liable to all the burdens and obligations of full citizens – especially military service"; Armstrong 2016: 287, "the sudden addition of such a vast amount of manpower ... allowed Rome's army to function on an entirely new scale." On the complexities and problems posed by the *civitas sine suffragio*, see Mouritsen 2007.

territory more than doubled in the aftermath of the settlement while the citizen population nearly tripled in Afzelius' estimate, from 126,400 to 347,300.[28] But while an increase in the pool of potential recruits for the army was undoubtedly a result of the senate's settlement following the Latin War, that the *patres*' primary aim was not military recruitment seems clear in light of the fact that Rome drew comparatively few soldiers from its new citizens *sine suffragio*. What evidence we have for how the Republic deployed them indicates that they fought in their own formations like Rome's other allies and separately from the legions composed of citizens *optimo iure*. Dionysius of Halicarnassus in describing the disposition of Roman forces at the battle of Asculum in 279 (20.1.4–5) distinguishes between the four legions deployed there (who are also described as 20,000 Romans at 1.8) and "the Latins, Campanians, Sabines … and other subjects." Dionysius' description is very likely drawn from Greek sources contemporary with the events and so carries considerable weight, particularly in light of the report that a few years earlier in 282 a *legio Campania* of 800 men had seized control of Rhegium.[29] This force was a contingent of Campanian citizens *sine suffragio*, very like the one that fought later at Asculum that was brigaded with the consul Fabricius' army in 282 but not enrolled in the legions he commanded.[30] These cases strongly suggest that Campanian troops (and presumably other contingents drawn from the citizens *sine suffragio*) were at this stage fighting in formations distinct from the legions, reflecting the usual way that Roman armies incorporated non-Roman contingents, which fought in their own semi-independent bands or maniples.[31] To judge from later practice, these units of allied and citizen *sine suffragio* soldiers together constituted a force in numbers roughly equal to or somewhat larger in size than the Roman legions they operated in conjunction with. As one component of this force, the troops forming the maniples of citizens without the vote will necessarily have been significantly fewer than the full citizens serving at the same time in the legions. How many fewer we have no way of determining, but the size of the Campanian force left to guard Regium, 800 men, may offer some indication of the ratio of citizens without the vote to the roughly 4,000 full citizens serving in a legion (although we cannot be sure that these 800 soldiers were the only Campanians attached to Fabricius' army in 282).

---

[28] Afzelius 1942: 152–4.
[29] Livy, *Per.* 15; Dion. Hal. 20.4.1–2. Rawson 1971: 24 on Dionysius' sources for these events.
[30] Rosenstein 2012: 55–6, incorrectly referring to the Campanians as "legionaries."
[31] Armstrong 2020; cf. Frederiksen 1985: 222–5. Note, however, Brunt's argument that by 225 Campanian conscripts had been fully integrated into the legions: 1971: 17–21.

One can note, too, Polybius' much-studied account of Rome's manpower resources in 225, drawn from Fabius Pictor, in which citizen forces are described as "Romans and Campanians," again suggesting that even at that date the Romans may have seen the Campanians and other citizens without the vote as constituting a group of potential recruits separate from those from which they drew their legionaries.[32] In other words, in imposing citizenship without the vote on the bulk of Rome's defeated allies in 331 the senate elected to treat them like other *socii* for purposes of military recruitment, levying only relatively small numbers of them for its armies, but as full citizens for purposes of *tributum*, imposing its payment on the great majority of them who qualified as *assidui* and were not exempt because of military service.[33]

Differences in language are often cited as the reason for the Campanians' exclusion from the legions, but perhaps as important in the senators' minds was their modest quality as infantry, at least to judge by their poor showing during the Second Punic War (note Livy 23.46.11: *peditem inbellem*).[34] At any rate, the decision to keep citizens without the vote out of the legions at this date indicates that the senate did not see the imposition of this status on Rome's former allies in Campania and elsewhere as a means of expanding the number of men it could call on to serve in the legions. With the addition of the former Latin cities and others to the body of citizens *optimo iure*, Rome had more than enough manpower to double the number of legions raised annually from two to four around 311, presumably reflecting a doubling of the number of men under arms each year. And no senator in 338 could have anticipated the massive mobilization that fighting Hannibal more than a century later would require.

What Rome needed, as its leaders contemplated the prospect of having to wage much longer campaigns in the future, particularly now that Campania had been incorporated into the *ager Romanus*, was an enlarged economic base to support those campaigns. In the settlement of the Latin War and the limited enfranchisement of the Campanians and others that followed they created a new and abundant source of *tributum* that at the same time would ease the burden of *tributum* imposed on all citizens, both *optimo iure* and *sine suffragio*, since the costs of war would henceforth be shared by a greater number of payers. The great advantage of using *civitas sine suffragio* in this way was the regularity of the extraction of wealth from

---

[32] Polyb. 2.24.14; Pictor as the source for Polybius' figures: Eutr. 3.5; Oros. 4.13.6.
[33] Cf. Tan 2020: 60–1; Mouritsen 2007: 152–3.
[34] Language difference: for example Brunt 1971: 19. Brunt 1971: 18, however, imagines that the *peditem inbellem* were *proletarii* unused to fighting.

them, as opposed to the one-off profits that came from taking spoils or imposing an indemnity payment.[35] Moreover, *assidui optimo iure*, whose considerable fighting qualities were well known, could now be recruited in greater numbers into the legions and so lost as *tributum* payers without diminishing the amount of *tributum* collected or overburdening the remaining *tributum* payers.

Thus the well-known wealth of Campania and the other areas where citizenship without the vote was imposed to a very great extent underwrote the long series of lengthy campaigns in Samnium and elsewhere after 338 that gradually and inevitably established Rome's dominion over the Italian Peninsula. These conquests eventually produced a great influx of wealth into the treasury at Rome, as revealed by the spate of temple building at the end of the fourth and beginning of the third centuries.[36] But those victories required years of costly fighting that rarely returned enough in booty to repay the *stipendium* of the armies that won them. Instead they were mainly financed by the *tributum* of the citizens and especially those citizens without the vote.

4.1 Appendix

The consequences of incorporating the *cives sine suffragio* into the political economy of the Republic via the *tributum* system were far-reaching and lie well beyond the scope of this chapter: For discussion of one important aspect, see Tan's chapter in this volume (Chapter 3). One question, however, that does need to be touched on here is how this change might have affected economic developments. It might be supposed that the imposition of *tributum* on so many new citizens – both those without the vote and those *optimo iure* – after 331 required each either to divert or intensify current agricultural production to meet this new purpose, since payment would ordinarily recur annually. One might wonder, therefore, whether it might be possible to trace a causal link between a need to grow more crops in order to pay *tributum* and the sorts of changes in agriculture discussed in the chapters by de Haas (Chapter 7) and Trentacoste and Lodwick (Chapter 8) in this volume.

While such a link cannot be ruled out in any specific instance, one must be very cautious about generalizing about farming practices in this (or any

---

[35] Cf. Tan 2020. I was able to read a version of this important paper prior to its publication, and I thank Dr. Tan for permission to cite it here.
[36] Orlin 1997: 199–200 for a list and Davies in this volume (Chapter 10) for discussion.

other) era. As already discussed, the productivity of any preindustrial farm will have depended on a variety of factors: the quality of the land; the microclimate in its location; rainfall in any particular year and the availability of other sources of water; the presence of livestock for manure; and the configuration of the household, among other things. In addition, the decisions that farmers made about intensification will have entailed considerations of the amount of food the family would need for the coming year as members were added and/or aged; how much of the crop needed to be put aside for storage as a hedge against future shortages; opportunities to market or exchange surpluses; and the availability of additional or surplus labor to undertake the work and possibly a source of cash to fund it. The need to pay *tributum* can have been at most only one among these various factors, and in so far as payment was after 331 distributed among a much larger number of *assidui* while down to circa 311 the number of troops being funded remained constant, the burden it imposed seems in most cases likely to have been minor.

A more intriguing possibility arises from the role labor availability played in farmers' decisions about what to grow and where to invest their efforts after 331. As I have demonstrated elsewhere,[37] by the late third century slave ownership was widespread among the Roman citizenry, the overwhelming majority of whom were farmers. Even members of the third census class – that is, citizens squarely in the middle range of the Middle Republic's socioeconomic hierarchy – commonly owned slaves. It seems very probable that Rome's wars in the late fourth and third centuries produced this state of affairs. During this period, Roman armies pushed into areas like Samnium that were far less amenable to the sorts of informal and more collaborative forms of incorporation into Roman hegemony described by Terrenato for the fifth and fourth centuries.[38] Violent conquest instead subjugated them, and although these victories usually did not repay the *tributum* that funded them, they did often produce substantial booty for the soldiers themselves. In an era of relatively limited material wealth, such booty may often have taken the form of prisoners. Some of these may have been sold abroad, but others will have been distributed as slaves to the soldiers themselves, who brought them back to work on their families' farms or sold them to other farmers who could profitably employ their labor: see Scheidel's chapter in this volume (Chapter 5). The presence of this additional agricultural labor on Roman farms (and Italian farms as well, assuming that allied soldiers shared equally in spoils) in the form of

---

[37] Rosenstein 2008: 5–7.   [38] Terrenato 2019.

enslaved war captives could therefore have been an important reason for a willingness on the part of farmers to increase their productivity where other factors favored this strategy. *Tributum's* role will in that case have been merely to facilitate the Republic's push to conquer more distant regions, where such spoils could be won.

5 | Building up Slaveries in Ancient Italy and the Central Sudan

WALTER SCHEIDEL

By the end of the Roman Republic, Italy had filled up with slaves: at least a million of them and probably more, even if not quite as many as once thought.[1] How had it come to that? For an answer, we cannot neglect the early formative stages of the Roman polity, the subject of this volume. But there we immediately encounter a forbidding dearth of evidence: Whereas the steady flow of slaves into Italy during the last two centuries of the Republic is well attested, less is known about the preceding period. Faced with this challenge, I adopt a somewhat unconventional approach. I begin with what is commonly thought of as being known but which, looked at more closely, can hardly count as being reliably established. I then sketch out different scenarios of what might have happened, put them into perspective by introducing a comparison that has not been employed before – with developments in sub-Saharan Africa up to the nineteenth century – and finish by reflecting on what one may hope to gain from this exercise.

5.1 Italy

For a while, Moses Finley had given us a comforting if unreliable sense of the overall contours of change by envisioning a trajectory from more "archaic" forms of dependence toward fully-fledged chattel slavery. Early on (say, in the fifth and fourth centuries BCE), Roman bondsmen tied down by *nexum* or Etruscan "serfs" would have been more common than slaves. As political and military comobilization ushered in more civic rights, liberties, and obligations, thoroughly "unfree" slaves came to be more starkly demarcated from "free" citizen-soldiers. Unshackled from personal dependencies, citizen armies proceeded to enslave their

---

[1] I am very grateful to the editors, the referees, and David Lewis, Nathan Rosenstein, Richard Roberts, and Mohammed Bashir Salau for their help, comments, and bibliographical suggestions.

For a conjectural reconstruction and critique of earlier (higher) guesstimates, see Scheidel 2005: 64–71, with Scheidel 2011: 291–3.

opponents across the Mediterranean and its hinterlands until – in Keith Hopkins' deceptively elegant reconstruction – slave labor eventually undermined the livelihood of much of the citizenry: but that is another story.²

We know so little about social change in early Italy that this model may well be correct, if only by chance. Yet we must be wary. Finley promoted an analogous storyline for ancient Greece, which has begun to wither under the criticism of scholars who are chipping away at his claim that "intermediate statuses" (between slavery and freedom) once used to be the dominant form of personal bondage. As a result, the worlds of Homer and Hesiod have been repopulated with "proper" slaves and the status transition narrative has lost some of its luster.³ That alone ought to encourage us to rethink its Roman version as well.

The most conventional approach is to look for references to slaves and slavery in fifth- and fourth century BCE Italy. The canonical tally is modest but suggestive of deep roots. Thus, slavery appears well established in the mid-fifth century BCE Laws of the Twelve Tables. A tax on manumissions is reported – albeit several centuries later – for the year 357 BCE. The Roman-Carthaginian treaty of (probably) 348 CE points to slave ownership among Romans and Italians. The abolition of *nexum*, dated to 326 or 313 BCE, might conceivably have been facilitated by an expansion of slavery. The question of where to register freed slaves was said to have triggered discord in 312 BCE, which presupposes their presence in nontrivial numbers. The *lex Aquilia* of the 280s BCE specified damages to slaves. Moreover, accounts of enslavement of war captives go back to the regal period, all the way to the reign of King No. 5. The plot thickens later on, first with the alleged mass enslavement of the population of Veii in the 390s BCE and a century later with the Third Samnite War. Livy, our key source, supplies more and more precise numbers for the latter than he does for

---

² Finley 1980: 83–9 = 1998: 151–7; 1999: 66–9. On the free citizenry's commitments (to war or other forms of mobilization) as a driver of slavery, see Scheidel 2008: 115–23, especially 117–18 for Greece and Rome. Another story: Hopkins 1978: 1–74, especially 30, "Roman peasant soldiers were fighting for their own displacement." This approach – essentially a variation on Appian, *BC* 1.7 – has not weathered particularly well: for example, Launaro 2011: 168–77; De Ligt 2012: 162–5.

³ Greece: Finley 1980: 88–9 = 1998: 156–7; 1981: 156–66; 1999: 66–9. Harris 2012 and Lewis 2018: 89–92, 107–24 offer the most sustained critiques; see also Lenski 2018b: 125–8. Lewis, in press reviews local varieties of slavery across Greece that are often considered forms of serfdom. Finley's use of the concept of "slave societies" (as opposed to "slave-owning" ones) is now at risk of ending up as a collateral casualty: for example, Vlassopoulos 2016: 81–5, 95–7; Lenski 2018a: 39–46; but also Lewis 2018: 94–6 for a more nuanced view. Harper and Scheidel 2018: 103–5 defend this taxonomy. See also below at n. 43.

earlier campaigns, which – depending on how we count – add up to between 58,000 and 77,000 slaves taken over the course of just five years of warfare (297–93 BCE).[4]

What are we to make of this? Deep roots do not equate to large scale. More importantly, those reports that do hint at a sizeable slave presence tend to be less than compelling, as Welwei forcefully argued back in 2000.[5] In the end, we will never know which – if any – of them to take seriously. At the same time, it would be rash to throw out the slave baby with the muddied bathwater of the annalistic tradition. If there is one thing about early Roman and Italian history that would seem hard to doubt, it is the ubiquity of armed conflict – and not just between the Romans and their endless line-up of enemies but also among Italy's inhabitants more generally.[6] Unless pretty much everything we are told about the nature of these hostilities was made up later, these clashes generated lots of captives, who were liable to be turned into slaves. That later Romans were unsure about the origins of the term *sub corona vendere* – applied to captives sold into slaves off the battlefield – suggests that this practice was quite ancient indeed.[7]

Habitual enslavement of captives, however, did not necessarily translate to a dramatic expansion of slave ownership in Italy. Alternative means of disposing of captives were available. Ransoming was one of them. Common in classical Greece, where interstate warfare likewise yielded lots of human loot, this practice was – albeit once again much later – reported for Italy in the 290s BCE. But relatively low levels of monetization in Italy at the time cast doubt on the viability of such arrangements. For all we can tell, mass bailouts would have been harder to engineer than in much more monetized classical Greece. High-weight low-value *aes signatum* or *aes grave* would have been an inadequate medium for such transactions, even if Livy claims that it was used in staggering quantities. The considerable degree of metrological variation that characterized these early issues – discussed in Liv Yarrow's chapter – might have posed further obstacles.[8]

---

[4] References: Bradley 1985: 4–6; 2011: 242–5; and also Volkmann 1990: 36–40 for enslavement in early wars. Cf. furthermore Nenci 1982 for the bold conjecture that the use of the verb *kolabrízesthai* in the Septuagint version of Job 5.4 might reflect the practice of enslaving and exporting Calabrians, intermediated by Greeks.

[5] Welwei 2000: 23–42.

[6] Even Terrenato 2019, who emphasizes the role of alliance building and cooptation in Roman state formation, does not reject the tradition regarding endemic bellicosity.

[7] Welwei 2000: 12–13.

[8] Ransom was common cross-culturally, especially for elites: Patterson 1982: 107. For Greece, see Garlan 1987: 15–18; Braund 2011: 117. Prachner 1995: 2–9 gives a gullible account of the ransoms reported for 295 and 293 BCE; but see Welwei 2000: 55–6.

In this environment, export of captives might have been a more attractive strategy. Hardly ever considered in modern scholarship – presumably because of the silence of the sources – exports would allow us to reconcile the practice of large-scale enslavement in war with concerns about the ostensible dearth of employment opportunities for slaves or better (and especially archaeological) evidence for their presence. Conditions would have been favorable. Prior to the completion of the Roman takeover, peninsular Italy formed a readily accessible and exploitable periphery relative to wealthier core regions such as the Greek communities of Sicily and Southern Italy and the dominion of Carthage and its North African associates (centered on present-day Tunisia).[9]

Analogous trade relations were well established in the eastern Mediterranean, where Greek poleis customarily imported slaves from peripheralized "slaving" zones in Thrace, the Black Sea basin, and western Asia Minor. Enslavement was generally undertaken by local parties who sold captives to Greek merchants.[10] For the classical and Hellenistic periods, these transfers are clearly visible in epigraphic documentation from places such as Athens, Delphi, and Rhodes. Unfortunately for our understanding of conditions in the Western Mediterranean, we lack analogous data from the western reaches of the Greek city-state culture.[11] Tantalizingly, a handful of individuals from Italy are mentioned in the earliest manumission inscriptions from Delphi: reported in the early second century BCE, their presence presumably reflects the dislocations of the Hannibalic campaigns. Manumission decrees from Buthrotum, which faced Italy across the Strait of Otranto, likewise date from the second century BCE. We can only speculate that earlier and more western

---

[9] Welwei 2000: 61 has been exceptional in even raising the possibility of exports; see also Scheidel 2012: 103. The Roman–Carthaginian treaty referenced by Polybius 3.24 envisions Carthaginian raiding and enslaving in Italy (Welwei 2000: 58). But what about slave exports organized by Romans or other Italians? All we can do is resort to speculation (with my thanks to Dan-el Padilla Peralta for these suggestions): For instance, the displays of gold at Roman funerals that were regulated by the Laws of the Twelve Tables (10.8) might have been made possible in part by the sale of debtors abroad (ibid. 3.5); or the adoption of Cisalpine Celtic styles of armor in peninsular Italy (Taylor 2020a) might have been furthered by the exchange of Italian slaves for northern goods. Yet we lack solid evidence for these or comparable transactions. Be that as it may, exports would go a long way in addressing the problem noted by Roselaar 2010: 73 that it would have been hard to sell large numbers of slaves during the early Republic "since at this time Rome did not have as much use for slaves as in later periods." Cf. Bernard 2018a: 169 for slave trade *within* fourth- and third-century-BCE Italy.

[10] See now especially Braund 2011: 120–3; Lewis 2018: 276–7.

[11] Nash Briggs 2003 seeks to make a case for slave exports from Gaul to Etruria in the archaic period.

documents, if they existed, might show more slaves from Italy – a vexing case of absence of evidence not to be mistaken for evidence of absence.[12]

By all accounts, the institution of slavery was entrenched among the western Greeks. Syracusan slavery is reasonably well attested, even if local "helots" loom large in the record, and mass enslavement of fellow Greeks was attributed to Dionysius I in the early fourth century BCE. During his raid of Pyrgi on the Etruscan coast in 384 BCE, he also took slaves who were then sold in Syracuse. It would have been quite remarkable if the Greeks of Sicily and Magna Graecia had not imported unfree persons from Italy on a more regular basis.[13]

A similar line of reasoning may be applied to Carthage. Recent work claims that Carthage was "awash in slaves." Slaves hailed not only from the Berber frontier but also from various Mediterranean islands – Corsica and the Balearic islands –, and Greeks could be enslaved in Sicily.[14] Italy would have been an obvious source of imports, and the Roman-Carthaginian treaties, which paid attention to coastal raiding, may indeed reflect relations of this kind.[15]

If one were inclined to step up conjecture, it would be tempting to speculate that the impact of Greek and Punic commercial capital might have intensified conflict in peripheral zones and directed it toward the enslavement of captives for export. Yvon Garlan has raised this possibility for the peripheries of the Greek Aegean in analogy to dynamics that are extremely well documented for early modern sub-Saharan Africa and may also have played out along the frontiers of the mature Roman Empire. During the Middle Republican period, war-riven Italy would have been a prime candidate for such processes to unfold.[16]

These conjectures are informed by circumstantial evidence and an appreciation of context and analogy. According them a measure of respect would require us to be less enthralled by what the surviving – and generally much later – texts happen to claim and to be more open to probabilistic reasoning about what was likely to happen in a particular environment,

---

[12] Lewis 2018: 278–80 discusses these datasets and their respective catchment areas, which could be quite limited. Except for the Hermokopidae auction texts from Athens in the late fifth century BCE, these inscriptions date mostly from the third and second centuries BCE. Bresson 2019: 258–64 provides an exhaustive list of manumission texts from Illyria, Epirus, and Akarnania: With few exceptions (mostly from Apollonia), they date from the second century BCE.

[13] Mass enslavement: Welwei 2000: 56–8. Helots: for example, Carlà 2014.

[14] Flaig 2009: 55–6; Lewis 2018: 259–66; Lenski 2018a: 26–9 (quote: 28).   [15] Welwei 2000: 58.

[16] Garlan 1987: 19–20 (capital); Braund 2011: 123 (motivation for local enslavement); and now also Lewis 2018: 282–6 for the pull of Greek demand stirring up conflict elsewhere (in Thrace and Phrygia?). For the Roman Empire, see below, n. 18.

even if it is not explicitly mentioned in what sadly passes for our evidence. After all, it would not be terribly surprising if Augustan-age writers had failed to be attracted to the image of the people of Italy being carried away into slavery, or if they had simply been unaware of such practices even if they had once existed. None of this calls for major leaps of faith.

Moreover, the export scenario would also make sense if – and I shall presently return to this "if" – we expect widespread slavery in Italy itself to have left a stronger mark on the material record. Commencing as it does around the mid-third century BCE, archaeological evidence of intensification of production and commerce (such as wine exports) appears only well after mass enslavement would already have been in full swing.[17] This alone raises the possibility that even if lots of captives were turned into slaves, not all that many of them need have stayed put.[18]

Yet while that is certainly possible and might even seem plausible – which shows just how little we know for sure –, such a reading risks conflating two distinct matters: commercialized slavery – where owners paid for slaves with money and exploited them for profit – and more familial forms of bondage that did not necessarily coincide with economic intensification and would consequently be harder (or perhaps even impossible) to detect in the archaeological record. Roman-style slavery provided a suitable template for the latter: witness the formal emphasis on slaves being incorporated into the *familia* and the custom of manumitted slaves being associated with the owner's lineage, a pattern that was common in other slave-owning societies in which slavery operated mainly at the household level and did not necessarily involve commercialized relations.[19]

This raises another and more heterodox possibility – that the very question of how or why slavery expanded in Roman Italy might be somewhat misconceived. What if slavery had already been common when the Romans set out to take over the peninsula? It is by no means out of the question that large numbers of slaves were already present at that time, pre-dating by far any subsequent commercialization and

---

[17] Thus most recently Bernard 2018b: 17–18.
[18] Ideally one would want to see slave exports corroborated by (preferably ample) Greek coin finds: compare attempts to explain the distribution of Roman coin finds in Dacia with reference to the slave trade: Crawford 1977, with Stan 2014.
[19] See Zeuske 2013: 156 (Rome), cf. 156–7 (Africa), and also generally 164, 168 for later intensification. See Saller 1994: 74–88 for the relationship between family, *familia*, and *domus* in Roman discourse, and Mouritsen 2011: 37–40 for Roman freedmen as quasi-sons and 42–3 for *libertae suae* (one's own manumitted female slaves) as respectable *concubinae* (consorts) and wives.

economic intensification.[20] Greek sources make it appear that slaves were numerous in Thrace, in a familiar context of political fragmentation and endemic conflict. They even ascribe 300,000 (supposedly "helot-like") slaves to the Illyrian Ardiaioi and 1,000 slaves or more to each of the two richest persons among the nearby Dardanians.[21] Never mind what are bound to be fake numbers: what matters is that Greek observers seem to have found the notion of large-scale slave ownership among their non- or proto-state "barbarian" neighbors perfectly plausible. If just one of them had made a similar offhand remark about early Italy, what would we make of it?

Tymon de Haas's discussion in Chapter 7 of this volume of platform sites and population growth during the Middle Republican period suggests that at the very least there would have been room for widespread domestic slavery. And as the *ager Romanus* grew, so would have employment opportunities for slaves.[22] Absent large-scale market production, slave labor could have helped sustain unceasing warfare by freeing up adult male household members and by helping to generate *tributum*.[23] The roots of Italian slavery may well have been both deeper and wider than we imagine. In this scenario, familial slaveholding on a broad scale would have coincided with and underpinned endemic warfare that was only later joined by growing commercialization. While the latter was likely to increase overall slave numbers – and in elite circles almost certainly did – this expansion need not have been particularly dramatic or discontinuous.

---

[20] Etruria is a strong candidate: Nash Briggs 2003.

[21] Lewis 2018: 100–1 provides references. Cf. Taylor 2001 for early indigenous slaveries, and Bresson 2019: 271–3 for the importance of slavery in northwestern Greece, adjacent to the Illyrian Balkans.

[22] Welwei 2000: 61–2; and see also Harris 1979: 59–60 and Scheidel 2012: 103. Roselaar 2010: 79 favors other options only because she remains wedded to the linkage between slave labor and marketized production. A similar perspective accounts for Terrenato's (2019: 213) view that "slavery at the time of the conquest of Italy should not be considered a very significant factor." That remains possible but cannot be substantiated.

[23] Roman military mobilization rates were already high early on (from 346 BCE): Scheidel 2006: 220–3. For *tributum*, see Nathan Rosenstein and James Tan's chapters (Chapters 3 and 4). I should note that any assessment of the burden of *tributum* suffers from our profound ignorance regarding its relation to overall income. Even so, if a levy of 0.1 percent of assessed wealth very roughly corresponded to a levy of 0.7 percent of private income (see Scheidel 2020: 345–8 for the underlying ratio for total wealth to GDP, which is unlikely to have been very different from the ratio of private wealth to income), the very few references to relevant annual rates (0.1–0.3 percent of wealth: Nicolet 1980: 158) suggest a very low tax on income, as do the schematic calculations for the late third and/or early second centuries BCE by Rosenstein 2016b (esp. 90–1: anywhere from 0.2 to 0.5 percent of wealth) and Taylor 2017: 163–5 (0.3 to 0.5 percent), both of which are consistent with effective annual income tax rates of between 1.5 and 3.5 percent and thus far lower than tithes or other direct taxes reported for Roman provinces in later periods. To be sure, we know even less about the relative burden in the fourth or early-third centuries BCE (cf. Rosenstein 2016b: 96).

Discontinuities might have been confined in the first instance to the ends of slavery – to the ways in which slave labor was employed.

5.2 Sudan

This is not a completely fanciful outline: although it is not expressly supported by evidence for ancient Italy, it does reflect developments that took place elsewhere. By far the best examples come from sub-Saharan Africa, where slavery had been widespread well before major commercializing trends took hold. Enslavement was routinely used as a strategy to incorporate disempowered strangers into households and lineages in ways that allowed household heads to bypass conventional kinship structures and the constraints on exploitation these entailed. For centuries, sub-Saharan slaveries shared with their ancient Roman equivalent a feature that was relatively rare among societies characterized by large-scale slave ownership: the fact that capture in war and raids served as a principal source of slaves for the same group that undertook the warring and raiding.[24]

In as much as it is appropriate to generalize, slavery in sub-Saharan Africa was grounded in domestic kin slavery that prioritized enslavement of women – who engaged in fieldwork and acted as sexual partners – as a means of attaching additional and subordinate women (alongside "honorable" wives) and their offspring to the elders in charge of households and lineages. Sexual relations and reproduction served as the most important means of gradual assimilation. These arrangements were not immutable: over time, one can perceive a grand arc away from kinship-based household settings and toward increasing institutionalization as slave labor assumed growing importance in the economy and slavery became de facto more detached from owners' households – a shift that occurred in no small measure in response to the pull of international trade relations.[25]

This outside influence had a long pedigree. Although the evidence for a trans-Saharan slave trade in antiquity remains scarce and often circumstantial, recent studies have made a plausible case for imports from Saharan

---

[24] See Patterson 1982: 106–22 for a global view of capture in warfare and raids as a source of slaves. Lovejoy 2012: 22 notes the emphasis on direct enslavement, in contrast to practices in the Islamic Middle East and the colonial Americas. In the following, I provide a bare-bones outline of African conditions in recognition of the fact that this volume is aimed primarily at those who are more familiar with ancient Mediterranean history. The relatively narrow bibliographical range reflects the status of recent scholarship.

[25] Lovejoy 2012: 13–16 outlines the overall setting. Change over time: ibid. 18–19.

and sub-Saharan areas into the Roman Empire that provided infrastructure for later and better-attested trade flows on a large scale.[26] Islamic influence made itself felt from the early Middle Ages onward, as societies of the Muslim "core" in the Middle East and North Africa region imported large numbers of slaves from sub-Saharan Africa (as well as from Europe and elsewhere). This in turn affected practices of slave ownership in Africa as well. Beginning with the Portuguese in the fifteenth century, the European (and transatlantic) slave trade built on and eventually greatly intensified these relations. Some local societies developed fully-fledged slave economies.[27]

Similarly to the Red Sea and East African coast, the Sahel and Sudan zones became a principal frontier of Islamic intervention. From the seventh to the sixteenth century, somewhere around 5 million slaves were traded from the Sudan northward.[28] The Sudan, a savanna belt of tropical grassland with lightly wooded rolling but generally low-lying terrain characterized by wet and dry seasons that governed the rhythms of farming and transhumant pastoralism, turned into a belt of Muslim polities that reached from the Senegal river in the west to Lake Chad in the east. State formation critically depended on access to horses, which enabled military power projection across the great plains of the northern savanna. In an institutionalized and self-sustaining cycle of violence and commerce, horses from farther north were exchanged for slaves from farther south, with the horses being used to capture more slaves.[29] But not all captives were traded away: others were put to work as laborers, soldiers, and administrators, and – above all – women were kept as concubines. The buildup of a substantial servile workforce supported an early plantation system in the Niger Valley (devoted to the production of staples such as millet, sorghum, wheat, and rice) and the employment of slaves in gold mines and saltworks.[30]

In terms of the retention of enslaved persons and the direction of slave exports, in the early modern period the Sudan stood apart from other African regions that became major suppliers of slaves to European traders. Its main counterpoint was West-Central Africa (Kongo and Angola) where the collapse of the Kingdom of Kongo (which had cooperated with Portuguese slave dealers) in the 1660s gave rise to warlordism and kinless

---

[26] Harper 2011: 86–91; Wilson 2012: 427, 432–5. Wright 2007 surveys the history of the trans-Saharan slave trade up to the nineteenth century.
[27] Islamic influence: Lovejoy 2012: 15–18. For the role of commercial credit first from Muslim North Africa and then from Europe, see Miller 2012: 116.
[28] Lovejoy 2012: 24–6.   [29] Smaldone 1977: 9–12; Lovejoy 2012: 29–31.
[30] Lovejoy 2012: 32–3.

warrior bands that replenished their ranks with enslaved boy-soldiers and exported other captives en masse. This region consequently came to account for the largest regional share of the transatlantic slave trade. Farther north, more successful state building both restricted and promoted exports, as emerging kingdoms such as Benin, Oyo, and Asante shielded their subjects while converting populations along their frontiers into slaves.[31]

In the savanna, the formation of the Songhay Empire in the sixteenth century caused slave exports to the Islamic core regions to peak as raids ensnared even more people. However, after Songhay succumbed to a Moroccan attack in 1591, the northern savanna came to lack large centralized states, apart from Borno in the Lake Chad basin.[32] The seventeenth and eighteenth centuries were characterized by endemic warfare: Conflict over land and manpower – variously staged among Muslims, between Muslims and others, and as jihad against all – produced a steady stream of the newly enslaved. In what is now northern Nigeria, the five major Hausa states – Gobir, Zamfara, Kano, Katsina, and Zazzau – fought dozens of wars while temporary hegemony passed between them, and Borno strove to maintain some measure of nominal control over some of them. As before, slaves resulting from these conflicts were either retained or sold across the Sahara.[33]

The slave trade was organized by Muslim commercial networks in which Hausa merchants (who were attached to individual city-states) played a major role. In long-standing circuits of exchange that were largely detached from the growing European-dominated Atlantic system, slaves were traded for cowries, glass beads, iron bars, foreign silver coin, textiles, horses, and weapons. The seventeenth and eighteenth centuries witnessed the formation of two distinct zones of slaving: the Islamic savanna belt with its consolidated holdings of slave labor, and areas closer to the coast where the pull of the Atlantic market transformed traditional kin-based slavery. Whereas the latter zone exported more slaves than it retained, the opposite appears to have been true in the savanna where demand for male slave labor was stronger. Political scaling-up in savanna polities such as Borno, Darfur, and Futa Jallon allowed large slave estates to be set up.[34]

---

[31] Kongo/Angola: Lovejoy 2012: 40–1, 76–80. State formation and exports: ibid. 46–67, 80–7.
[32] For the fall of Songhay, see Gomez 2018: 315–67.
[33] Lovejoy 2012: 68–74. Hausa wars and polycentrism: Smaldone 1977: 17. For Hausa city-state culture, see Griffeth 2000.
[34] Lovejoy 2012: 91–5 (networks), 107 (means of exchange), 112 (zones), 113 (population), 115 (uses), 117–18 (larger states).

In this environment, war, slaving, and state formation were increasingly bound up with jihadist movements. From the late seventeenth century onward, a series of jihads sought to overcome warring states that were run by, and for the benefit of, narrow military elites whose predatory behavior prompted visions of a more unified and purified Islamic community.[35] Inspired by religious scholars, these movements had a strong ethnic component: Fulbe (Fulani), many of whom traversed the savanna as transhumant pastoralists, were almost invariably deeply involved in these campaigns.[36] The combination of pastoralist specialization, Islamic faith, and a common language lent the Fulbe a distinctive identity that could be harnessed by its elites, who controlled herds as well as landed estates and were well placed to organize larger operations. Structural tension between urban polities, such as the Hausa city-states, and Fulbe herders who were mobile and wary of taxation shored up the herders' capacity for collective action.[37]

In the Hausa region, endless warfare had forced many Muslims into slavery, a predicament that galvanized fundamentalists into action.[38] The most successful of them, the charismatic Fulbe scholar and imam Uthman dan Fodio, gathered followers to challenge the Hausa state of Gobir from within. In 1802 he declared the enslavement of fellow Muslims unlawful. Supported by Fulbe clan leaders and clerics, he launched open jihad two years later. Fomenting and exploiting local risings across a growing area, Uthman dan Fodio set up a franchise operation whereby he bestowed "flags" on other rebel leaders to legitimate their own operations.[39]

During four years of intense conflict (1804–8), he and his followers managed to establish a caliphate in the central Hausa region: Existing governments were overthrown and replaced by semi-autonomous emirs largely drawn from the Fulbe elite. The well-established kingdom of Borno farther east survived the caliphate's assault in a diminished state. Further expansion targeted the south, where a rebellion of Ilorin slave soldiers in 1817 had brought down the Oyo kingdom. The empire – the Sokoto caliphate – that resulted from these campaigns was heavily segmented: Effectively though not formally split since 1817 between Sokoto and Gwandu, it was made up of two central districts

---

[35] Lovejoy 2016 is the most comprehensive account; see especially 37–8 for a list of major movements from the 1670s to the 1840s.
[36] I use the (anglicized) Fulfulde term Fulbe instead of the Hausa term Fulani.
[37] Smaldone 1977: 23; Lovejoy 2016: 45–6, 51, 58–9, 61.   [38] Lovejoy 2016: 62.
[39] For the jihad of Uthman dan Fodio, see Smaldone 1977: 19–37 and Lovejoy 2016: 68–101, esp. 68–9, 74–5, 80–3, 97.

(centered on these twin capitals) and thirty-three emirates that in turn contained several hundred subemirates.[40]

Officially, Uthman's regime subscribed to a strict program of eliminating the social injustices attributed to previous governments, imposing full observance of Islamic rules, and preventing innovation that conflicted with such norms.[41] Slavery was a touchstone issue: Followers of the caliphate were not supposed to enslave fellow Muslims but were permitted to fight fellow believers who failed to submit. The latter provision resulted in the capture and enslavement of huge numbers of Muslims. This conundrum, compounded by problems of rule enforcement, led to controversies about who counted as a proper "Muslim" and allegations of hypocrisy in treating members of the Islamic community.[42]

A movement that had been inspired at least in part by opposition to "illegitimate" enslavement thus brought about an unprecedented expansion and intensification of slave labor. The initial jihad destroyed major urban centers in the core region, which were sometimes replaced by new foundations. Turnover was at its most severe in the Sokoto and Gwandu areas: Before long, the majority of the population (perhaps as many as four fifths) of these centers came to consist of slaves who had been locally captured or forcibly relocated. Overall slave numbers across the empire were undoubtedly very large, even if we need to bear in mind that modern estimates are largely guesswork based on sporadic claims by contemporary observers and only imperfectly checked by European counts in the wake of the early-twentieth-century colonial takeover. According to the current consensus, somewhere between a quarter and one half of the caliphate's population was of servile status. Assuming a total of roughly 10 million inhabitants, this guesstimate translates to several million slaves – at least as many as in nineteenth-century Brazil and possibly even as many as in the United States on the eve of the Civil War. Notwithstanding wide margins of error, we can be confident that throughout the nineteenth century, Sokoto was one of the largest slave societies in history.[43]

---

[40] Prominence of the Fulbe in jihad: Lovejoy 2016: 93–8. Setup of the caliphate: Lovejoy 2005: 2–3, 230; 2016: 101, 109. The split was a result of an administrative division going back to Uthman's reign: However, the subsequent rulers in charge of Sokoto and its dominion were the sole sultans whereas Gwandu was (merely) an emirate in charge of other, western emirates. Expansion to the south: Lovejoy 2012: 206–8.

[41] Lovejoy 2005: 156; 2016: 88, 99. This inspired later movements, from the Mahdi in the eastern Sudan up to present-day Boko Haram (Lovejoy 2016: 99–100).

[42] Lovejoy 2005: 23–4; 2016: 92–3. Fugitive and rebel slaves played an important role as followers and allies of the emerging Sokoto system: Lovejoy 2005: 235–43.

[43] Numbers: Lovejoy 2005: 1–3, 14, 231 (156 and 163, reproduced from much earlier articles, are outdated); 2012: 191–3, 202, 204; 2016: 102, 105–6, 109; Salau 2018: 52. Attrition at the core: Lovejoy 2005: 178–9. Settlements: Lovejoy 2016: 106–7. For the application of the concept of

Violent conflict is considered the principal source of slaves: the enslavement of opponents in the initial struggle to set up the caliphate as well as in later campaigns against rival polities and rebels; the takeover of existing slaves who had not joined pro-Sokoto risings; and far-reaching raids into non-Muslim areas. After the consolidation of much of the caliphate's territory in the early 1820s, routinized raiding – slave-catching expeditions – accounted for most of any new supplies.[44] While these operations ensnared numerous Muslims, injunctions against the export of coreligionists to nonbelievers appear to have been more faithfully observed. Consequently, with the exception of the well-established trans-Saharan trade, exports were curtailed, even if some victims of campaigning closer to the Atlantic coast did eventually end up in Brazil.[45]

Sokoto's slave trade was therefore primarily a domestic affair, a mixture of commercial transactions, tributary transfers, and redistribution to followers. Much of this mobility was centripetal: Every year, the subordinate emirates dispatched thousands of slaves as tribute to Sokoto and Gwandu.[46] Officials generally received land and slaves instead of salaries. Slaves worked both for this greatly enriched Fulbe elite and for wealthy Hausa merchants who had accommodated themselves to the new regime.[47] The sheer scale of empire boosted the scale of slave ownership at the top: Dignitaries could own more than 1,000 slaves each, who were often handed over to them as a reward for their services and loyalty, while individual Hausa investors managed to purchase dozens or hundreds. In what was a thoroughly hybrid system, redistribution served as the principal means of access to slave labor for the new state class of leaders and key associates whereas the civilian wealth elite relied on market transactions.[48]

Slaves were forced into a variety of occupations. Traditional forms of employment as domestic servants and concubines remained of great significance but were complemented by large-scale commercialized production.[49] Textile production played a major role: The emirate of

---

"slave society" to the Sokoto caliphate, see Lovejoy 2012: 21 (but cf. now 2018: 220–1); Lewis 2018: 97; Salau 2018: 19; and cf. also Lenski 2018a: 32–4. See above, n. 3.

[44] Lovejoy 2012: 160, 204; Salau 2018: 91–4.

[45] Retention: Lovejoy 2005: 5, 20; 2016: 161 (and 133–66 on jihad and the slave trade in general). Trans-Saharan trade in the nineteenth century: Lovejoy 2005: 15. Drive toward the coast: ibid. 58. Brazil (Bahia): ibid. 55–80.

[46] Lovejoy 2005: 14, 171; 2012: 193, 203–4.

[47] Lovejoy 2005: 16, 171; 2012: 202; see also Salau 2018: 54 (land assignments), 124 (land and slaves in lieu of salaries). Slaves assigned to the elite from booty: Smaldone 1977: 92.

[48] Lovejoy 2012: 205; Salau 2018: 75–80. In addition, merchants could join campaigns and share booty, or engage in kidnapping: Salau 2018: 53.

[49] Concubinage: Lovejoy 2005: 117–52. Other sectors: ibid. 15–16, and see n. 52. Stilwell 2000 discusses the status of royal slaves.

Kano was credited with 15,000 dye pits, staffed by 50,000 slaves, who manufactured goods for exports across the Sudan.[50] In addition, unprecedented numbers of slaves worked in agriculture: millet, sorghum, indigo, cotton, and grain were the main crops.[51] In elite circles, farming was frequently organized within large estates that deserve the label "plantation" (at least when defined as "large-scale agriculture with slave labor, often organized in gangs," as Paul Lovejoy does), even if Sokoto society lacked a single specific term for these entities.[52]

On these estates, slave labor was centralized under overseers (free or enslaved) and slave drivers in charge of gangs, analogous to the mode of organization described by the Roman agronomists and widely practiced in the New World. Slaves were subject to direct supervision when they worked for their owners but were also expected to grow their own crops to complement their rations. Slave villages that enjoyed a greater degree of autonomy represented the main alternative form of organization. Agricultural work was concentrated in the rainy season, whereas the dry season was given over to manufacturing, construction, or textile production.[53]

Much of the output was used to support palaces and elite retinues as well as military forces. The central emirates shipped grain and cotton for consumption and processing to commercial centers such as Kano, which required more than they produced.[54] Goods were also sold in local markets. The plantation system thus sustained both domestic consumption and transregional commerce.[55]

Overall, mass slavery was fundamental to Sokoto's political economy. The ruling class recruited slaves by means of routinized organized violence and employed them to preserve its social power with the help of the massive economic benefits derived from their accumulation, exploitation, and sale. Enslavement of captives had become institutionalized via war and raiding – what Jack Goody called the "means of destruction" – tributary allocation and redistribution, and market exchange. Unlike in

---

[50] Kano: Lovejoy 2005: 183; 2012: 203. For the textile sector, see Lovejoy 2016: 127–32.
[51] Crops and regional variation in production: Lovejoy 2005: 163, 168, 173–5; Salau 2018: 84. For the development of Kano and its concentration of textile (export) industries, see Salau 2018: 70–3.
[52] Salau 2018 is now the most comprehensive study. Expansion of plantation economy: Lovejoy 2005: 176–99; 2012: 203; Salau 2018: 61–73; also in general Lovejoy 2016: 110–27. Plantation sector: Lovejoy 2005: 153–206 (definition [quote]: 154, no term: 161). Salau 2018: 24–9, esp. 27–8 argues for the applicability of the concept of "plantation."
[53] Organization of the plantation sector: Lovejoy 2005: 165–7; 2012: 212–16; Salau 2018: 74–89.
[54] Lovejoy 2012: 214, 277.   [55] Lovejoy 2005: 169–73; Salau 2018: 129.

other parts of sub-Saharan Africa, the demands of the regional economy trumped the pull of the Atlantic export trade. This was true both with regard to the transfer of slaves and to the so-called "legitimate trade" that had local slaves produce commodities for long-distance export to Western societies that had formally turned away from slave labor or the slave trade. This latter type of commerce was once again much more common along the coasts than in the Sudan. As Lovejoy poignantly observes, the greatest concentration of slaves in nineteenth-century Africa thus coincided with the weakest articulation between slavery and commercial capitalism.[56]

5.3 Comparisons

Separated by 2,000 miles and 2,000 years, the Roman Republic and the Sokoto caliphate nevertheless had much in common.[57] This was true despite significant ecological differences that motivated societies to prioritize access to land in Italy and to manpower in the Sudan.[58] In both cases, war yielded masses of slaves. To be sure, motivations for warfare varied. Yet although the Romans are not known to have waged jihad, the religious drive behind their initial aggression must not be underrated and may well have been more crucial than later secularized accounts reveal: During the fourth and third centuries BCE, their wars paid for an awful lot of temples.[59] Conversely, religious devotion in Sokoto clearly had its limits, as fellow Muslims were routinely captured and enslaved for material gain.

Most importantly, war was a steady state: Annual levies to raise forces for raids and punitive expeditions were as common in Rome as they were in the caliphate. In both cases, warfare acted as a vital means of coercive redistribution, of land as well as labor. Martial prowess was a crucial criterion for elite advancement, required to obtain titled office, whether as a Roman senior magistrate or a Sokoto emir. "War, booty, and political

---

[56] Institutionalization: Lovejoy 2012: 278. Regional vs. export economies, slave numbers, and capitalism: ibid. 285. On the "legitimate trade" in general, see ibid. 141, 165–90.

[57] These similarities make it all the more surprising that comparisons have so far been almost nonexistent: for very brief observations, see Scheidel 2012: 96; Lenski 2018a: 34. In the following, I largely limit references to the African side of the comparison (cf. above, no. 24).

[58] Salau 2018: 98. The latter was qualified by increasing demand for land due to nineteenth-century population growth.

[59] Rüpke 1990; Padilla Peralta 2020a. Cf. also Driediger-Murphy 2019: 8–9 for Rome as a "deeply, consistently, passionately religious society" led by an elite whose members could be "religious extremist[s]."

dominance constituted mutually reinforcing elements" not merely for the caliphate's ruling class but just as clearly for Rome's senators and knights.[60]

Military styles differed in keeping with ecological differences, which lent greater importance to cavalry in the Sudan.[61] Even so, during the caliphate's formative phase, Sokoto warfare bore some resemblance to Roman traditions by being relatively (that is, by local standards) egalitarian in nature. According to the classic modern account, it displayed "distinctive features of the raiding citizen army," a notion that is readily applicable to the early Roman legions too: It was only later in the nineteenth century that growing social differentiation favored elite cavalry and their retainers, just as Roman warfare became less democratic over time, albeit much more slowly and far less starkly so.[62]

In terms of political organization, both imperial powers are best described are complex conglomerates, made up of hundreds of *municipia*, *coloniae*, and allied polities in Italy and of hundreds of subemirates in the caliphate. Both of them invested in networks of fortified settlements, colonies in Italy and ribats in the caliphal state. Direct governance was effectively confined to the central regions, to Rome and its hinterland (where residents could routinely participate in the business of politics and ritual and public goods were dispensed) and to the twin capital districts of Sokoto and Gwandu. In both cases, the political centers and the economically most vibrant areas were not the same: witness the relative commercial importance of Campania and Kano.[63]

The two societies resembled each other even more closely with respect to slavery. Slaveholding had originally been embedded in familial relations. In both cases we encounter the notion of inherently "free" persons who could not legitimately be enslaved, Roman citizens and ethnic Fulbe.[64] At the same time, slavery was not racialized: Everyone outside the core groups was fair game, including, de facto, fellow Muslims. Assimilation persisted in the face of the violent acquisition of slaves and intensifying exploitation at arm's length: Slave women in the Sudan and Roman freedpersons who

---

[60] Smaldone 1977: 58, 93, 139, 141, 149 (quote); see also Salau 2018: 128.
[61] That said, the importance of cavalry warfare and its role in establishing elite status in early Rome until (at least) the fourth century BCE must not be underrated: for example, Davenport 2019: 39–42.
[62] Smaldone 1977: 129 (quote). The intensity of warfare peaked from 1804 to 1837, then abated (ibid. 157), a process that coincided with disequalizing organizational changes (ibid. 129–33).
[63] Conglomerates: Lovejoy 2005: 15. Ribats: Smaldone 1977: 61; Lovejoy 2005: 180; 2016: 97; Salau 2018: 51–4.
[64] Lovejoy 2005: 22. But in general, enslavability was determined by religious affiliation rather than race or ethnicity: Salau 2018: 31–46, especially 45.

assumed elements of their patrons' names are the most notable examples.[65] Slaves were present across so many different sectors that they did not form a distinct class. And unlike in many other large-scale slave systems outside the New World, slave labor played a prominent role in agriculture.[66]

More trivial parallels merit only passing notice. These include slaves gaining permission to work on their own account (what the Romans called *peculium*) in exchange for payments to their owners, which in Sokoto were known as *murgu* (if paid in cash or cowries) and *wuri* (if delivered as a share of income), and slaves' associated opportunity to save funds with an eye to purchasing their own freedom (in a process known as *fansa* in Sokoto). Manumitted slaves became clients. First-generation slaves (*bayi* in Sokoto) were distinguished from (more highly regarded) home-born slaves (*vernae* in Rome, *cucanawa* in Sokoto). Field hands were conceptually differentiated from domestics. General overseers (such as *procuratores*) would monitor estate managers (*vilici*), who were generally slaves.[67]

Moreover, the African experience sometimes offers suggestions on issues for which we lack specific information regarding early Rome. For example, in the Sudan slave exports played a greater role prior to the formation of the Sokoto Empire. This might make us wonder whether this had also been true of Italy prior to the Roman takeover: Sub-Saharan Africa provides a real-life example of my earlier conjecture along these lines. Upon imperial consolidation, most slaves were retained within the respective conquest states.

Market mechanisms for the transfer of slaves existed in both societies. Yet the considerable significance of nonmarket redistribution in the caliphate raises the question of whether similar processes also occurred in Middle Republican Rome and Italy. The Sokoto elite was allocated slaves outright (alongside land grants): Emirs and lesser officials received the most generous shares and were free to keep these slaves, pass them on to their

---

[65] Assimilation under Sokoto: Lovejoy 2012: 220–4, who mentions manumission via death-bed grants, self-purchasing, ransom, and favors to concubines with children (223), all of which have Roman parallels; likewise, the fact that most slaves were not thus privileged (224).

[66] Farming, not a class: for example, Lovejoy 2005: 16–17. Hausa partible inheritance laws fueled the need for ongoing raids to replenish fragmenting domains (Smaldone 1977: 148; also Salau 2018: 98): A similar mechanism might be hypothesized for Roman society.

[67] Lovejoy 2005: 44, 207–9 (*murgu*), 210 (*wuri*, a tithe), 43, 209 (*fansa*); Salau 2018: 102 (*cucanawa*), 85 (rural vs domestic), 81 (levels of hierarchy). Cato, *On Agriculture* 59 (one new piece of clothing to be issued to farm slaves every other year) was even stingier than some Sokoto owners: Lovejoy 2012: 213 (once per year). Treatment of slaves in Sokoto could be severe, once again mirroring Roman practices: Lovejoy 2005: 247; 2012: 215–16. Slave revolts were rare: Salau 2018: 112.

retainers, or sell them off.⁶⁸ Under the Roman system of aristocratic oligarchy, commanding officers enjoyed great discretion regarding the distribution of war booty. In principle, there was little to prevent them from keeping some captives for their own use and that of their peers who accompanied them on campaigns, or from distributing them to their soldiers. A few accounts of doubtful reliability hint at such practices: Just as the caliphate's soldiers expected booty to be shared on the battlefield, similar conventions may have applied among Romans. References to Roman soldiers receiving slaves not only reach back to the campaigns of Coriolanus and the sack of Fidenae in 425 BCE but also, and comfortingly for those skeptical of such semimythical tales, still show up in Caesar's account of his campaigns in Gaul in the 50s BCE.⁶⁹

We have to allow for the possibility that the redistribution of captives taken in military operations played a greater role in the early stages of Roman state building than the sources indicate. This conjecture would make it easier to reconcile references to mass enslavement with low levels of monetization and commercialization. It shows how slaveholdings great and small could have been built up without cash changing hands, enabling farmer-soldiers to take home one or two extra workers, and aristocrats to grab many more. Absent the need to recover initial investments, such slaves could have been employed to sustain households at various status levels, by contributing to elite ostentation and largess, by freeing up commoners for continuous war-making, and by generating extra resources for paying *tributum*.⁷⁰ Such arrangements, elements of which are well attested for the Sokoto Empire, would also have been perfectly consistent with Roman needs and mores. We might even ask whether the Sokoto practice of using slaves as a means of payment for larger transactions might have been anticipated in cash-poor Italy.⁷¹

In coastal sub-Saharan Africa, the employment of slave labor for the manufacturing of export goods was a late feature, motivated in the first instance by British measures against the international slave trade. The massive scale of Sokoto's domestic market farther inland absorbed much

---

⁶⁸ Lovejoy 2005: 163, 171–3, 232.
⁶⁹ Sokoto: Smaldone 1977: 91–2. Rome: Volkmann 1990: 37 (fifth century BCE), 52, 147 (Caesar). Although Welwei 2000: 25 expresses doubts about the Fidenae allocations, reportedly limited to officers and cavalrymen (Livy 4.34.4), he deems this practice plausible for the period of the Samnite Wars (156).
⁷⁰ As I speculated in Scheidel 2012: 103, "[i]n a period of little regular state income and primitive accumulation through plunder, slaveownership represented one of the few opportunities for elites to privatize the gains from empire."
⁷¹ Smaldone 1977: 148.

of the greatly increased output of the textile industry, even as some of it ended up in other parts of Africa as far away as Libya.[72] This serves as a reminder that the production of goods for export is not a logical corollary of mass slavery. Thus, at the very least, there is no need to interpret the commencement of such exports in Italy in the mid-third century BCE as indicative of the relative insignificance or small scale of slavery in previous generations. Likewise, access to cash was not a necessary precondition for slave ownership on a large scale: The use of cowrie shells, iron bars, and foreign silver coins to arrange transfers for many of the millions of slaves kept in the caliphate leaves ample room for us to imagine a substantial slave trade within Italy conducted with the help of basic bronze monies and imported Greek coins.

In practical terms, the main value of this type of conjectural reasoning by analogy lies in the fact that it provides food for thought. My very brief comparison between early Rome and the Sudan up to the Sokoto caliphate is meant to draw our attention to features that are given short shrift or not mentioned at all in the existing record for Italy in the fourth and early third centuries. One of them is the fact that conditions in the Western Mediterranean at the time would have favored the export of war captives from the Italian Peninsula. The allocation of such captives to war leaders and soldiers in the wake of military operations is another. In the Sokoto caliphate, both land and people were forcibly appropriated and redistributed. Roman sources routinely refer to the seizure and transfer of enemy territory but show far less interest in the assignment of war captives. Instead we are treated to tales of ransom or local sale that may well be anachronistic in that they are more readily compatible with – and thus perhaps influenced by – the customs of a later, more cash-rich age. It should give us pause that ostensibly plausible means of disposing of captives are not mentioned at all, or not enough, while less credible ones receive more attention. A comparative perspective deepens such concerns.

The Sokoto experience demonstrates that it was perfectly feasible to establish slavery on a large scale in the absence of widespread intensification of productive activities and a developed export trade for slave-made goods. The more slavery was fueled by capture in war waged by slave owners and their subordinates, the less it would have depended on commercial incentives. This was true of early Rome and the Sudan, but far less so of better-known slave societies such as classical Greece – where domestic captives were often ransomed and actual slaves were primarily imported

[72] Candotti 2010: 196–206.

from less monetized and commercialized regions – and not at all of the colonial plantation systems of the Americas, where commercial capital was king and the creation of slaves was effectively outsourced to business partners on a different continent.

To be sure, analogies are not history, and possibilities or probabilities are not what actually happened. Evidence for one case cannot and must not be used to fill gaps in the evidence for another. That is not the point of comparison.[73] In the present context, comparison helps us transcend the biases of the existing record; alerts us to plausible options – made plausible by the simple fact that they reflect actual outcomes elsewhere and are not merely the product of our imagination; and makes us think harder about these biases and options as we go about our business. While fraught with its own set of pitfalls and temptations, this approach seems preferable to the conventional game of reshuffling and massaging the same factoids over and over again, a frustrating pursuit that has kept students of the literary record of early Roman history busy for many generations without yielding much of substance – in marked contrast to archaeological research.

But there is more to this particular comparison. While comparative perspectives have gained ground in the study of Greek and Roman slavery, they have been dominated by references to the well-researched slave societies of the New World – and above all to the United States, even if practices of slavery in Brazil and other parts of Latin America may have had more in common with their Roman antecedents.[74] This is hardly surprising given the sheer amount and accessibility of pertinent scholarship, and is without any doubt worth developing in much greater depth. That said, this orientation toward colonial or colonial-origin slavery reinforces Eurocentric notions of what matters most, sidelining alternative sources of inspiration and reflection.

Sub-Saharan Africa was not merely a source of slave labor for Western plantation owners; it also housed major slave societies that followed their own developmental dynamics. In the Sudan, the institution of slavery evolved at some remove from the pull of Western markets, in closer interaction with the slave-owning Islamic societies of the Middle East and North Africa region – not coincidentally, yet another

---

[73] For the uses and different flavors of comparative history, see the survey by Lange 2013, and more narrowly Scheidel 2018, directed at ancient historians.
[74] Lenski's 2018b: 129–45 critique of Finley's lumping together Athens, Rome, and the Antebellum South targets merely the tip of the iceberg: comparison benefits from the widest possible scope. Bradley 1994, with his emphasis on slavery in Brazil rather than the United States as a *comparandum* to Roman slavery, made a step in the right direction, but much more remains to be done.

much-neglected candidate for fruitful comparison – and, in the nineteenth century, expanded in response to domestic concentration of power. Embedded as they are in disciplinary traditions that have long prioritized European or Western experiences in terms of approach as well as content, historians of the Roman world stand to gain from opening up to African history. The intellectual case for comparative engagement is strong. So is the moral one.

PART II

Material Sources

6 | The Strangeness of Rome's Early Heavy Bronze Coinage

LIV MARIAH YARROW

6.1 The Money Problem

Roman coinage is one of the most important and certainly most tangible 'firsts' of the Middle Republican period. This chapter suggests we have not yet looked as hard as we should at the historical implications of cast coinage, as opposed to the relatively well studied (if controversial) early struck coinages.[1] Yet even as these early cast bronzes are some of Rome's earliest 'coins' in a formal sense, in many ways they are quite alien in both form and function to any modern sense of that word.

Typically, we tend to think about money as either having intrinsic value or operating by fiat. For instance, your average person might assume that a gold or silver coin should have the same value as its metal content, and yet that same person is likely equally comfortable with a piece of paper that says it is legal tender because we use it in all the same ways we use a precious metal coin with an assumed intrinsic value. The vast majority of our economic transactions are simply bookkeeping tallies of credits and debits facilitated by various financial institutions authorized by and to varying degrees overseen by our governments. There is no big vault with all the physical money in it that is represented by what we spend or save via coded electronic messages. Understanding fiat money isn't hard – we use it all the time. The intellectual challenge is understanding how far back in history one can observe similar monetary practices. We tend to assume that without tangible money ancient people were reduced to barter, and that even with money ancient peoples expected physical objects to have intrinsic value. One purpose of this chapter is to help further dispel these ideas.

We are relatively confident that Rome partook in the wider northern and central Italic tradition of using bronze as money, at least in the sense of a unit of account and measure of value, long before it ever issued coinage. The usual evidence cited for this is the list of fines in the Twelve Tables.

---

[1] Coarelli 2013 with Burnett and Crawford 2014 and Bernard 2017. Generally, specific issues are referred to following convention by their *RRC* classification number in Crawford 1974.

However, the tables do not explicitly mention the unit or material to which the number corresponds.² Support for this hypothesis has been seen in Latin vocabulary, including such phrases as *pendere poenas* ('to weigh fines') or the word *stipendium* (a 'weighed heap').³

James Tan's chapter in this volume (Chapter 3) demonstrates the degree to which the Romans were capable of using complicated systems of account to track credits and debits for the *tributum-stipendium* system long before they issued coinage. A monetized economy requires a means by which accounts may be kept, value stored, and payments made; coinage itself is not required. Multiple things can function as money – grain, metal, cattle, but also just the credit and debts themselves. The unit of account was primarily bronze, and bronze could be used to store value and also to make payments, but in most instances credits and debits reckoned in bronze units are likely to have been the most common means of transaction.

Imagine this scenario: you bring me three sacks of wheat worth three *asses*, and I credit two *asses* towards your next *tributum* payment and then give you one *as* worth of wine, and now we're even. No physical money changes hands, but the transaction still presumes a common monetary system. Or perhaps you take your remaining wheat home and save it or even eat it, or you ask if I'd buy it, and you get a hunk of bronze.

The next problem is the nature of that piece of bronze. What makes it valuable? Is it fungible? To be fungible it must be possible to swap it with any other similar piece of bronze of the same value. Bullion is by nature fungible. It doesn't matter what shape your gold is in, bars, ingots, torques, coins, it is all fungible (assuming similar levels of purity, of course).

Is that piece of bronze bullion? Does it have intrinsic value as raw material? Historians have long assumed the answer to that question is yes, but the more we know about the evidence the less that seems to be the case, and the more complex it makes our understanding about the moment Rome began making coins.

Early Roman cast bronze monetary instruments are today called *aes rude* and *aes formatum*. *Aes rude* is the term used for bronze pieces of just about any metallurgical formula, which we presume to have been used as money and which appear shapeless to modern eyes. *Aes formatum* is much the same but the shape of the pieces seems more deliberate, usually taking the form of ingots or discs, often referred to as 'loaves' or 'buns', perhaps even

---

² See Crawford 1996: 2.606 discussing reconstruction and emphasizing significance of Festus 508L.
³ Kroll 2008; Varro, *LL* 5.169–83.

with some minimal design element but not apparently conforming to any weight standard.[4]

Metallurgical testing has revealed considerable variety to the composition of *aes rude*, and this makes it harder to believe that *aes rude* functioned as bullion. Some of the best-studied material is that retrieved in controlled excavations from Ghiaccioforte, the site of a small oppidum in Etruria (near modern Scansano) occupied in the late fourth century BCE but destroyed circa 280 BCE, in the period shortly before the introduction of Roman *aes grave*. Analysis of twenty specimens from Ghiaccioforte showed at least five different metallurgical groupings, while the characteristic that most stands out is the number of pieces with high iron content where iron has been dissolved into the bronze.[5] The alloying of iron and copper is not naturally occurring and requires significantly high temperatures of circa 1536°C (2696.8°F). Furthermore, for practical purposes such ferruginous alloys are useless for producing other metal objects by means of casting or hot and cold working, meaning pieces with this profile had little intrinsic value as raw material.[6] The Ghiaccioforte finds do not appear to be anomalous, as scientific analyses of a Sardinian hoard of *aes rude* and of *ramo secco* in the British Museum likewise reveal high iron contents.[7]

The variable and ferruginous metallurgical profiles of *aes rude* and *aes formatum* suggest we need to let go of a bullion or intrinsic-value model in which these objects functioned as stocks of raw materials and begin to think about how this material might have functioned as a type of fiat money. However, the bullion and intrinsic-value model for *aes rude* and *aes formatum* underpins most of our thinking about Rome's earliest bronze coinage, the heavy cast coins we call *aes grave*, meaning heavy bronze.[8] This link not only derives from the metal and weight of this earliest bronze coinage, but also from the fact that *aes rude*, *aes formatum*, and early *aes grave* all appear in the same find contexts and seem to function in very similar ways. At Praeneste, a single piece of *aes rude* was commonly deposited alongside other grave goods; in the 2004–7 excavations at the Colombella necropolis *aes grave* pieces (presumably of local manufacture)

---

[4] A new typology of this class of object based on a re-evaluation of the Mazin hoard (Croatia) has been recently proposed, Bertol and Farac 2012, but one focused on Italian finds is still needed; cf. Thurlow and Vecchi 1979: plates 2–9, Vecchi 2014: 76 with plates 83–90 and Haeberlin 1910: plates 1–9.
[5] Baldassarri et al. 2007.   [6] Ingo et al. 2006: 217.
[7] De Caro, Ingo, and Salvi 2005; Burnett, Craddock, and Meeks 1986.
[8] We do not (yet) have published scientific results of the metallurgical composition of Roman *aes grave*, although hopefully testing will be forthcoming which could help determine its typical profile and possible iron content.

were found in a rich layer of ancient deposition separate from the tombs themselves.[9] At the sanctuary at Pyrgi, ritual deposits have been found containing *aes formatum* buried in an *olla*, and also quadrans from an early series of Roman *aes grave* (RRC 14) was similarly buried in an *olla*.[10] Votive offerings found at Nemi or Vicarello contained both *aes rude* and *aes grave* as well as later struck coinage.[11] Notably, *aes rude*, *aes formatum*, and early *aes grave* are commonly found in association with sacred or ritual spaces.[12] If we think that *aes grave* connects functionally in some way to the earlier bronze classes of *aes rude* or *aes formatum*, then the apparent lack of a bullion function to the earlier material makes it harder to assume that the heaviness of *aes grave* relates in turn to its intrinsic value.

This paper analyses available metrological data for the three earliest issues of *aes grave* to further demonstrate the limited value of a bullion or intrinsic-value model for early Roman bronze cast coinage. Once these limitations are fully realized, we are left to confront the 'strangeness' of the phenomenon of creating such a heavy coinage as a type of fiat money. As coins, these *aes grave* were, after all, serially made objects, and their reproduction on supposed standard weight units has been seen to differentiate them from the *aes rude* and *aes formatum*, which preceded them. The following shows that this idea of uniform or standardized weights is less sound than is often thought. This perhaps strengthens the relationship of early *aes grave* with those bronze objects, which preceded it, but it continues to pose interesting historical questions. What made it desirable to

---

[9] These *aes grave* finds are not yet published but are already on public display at the local museum because of their historical importance; photographs are available on the author's personal website: Liv Mariah Yarrow, 'Aes Rude and Aes Grave, Praeneste Finds', *Adventures in My Head* [blog], 26 October 2019, https://livyarrow.org/2019/10/26/aes-rude-and-aes-grave-praeneste-finds/. The two specimens on display are both of the bull-head/prow type (HN Italy 359 = Vecchi 276 = Haeberlin 157–8). One of the pieces has been pierced so as to allow it to be hung on a string and perhaps worn. The excavator, Prof. Gatti, kindly discussed the context finds with the author in private correspondence and shared further images of the finds; this deposition layer also contained a Roman *as* with minimal wear of the McCabe's Group E type which is related to *RRC* 106 and likely made in Etruria (McCabe 2013: 145–8), thus suggesting the deposition layer closed during or after the Second Punic War. Haeberlin no. 9 was also found at Praeneste and another specimen was part of the Ariccia 1848 hoard (*RRCH* 13; c. 28 km SW of Praeneste). The museum also displays many complete grave goods assemblages from recent excavations (cf. Gatti 2009), but the common appearance of a single piece of *aes rude* in these burials was already well documented by Fernique 1878 and Vaglieri 1907. Fernique 1878 descriptions are particularly interesting because they record the finding in a level below the *aes rude* of a coin likely to be of the HN Italy 644 type (c. 325–275 BCE), thus strongly supporting the use of *aes rude* well into the third century.

[10] Baglione et al. 2015: 225; Drago Troccoli 2013; and Ambrosini and Michetti 2013.

[11] Crawford 1983; Tocci 1967–8.   [12] Cf. Jaia and Molinari 2011 for discussion.

have such a physically large monetary object when other types of small struck coinage were well known from neighbouring culture groups?

6.2 Rome's Earliest Bronze and Its Denomination Structure

Rome's very earliest bronze coinage is all cast and consists of three issues (Table 6.1). Casting is a slower manufacturing technique than striking but allows for larger coins to be produced. The hoard evidence makes clear that all three issues were produced well before other cast bronzes. Far fewer specimens of *RRC* 19 survive, but two hoards help us securely group it with the other two issues. Neither the exact nor relative chronology of these three issues has been firmly established. Modern scholarly treatments of the evidence begin from the work of Haeberlin's *Aes Grave: das Schwergeld Roms und Mittelitaliens einschliesslich der ihm vorausgehenden Rohbronzewährung* (1910), which documented the location and weight of every specimen then known, reviewed all previous publications, and published multiple illustrations of each type. Haeberlin was an avid collector and many of the specimens he documents were from his own collection. The material was treated holistically alongside the other coinage with a primarily chronological interest by Thomsen in *Early Roman Coinage: A Study of the Chronology* (1957–1961). Crawford's landmark study of the whole of *Roman Republican Coinage* (1974) remains the most consulted reference work, and for the *aes grave* he was much influenced by both Haeberlin and Thomsen. In particular, Crawford followed Thomsen in placing the Dioscuri/Mercury series (*RRC* 14) some five to ten years earlier than the Apollo/Apollo series (*RRC* 19), but, as we shall see, this ordering is based on assumptions about the development of the weight standards for this early coinage.

There is some shared iconography between these issues and black glaze ware (*vernice nera*) of the third-century *atelier des petites estampilles* produced around 280–260 BCE.[13] A temporal connection between this pottery class and early *aes grave* is strengthened by the discovery of a ritual deposit of both examples together both at the Sanctuary of Sol Indiges (Torvaianica) and at the Sanctuary at Pyrgi.[14] The iconographic parallels, however, are not a secure means of dating the *aes grave*: these same pottery

---

[13] Cf. Stanco 2009: fig. 5 no. 25, fig. 13 nos. 67–73 and 84–8; Jaia and Molinari 2011: 87 briefly touch on the iconographic parallels.

[14] Jaia and Molinari 2011, especially plate 7; Ambrosini and Michetti 2013: 131–3; a temporal connection was posited by Burnett 1989: 64. For discussion of production and association with temple economies, see Di Guiseppe 2012: 62–70, 89–90, and 95.

Table 6.1 *Overview of denominations and types*

	Denominations			Types		
Name*	Relative value		Symbol	RRC 14/1–7	RRC 18/1–6 All mirror-image designs	RRC 19/1–2
As	1 as	12 uncia	|	Beardless Janus** and Mercury	Apollo	Dioscurus and Apollo
Semis	1/2-as	6 uncia	S	Mars and Venus†	Pegasus	Roma and Faunus‡
Triens	1/3-as	4 uncia	••••	Dolphin and thunderbolt	horse head	n/a
Quadrans	1/4-as	3 uncia	•••	Palm of right hand and two kernels of grain	boar	n/a
Sextans	1/6-as	2 uncia	••	Scallop shell (outside) and caduceus	Dioscurus	n/a
Uncia	1/12-as	1 uncia	•	Knucklebone and only denomination symbol	one kernel of grain	n/a
Semuncia	1/24-as	½ uncia	Σ	Acorn and only denomination symbol	n/a	n/a

Prepared by the author.

* The ancient names of coin types are relatively well attested in later sources; the earliest and most complete overview is Varro, *LL* 5.169–73.

** Cf. Molinari 2014 with reference to earlier scholarship.

† For this identification, see Haeberlin 1910: 94; Thomsen 1957–61 (1957): 59; *pace* Crawford 1974: 133. Likewise, other 'Minerva' identifications on the *aes grave* by Crawford must be corrected to Mars: RRC 21/2, 25/5, and 27/6.

‡ I endorse Massa-Pairault 2011's identification of the reverse as based on the iconography of Lycaean Pan; it may derive from the iconography on the tetradrachms of Antigonos II Gonatas (after 274 BCE). Antigonos' iconography of Pan itself derives from the iconography of the fourth-century obols of the Arcadian league, cf. Warren 1989: 294 no. 54.

impressions also share strong visual parallels with the designs found on non-Roman *aes grave* that are typically dated to the First Punic War and some even down through the Second Punic War.[15] In the opinion of this

[15] Parallels include (an illustrative, not complete, list): five-pointed star: Stanco 2009: fig. 5 no. 21 with Vecchi 2014: nos. 306–7; frog: Stanco 2009: fig. 5 no. 30 and fig. 13 no. 66 with Vecchi 2014:

author, it is most likely that the shared iconography on both pottery stamps and on *aes grave*, in both Roman and non-Roman contexts, is influenced by the types of symbols found in other cultural contexts, including intaglios used as signet rings, the impressions of which were markers of identity, as well as guarantors of the authenticity of communications, contracts, and more.[16]

Otherwise, our best evidence for dating the early heavy bronze comes from the work of Jaia and Molinari's publication of two foundation deposits containing both *RRC* 14 and 18, but no later issues, at the fortified Sanctuary of Sol Indiges along the coast below Lavinium.[17] They emphasize how other hoards containing *RRC* 14 and 18 cluster around the coastline south of Rome.[18] They suggest that *aes grave* was created in the first instance as part of Roman efforts to improve coastal defences ahead of an anticipated clash with Carthaginian naval power in the Tyrrhenian Sea. As for the function and appearance of the coinage, Jaia and Molinari follow the long-standing and little-questioned hypothesis of Burnett, who suggested that Romans adopted the fixed-weight standard, circular shape, and double-sided design of Greek coinage prevalent in Southern Italy for many centuries, and then adapted it to the Central and North Italian tradition of using cast bronze as a monetary instrument.[19]

The bullion model discussed in the previous section is at the heart of the argument for dating *RRC* 14 earlier than *RRC* 18, despite the implication that the second series was heavier than the first. Based on Haeberlin's observed specimen weights, Thomsen assumed that the Beardless Janus and Mercury *as* (*RRC* 14/1) was intended to weigh 288 Roman scruples, that is precisely one Roman pound, and the Apollo and Apollo *as* (*RRC* 18/1) was intended to weigh 300 scruples. A scruple is the 1/288 part of a whole. Because Thomsen believed *RRC* 14 was closer to the weight of the

---

nos. 219, 225, 291, and 342; triskeles: Stanco 2009: fig. 5 no. 29 with Vecchi 2014: no. 291; star and crescent: Stanco 2009: fig. 5 no. 22 with Vecchi 2014: nos. 282, 364–7; insect (cicada?): Stanco 2009: fig. 5 no. 35 with Vecchi 2014: nos. 220 and 226.

[16] For example frog intaglios: Walters inv. no. 42.1136 (= Marlborough gems no. 449); Thorvaldsen inv. no. I1487; British Museum 1865,0712.114 (an italic scarab); cf. frog stamps and *aes grave* imagery cited in previous note. For intaglios as markers of identity, see Yarrow 2018 with earlier bibliography.

[17] Jaia and Molinari 2011; cf. Bernard 2018a: 175–81.

[18] See Yarrow 2021: 12–13, especially n. 6 for details of a hoard dispersed in trade in the 1980s and 1990s which likely comes from this same geographical area, but the exact find-spot is now sadly lost. The reported contents of this hoard seem to suggest a similar date between *RRC* 14 and the Roman currency bars (the so-called *aes signatum*). It is surprising that no specimens of the *RRC* 18 type are noted among the hoard contents, but given this report is clearly less concerned with the accurate recording of the *aes grave* and *aes rude* elements than of the currency bars, we might assume they may have gone unreported.

[19] Burnett 1989: 55–7.

Roman pound, which he presumed to have been a stable unit, he extrapolated it must then be closer in time to the preceding bullion-based weight system. RRC 18 to his mind *must* have been later because it is more than a Roman pound – as he understood it – and thus could not grow out of a monetary system based on weight.[20]

More recent scholarship, however, challenges the assumption that one precise modern weight ought to be assigned to the Roman pound.[21] This would support the general view and approach used by Crawford. He surveyed various estimates for the Roman pound, ranging from 322.56 to 327.45 g, that have been proposed by earlier scholars based on different source materials – coins, stone weights, balances, metal weights. In the end he used circa 324 g, in part because it is easily divisible by 12, with the caveat that it was not reasonable to assume 'that the Romans were able to maintain the weight of their pound absolutely constant, at all times and in all places'.[22]

Any model that emphasizes the intrinsic value of the coin itself seems a poor fit for our physical evidence of the *aes grave*. There are intentionally halved and otherwise intentionally fragmented pieces of non-Roman *aes grave*, but this practice is far from common.[23] I know of only one cut Roman aes grave, a semis found outside peninsular Italy, as well as one additional fragment observed in trade.[24] One of the features that clearly

---

[20] Thomsen 1957–61: (1961), 71.

[21] Riggsby 2019: 83–129, esp. 100–7. The Pondera Online Project documents 20,000 weights produced between the mid-sixth century BCE and the mid-fifteenth century CE, many from archaeological contexts and previously unpublished (pondera.uclouvain.be). To this author's knowledge the most complete set of basalt weights found in Latium and with an archeological provenance is the set found in the presumed ancient forum of Praeneste in 1907, now on display in the local museum. All seven weights conform with less than a gram deviation to a Roman pound of 327.4 g, but thus far no precise date for the find is established (Liv Mariah Yarrow, 'A Highly Precise Set of Weights', *Adventures in My Head* [blog], 26 October 2019, https://livyarrow.org/2019/10/26/a-highly-precise-set-of-weights).

[22] Crawford 1974: 591.

[23] For example Haeberlin 1910: pl. 78.10 of the Iguvium HN Italy 26 (Vecchi 2014: 206) type halved; Haeberlin 1910: pl. 79.2 of the Iguvium HN Italy 29 (Vecchi 2014: 210) type quartered. 77.6 = Ariminum sword/scabbard type maybe halved. Garrucci 1885: pl. IV.15 may be a quartered cast coin found in the votive deposit at Vicarello, but the drawing leaves the type uncertain.

[24] Werz 2015 A fragment is illustrated by Haeberlin 1910: pl. 94.6, but appears broken because the bronze was friable, not as an intentional modification; note also that this is the only known specimen of this specific Crawford subtype 37/1b; cf. Haeberlin 1910: pl. 56.4 a fragment of a specimen of the RRC 37/1c. Garrucci 1885: pl. IV.15 may be a quartered cast coin found in the votive deposit at Vicarello, but the drawing leaves type uncertain. By contrast nearly all Roman currency bars (so-called *aes signatum*) to appear in trade today are broken pieces of whole bars, and fragments of Roman currency bars are also very common among our hoards; in the Mazin hoard, we even seem to have two fragments from the same original elephant and pig bar, on which Mirnik 2009: 457. On why the term *aes signatum* is an inappropriate descriptor of the objects, Crawford 2009.

separates early Roman *aes grave* from other heavy bronze (*aes rude* and *aes formatum*), and also struck bronze and silver in use in central Italy, is its relatively elaborate base-12 denomination system (cf. Table 6.1 above). The inclusion of denomination marks on the coins themselves makes clear the importance of the denomination system to this new form of coinage. A denomination system is in some ways the opposite of a bullion system based on weight. The coin itself proclaims its worth, and the entity issuing the coin expects that the receiver will value the coin as it is marked, that is, without weighing.

The type of bronze denomination system adopted by Rome does have some precedents in Sicily.[25] However, the pellet denomination mark had not been in regular use for more than 100 years when Rome implemented its own similar system on its new heavy bronze. Bronze coins *without* denomination marks were widely struck and widely circulated throughout Southern Italy and Greece in the intervening period, but rarely in so many different denominations. It is rare to see more than two or three different bronze denominations issued by any one mint at any one time. Rome's currency system stands out from other contemporary struck coinage particularly because of the number of fractions of the whole unit that were made. It would become the norm for many other *aes grave* coinages produced in Northern Italy, especially Etruria and Umbria.[26]

One of the oddities of the earliest three issues of Roman *aes grave* is that they don't *seem* to have the same target weight for the whole unit or *as*. Generally speaking, the *asses* of RRC 18 and 19 are heavier than those of the series RRC 14 by approximately 10–15 g. Crawford was worried about how the apparent weight standards between these early issues varied, but he did not come to any fixed conclusion about what it meant. Although he followed Thomsen's sequence, he particularly didn't like that RRC 18, which appears to be later in time, also seems intended to weigh more. He could accept weight decreases as an economic move, but the apparent temporary weight increase seemed to him less easy to explain.[27]

---

[25] For example the coinage of Akragas, cf. SNG ANS 1029, or Himera, cf. SNG ANS 179–80.

[26] Our evidence for dating these other series is highly inexact, but generally speaking we believe them to be later than the Roman series and to take their inspiration from Rome. The earliest of the non-Roman *aes grave* is likely to be the unattributed oval series (maybe from Volsinii?) Vecchi 196–201; other key examples of early non-Roman *aes grave* with pellets include those from Iguvium (Vecchi 203–15); Tuder (Vecchi 216–22); Tarquinii (Vecchi 120–7); and Volaterrae (Vecchi 128–34). There are also silver issues from Etruria that have denominations marks, likely struck at Pisa, Luca, and/or Populonia (HN Italy 95–101, 104–6, and 117–80).

[27] RRC 1.44–5 esp. no. 3 and RRC 2.595.

Crawford follows Haeberlin's assessment of relative weight standards for *aes grave*.[28] Haeberlin had collected data on far more specimens than are readily accessible for study today, and Crawford deferred to those numbers. Haeberlin derived his weight standard by applying a mean average to all his collected weights after excluding any specimens that he judged as outside his anticipated norms. Given our advances in statistical analysis over the last 100 years, it is worth revisiting Haeberlin's calculations to determine the validity of the weight standards he proposes.[29]

The reinvestigation of the published weights also allows us more accurately to describe the uniformity (or non-uniformity) of the data. Could a Roman or anyone else trust the face value of one of these coins? Did its face-value denomination communicate something meaningful about its weight? These questions are important for assessing the idea that these coins functioned as bullion or stores of raw material based on their weight.

Exploring data variability can be done both through data visualization (charts) and statistical analysis. Both are useful for trying to understand what level of variation might be historically meaningful. *Coinage of the Roman Republic Online* (CRRO) is an online, open access database documenting more than 60,000 coins from more than 50 collections. The weights recorded there are those reported directly by each major collection. *CRRO* represents the best aggregate of modern data, while many specimens recorded in *CRRO* were also observed by Haeberlin. Throughout the following sections, I report both *CRRO* and Haeberlin numbers. Haeberlin had access to far more material, but *CRRO* numbers are verifiable in a way that Haeberlin's are not.

6.3 *RRC 14* Analyses

Table 6.2 displays a wide range of statistical data on the reported weights of coins in the series *RRC* 14. Most of these ways of describing the information help us think about how consistent the weights of individual specimens are in relationship to what the target weight may have been and help us see if there was in fact a consistent target weight for the whole issue and/or within each denomination.

---

[28] Haeberlin 1910.
[29] For the use of statistics to explore the weights of bronze coins, cf. Bransbourg 2011.

Table 6.2 Comparison of CRRO and Haeberlin weights for RRC 14/1 by denomination*

Type	RRC 14/1 (as)		RRC 14/2 (semis)		RRC 14/3 (triens)		RRC 14/4 (quadrans)		RRC 14/5 (sextans)		RRC 14/6 (uncia)		RRC 14/7 (semuncia)	
Data source	CRRO	Haeb.	CRRO	Haeb.	CRRO	Haeb.	CRRO	Haeb.	CRRO	Haeb.	CRRO	Haeb.	CRRO	Haeb.
No. of specimens	20	95	20	108	41	160	31	136	42	202	14	102	7	75
Mean ('average')	316.3	317	158.2	159.9	101.8	106.1	76.1	80.4	51.6	54.7	25.3	26.77	17.6	17
Median ('midpoint')	319.7	319	162	159.1	101	105.5	77.3	80	51.2	53.5	24	26.1	17.4	17.15
Standard Deviation	29.9	24.4	14	11.6	14.6	10.2	9.5	6.9	72	6.4	4.6	4.1	3.5	3.22
Relative SD	9%	8%	9%	7%	14%	10%	12%	9%	14%	12%	19%	16%	20%	19%
Interquartile Range	29.27	27.19	15	13.6	13.2	11.4	7.7	8.9	7.6	7.6	5.4	4.7	3.9	4.4
Relative IQR	9%	9%	9%	9%	13%	11%	10%	11%	15%	14%	22%	18%	23%	26%
Mean Absolute Deviation	15.97	13.69	7.7	6.9	6.9	5.6	4.5	4.5	3.7	3.7	2.5	2.39	2.1	2.1
Relative MAD	5%	4%	5%	4%	7%	5%	6%	6%	7%	7%	10%	9%	12%	12%

Prepared by the author.

* I have used a 'relative' IQR by dividing IQR by the median (the midpoint of the data), and a 'relative' MAD created by dividing the MAD by the mean (simple average). To the best of my knowledge, these are not widely applied statistical approaches but are mathematically and methodologically sound.

The relative standard deviation is a statistical method of comparing variance between different data sets.[30] In graph A of Chart 6.1, notice that weights reported by Haeberlin have a consistently lower degree of variance than those from *CRRO* – perhaps unsurprising given how many more specimens he observed and thus the greater strength of his sample size. Generally speaking, we find a greater variance among the weights of the smaller denominations. In historical terms, this means that the face value of a higher denomination *RRC* 14 specimen is significantly more likely to conform to the notional weight standard than that of a small denomination. To put this another way, we can see that the mint took far less care to control the weight of small denomination coins than it did for larger denominations. The *triens* however does not seem to fit the overall pattern, as it shows greater variation than the quadrans, possibly because it may have been produced in greater numbers than the quadrans. The standard deviation is more influenced by outliers in the data than other statistical measures of variability. We can use these other measurements as a check on the validity of any assertions based on this statistic. One such alternative measure is Interquartile Range, which assesses the size of the range into which the middle 50 per cent of the data falls. Graph B of Chart 6.1 shows a very similar pattern, adding confidence in our conclusion that less care was taken to control the weights of small denominations, and that, again, the *triens* shows greater weight variation than the quadrans. Chart 6.2 graphs the 'relative' Mean Absolute Deviation, a third approach for measuring the variability in the data. The Mean Absolute Deviation calculates the average distance of the individual data points from a particular point, in this case the mean (simple average). Like the Interquartile Range illustrated in Chart 6.1, Graph B, this the measure is less affected by outliers in the data. Again, the same pattern is visible: less variability in large denominations, greater variability in larger denominations. The trend lines are however more gradual, and for Haeberlin's data the *triens* here seems to fit the pattern. This warns us against concluding that the *triens* was actually cast with less care than the *quadrans*.

Were all the denominations aiming at the same or at least a similar weight standard?

To answer this question, I have multiplied each mean and median by the fraction of the full unit which the denomination represents: the *semuncia* was multiplied by twenty-four, the *uncia* by twelve, the *sextans* by six, and

---

[30] Another name for this calculation is the coefficient of variance; it is calculated by dividing standard deviation by the mean (simple average).

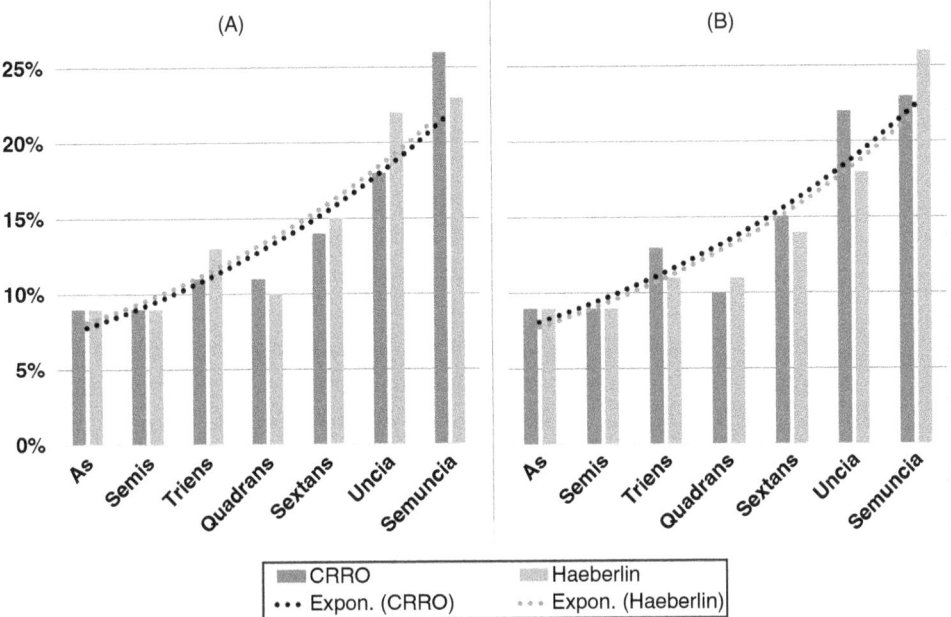

Chart 6.1 A-B: Relative standard deviations (A) and relative interquartile ranges (B) of *RRC* 14 weights as reported in *CRRO* and Haeberlin.
Prepared by the author.

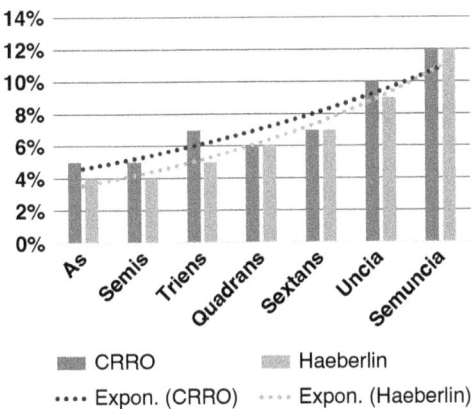

Chart 6.2 Relative mean absolute deviations of *RRC* 14 weights as reported in *CRRO* and Haeberlin.
Prepared by the author.

so on. The table records the results. As one can readily see, the *semuncia* produces a full unit equivalent much, much larger than any of the other denominations, perhaps because of the technical limitations of casting such a very small denomination. Haeberlin's specimens would suggest the full unit average weight was between 317 and 328.2 g, with the *sextans* resulting in the heaviest full unit and the *as* the lowest. *CRRO*'s data on the other hand produces a range between 303.6 and 316.4 g, with the *as* and *semis* giving the heaviest full unit average weights and the *uncia* the lowest. The mean (simple average) is, however, a poor tool for determining the possible original target weight.

Histograms are one means of visualizing the weight distributions of individual specimens of each denomination. The shape of data changes depending on the number of 'bins'. Each bin is the same size as every other bin on the same histogram; more bins mean narrower bins and a finer-grained analysis. The more data points within a particular bin, the higher that bin on the chart. The selection of number of bins is, in and of itself, an interpretive choice and the comparison of histograms of the same data set but with different numbers of bins can suggest different patterns.

In Chart 6.3, Graphs A and B both show the weights of the ninety-five specimens of *RRC* 14/1 reported by Haeberlin, the only difference is that A uses ten bins and B twenty bins. The ten-bin histogram (Chart 6.3, Graph A) shows the strong tendency for weights to be in this 304–336 g range, but the twenty-bin histogram (Chart 6.3, Graph B) helps us see better that steep drop-off after 344 g. In histograms we see that there is a more gradual

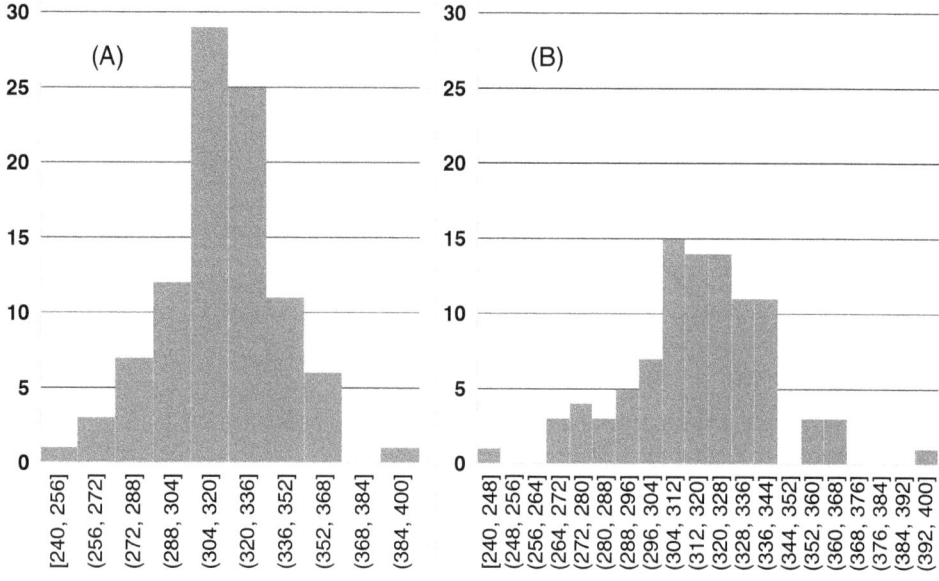

Chart 6.3 Ten-bin (A) and twenty-bin (B) histograms of the *RRC* 14 as based on Haeberlin. Prepared by the author.

distribution of lower weight specimens but also that not only do the weights drop off sharply, but overweight specimens are more likely to be true outliers.

Chart 6.4 shows the weight distributions of specimens of the *semis* to *uncia* of *RRC* 14. The number of bins used in each of these five histograms is my own interpretative choice. While exploring the data, I experimented with any number of bins for each data set, going as low as four and as high as thirty. I selected for illustration for each denomination the number of bins that showed the most pronounced peak followed by a noticeable drop. The goal is to illustrate the distribution around the peak but also to use that peak as a potential indicator of the typical or target weight of the denomination. In the interests of space, histograms of the *CRRO* data are not illustrated, but the observed results are reported by way of comparison.

Based on these histograms, one can describe the typical and likely target weight of each denomination as follows. The numbers in parentheses are the upper and lower ranges suggested by histograms of the *CRRO* data for comparison purposes.[31]

The first thing this table (Table 6.4) demonstrates is that the *semuncia* is a significant outlier and cannot be meaningfully fit into a typical weight range for the full unit, as is the case with the other denominations. This raises questions as to whether a single weight standard was ever intended to apply to all denominations. However, if we allow that the *semuncia*'s status as an outlier might be due to challenges in the manufacturing process, we can look for a range applicable to the other denominations. This next table (Table 6.5) summarizes possible target ranges and to which denominations they fit the observed evidence.

A range of 316–324 g could apply to all denominations (except the *semuncia*, cf. Table 6.3) and thus might be considered the best fit if we want to assume that the target full unit equivalents were intended to be the same across all denominations. However, the significant variability in the data for the smaller denominations observed above (cf. Charts 6.1–2) would make it reasonable to question whether not only the *semuncia* but also the *uncia* forms a good indicator of the original unit applied to the series as a whole. Again, the smaller units reveal greater difficulty in assessing uniformity. Excluding the *uncia*, we might consider the typical range for *RRC* 14 to be circa 316–330 g.

---

[31] For the histograms of the *CRRO* data I used a six-bin for the *semis*, ten-bin for both *triens*, and eight-bins for both *quadrans* and *sextans*. The *CRRO uncia* histograms were largely inconclusive, but numbers from the six-bin are given. *CRRO* only has six specimens of the *semuncia*: too few to make a meaningful histogram.

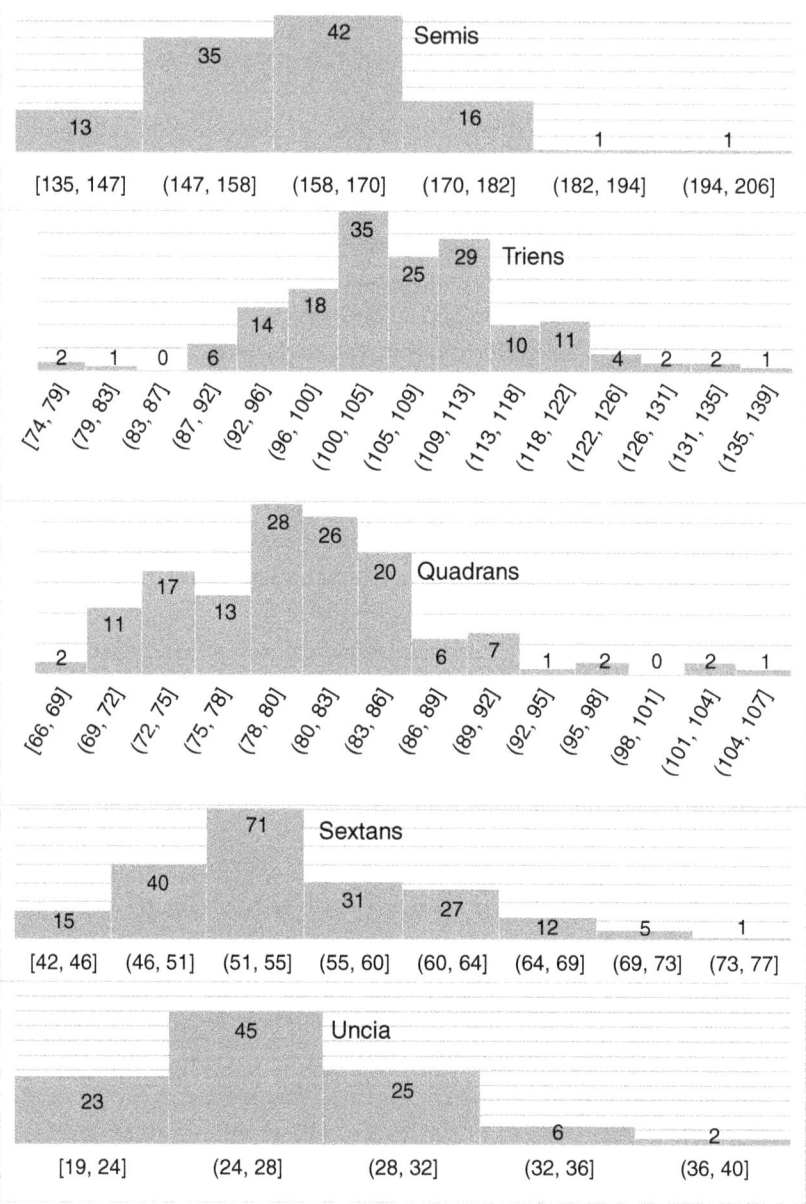

Chart 6.4 Histograms of *semis* through *uncia* for *RRC* 14 based on Haeberlin. Prepared by the author.

How is this different than Crawford's reported weight standard of circa 322 g, or why might it be better than using the range of mean weights, 317–328 g (cf. Table 6.3)? First and foremost, it acknowledges the lack of precision we observe in the objects themselves. The Romans were certainly capable of producing

Table 6.3 Comparison of CRRO and Haeberlin mean and median weights for RRC 14/1 by denomination, standardized by denomination

Type	RRC 14/1 (as)		RRC 14/2 (semis)		RRC 14/3 (triens)		RRC 14/4 (quadrans)		RRC 14/5 (sextans)		RRC 14/6 (uncia)		RRC 14/7 (semuncia)	
Data source	CRRO	Haeb.	CRRO	Haeb.	CRRO	Haeb.	CRRO	Haeb.	CRRO	Haeb.	CRRO	Haeb.	CRRO	Haeb.
No. of specimens	20	95	20	108	41	160	31	136	42	202	14	102	7	75
Mean ('average') as full unit equivalent	316.3	317	316.4	319.8	305.4	318.3	304.4	321.6	309.6	328.2	303.6	321.2	422.4	408
Median ('midpoint') as full unit equivalent	319.7	319	324.0	318.2	303	316.5	309.2	320	307.2	321	288	313.2	417.6	411.6

Prepared by the author.

Table 6.4 *Summary of typical weight ranges of RRC 14 denominations as observed using histograms (Charts 6.3–4)*

Denomination	Lower end of range	Upper end of range	Full unit equivalents	
As	304	336	304	336
Semis	158 (160)	170 (170)	316	340
Triens	100 (99)	113 (108)	300	339
Quadrans	77 (76)	86 (82)	308	344
Sextans	50 (48)	55 (56)	300	330
Uncia	24 (22)	28 (25)	288	336
Semuncia	16	20	384	480

Prepared by the author.

Table 6.5 *Summary of possible typical full unit weight ranges for RRC 14/1 and the fit with each denomination*

Possible range (g)	As	Semis	Triens	Quadrans	Sextans	Uncia
304–324					X	X
308–328		X	X	X	X	
308–336	X		X	X		
316–324	X	X	X	X	X	X
316–330	X	X	X	X	X	
316–336	X	X	X	X		
316–340		X	X	X	X	

Prepared by the author.

objects all conforming to a fixed standard in this period. That they chose not to prioritize conformity is a significant finding. Reporting the weight standard as a typical range of 316–330 g or 316–324 g helps reveal the amount of imprecision the Romans were willing to accept in their new monetary system. Ten to fifteen grams or 3–5 percent of the target weight of the *as* was 'close enough'. This 'close-enough' attitude and the inability to fit the *semuncia* into a weight standard that could be shared by the rest of the series further problematizes the idea that *RRC* 14 was intended to circulate as bullion based on intrinsic value.

6.4 RRC 18 Analyses

This section is concerned with similar questions as the last: How much variation is in the reported weights of what is traditionally understood as the second series of heavy bronze, *RRC* 18, and is it possible to find a typical or even target weight range for the series or its denominations (cf. Tables 6.6–7)? We can also use this approach to assess Thomsen's determination of the relative chronological relationship of *RRC* 14 and 18 based on assumptions about their respective weight standards.

By all statistical measures (Charts 6.5–6), the smaller denominations of *RRC* 18 show increased variation, just as we saw with *RRC* 14. Thus it seems fair to conclude that less care with regard to conformity to a weight standard was taken in the manufacture of the smaller denominations of Rome's earliest *aes grave*

The comparison of the variation of coins in series *RRC* 14 and *RRC* 18 provides a good reminder that statistical analysis is only as good as the available data. Looking at both interquartile range (IQR) and mean absolute deviation (MAD), *CRRO* data reveals more variation for *RRC* 18 than *RRC* 14, whereas Haeberlin's data shows the reverse with less variation for *RRC* 18 than *RRC* 14. Both cannot be true of the original population, by which I mean all coins originally made. One dataset *must* be a more accurate reflection of that original population than the other. The differences in the patterns expressed by data from *CRRO* and Haeberlin are also problematic when trying to test whether or not *RRC* 18 was intended to conform to a higher weight standard than *RRC* 14, a fact thus far widely accepted by scholarship. Chart 6.7, Graph A illustrates that this is true for the Haeberlin data in general, but the degree to which *RRC* 18 specimens have a higher mean weight than *RRC* 14 specimens varies greatly by denomination. Chart 6.7, Graph B illustrates the *CRRO* data and shows far less consistency. It is notable in both instances that the *quadrans* has a mean weight that is so much higher than other denominations.

As in the last section, data for *RRC* 18 can also be visually analysed by the use of histograms. The following charts are based on Table 6.8 and unillustrated histograms of *CRRO* data (cf. Chart 6.8). For all denominations a typical weight range of 324–336 g for the full unit is observed. Crawford suggests a target weight of 'about 334 gr.' for *RRC* 18, but this seems high given the available data. If we measure it against the mean weights for each denomination as reported by Haeberlin (Chart 6.7, Graph A), we find a mean average deviation of 6.66.

We can also notice how closely the typical weight ranges for all denominations correspond for both *RRC* 14 and 18 (see Table 6.9). While on average *RRC* 18 specimens do seem to be slightly heavier than *RRC* 14, the data patterns do not suggest that this was necessarily a very meaningful difference as both issues produced specimens that significantly differed from any apparent target or weight standard. If we wanted to describe the

Table 6.6 Comparison of CRRO and Haeberlin weights for RRC 18/1 by denomination

Type	RRC 18/1 (as)		RRC 18/2 (semis)		RRC 18/3 (triens)		RRC 18/4 (quadrans)		RRC 18/5 (sextans)		RRC 18/6 (uncia)	
Data source	CRRO	Haeb.	CRRO	Haeb.	CRRO	Haeb.	CRRO	Haeb.	CRRO	Haeb.	CRRO	Haeb.
No. of specimens	20	75	29	100	28	111	32	132	30	163	27	105
Mean ('average')	316.8	339.2	153.7	162.5	106.2	111.0	78.1	81.8	54.9	56.6	25.4	27.4
Median ('midpoint')	324.3	339.1	153.4	163.2	103.7	110.7	79.2	82.6	54.4	55.0	25.4	27.3
Standard deviation	25.2	15.1	13.9	12.2	11.1	7.9	10.5	9.4	8.9	6.5	4.8	3.2
Relative SD	8%	4%	9%	7%	11%	7%	13%	11%	16%	12%	19%	12%
Interquartile range	32.2	21.3	19.2	16.0	11.2	10.5	10.8	8.7	6.8	8.5	6.1	4.0
Relative IQR	10%	6%	13%	10%	11%	9%	14%	11%	13%	15%	24%	15%
Mean Absolute Deviation	16.1	11.3	9.6	7.4	5	5.2	6	4.2	4.7	3.6	3.2	2.3
Relative MAD	5%	3%	6%	5%	5%	5%	8%	5%	9%	6%	13%	8%

Prepared by the author.

Table 6.7 Comparison of CRRO and Haeberlin mean and median weights for RRC 18/1 by denomination, standardized by denomination

Type	RRC 18/1 (as)		RRC 18/2 (semis)		RRC 18/3 (triens)		RRC 18/4 (quadrans)		RRC 18/5 (sextans)		RRC 18/6 (uncia)	
Data source	CRRO	Haeb.	CRRO	Haeb.	CRRO	Haeb.	CRRO	Haeb.	CRRO	Haeb.	CRRO	Haeb.
No. of specimens	20	75	29	100	28	111	32	132	30	163	27	105
Mean ('average') as full unit equivalent	307.4	325	318.6	333	312.4	327.2	329.4	339.6	304.8	328.8	307.4	325
Median ('midpoint') as full unit equivalent	306.8	326.4	311.1	332.1	316.8	330.4	326.4	330	304.8	327.6	306.8	326.4

Prepared by the author.

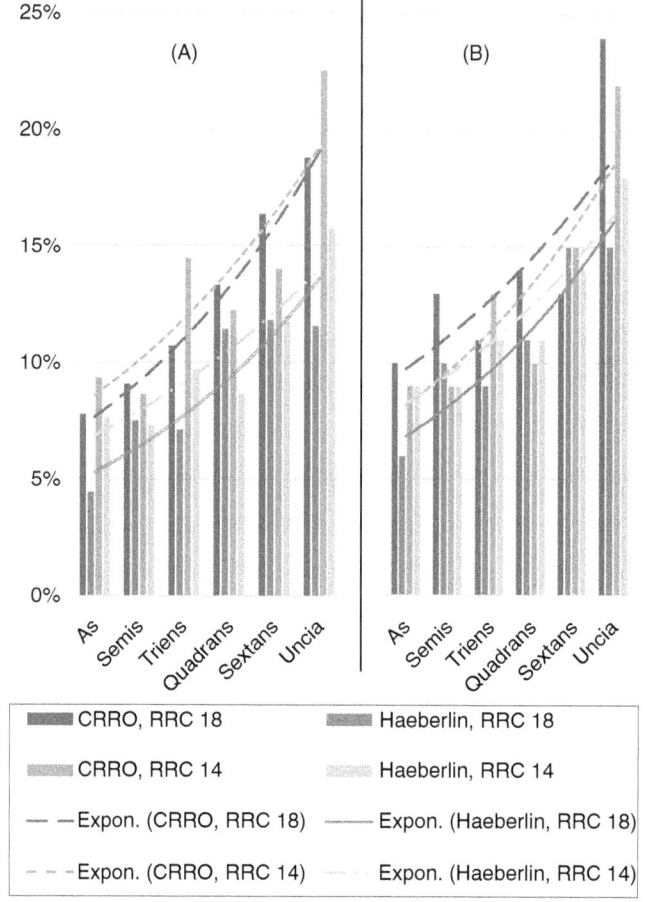

Chart 6.5 Comparisons of *RRC* 14 and 18 as reported in *CRRO* and Haeberlin showing (A) relative standard deviations and (B) relative interquartile ranges.
Prepared by the author.

weight range of both, we could comfortably describe them together as generally conforming to a 324 g ±12 standard. For *RRC* 18, Haeberlin's data produces a mean absolute deviation of 3.33 for each denomination's mean weight when measured against a 324 g weight standard, a 50 per cent better fit than for Crawford's 334 g number. The same calculation using the median weight of each denomination also produces a better fit, but only 6 per cent better. However, because of the exceptionally high variation in the data, these types of measure are not particularly meaningful. The most important point is that, even if there was a notional weight standard, this did not result in any great concern regarding uniformity of weights in the manufacturing process.

Table 6.8 *Summary of typical weight ranges of RRC 18 denominations as observed using histograms (cf. Chart 6.8)*

Denomination	Lower end of range	Upper end of range	Full unit equivalents	
As	324 (323)	348 (343)	324	348
Semis	161 (148)	170 (166)	322	340
Triens	102 (100)	116 (105)	306	348
Quadrans	80 (78)	87 (84)	320	348
Sextans	52 (52)	56 (58)	312	336
Uncia	25 (24)	30 (29)	300	360

Prepared by the author.

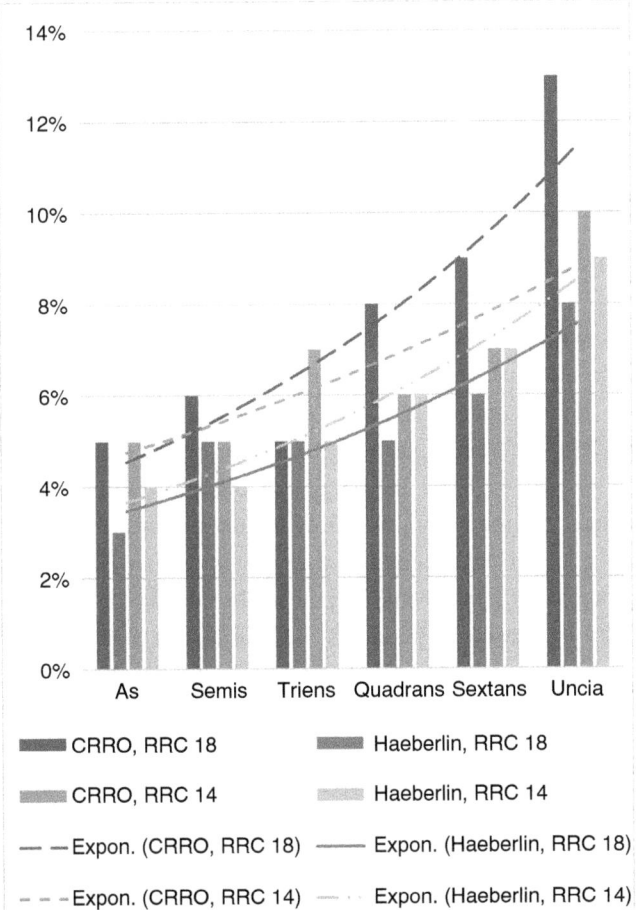

Chart 6.6 Comparison of *RRC* 14 and 18 as reported in *CRRO* and Haeberlin showing relative mean absolute deviations.
Prepared by the author.

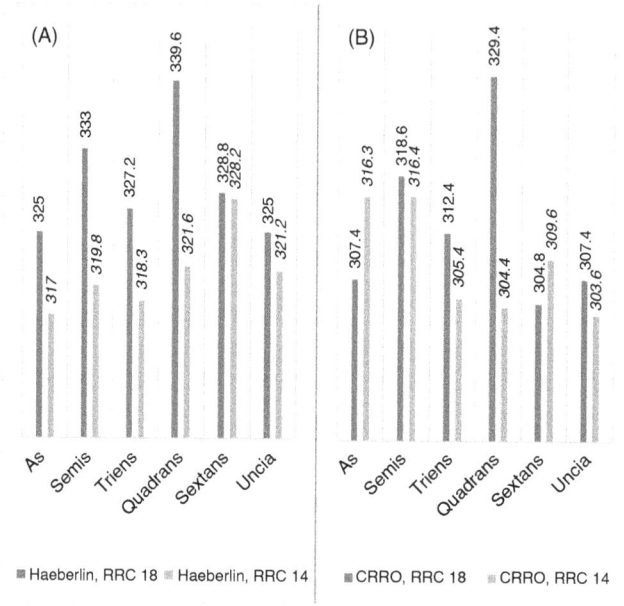

Chart 6.7 Mean weights by denomination as reported by Haeberlin (A) and *CRRO* (B). Prepared by the author.

6.5 RRC 19 'Analyses'

One cannot really analyse coins of the third series of heavy bronze (*RRC* 19) in this same manner because of the small number of recorded specimens. There is only one known specimen of the *as* from the Santa Marinella hoard (330.70 g). For the *semis*, we have three examples recorded by Haeberlin (170.17 g, 164.49 g, and 161.05 g) and one more gifted to the American Numismatic Society (ANS) in 1944 (161.04 g). These five specimens suggest 329 g might have been the average full unit weight, with a standard deviation of 7.5 (2.3 per cent) and mean absolute deviation of 6.8 (2.1 per cent). All known specimens could fit well within the typical weight ranges observed using histograms of *RRC* 14 and 18 data.

6.6 Historical Implications

Based on the preceding statistical analyses of *RRC* 14 and 18, I am comfortable with a generalizing statement that both coin series were conceived of in antiquity as conforming to a system where an *as* was equal to a Roman pound. This was likely also true of *RRC* 19, although there is too little evidence to be certain. Even if *RRC* 18 tends to be slightly heavier than *RRC* 14, this turns out

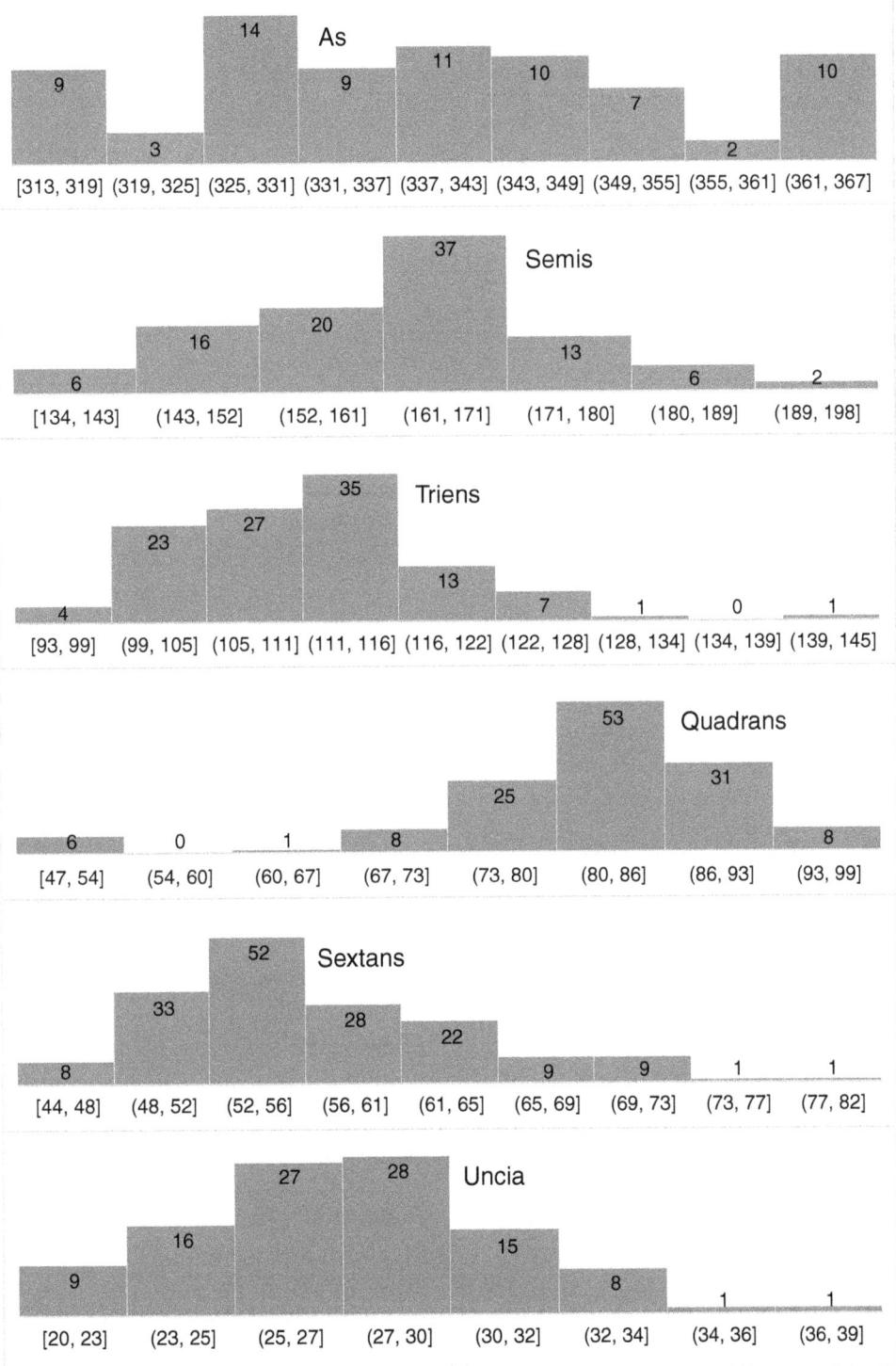

Chart 6.8 Histograms of *as* through *uncia* for *RRC* 18 based on Haeberlin. Prepared by the author.

Table 6.9 *Summary of typical weight ranges of* RRC 14 *and* 18 *denominations compared (cf. Tables 6.4 and 6.8)*

	RRC 18		RRC 14	
	Lower end of range	Upper end of range	Lower end of range	Upper end of range
As	324 (323)	348 (343)	304	336
Semis	161 (148)	170 (166)	158 (160)	170 (170)
Triens	102 (100)	116 (105)	100 (99)	113 (108)
Quadrans	80 (78)	87 (84)	77 (76)	86 (82)
Sextans	52 (52)	56 (58)	50 (48)	55 (56)
Uncia	25 (24)	30 (29)	24 (22)	27 (25)

Prepared by the author.

to be a very slight and arguably insignificant difference. The designation of RRC 18 (and RRC 19) as a 'supralibral' standard in contrast to the libral standard of RRC 14 should be abandoned. Given that it was this supposed 'supralibral' quality that led Thomsen (followed by Crawford) to date RRC 18 and 19 later than RRC 14, we can no longer support this chronological seriation on these grounds. It would be better to assign all three series to approximately the same period, some time in the decade prior to the First Punic War, and remain agnostic about resolving their sequence further until better evidence or hoard data emerges.

The other major conclusion is that conformity of the individual specimens to a precise standard does not seem to have been a production concern. For individual specimens of RRC 18, for example, the full unit equivalent of their weight could be anywhere between circa 290 and 370 g, and the specimen could still be said to fall within the observable norm. Likewise, for individual specimens of RRC 14 the full unit equivalent of their weight could be anywhere between circa 290 to 345 g, and the specimen could still be said to be within the observable norm. Chart 6.9 illustrates this using a box and whiskers diagram. The box contains 50 per cent of known specimens, the line through the box represents the median, and the cross marks the mean. The whiskers show the extent of the data, and the dots outliers.

These coins therefore reveal considerable variation such that we should question whether the type and degree of variation in weight was meaningful to the function or sociohistorical value of these coins. A practical explanation for the variation we observe is identifiable in the casting process, which controlled for diameter, not weight. The channels through which molten bronze was poured into moulds created branches or 'spues'. When the newly cast coin was broken off the branch, the break produced a very visible indentation or protrusion on almost all specimens. The depth of the carving of the design in each individual mould would also affect the volume of metal in the individual specimen, even if the diameter of each mould was the same. The Romans could manufacture with precision, as their contemporary struck coinage would confirm, but it was apparently not a concern to control this casting process to achieve more uniform results. With the *aes grave*, it was easier and seemingly acceptable for the intended purpose to manufacture a highly variable final product.

As mentioned in the first section of this chapter (Section 6.1), we assume that these early cast Roman bronzes were intended to suit the needs of populations habituated to the use of *aes rude* or *aes formatum* as money. In archaeological contexts, primarily votive deposits, we find very small pieces of *aes rude*. The thirteen specimens recovered from Nemi range from 13.39 g to 211.1 g, but with most falling under 45 g and about one third under 20 g.[32] Reports of *aes rude* from Vicarello on deposit at the Vatican have specimens in the 11–43 g range.[33] There are also many very small specimens of *aes rude* in museum collections but without archaeological context.[34] The existence of very small pieces of *aes rude* suggests that it may not have been uncommon for transactions done by weighing these pieces to be precise down to measurements as small as 10–20 g. But if such accuracy was a goal, this makes the variation seen in early Roman *aes grave* denominations harder to understand on a bullion-based model. With small but heavy denominations such as the *semuncia*, it may have been more costly in raw-material terms to produce these coins than their denominational face value.

Why then make such heavy cast coins? Would not adopting smaller struck coinage be more convenient? The answer is probably not economic, but rather cultural and social.[35] *Aes rude* and *aes formatum* were widely used monetary instruments, which served as means of storing wealth, measuring value, and conducting exchange. As valued objects we often find them deposited as religious offerings as well. Roman *aes grave* is heavy because it serves the monetary needs of peoples acculturated to heavy bronze money, but that does not directly follow that they conceived of bronze monetary objects as raw materials or commodities.

---

[32] Crawford 1983.
[33] Tocci 1967–8. Large finds are also known in religious contexts: at Pyrgi, a pot hoard of *aes rude*, likely a ritual deposit connected to a nearby altar, contained five very large pieces ranging from 152.61g to 760.2 g (Drago Troccoli 2013).
[34] For example, more than two dozen weighing under 20 g at the BnF.
[35] Cf. Bernard 2018b.

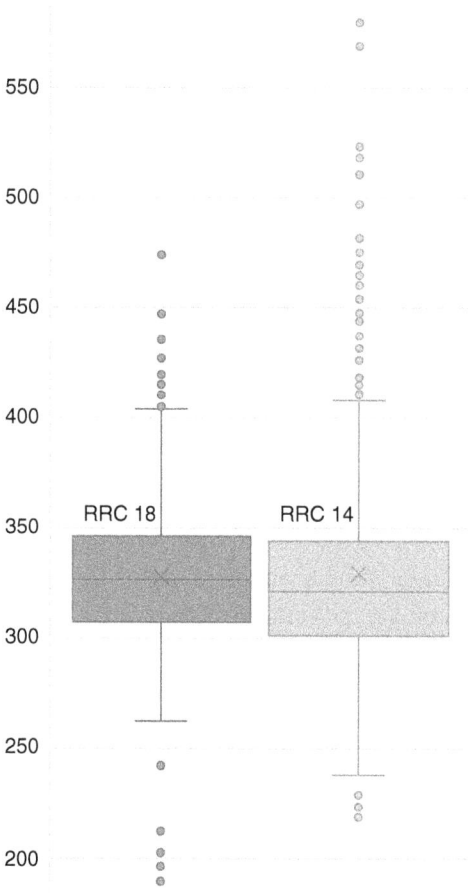

Chart 6.9 Box and whisker chart showing Haeberlin weights for *RRC* 18 and *RRC* 14 with fractional denominations given as their full pound equivalents.
Prepared by the author.

As to the question of why the early issues had such a complex denomination system, it may be that the *aes rude* and *aes formatum* already had some form of denomination system in place. New work statistically analysing the weights of hacksilver, seemingly unstandardized pieces of silver commonly found at Near Eastern Bronze Age sites, has demonstrated that individual pieces indeed tended to conform to known weight standards and that the individual pieces likely circulated as a 'bullion-currency' or what we might call pseudo-denominations.[36] Similar analysis of *aes rude* may reveal that it shows tendencies to conform to local weight standards, and more research is needed.

[36] Ialongo, Vacca, and Peyronel et al. 2018.

What does all this mean for the historian? Rome's *aes grave* is strange, and perhaps stranger than we have appreciated to date. It does not seem to have been valued as bullion, but rather as a symbolic monetary object. At the point of manufacture, we can say that Rome wanted its bronze money to look like coinage but still wanted it to conform in weight variability to its antecedents. This conclusion should serve to destabilize some of our ideas about the fixed nature of exchange in this period and aligns well with the more fluid economic picture painted by Tan in Chapter 3. This is not because the specific metal content itself gave it value, but because the heft of the individual pieces was a cultural norm, one not easily set aside. Ultimately, this ends up being a vindication of Burnett's hypothesis that the Romans applied the circular shape and double-sided design of Greek coinage prevalent in Southern Italy to the Central and North Italian tradition of using cast bronze as monetary instruments.[37] The important caveat is that the weight standards (such as they are) and denominational system are likely an outgrowth of the pre-existing monetary habits of the region.

---

[37] Burnett 1989: 55–7.

7 | Rural Transformations in Middle Republican Central Italy

An Archaeological Perspective

TYMON DE HAAS

7.1 Introduction

The period between the conquest of Veii in 396 and the outbreak of the Second Punic War in 218 was a crucial phase in the establishment of Roman hegemony. With the submission of various mountain peoples and the settlement with the Latins in 338, the conclusion of the Samnite Wars in 290, the subjugation of Etruscans and Gauls after 308 and 283 respectively and, finally, the capture of Tarentum in 272, this period witnessed the affirmation of Roman power over the Italian Peninsula, while it also saw the renewed rise of Rome on an international stage and the start of Rome's expansion overseas.[1]

In this context, profound changes occurred in the rural landscapes of Central Italy. The increasing scale and duration of warfare put a major strain on rural manpower and involved the large-scale plundering and scorching of rural areas. Moreover, in this pre-industrial setting, the economy largely depended on agricultural surpluses, which were therefore crucial to sustain the growing population of Rome and warfare, as Rosenstein's contribution to this volume also stresses (Chapter 4).[2] Finally, the Licinio-Sextian Laws of 367, intended to resolve the increasing social tensions at Rome ("the Struggle of the Orders") that arose from growing social, economic, and political inequality between patricians and plebeians, imply fundamental changes of land ownership: while "gentilicial land" was previously controlled by clan leaders, these reforms represented a new legal framework in which land was either public or private. Plebeian small farmers now obtained the social and legal position to privately own land. At the same time their independent position was far from secure: they were under constant risk of becoming bonded by debt and losing their land to elites, who may also have started to employ slave labor on their agricultural estates.[3]

---

[1] All dates are BCE. For the historical narrative: Cornell 2008; Raaflaub 2010. On treaties with Carthage and early expeditions to Sardinia and Corsica, Bradley 2008: 45; Stek 2018: 154 with references.

[2] On *tributum* as a means to collect these surpluses: Tan in this volume (Chapter 3). For the nature of warfare and its impact on the countryside: Erdkamp 2010; Attema 2000.

[3] Roselaar 2010: ch. 2; Capogrossi Colognesi 2012; Scheidel in this volume (Chapter 5).

Thus, the Middle Republican period, here roughly defined as the (mid-) fourth to third century, was a highly dynamic period – in terms of historical events, of economic and demographic change, and of underlying sociopolitical processes. The interplay of these events and processes must have had a profound impact on the countryside and implies major changes in the settlement and exploitation of the rural landscapes of central Tyrrhenian Italy (Figure 7.1).[4]

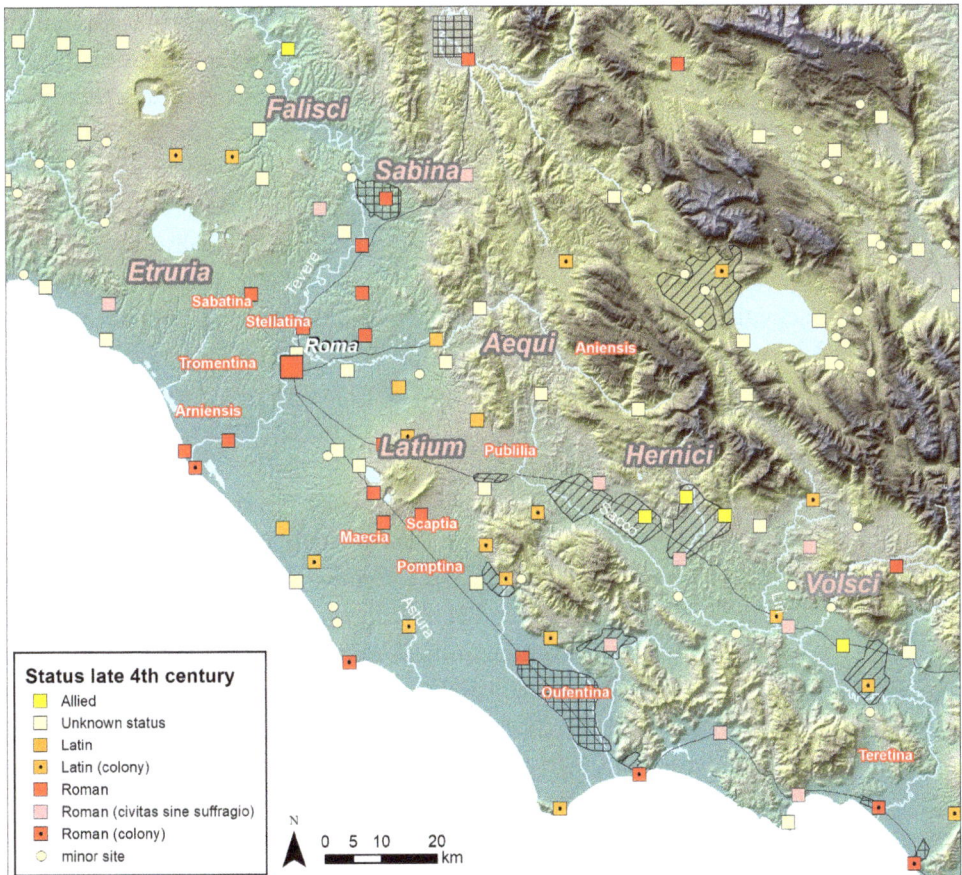

Figure 7.1 The sociopolitical landscape of Central Tyrrhenian Italy in the late fourth century. Drawn by the author.*

* For the administrative status of towns as displayed in Figure 7.1: Beloch 1926: map 2, complemented by *RE* online; Stillwell et al. 1976; Hornblower and Spawforth 2005; Cornell 2008, whom I have followed in assuming that some sites believed to be *civitates sine suffragio* by Beloch had full citizenship. For locating rural tribes: Ross Taylor 1960, with updates in Richardson 2007, and Linderski 2013.

[4] Terrenato 2007.

Archaeologically, this impact is not easy to detect: While excavations give detailed information on specific sites, they provide keyholes into rural history that cannot be considered representative for broader regional developments. In this sense, regional field surveys offer a more useful line of evidence, as they provide rural settlement data from different regions and historical contexts, both in Rome's direct surroundings and in still-contested areas at greater distances; such data therefore allow assessing changes in rural landscapes at a much larger scale, but without ignoring possible local variability. However, these data also come with limitations: They lack stratigraphic context, and the local and regional settlement patterns and trends they provide therefore have a limited chronological resolution – usually of one or more centuries. Moreover, such trends are the product of both demographic and economic processes, and growing or declining site numbers may thus to some undefined extent reflect either real changes in population or changes in consumption practices, or both (sites become more visible as more pottery is used). Finally, the interpretation of ceramic surface scatters, which are often palimpsests of human activities spanning centuries (if not millennia), remains a challenge. For these reasons it should be clear that one can indeed only rarely relate increases in rural settlement to short-term history (e.g. phases of conquest and colonization) or interpret changes in rural site patterns and typologies in terms of land ownership.[5]

That being said, recent archaeological work has substantially improved our understanding of the early Roman countryside. Gabriele Cifani's review of excavation data provides a comprehensive idea of the range of Archaic and Early to Middle Republican rural site types in Central Italy, and the landmark excavations at the Auditorium site have highlighted the presence of elite estate centers in the country outside Rome.[6] Moreover, the exceptional wealth of archaeological survey data that has accumulated over the past decades provides an excellent source to understand general socioeconomic developments in this crucial phase of Roman history.

The aim of this chapter is therefore twofold: first, to review the period's archaeological evidence for changes in rural settlement, land use, and infrastructure in central Tyrrhenian Italy; and second, to evaluate the socioeconomic implications of these changes in their broader historical context. To this end, I start out with a discussion of rural settlement

---

[5] Archaeology and time: Smith 1992; Foxhall 2000; Bailey 2007. On site classification: papers in Attema and Schoerner 2012. On linking settlement data and colonization events: De Haas 2011.
[6] Cifani 1998; 2002; 2008. For the Auditorium site: Carandini, D'Alessio, and Di Guiseppe 2006; Terrenato 2001.

developments on the basis of three major survey projects (Section 7.2), which highlights both general trends and local specificities. I then proceed with a discussion of the evidence for reclamation projects from centuriations (Section 7.3). While the dating of many of these systems remains debated, it is argued that some were surely laid out in the (late) fourth and early third centuries. I discuss in more detail the centuriation in the Pontine plain to argue that these systems, in combination with major road-building projects, imply very substantial and sustained investments in the countryside. Section 7.4 then discusses the demographic, economic, and social implications of rural developments in relation to urban contexts, arguing that despite the ongoing efforts in warfare, Central Italy witnessed growth both in population and the economy, which in turn contributed to Rome´s subsequent expansion. Section 7.5 then tentatively links the observed socioeconomic developments to the ongoing historical debates on the effects of Roman expansion, the Struggle of the Orders, and changes in land ownership.

7.2 Rural Settlement Developments in Central Italy

As already suggested, there are many datasets we may draw on to reconstruct rural settlement developments: Italian topographic surveys, most prominently the *Forma Italiae* and the *Latium vetus* publications, have covered large parts of central Tyrrhenian Italy.[7] But while such inventories provide invaluable and detailed inventories of sites and associated architecture, they have not systematically collected and published ceramic data – which are crucial for a detailed diachronic analysis of changes within the period discussed here.[8] I therefore limit myself to data from three major systematic surveys: the University of Rome's Suburbium Project, which conducted field surveys in the direct surroundings north and east of Rome; the British School in Rome's South Etruria Survey (SES), later restudied within the Tiber Valley Project; and the University of Groningen's Pontine Region Project (PRP).[9]

The published quantitative data of these projects cannot be compared directly, as each of the three projects has used slightly different field

---

[7] www.formitaliae.it/fi/index.html. *Latium vetus* project: Quilici and Quilici Gigli 1993.
[8] Cf. Attema 2017.
[9] Suburbium Project: Carafa and Capanna 2009 and 2019. South Etruria Survey/Tiber Valley project: Potter 1979; Di Giuseppe 2018; Patterson, Di Guiseppe, and Witcher 2020. Pontine Region Project: Attema 1993; Attema, Burgers, and Van Leusen 2010; De Haas and Tol, in press.

methodologies as well as different interpretive and chronological frameworks. Thus, while Suburbium data have recently been published at a chronological resolution of fifty years, both the SES and most of the PRP surveys present settlement trends in bins of c. 150 years. These bins, in turn, are not entirely the same: Where the Middle Republic runs from 350 to 250 in the SES, it runs from 350 to 200 in the PRP. Also, where the SES includes information on settlement sites and associated artifacts only, the PRP data includes nonsettlement sites and offsite data; the Suburbium Project, finally, presents not sites but so-called topographic units, several of which may form what in the PRP or SES would be defined as a single settlement or nonsettlement site.

While these differences render any attempt at direct comparison impossible, we can compare confidently the general patterns and trends these various datasets show. That such general interpretations are compatible is suggested by current work by members of these three projects on an integration of the respective databases within the so-called Rome Hinterland Project. While this integration had at the time of writing not yet been achieved and I do not draw directly on these integrated data here, the team has been able to establish that the ceramic chronologies behind the periodizations used in the published analyses are compatible.[10] Hence, although a direct comparison of settlement trends over time is not possible, these three datasets from a methodological point of view are suitable for comparative analysis.

In selecting suitable data from these projects, I focus on those subsets for which diachronic analyses have been published with a chronological resolution suitable to evaluate the fourth and third centuries as part of longer-term developments in settlement. The areas included in my comparison represent diverse historical contexts (areas that had long been part of the *ager Romanus*, areas that were incorporated in the *ager Romanus*, areas pertaining to old Latin cities and colonies, areas controlled by new Latin colonies, and areas controlled by other allied or independent polities), and therefore allow us to evaluate to what extent broader trends and patterns relate to specific local historical or geographical contexts. In this light it is especially relevant that these projects all use 350 as a separation point in their periodizations, which allows us to roughly discern situations before and after the watershed events of the mid-fourth century (the Licinio-Sextian Laws of 367, extensive territorial reorganization in 338).

[10] Attema et al. 2022; http://comparativesurveyarchaeology.org/.

Finally, the chosen areas also represent distinct geomorphological contexts, including sections of coastal plain in south Latium, rugged limestone uplands and intermediate hills and footslopes, as well as sections of the Tiber Valley.[11] Figure 7.2 presents the study areas, which include the Northern Suburbium, the territories of Veii, Capena, and Falerii in Southern Etruria, the territory of Eretum in Sabina, the territories of Antium and Norba in south Latium, and the inner Pontine plain further to the southeast.[12] Rather than reviewing settlement developments in these areas separately, I explore developments thematically to evaluate to what extent three aspects of rural settlement correlate with different historical and/or geographical contexts:[13] first, changes in settlement numbers, which may reflect processes of settlement and population expansion and contraction; second, patterns of settlement continuity and change, which may inform us on changes in land ownership; and third, changes in site typologies, which may relate both to ownership and agricultural exploitation strategies (see also Table 7.1 for an overview). Finally, I also comment on the ceramic assemblages of sites investigated by the PRP, which point out changes in networks of exchange.

Before turning to the data, there is one important methodological issue that may affect the trends and patterns of (dis)continuity. For the Archaic period and fifth/early fourth centuries in particular, our site dating is usually based on types of coarse ware ceramics and associated fabrics, which can usually only be dated roughly, and in some cases it is unclear to which phase they should be assigned.[14] The scarcity or even lack of dated ceramics of the fifth and early fourth centuries may thus be explained in different ways: It may imply that there was no rural settlement, or that people used less pottery and are therefore archaeologically less visible.[15] Some would argue that both issues are particularly influential and render a comparative analysis of trends useless.

Both issues do indeed impose limitations on the interpretations we can attach to such analyses, but they do not render them pointless. As already suggested, for the three datasets used here, ceramics have been dated in similar ways, which means that sites have been assigned to different periods

---

[11] Physical geography: Stoddart 2010; Teichmann 2017.
[12] This leaves out SES surveys around Sutri and Cures Sabini, which both yielded limited quantitative data, and in the case of Cures were published with a different periodization. Surveys in the eastern Suburbium remain largely unpublished, and PRP survey data from before the year 2000 have not been processed in sufficient detail to be included.
[13] An evaluation of changing distribution patterns would yield useful additional insights (for example into patterns of continuity and change and in relations between site types), but this requires the kind of detailed spatial data integration currently being prepared within the Rome Hinterland Project.
[14] Attema et al. 2017.   [15] Millett 1991.

Table 7.1 *Summary of published settlement data from the Suburbium Project, the Tiber Valley Project, and the Pontine Region Project*

Region	Area	Terrain	Context	Trends	Continuity/discontinuity	Typology	Source
Suburbium	Northern Suburbium	Hilly terrain on the Tiber Valley	*Ager Romanus* since the fifth century	Stability, slight growth in northernmost part between 400 and 350	High proportion of abandoned and newly founded sites in the first half of the fourth century, continuity in second half of the fourth century	Small sites (farms). Larger farms with more luxury ceramics from fifth century, peak in late fourth century	Carafa and Capanna 2019
South Etruria	*Ager Veientanus*	Hilly terrain, volcanic soils	Conquered and included in *ager Romanus* in early fourth century	Modest growth after 350 (221 to 287 sites)	25% new, 40% continuity, 35% resettled after gap; 15% of pre-existing sites abandoned	Continuity on Late Republican villas suggests early villas from sixth century onwards. If correct, suggests increasing numbers after 350	Di Giuseppe 2009 and 2018
	Ager Faliscus	Hilly terrain, volcanic soils	Independent polity	Dramatic growth after 350 (46 to 131 sites)	c. 55% new, 36% continuity, 9% resettled after gap; 8% of pre-existing sites abandoned		Di Giuseppe 2009 and 2018
	Ager Capenas	Hilly terrain, volcanic soils	Conquered and included in *ager Romanus* in early fourth century	Dramatic growth after 350 (43 to 142 sites)	40% new, c. 20% continuity, c. 40% resettled;* c. 27% of pre-existing sites abandoned		Di Giuseppe 2009 and 2018
Sabina	Eretum	Hilly terrain on the Tiber Valley	Frontier area between *ager Romanus* and Sabines	Dramatic growth after 350 (17 to 52 sites)	63% new, c. 35% continuity, c. 2% resettled; c. 3% of pre-existing sites abandoned		Di Giuseppe 2009 and 2018
	Cures Sabini	Hilly terrain on the Tiber Valley	Conquered and included in the *ager Romanus* in early third century	Growth after 350 (300?)**	40% new, c. 20% continuity, c. 40% resettled; c. 2% of pre-existing sites abandoned		Di Giuseppe 2009 and 2018

Region	Area	Terrain	Historical context	Growth	Site patterns	Later developments	References
South Latium	Between Antium and Satricum	Marine terraces, undulating terrain	Latin centers-of-old with renewed Latin and citizen colonies in fourth century	Growth after 350, degree dependent on reading of the data	New sites and continuity on most pre-existing sites	Abandonment of villages after 350	De Haas 2011; Tol 2012
	Norba	footslopes with mixed soils and rugged limestone uplands	Early fifth and fourth century Latin colonies	Modest growth after 350	New sites and continuity on most pre-existing sites	Rise of platform sites in (early?) third century	De Haas 2011
	Lower Pontine plain	Low-lying marsh with peaty and clayey soils	Late-fourth-century reclamation associated with tribus Oufentina (318) and Via Appia (312)	Radical growth after 350	Almost exclusively new sites	Smaller and larger farms	De Haas 2011; de Haas and Tol 2017

Prepared by the author.

* These percentages have been calculated by applying the percentages in Di Giuseppe 2009, fig. 6 to the site numbers in Di Giuseppe 2018.

** The data for Cures are quantitatively speaking very modest, and the periodization does not discern between Archaic and Early Republican/Classical sites (Di Giuseppe 2018, fig. 49).

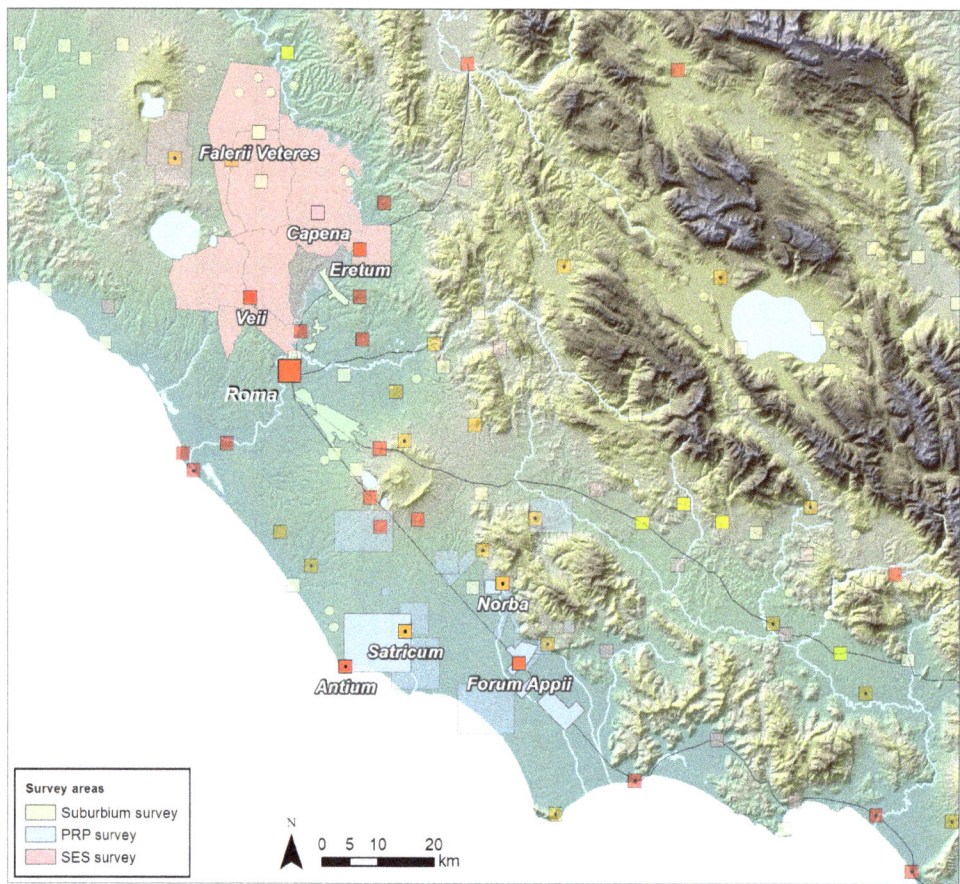

Figure 7.2 Selected survey areas from the SES, Suburbium Project, and PRP surveys. Areas marked by transparent boxes are additional survey areas of the three projects that are not considered here. For a key to the symbols, see Figure 7.1. Drawn by the author.

in comparable ways. Furthermore, all three projects have indeed identified (similar) fifth-century ceramics, which means this period is not "invisible" because of a lack of ceramic consumption. This of course leaves open whether the scarcity of such ceramics implies that there were fewer sites, or that people consumed *less* pottery; it in fact seems likely that we underestimate the actual number of sites of this period. However, as we will see, the observed changes are so clear and consistent that they cannot be explained solely by such biases in the data. In other words, the trends that will be discussed in Section 7.2.1 may exaggerate the degree to which rural settlements declined and subsequently grew, but the trends themselves are meaningful.[16]

[16] Cf. Patterson et al. 2020: 93–4.

7.2.1 Settlement Trends

Let us start with settlement trends, which inform us on both demographic and economic developments (even if, as suggested earlier in Section 7.1, both are difficult to disentangle). Taking into account developments between the Archaic and Middle Republican period, we can discern three basic patterns (Chart 7.1).

The first main pattern can be observed in Rome's Northern Suburbium, where numbers of rural sites are stable or even gradually grow throughout the fifth and fourth centuries. While this pattern suggests a higher degree of stability in rural settlement and exploitation, this seeming continuity does hide clear ruptures: in the first half of the fifth and the first half of the fourth century, over 15 percent of the sites were abandoned, and an equal

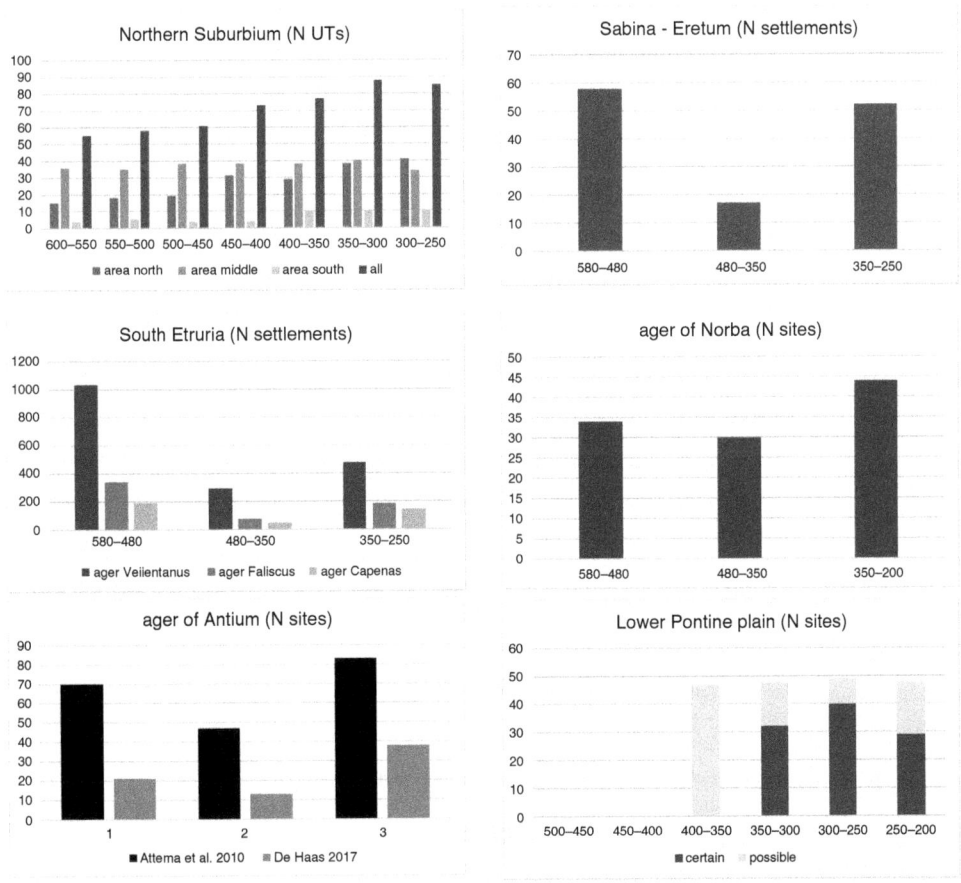

Chart 7.1 Settlement trends in different parts of Central Tyrrhenian Italy. Prepared by the author.

percentage were newly founded.[17] Such ruptures seem to reflect the abandonment of individual farm estates and the establishment of new ones. These new estates are very similar in terms of size and remains, and thus do not indicate changes in the status and size of landholdings, but rather in the actual owners (e.g. smallholders replaced by different smallholders).

The second – and most common – pattern is characterized by relatively large numbers of rural sites in the Archaic period, a marked decline in site numbers in the fifth and early fourth centuries, and a recovery in the later fourth and third centuries. This pattern can be detected around many Archaic urban centers in south Etruria, the Sabina, and the Pontine plain. It should be noted that this pattern hides considerable local variation in the degree of continuity (with a very high degree of discontinuity around Veii and Capena, and higher degrees of continuity around Falerii, Norba, and Antium) although also here the majority of later fourth-/third-century sites were new foundations.[18]

The third and final main pattern is witnessed in the lower Pontine plain, which appears to have been colonized *ex novo* in the later fourth century (see also Section 7.2.2).[19] Such expansion into parts of the landscape that had previously not settled can also be seen in other areas, where particular landscape zones (the coastal strip southeast of Antium, the Lepine uplands north of Norba) were now becoming more systematically settled and exploited. This pattern can also be observed in other more marginal landscapes, such as around Cures and Eretum in the Sabina, where only few rural sites existed before and a very high number of new sites were founded.

These three main patterns and the local variability they hide can only in some cases be linked directly to historical processes: Similar processes may translate into different archaeological patterns, and different processes can cause similar archaeological patterns. For example, archaeologically observed site continuity may hide changes in ownership (e.g. when a farmer could not pay his debts or sold his estate). Conversely, a historical process – colonization is a good example – may leave different archaeological patterns: an expansion of site numbers, for example around

---

[17] Carafa and Capanna 2019, fig. 4.

[18] Around Veii and Capena, only 40 and 30 percent respectively of the fifth-to-early-fourth century sites show continuity into the later fourth and third centuries (Di Giuseppe 2009: 443–4 and 2018: 110–12; Cf. Patterson, Di Guiseppe, and Witcher 2004: 11–13 and fig. 3). Antium/Satricum: De Haas 2011: figs. 7.5B, 7.11, and 7.15 and Tol 2012: maps 7.7 and 7.8; for Norba: De Haas 2011: figs. 9.7B, 9.13, and 9.16.

[19] De Haas 2011; Tol and De Haas 2016. This marshland was surely frequented before, but material remains are sparse and settlement contexts extremely rare.

Veii and Antium, might signal that colonists established new farms alongside pre-existing estates, but such colonists could also take over such pre-existing estates (thus leading to observed settlement continuity). Only in parts of the landscape that had been settled less densely or hardly at all before (Capena, Falerii, the Sabine area, and the lower Pontine plain), we may confidently link new settlements to an influx of colonists.[20]

That being said, the characteristics of rural site changes in the fifth and fourth centuries (reduction and expansion in site numbers, impoverishment and different degrees of continuity) surely are compatible with the general historical contexts, in which warfare and expansion – implying destruction of farms and the settling of new people – and changing social relations – dependency and debt[21] affecting patterns of land ownership – were drivers for changes in settlement patterns, but in which we may also expect a (variable) degree of continuity as local landowners were allowed to retain their land.

7.2.2 Site Typologies

The combined evidence of surveys, topographic studies, and excavations suggests that changes also occurred in terms of the types of sites in the countryside, and that these changes in turn bear witness to socioeconomic and productive changes. One such change concerns the increasing evidence for the rise of elite-controlled, and to some extent also monumental estates. Such estates existed from at least the fifth century onward, as is clearly illustrated by the aforementioned Auditorium site. Based on both the larger size and the proportions of luxury fine wares of some ceramic scatters, it has been suggested that similar estates can also be identified in the survey data for the Northern Suburbium. Such estates would equally have arisen in the fifth century, and their numbers would have grown in the second half of the fourth century, at the expense of the numbers of smaller and simpler farms.[22]

---

[20] The gap between the rise of these new and resettled sites in the later fourth century and the conquest of these areas in the early fourth century has been explained as reflecting a situation in which conquered land was initially turned into *ager publicus*, which was only from the second half of the fourth century onward distributed and resettled (Di Giuseppe 2018, 122 with references). This 'diffuse' model of rural changes seems to align well with the flexible agendas and strategies Rome would, according to some recent studies, have followed (Stek 2017; Terrenato 2019).

[21] Cf. Tan in Chapter 3 on the role of *tributum* in potentially exacerbating debt issues.

[22] Carafa and Capanna 2019, who consider sites over 1,000 m^2 and with more than 4 percent fine wares in their assemblages to be such larger elite estates. While not unlikely in light of what we know from the excavated Auditorium site and a few other cases, this hypothesis does require further support through ground-truthing.

Using a different line of argument, Di Giuseppe has suggested that elite estates were also quite common in south Etruria. She has observed that sites that became villas in Late Republican times show a higher degree of continuity between the Archaic and Late Republican times than simpler farm sites. Without suggesting a direct typological or architectural continuity, she argues that these locations did represent relatively large and high-status rural sites in earlier periods. If correct, this would also suggest a considerable increase in the numbers of elite rural estates after 350 for south Etruria (and perhaps the Sabina).[23]

For south Latium, yet other archaeological indicators attest to changes in rural site typologies. For example, both in the area around Satricum and in the Lepine uplands, nucleated sites (villages and hilltop settlements) that had arisen in the sixth and fifth/early fourth centuries dissolved, and small farms seem to have taken their place in the landscape in the later fourth century.[24] In the Lepine mountains sites referred to as *basis villae, villa a piattaforma* or, more neutrally, platform sites arose. These sites consist of a farm building constructed with perishable materials but built on top of monumental, yet modest, earthen platforms enclosed by polygonal masonry walls. These constructions imply that the owners could mobilize and invest considerable resources in construction, and it seems likely that they represent rural estates owned by local elites. These elites invested not only in their farm buildings, but also in agriculture: On a number of these sites press beds have been found, suggesting they were involved in specialized wine, or perhaps more likely, olive oil production. Furthermore, agricultural terracing with facings in polygonal masonry also occurs widely in the Lepine foothills and uplands, suggesting investments were made in agricultural production, again most likely for olive cultivation. The regular spacing and association of platform sites with roads support the hypothesis that they represent larger estates, producing for a growing urban market.[25]

It should be emphasized that the chronology of these platforms and associated agricultural features remains unclear, owing to a lack of excavated well-dated contexts. However, considering both the ceramic assemblages found on the surface and the stylistic similarities of the platform walls to those of the fortifications and interior terracing of nearby

---

[23] "... è difficile resistere alla tentazione di credere che quelle che abbiamo chiamato finora 'future ville' fossero già ville, o comunque insediamenti di un certo rilievo" (Di Giuseppe 2005: 21). Cf. Di Giuseppe 2018: 54–8 and fig. 15 for the increase after 350. The typological links between early elite sites and later villas is of course much more doubtful, and continuity of occupation does not equal continuity of ownership or socioeconomic status. See also Patterson et al. 2020: 91–3.

[24] De Haas 2011: 183–93.   [25] De Haas, Attema, and Tol 2012.

towns such as Norba, Cora, and Setia, it seems most likely we should place their construction in the (early?) third century.[26] It should be noted that ceramic evidence from surveys suggests that many of these sites already existed in the sixth and fifth centuries. Following Di Giuseppe's argument, they may already have represented elite estates in the fifth and fourth centuries, monumentalized in the third century.

Also in other parts of south Latium, rural sites of different sizes existed. This is particularly clear in the lower Pontine plain, where we have investigated c. thirty Middle Republican farm sites without later occupation phases, which provide reliable information on the size of farms in this particular period. These sites varied in size between c. 0.05 and 0.35 ha, with a main peak around 0.1–0.15 ha and a smaller group of sites of substantially larger size (Chart 7.2).[27] This bimodal size distribution suggests we are dealing with at least two classes of farms – or perhaps more realistically, a continuum of smaller and larger farms that exploited plots of varying size in this reclaimed area (see Section 7.3).

In sum, the evidence suggests that both the numbers of small, simple farm sites and larger rural sites with an elevated socioeconomic status increased in the later fourth and third centuries. Although in some areas such larger sites replaced smaller farms, in general both seem to occur side by side. Likely, the larger sites also controlled larger proportions of the landscape, and were

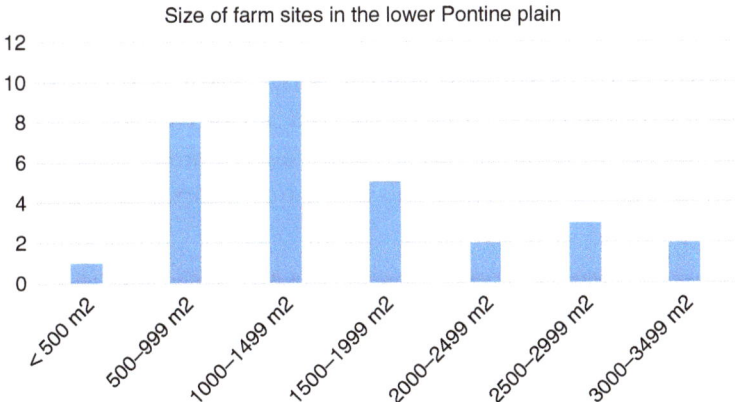

Chart 7.2 Size of late fourth-/third-century farm sites in the lower Pontine plain. Prepared by the author.

[26] De Haas, Attema, and Tol 2012, with extensive discussion of various chronological and socioeconomic interpretations of similar sites in Sabina, South Lazio, and northern Campania. Cf. Panella 2010: 59–60 for possible models in Sicily and the Punic World.

[27] The sites in Chart 7.2 were all abandoned after the third century, not occupied before that time, and their extent could be established clearly in the field.

associated with agricultural intensification and specialization.[28] Employment of slave labor on these sites seems plausible (but archaeologically impossible to prove),[29] but if we follow Scheidel's argument, slaves would in fact already have been much more widespread before the general increase in the number of these sites in the late-fourth and third centuries – and perhaps also at less conspicuous sites. So, while slave labor probably played a role in the rise of commercial farming, it was surely not a new phenomenon or a likely incentive.[30]

7.2.3 Ceramic Assemblages and Economic Change

These changes in settlement typologies and associated landholdings can be related to processes of urbanization and socioeconomic integration that involved areas far beyond Latium.[31] We may refer to both the rise of local urban markets, and increasing levels of long-distance exchange: In the bay of Naples, an area with a long tradition of craft production and very favorably situated in terms of overseas trade routes, commercial wine production expanded massively.[32] Similar processes of agricultural specialization in wine and oil production occurred in Rome's Suburbium, though here primarily to supply the growing market at Rome.[33] Another indicator for such expanding economic networks concerns the rise of black gloss ceramic productions, which both served the many local urban markets and dominated an international market from the later fourth century onward.[34]

While the ceramic assemblages of the SES and Suburbium projects have not been fully published yet, reflections of these developments are visible in the ceramic data of the PRP. For example, early Graeco-Italic amphorae attesting to the consumption of imported wine are found in the ceramic assemblages of both smaller and larger (platform) sites around Norba and in the lower Pontine plain, and early-to-mid-third-century black gloss fine

---

[28] In the case of olive cultivation and viticulture we are clearly dealing with intensification processes, but the exploitation of marginal areas may also have involved processes of extensification (e.g. through animal husbandry). Obviously, cultivation of (a wide range of) cereals remained the dominant form of arable farming in this period (cf. Trentacoste and Lodwick, Chapter 8 in this volume).

[29] Cf. Panella 2010, who assumes slave labor played a substantial role in the development of commercial farming in the late fourth century.

[30] Scheidel in this volume (Chapter 5).

[31] Urbanization: Sewell 2016; Economic expansion and integration: Kay 2014; De Haas 2017a.

[32] Olcese 2017, 311–14. Economic motives were surely among the reasons behind the treaty of alliance Rome struck with Neapolis, one of the main port cities of the central Mediterranean, in 326.

[33] Panella 2010.

[34] Morel 1969; Ferrandes 2006; Stanco 2009; Cibecchini and Principal 2002; Di Giuseppe 2012.

wares occur commonly on rural sites, with the oldest fragments dating back to the mid-to-late fourth century.[35] This massive consumption of fine table wares and imported wine surely reflects an increasing connection of rural estates to regional markets; accepting them as a proxy for rising standards of living, they may also reflect increasing levels of prosperity.[36] An initial study of Middle Republican coarse wares seems to suggest these ceramics were also exchanged over considerable distances within central Tyrrhenian Italy.[37]

7.3 Reorganized and Reclaimed Landscapes: The Evidence from Centuriations

Besides settlement data, profound changes to rural landscapes are also suggested by infrastructural works, especially centuriation.[38] These field systems have been reconstructed on the basis of traces visible in aerial photographs and cartographic sources throughout Central Italy.[39] However, in assessing this evidence in the historical context of the fourth century, there are two issues. First, the approach used by French scholars to identify these systems has rightly been criticized for not properly taking into account local geomorphological and postdepositional contexts, which has led to unreliable and even false identifications.[40] Second, the dating of these systems is usually derived from assumed connections with historical colonization and land-distribution events, without any archaeological evidence to support such claims. The lack of standardization of the measurements used in these field systems might imply they relate to indigenous and/or pre-Roman contexts, or alternatively to later land reforms.[41] Thus, the paradigmatic interpretation of centuriation as a Roman, colonial phenomenon is now criticized.

---

[35] Recent overview with discussion of microregional variations: Tol 2017. See also Attema et al. 2022.
[36] De Haas, Tol, and Attema 2011; Jongman 2014.   [37] Borgers, Tol, and De Haas 2018.
[38] Technically, the term centuriation refers to one specific type of field system based on rectangular modules (canonically of 10 x 10 *actus*). In the following I use this term as an umbrella for all cadastral systems, including land division in elongated strips, *strigatio*. For an introduction: Dilke 1972.
[39] Bussi and Vandelli 1985; Chouquer et al. 1987 (revised in Libertini 2018). For the *corpus agrimensores*: Campbell 2000.
[40] Discussion of French and Italian schools of research: Franceschelli 2015. Critique of the French School: Quilici 1994: 130–1.
[41] For a critical discussion of the ideological underpinnings of the colonial model: Pelgrom 2018. See also Terrenato 2019: 226–9.

To some extent, I agree with these critiques: Rather than assuming a priori a link between early Roman expansion and centuriation, this link should be substantiated by the archaeological evidence in the form of rural settlement associated with these systems and/or direct dating of associated features (ditches, canals, roads).[42] The ascription of centuriation systems to the fourth and early-third centuries, presented in Figure 7.3 and Table 7.2, should therefore be assessed cautiously.[43]

At the same time, for several cases there is convincing evidence to support an early date for centuriation. A case in point is again the Pontine plain, where – as we have seen – sudden and widespread settlement appeared in the later fourth century, which could only have taken place upon reclamation of this marshland.[44] For Cures Sabini, third-century sites have been found throughout the centuriated area as well; for Reate, surveys on the eastern edge of the centuriated area show a peak in settlement in the Republican period (more specifics are unfortunately not given).[45] Around Privernum, surveys have identified numerous sites of the fourth and third centuries that may be linked to the *strigatio*.[46]

These more convincing cases suggest that the rural settlement expansion in the later fourth and early third centuries went hand in hand with large-scale interferences in the physical landscape. In this light, the use of different field systems (*centuriatio* and *strigatio*) may be of specific interest.[47] Pelgrom has recently argued that *centuriatio*, rather than generally being applied to areas settled by Roman citizens, was used in close proximity to Rome in fertile lowland areas, perhaps not only for handing

---

[42] Issues of archaeological dating: Franceschelli 2015: 204–5.

[43] For example, the presumed traces of *strigatio* south of Norba continue between areas separated by cliffs of c. 200 m high, or on closer inspection represent recent roads and tracks without older predecessors (Van Leusen et al. 2003–2004: 312); cf. Terrenato 2019: 228 for a similar argument concerning Aletrium, and Stek 2018: 162–3 for Alba Fucens.

[44] De Haas 2017b.

[45] Cures: Muzzioli 1985, corroborated by the Corese survey (Patterson, Di Guiseppe, and Witcher 2020: 106). It is assumed that the centuriated area was *ager quaestorius*, land leased out by the state in large blocks. Reate: Coccia and Mattingly 1995: 115–16. Recent surveys around Interamna await final publication; Launaro and Leone 2018: 335–6 suggest that site numbers were relatively low between 350 and 200, but do not discuss the period before 350.

[46] Cancellieri 1983: 35–7.

[47] These systems were previously thought to reflect different levels of investment: the Roman state would more precisely register land holdings around citizen colonies and in *viritane* distributions through *centuriatio* because this was useful for taxation, whereas for Latin colonies this was deemed less useful as these colonists were not Roman citizens and hence were not taxed by Rome. This explanation seems unsatisfactory, as it does not explain why in some *viritane* distributions (Privernum, the Sacco valley) *strigatio* and not *centuriatio* was used.

Table 7.2 Land-division systems ascribed to the later fourth/early third centuries

Area	Type	Module	Ascribed date	Archaeological dating evidence	Size (km²)	Source
Privernum	strigatio	13 actus	340?	Associated settlement expansion in later fourth/early third century	26	Chouquer et al. 1987; Libertini 2018; Cancellieri 1983
Ferentinum	strigatio	10 actus	338?	-	53	Chouquer et al. 1987; Libertini 2018
Alatrium	strigatio	12 actus	second half fourth century	-	87	Chouquer et al. 1987; Libertini 2018
Norba?	strigatio	12 actus	late fourth century	-	16	Chouquer et al. 1987; Libertini 2018
Pontine plain	centuriatio	10 actus	late fourth century	Sharp rise in rural settlement in (late) fourth century; radiocarbon dating of centuriation features	121	Cancellieri 1990; De Haas 2011 and 2017b
Tarracina	strigatio (centuriatio?)	2 actus (20 actus)	late fourth century?	-	7	Chouquer et al. 1987; Libertini 2018; Cancellieri 1983
Interamna Lirenas	strigatio	13 actus	312	Expansion in rural settlement?	55	Chouquer et al. 1987; Libertini 2018
Artena	strigatio	16 actus	late fourth/early third century?	-	8	Quilici 1991
Anagnia	strigatio	10 actus	306	-	54	Chouquer et al. 1987; Libertini 2018
Alba Fucens	strigatio	12 actus	303	-	113	Chouquer et al. 1987; Libertini 2018
Minturnae	centuriatio	4 actus	296?	-	3	Chouquer et al. 1987; Libertini 2018
Sinuessa	centuriatio	16 V	296?	-	6	Chouquer et al, 1987; Libertini 2018
Reate	centuriatio	20 actus	early third century	Associated settlement expansion in Republican	50	Camerieri, De Santis, and Matteoli 2009
Cures Sabini	centuriatio	10 actus	early third century?	Associated settlement expansion in third century	43	Muzzioli 1985

Prepared by the author.

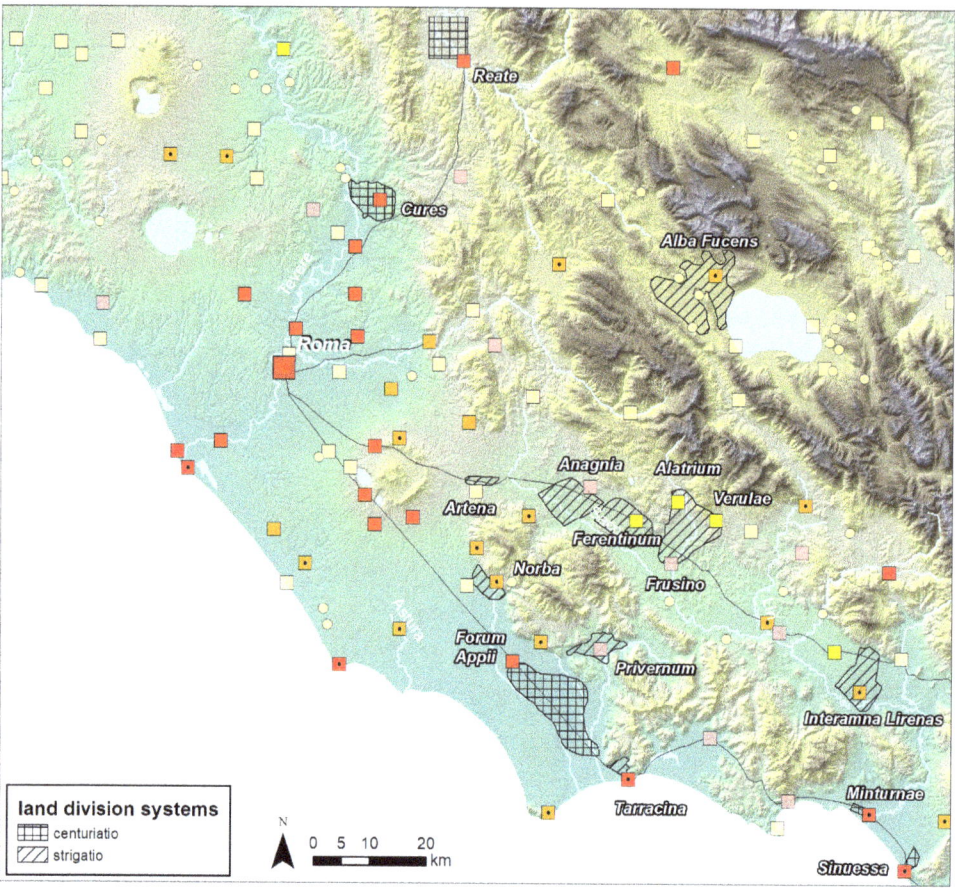

Figure 7.3 Land-division systems hypothetically ascribed to the fourth and early third centuries BCE. Drawn by the author.

out small plots but also for selling and leasing of public land.[48] While this hypothesis fits with the economic context sketched in this chapter, I would suggest that it is not primarily proximity to Rome or the commercial aim of registering landholdings more precisely that explains the use of different systems, but rather physical geographical conditions. With the exception of Cures, *centuriatio* is used in contexts where natural drainage conditions are

---

[48] Pelgrom 2018. There are problems with this hypothesis: The fact remains that *centuriatio* did not occur in all areas where such *viritane* distributions took place; one can think, for example, of the areas in the Sacco Valley, which were certainly not further away from Rome and probably also no less fertile than centuriated areas around Reate and in the Pontine plain. Also, the connection with the selling and leasing of land in the third and second centuries that Pelgrom suggests is chronologically problematic for the Pontine case, where the initial phase of colonization and *centuriatio* is dated earlier.

poor and radical measures are needed to reclaim land. As palaeo-environmental studies show, this is the case not only for the centuriated area in the Pontine plain, but also at Reate, Minturnae, and Sinuessa in the lower valley of the Garigliano river.[49] All these areas were characterized by badly drained marshlands that needed well-designed drainage systems, for which centuriation was apparently the more suitable approach. It seems likely that such concerns were less pressing in other areas.

7.4 The Socioeconomic Implications of Centuriation: The Pontine Case

To illustrate the scale and impact of these projects, let us take a closer look at the Pontine case (Figure 7.4). Early Roman interventions in this marshland did not only comprise the centuriation itself, which covered at least 120 km^2 with an intricate system of main canals of c. 5–6 m wide, secondary canals draining water into these main canals, and yet smaller ditches that drained individual plots of land.[50] The main canals of the centuriation drained into the Decennovium, a major canal c. 15 m wide that runs along the Via Appia for some 30 km between Forum Appii and Tarracina. The Via Appia, yet another part of early Roman interventions, was in this stretch built on a substantial dike (presumably using soil dug out from the Decennovium). Besides this main drainage axis, parts of the river Oufens were canalized, and an additional canal, the Rio Martino, was dug through the marine terraces that encloses the lower plain to the south in order to divert part of the run-off from the Lepine mountains toward the sea. This canal, c. 10 km long, would have required complex engineering and deep digging, as it cuts through ancient beach ridges with a height of up to c. 35 m. above sea level (the lower plain itself is situated only a few meters above sea level). All in all, these interventions radically changed the hydrology and environmental conditions in the lower plain.

Labor-cost studies provide insight into the economic implications of these interventions. This approach aims to quantify the costs of man-made structures, usually expressed as labor time estimates, based on an assessment of the procurement and transport of raw materials as well as the construction process itself, and using labor inputs derived from experimental and/or

---

[49] Pontine plain: Sevink et al. 2013; Feiken 2014; De Haas 2017b. Reate: Calderini et al. 1998; Camerieri, De Santis, and Matteoli 2009. Garigliano basin: Bellotti et al. 2016.

[50] De Haas 2017b for the evidence and a hydrological model.

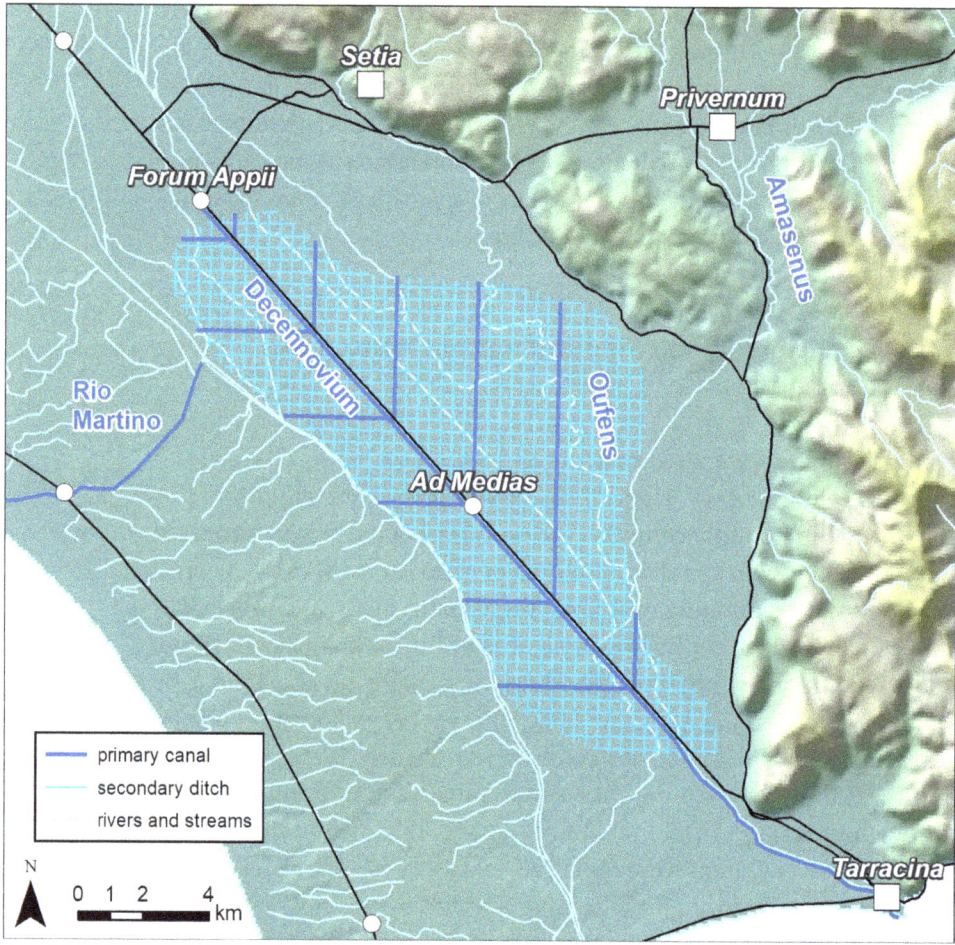

Figure 7.4 Reconstruction of the main and secondary canals of the Pontine centuriation in relation to natural streams and rivers. Drawn by the author.

comparative historical contexts.[51] While most often applied to buildings, this approach can also be used to quantify costs of dug-out features such as ditches and canals. In fact, considering the relative simplicity of such digging, many of the uncertainties surrounding the construction process of buildings (provenance and transport costs of raw materials, relative costs of applying different materials) do not apply to these projects (even if soil properties that affect the speed and ease of excavation also vary substantially). This means that the margins of error in the calculations are relatively small, and that the outcomes

---

[51] On the approach: Abrams and Bolland 1999; McCurdy and Abrams eds. 2019. Applications to the Roman world: Thornton and Thornton 1989; DeLaine 1997; Bernard 2018a.

are useful as an indicator of the order of magnitude of investments. They can, moreover, shed light on the scale of these projects from a cross-cultural comparative perspective.[52]

I use this approach to quantify the costs of the main features of the centuriation and the Decennovium, excluding the construction of the Via Appia, Rio Martino, and other related canalizations. Furthermore, I limit myself to the main canals that seem crucial for the draining of the area and the supposed ditches surrounding the primary blocks of land as indicated in Figure 7.4; all smaller ditches between and within individual plots are also excluded.[53] Also, this approach assumes that the work on this project was executed efficiently, constantly, and without any unforeseen complications. The resulting labor inputs therefore represent an absolute minimum estimate for the centuriation, which in turn was part of a much larger project.

Table 7.3 provides an overview of the inputs for the cost calculations (cf. reconstruction in Figure 7.4). The volume of the Decennovium is based on the measured length and width of the canal; its depth is my own estimation.[54] For the main canals, geophysical prospection data and analysis of aerial photographs suggest a width of up to 6 m, but allowing for collapse of the cut and for the fact that along its edges the canals were less deep, I use an average width of 5 m. Coring data suggest depths of c. 1–1.4 m, but it seems likely that because of erosion and deflation the top layer through which these canals were dug was originally thicker; to correct for this, I propose an average maximum depth of

Table 7.3 *Quantification of the volume of main and secondary canals within the Pontine centuriation*

Feature	Total length (m)	Average depth (m)	Average width (m)	Volume (m³)
Decennovium	30,000	2	13	780,000
main canals	42,300	1.5	5	317,250
secondary canals	639,476	0.5	1.5	479,607
TOTAL				**1,576,857**

Prepared by the author.

[52] Cf. Turner 2018.
[53] Some of these main blocks may not have been delimited by ditches but by roads, cippi, or vegetation, or perhaps not at all. The cost of such delimitations would have varied a lot; I take the modest labor inputs for ditches as a reasonable average.
[54] Not all main canals included in this reconstruction have been identified so far; their existence will hopefully be confirmed by ongoing ground-truthing by the author. The total width of the Decennovium is c. 15 m, but allowing for substantial tapering of the profile toward the base of the canal I here use an average of 13 m.

150 cm. For the secondary ditches, we have some geophysical prospection and coring data that suggest these were on average perhaps 1.5 m wide and 50 cm deep.[55]

Together, these figures suggest a total of more than 1.5 million m³ of heavy clayey soils being moved. Drawing on comparative labor rates as compiled by Turner (2018), we may estimate soil extraction rates at 1.5–2.2 m³ per person-hour (assuming the use of metal tools and applying rates for compact soils).[56] This gives us the approximate minimum and maximum labor costs as tabulated in Tables 7.4 and 7.5; considering the very heavy clay soils in the Pontine plain, the actual inputs probably more likely approached the maximum estimates of Table 7.5. These figures suggest a labor investment of between 235,000 and almost 350,000 (10-hour) workdays. Overhead for planning and management may add another 5–10 percent labor input, which gives a massive investment of 250,000–380,000 workdays.

These overall figures in turn suggest that we are here dealing with a project that implied a labor force of hundreds, if not thousands of laborers being employed over substantial periods of time; with a workforce of several thousands the digging could have been executed within one year, or several years at a labor force of 500–1500. As already suggested, this is a best-case scenario; for example, if not the entire workforce but only half of it disposed of metal shovels and the other half instead had to use wooden implements, the labor inputs could easily double.[57] Also, while 10-hour workdays may have been common, laborers could probably not

Table 7.4 *Minimum labor-cost estimates, assuming 1.5 person-hour per excavated m³ of soil, 10-hour workdays, and 220 workdays per year (cf. Turner 2018)*

Feature	Total volume	Hours	days	Duration (5000 laborers) days	years	Duration (1000 laborers) days	years	Duration (500 laborers) days	years
Total labor									
Decennovium	780,000	1,170,000	117,000	23	0.1	117	0.53	234	1.1
Large canals	317,250	475,875	47,588	10	0.05	48	0.22	95	0.43
Secondary canals	479,607	719,411	71,941	14	0.06	72	0.33	144	0.65
TOTAL	1,576,857	2,365,685	236,569	47	0.2	237	1.1	473	2.2
TOTAL incl 10% overhead		2,602,254	260,225	52	0.22	261	1.21	520	2.42

Prepared by the author.

[55] Corings: De Haas 2017b; Tol et al. 2020. [56] Turner 2018: Table 9.2.
[57] Turner 2018: Table 9.2

Table 7.5 *Maximum labor-cost estimates, assuming 2.2 person-hour per excavated m^3 of soil, 10-hour workdays, and 220 workdays per year (cf. Turner 2018)*

Feature	Total volume	Total labor Hours	Total labor Days	Duration (5000 laborers) days	Duration (5000 laborers) years	Duration (1000 laborers) days	Duration (1000 laborers) years	Duration (500 laborers) days	Duration (500 laborers) years
Decennovium	780,000	1,716,000	171,600	34	0.15	172	0.78	343	1.56
Main canals	317,250	697,950	69,795	14	0.06	70	0.32	140	0.64
Secondary canals	479,607	1,055,135	105,514	21	0.1	106	0.48	211	0.96
TOTAL	1,576,857	3,469,085	346,909	69	0.3	347	1.6	694	3.2
TOTAL incl 10% overhead		3,815,994	381,599	76	0.33	382	1.76	764	3.52

Prepared by the author.

productively work for such long periods.[58] In practice, moreover, excavation in the marshy environment would probably have shortened the work year, and diseases such as malaria would also have lowered productivity and led to loss of lives, as was also the case during reclamations in the 1930s.[59] Considering the complexity of the hydrology of the area, it seems highly likely that the works did not go entirely according to plan, or that extreme weather conditions caused further delays.

Finally, as already highlighted, the calculations have only taken into consideration the main elements of the system, excluding both smaller ditches and gullies and the construction of the Via Appia and Rio Martino canal. While such small ditches may well have been dug upon arrival by colonist farmers that settled the area, some of them could equally have been dug in advance by the same labor force that was responsible for the main canals. Equally, the construction of the Via Appia was closely linked to the construction of the Decennovium and must therefore have been organized in conjunction with the wider project. The same seems likely for the digging of the Rio Martino.

Thus, in all likelihood the reclamation of the Pontine marsh would have involved a workforce of several thousands, working for at least several years.[60] In turn, the Pontine centuriation was only one of several such

---

[58] Cf. Bernard 2018a: 78; Bernard 2022.
[59] De Haas 2017b: 479 with references. While the reclamation project of the Fascist regime exceeded the Roman efforts in the region substantially in scale (a much larger area was reclaimed), the Romans relied fully on human labor inputs, which may have approached those of the early twentieth century and surely exceeded those of earlier projects initiated by the papal state.
[60] Cf. Bernard 2018a: 130–1 for the costs of Rome's Middle Republican walls estimated at c. 7,000,000 person-days.

projects (Table 7.2); the two other large centuriations (Cures and Reate) cover an additional 100 km^2, while all systems that have been ascribed to the period between 338 and 268 together cover at least 634 km^2 (although again, some of these may pertain to later periods). Furthermore, systems outside the area discussed here in the Apennine uplands and Campania would raise this overall figure further.[61] Although in most areas the construction of these systems was less challenging in terms of hydrological conditions (and therefore required fewer canals to be dug) than in the Pontine plain, the overall labor inputs would still be massive.

Considering their close geographical links, it seems likely that the development of these land divisions was carried out in conjunction with another type of major infrastructural work, road building.[62] The most notable of such roads was of course the Via Appia, initiated in 312 and covering some 185 km from Rome to Capua across marshlands, hills, and mountainous landscapes. Although the quantification of such projects is complex and beyond the scope of this chapter, the labor inputs probably exceeded those for land divisions significantly.[63] Taken together, infrastructural projects surely involved the continuous investment of state revenues and the operation of a substantial labor forces throughout the later fourth and third centuries.[64] It is beyond the scope of this chapter to evaluate what types of labor these projects involved, but it seems plausible that one could draw on both slave and wage laborers and perhaps also corvée labor.[65]

---

[61] Apennine area north of Reate (Nursia, Villa S. Silvestro): Camerieri 2013. Campania (ager Falernus, Cales): Libertini 2018: 125–33 and 278.

[62] Laurence 1999. For the links between road building and Roman expansion: Coarelli 1988; Bradley 2014.

[63] Berechman (2003: Table 2) estimates a total of 308,429 person-hours for *a single* km of Via Appia, which would imply for the 30-km stretch through the Pontine's centuriated area a stunning 9,252,870 person-hours or 925,287 workdays (a factor of three times the total costs of the ditches and canals as calculated here). However, roughly a third of the costs in Berechmann's calculations comes from the surface preparation with large basalt lava blocks. As the early road probably did not have such a pavement, costs may be reduced considerably. Moreover, Berechmann used higher overhead costs (15 percent), and inputs in the construction of drainage gullies would not have to be included, as the Decennovium provided drainage for the road. Thus, it seems we should, for this area, lower his estimated inputs by as much as 30 or 40 percent (which gives figures more in line with Bernard 2018a: 130–1).

[64] A superficial comparison suggests the labor inputs of all these projects combined would be comparable to the largest reclamation projects undertaken by the Aztec Empire, which involved the continued input of several thousands of (corvée) laborers over several decades (Arco and Abrams 2006), or major ditch- and dike-construction programs in Medieval Europe (Squatriti 2002).

[65] Bernard 2018a: chs. 4 and 6.

7.5 Contextualizing Rural Developments: Demographic and Socioeconomic Implications

Having presented the archaeological evidence for changes in the Central Italian countryside, let us reflect on what this evidence implies about demographic, economic, and social changes in the fourth and third centuries.

7.5.1 Demography

It is generally accepted that settlement trends may cautiously be used as a proxy for rural population change over time. We may of course debate to what extent the increase in site numbers observed in almost every part of Central Italy after 350 also reflects an increasing visibility of sites due to increased ceramic consumption (especially of black gloss fine wares). However, it is difficult not to consider the general increase in site numbers and the occupation of "empty" marginal areas as a reflection of rural population growth in the fourth century.[66] There are local and regional variations in the timing and extent of this growth: It seems to have taken place earlier and more gradually in the direct surroundings of Rome; further away from Rome, it generally took off later (after 350), but was much more pronounced. Newly reclaimed areas in particular absorbed substantial numbers of people, who may well have migrated from Rome and its direct surroundings. It seems reasonable to suggest that conditions for rural expansion were more favorable earlier on in areas close to Rome and the major Latin and Etruscan towns, and only with increasing levels of territorial control and decreasing threat of seasonal raiding did they improve in more marginal landscapes, such as the Sabine uplands and the Pontine plain.

The growth of rural populations takes on additional significance in light of urban developments. Urban centers in Central Italy, many of which had witnessed a period of decline and contraction in the fifth century, generally seem to have recovered in the fourth century. This is, for example, clear in

---

[66] *Contra* Terrenato 2019: 98–9, who argues that demographic growth cannot explain the global nature of this phenomenon. He suggests the growth reflects improved economic conditions and/or a shift from nucleated (village-based) to dispersed settlement patterns caused by changes in land ownership. While improved economic conditions surely play a part in making Middle Republican sites well visible (see Section 7.2 above), the evidence seems to suggest that nucleated settlements also grew in numbers in this period. Also, I doubt whether such alternatives would be a more likely explanation for the global nature of the phenomenon.

an increase in fortification construction and a major growth in the numbers of urban sanctuaries.[67] Moreover, new settlements with urban characteristics also arose; one may think of newly founded colonies, but also of *fora* and other minor centers that were founded in this period.[68]

This increase of regional urban and rural populations is probably matched by population growth in the city of Rome itself, which by the third century is believed to have housed several hundreds of thousands of inhabitants.[69] Taken together, the evidence suggests an, in my view, substantial growth of regional population levels in the later fourth and third centuries, which seems perfectly compatible with the historical context. After long periods of warfare and plundering, Roman expansion led to more stable socioeconomic conditions in this core region: Apparently, the negative demographic effects of prolonged warfare in previous periods had been offset by natural growth and migration into this area.

7.5.2 Socioeconomic Change

In this context of urban and rural population growth, it is perhaps not surprising that we can cautiously identify archaeological evidence for economic diversification and growth. For the countryside, we witness both an intensification of exploitation (increasing densities of sites) and an expansion of agriculture into previously marginal areas – in which state investments in drainage and infrastructure played an important role. Furthermore, even if the evidence is at present limited, the later fourth and early third centuries may also have witnessed the spread of larger estates and market-oriented specialized production strategies. Platform sites, showing investments in rural architecture and (admittedly badly dated) evidence for specialization in olive oil production, may be examples of this. It is highly likely that these estates were owned by local elites and supplied local and regional urban markets.

While similar evidence for investments in rural estates lacks in other areas, both survey and excavation data clearly show evidence for diversification in terms of both the size and prosperity of rural sites. Smaller and larger farms occurred side by side, and the ceramic assemblages show

---

[67] Fortifications: Sewell 2016; sanctuaries: Bouma 1996.

[68] See also Palombi (Chapter 9) in this volume. Minor centers: Tol et al. 2014; Tol and De Haas 2016.

[69] Estimates for early-fourth-century Rome lie between 75,000 and 150,000 (Bernard 2018a: 103–6): Rosenstein in this volume (Chapter 4) asserts a population of c. 125,000 in 341 BCE, while Panella (2010: 68–9) gives ranges from 200,000 to 750,000 inhabitants for the city and its Suburbium in the third century BCE.

differential levels of fine ware consumption. The general spread of fine table wares and (rarer) wine amphorae on both smaller and larger rural sites more generally reflects increasing levels of prosperity for many rural dwellers.

These developments were of course tightly bound to urban developments. Increasing urban populations imply an increasing demand for rurally produced foodstuffs, but also an increasing market for craft goods. Such demand triggered processes of specialization in both urban and rural contexts, as is clear from the rise of specialized ceramic production workshops in both town and country. Perhaps the main trigger was that of urban construction projects, which caused increased demand for both raw materials (stone, timber, clay) and labor, both skilled and unskilled.[70]

The development of a regional infrastructure further stimulated economic expansion and integration. Roads lowered transport costs and enhanced connectivity between rural areas, local centers, and Rome, and link in with the occurrence of regional and extraregional ceramics (fine wares and Campanian wine amphorae) that seem to signal the start of a process of market integration.[71] While the construction of major roads probably drew on forced labor (slave and corvée), it likely also provided a considerable labor market over prolonged periods of time of which both urban and rural poor could benefit.[72]

7.6 The Historical Context

The archaeological evidence from field surveys and Roman land-division systems as discussed in this chapter suggests that the late fourth and early third centuries were a key moment of transformation in the rural landscapes of central Tyrrhenian Italy. Let us now explore how the observed transformations tie in with the broader historical context, focusing on the impact of Roman territorial expansion, the consequences of the Struggle of the Orders, and related issues concerning the rise of larger elite estates and agricultural changes.

First, let us consider the impact of early Roman expansion on rural landscapes, an issue that has received a lot of attention in recent

---

[70] Ceramic production: Di Giuseppe 2012; Tol and Borgers 2016. Construction and labor: Bernard 2018a.
[71] Cf Morel 2007; De Haas 2017a.
[72] Bernard 2018a: 109–13 on corvée labor; cf. Scheidel in this volume (Chapter 5) on slave labor.

scholarship.[73] It is obviously beyond the possible to use the archaeological record to reconstruct or illustrate the short-term history of events relating to early Roman expansion directly. On a more general level, however, the archaeological evidence seems to reflect the gradual outward movement of warfare, and the increasingly stable conditions in Central Italy. With the exception of Rome's direct surroundings, the archaeological evidence from areas that witnessed prolonged struggles and seasonal raiding in the fifth and earlier fourth centuries is generally poor and scarce. It is in the later fourth century that most, if not all, of these areas show more and richer rural settlements, here interpreted primarily as a sign of demographic and economic expansion. These changes are of course not a direct consequence of warfare or expansion: In some cases there is a considerable chronological gap between conquest and settlement expansion. They do, however, reflect the more stable conditions that arose in central Tyrrhenian Italy in the wake of Roman expansion. Especially in marginal landscapes, the direct consequences of Roman expansion could be profound – and more visible archaeologically.

We could suggest that there were reciprocal links between ongoing military expansion and the socioeconomic developments observed in Central Italy: As I have argued, state investments in road building and centuriation played their part in stimulating economic expansion.[74] These investments, in turn, increased state revenues as well: Assigning land to colonists would increase the number of citizens liable for taxation, and the selling and leasing of land provided the state with additional sources of income that could be reinvested in military expansion and infrastructure. Conversely, as more conquered peoples outside Central Italy received Roman citizenship, the burden of *tributum* was divided between more and more people, which may have enabled more people to reinvest part of their income in agricultural production, thus also stimulating processes of intensification and specialization. The resulting surpluses were in turn also needed to support the army as it engaged in longer campaigns, further away from Rome, after c. 340.[75] Thus, conquest stimulated economic growth, and economic growth stimulated conquest.

The second issue to return to concerns the links between rural settlement developments and the Struggle of the Orders. It has been suggested that the spread of farm sites reflects the rise of private land ownership by

---

[73] De Haas 2011; Casarotto, Pelgrom, and Stek 2016; Stek 2017.
[74] Cf. Cifani 2021, framing this growth in Keynesian terms.
[75] As suggested by Rosenstein in Chapter 4, and Tan in Tan 2020 and Chapter 3 of this volume on the *dilectus-tributum* system and the exaction of *tributum* from *cives sine suffragio*.

smallholder peasant farmers, following on the presumed reforms of 367. Assuming these reforms are a historical reality, I remain skeptical whether we can directly relate the general expansion of rural settlement to the land reforms of the Licinio-Sextian Laws: There is a considerable chronological gap between these reforms and the expansion in rural settlement, which in most areas occurred in the late fourth and early third centuries. Also, this expansion concerned as much 'Roman' land as it did areas on which these reforms should not have had an impact (e.g. Latin territory in south Latium). More generally, we should keep in mind that because of the chronological resolution of the archaeological data, we may conflate episodes of crisis and expansion of such smallholders, and that the trends observed here are part of a much broader phase of rural expansion witnessed in many parts of the Italian Peninsula and, indeed, the wider Mediterranean. There may therefore be alternative (or complementary) economic and demographic processes at work.

At the same time, the development of rural areas may well have contributed to relieving social pressure at Rome: The massive infrastructural projects (although likely drawing mainly on forced labor) could provide employment for poor plebeians, and in tandem with land distributions offered opportunities for populists to exert their political agendas.[76] Many of the new farms that we see archaeologically may well have been settled by Roman plebeians who obtained a piece of conquered land. Conversely, the proximity to Rome, both as a growing market and sociopolitical arena, may have attracted non-Romans (gentilicial groups) to migrate toward and invest in the countryside.[77]

This also leads me to consider land ownership and social status, which remain difficult to trace archaeologically. From the historical perspective, we know that within an area new allotments could be made while groups could also maintain their landholdings. To trace such processes, we need a more detailed, local archaeological perspective (and more thorough publishing of survey data). In most areas discussed, the social changes reflected in our written sources remain elusive: Independent smallholder farms, tenant farms, or even farms tied by debt bondage or operated by a slave labor force would leave very similar archaeological signatures. Equally, the redistribution of land after conquest could well have implied the settlement of new owners at existing farm sites, while other pre-existing farms remained in the hands of local people; different historical processes can thus lead to archaeologically observed continuity of occupation.[78]

---

[76] Terrenato 2019.   [77] Cf. Wright and Terrenato in this volume (Chapter 2).
[78] Cf. Di Giuseppe 2018: 104–12.

Thus, only in exceptional circumstances, especially in newly colonized territories, the evidence may allow a cautious evaluation of such issues. I again point at the case of the Pontine marshes with its well-preserved traces of Middle Republican colonization. The ceramic assemblages, with their fine table wares and imported wine amphorae, likely reflect independent landowners that were reasonably well off and are thus more compatible with private owners than with poor tenant farmers or slaves. The existence of larger and richer sites, moreover, clearly reflects a countryside that included both smaller and larger estates side by side.

In light of the above, it seems pointless to try and use the archaeological evidence to search for the transition from gentilicial to private land, the rise of historically attested ("Catonian") villas, or the start of slave-based agricultural production. Rather, the evidence suggests we deal with a diverse and dynamic Middle Republican countryside, in which Imperial expansion, warfare, and colonization were detrimental for some but offered opportunities for others; where elites of old continued to control estates, where many smallholders undoubtedly struggled to maintain their families, but where some farmers were also able to expand their production and improve their socioeconomic status; and where slaves became an increasingly important part of the labor force, even if perhaps not as a driver of economic change, as envisaged in traditional models describing the rise of villas and the slave mode of production.[79] Rather than debate the labels applied to our rural sites, it seems more important to note that the evidence firmly places an expansion of larger-scale, specialized production for the urban market, using additional labor (slaves and seasonal free labor), in the late fourth and third centuries – without denying continuities with previous periods.[80]

7.7 Concluding Remarks

While the archaeological evidence discussed in this chapter does not allow either detailed local or generalizing historical interpretations of rural developments, it does provide crucial new insights into rural settlement

---

[79] Scheidel in this volume (Chapter 5). Cf. Torelli 2012, placing the rise of villas based on slave labor in the context of the later fourth century, deriving from slave-based estates in Magna Graecia.

[80] Morel 2007; Becker and Terrenato eds. 2012. Trentacoste and Lodwick in this volume (Chapter 8) highlight the continuities in crop choices, including viticulture and olive cultivation, in the fourth and third centuries.

and economy in the Middle Republican period. This period is characterized by overall radical change, but with distinct local traits dependent on longer-term historical trajectories, urbanization processes, and geographical particularities. Areas close to Rome apparently show a higher degree of stability of occupation and exploitation, even if the data may hide considerable transformations; areas around Etruscan and Latin centers of old, in general already settled in the sixth century, were more radically (but variously) affected by warfare and Roman expansion in the fifth and first half of the fourth centuries; and marginal landscapes were increasingly settled and exploited from the later fourth century onward.

While these distinct local trajectories reflect *variability* in territorial and agricultural organization,[81] there are clear commonalities as well: There is undeniably a major expansion and increasing differentiation in rural settlement in the fourth/third centuries, which surely reflects a combination of economic and demographic expansion as well as social changes, even if these are archaeologically less tangible. As the stage of Roman expansion moved away from central Tyrrhenian Italy, sociopolitical stability enabled a phase of renewed urbanization, the rise of local and regional urban markets, and investments in the exploitation of the countryside, including formerly marginal landscapes. Treaties of alliance and infrastructural developments created increasingly favorable conditions for interregional exchange as well, and the inflow of wealth into Central Italy led to investments in agricultural (and artisanal) production – both by the state and by private individuals. The processes of economic expansion and integration so intensively studied for later periods thus clearly have their roots in this crucial phase of Roman history.

---

[81] Cf. Capogrossi Colognesi 2012.

8 | Towards an Agroecology of the Roman Expansion

Republican Agriculture and Animal Husbandry in Context

ANGELA TRENTACOSTE AND LISA LODWICK

8.1 Introduction

A significant increase in agricultural production underpinned the many socioeconomic transformations that define first-millennium-BCE Italy. Expansion of nonfarming urban communities, specialized craftspeople, and organized armies all required greater surpluses – food and materials which could, in turn, be mobilized for socioeconomic gain.[1] Contributions in this volume highlight an active and changing approach to rural production during the Middle Republican period. New patterns of land reclamation and land use,[2] as well as more centralized means of resource extraction and mobilization,[3] demonstrate significant changes in farming and distribution strategies. The echoes of rural change may also be reflected in this period's urban renewal projects and the labor systems that supported them.[4] However, while the impact of agricultural production strategies is widely documented, the nature of these strategies is poorly understood. Clearly more plants and animals were being produced, but how, precisely, were these surpluses created?

Rural change is almost invariably described as a process of *intensification*, where increases in surplus production were achieved through greater labor input per area of land.[5] Yet, greater rural settlement infill and greater archaeological visibility of land use do not necessarily imply more intensive cultivation practices.[6] Rather, *extensification* – cultivation of larger areas of land with relatively low labor inputs per unit area – has been identified as a key means of increasing arable agricultural production in ancient communities that were subject to economic growth and

---

[1] For example, Riva 2017; Rives 2019. Also Tan, Chapter 3 in this volume.
[2] Manfredi and Malnati eds. 2003; Sewell 2016; Pelgrom 2018; Stoddart et al. 2019; De Haas, Chapter 7 in this volume.
[3] Tan, Chapter 3 in this volume. Rosenstein, Chapter 4 in this volume.
[4] For example, Bernard 2018a: 76–117; Palombi, Chapter 9 in this volume. Davies, Chapter 10 in this volume.
[5] For example, Kron 2017.
[6] As recent research by the Roman Rural Peasant project has demonstrated: Bowes et al. 2017.

greater centralization.⁷ Relatively extensive cultivation strategies can also be accompanied by an increase in the number of small sites across the landscape, as is documented in Roman Italy and Roman Britain.⁸ Thus, while Republican rural settlement infill during the fourth century BCE may reflect more intensive patterns of land use,⁹ it does not necessarily imply that crop cultivation and animal husbandry practices also became more intensive.

These aspects of farming regimes represent far more than subsistence strategies. Cultivation practices dictate the relative value of land versus labor, with significant social implications.¹⁰ Shifts to more intensive or extensive agricultural strategies could have profound impacts on community structure,¹¹ including the dynamics of rural settlement organization, urbanization, and Roman expansion. Extensive farming regimes would have a direct impact on how "land hungry" different communities were, because production in such systems is primarily limited by the amount of land available. This has particular relevance for potential pressures on Roman expansion, and the suggestion of land acquisition as a primary motivator for Republican warfare.¹² Equally, farming strategies would have implications for rural labor dynamics. Low costs/values of labor compared to land would promote investment in large-scale land improvements like irrigation, drainage, and terracing.¹³ Should the physical supply of land become restricted, the relative importance of material wealth – including slave labor – to invest in land improvements would escalate, with consequences for social inequality.¹⁴

Agriculture is not a monolithic process, but a dynamic activity whose character and consequences are intrinsically bound up with major themes in Middle Republican research. Plants and animals can be produced in different systems conditioned by the availability and value of land, labor, and wealth. Crops and animals can also be produced through a diverse spectrum of different farming regimes. Notably, staple taxa like wheats and pigs can be produced in a range of both intensive and extensive systems (also simultaneously),¹⁵ which depend as much on social and economic

---

⁷ Styring et al. 2017a; Styring et al. 2017b.
⁸ Italy: Bowes et al. 2017. Roman Britain: Smith et al. 2016; Allen and Lodwick 2017; Lodwick et al. 2020.
⁹ See de Haas, Chapter 7 in this volume. ¹⁰ Bogaard, Fochesato, and Bowles 2019.
¹¹ In terms of labor and inputs: intensive, labor-dependent, higher yield per area vs. extensive, land-dependent, lower yield per area. Both strategies will increase overall agricultural output. See van der Veen and O'Connor 1998 for further discussion. Also Halstead 2014: 238–51.
¹² Rosenstein, Chapter 4 in this volume. Harris 1979: 60.
¹³ For example de Haas, Chapter 7 in this volume.
¹⁴ Bogaard, Fochesato, and Bowles 2019. Relevant to Scheidel, Chapter 5 in this volume.
¹⁵ MacKinnon 2001; Bogaard et al. 2017.

influences as on ecological requirements.[16] Republican agriculture has been discussed at length from a historical perspective as well as an architectural one,[17] but bioarchaeological evidence is needed for a quantitative, regional investigation of farming regimes, and to provide insights into precisely *how* increases in production were achieved. This approach is especially relevant to Italy, where the diverse topographic, ecological, and cultural landscape doubtless encouraged a spectrum of contemporary agricultural strategies.

Progress on these themes has been limited by the scarcity of high-value assemblages of plant and animal remains, that is, assemblages with a robust sample size that are well dated, well collected, and well published. Although chronological challenges are inherent to bioarchaeological remains,[18] the primary obstacle has traditionally been a lack of engagement on archaeological excavations with ancient farming as an interesting and relevant research theme – an agenda that might merit the labor-intensive processes of assemblage collection and analysis. Although environmental sampling has been undertaken since the 1980s and 1990s,[19] the low quantities of botanical material recovered – due to limited sampling or low densities of that material – have meant that, until recently, it has been consigned to short reports and appendices. Despite assurances that archaeobotanical data are accruing,[20] arable cultivation and processing have received limited study across protohistoric research.[21] There has been some interest in crop diversification in imperial Italy, but few syntheses have considered the formative centuries of the Early and Middle Republic.[22] However, with an adequate dataset, developments are likely to be found. Broader syntheses including micro- and macrobotanical remains have identified shifts at the landscape scale,[23] and zooarchaeological data also point to a significant reorganization of animal production and consumption strategies between

---

[16] For example, Styring et al. 2017b.

[17] Including a view integrated with archaeological evidence. White 1970; Frayn 1979; Spurr 1986; Marzano 2007; Becker 2013; Goodchild 2013; Kron 2017 and references therein.

[18] Unlike pottery, such remains can only be directly dated using radiocarbon. Unless they derive from a precisely dated context (rare for the fills and waste deposits where such materials typically accrue) plant and animal remains are typically dated on the scale of a century or two. This resolution can be overcome through syntheses and taphonomic studies, where sufficient material is available.

[19] For example, Martin Jones' work at Settefinestre: Jones and Sheldon 1985. [20] Witcher 2016.

[21] Bosi et al. 2020 is a notable exception. Ongoing research at Gabii also promises valuable new results: Motta 2016; Gavériaux et al. 2022.

[22] For example, Heinrich 2017 only considers pre-Roman Pompeii and Liguria: Robinson 2002; Arobba, Caramiello, and Del Lucchese 2003. Lentjes 2016 is a notable exception.

[23] Mercuri et al. 2015.

the Iron Age and Republican period, with further changes in imperial times.[24] The zooarchaeology of Republican Italy, however, has not been systematically investigated in fifteen years.[25]

Our aim here is to present a first step toward an agroecology of the Roman expansion, through a new interdisciplinary synthesis of bioarchaeological evidence that links the prehistoric and historic periods, which highlights, in our view, key points of change and potential pathways for future research, both in environmental studies and more broadly for Republican Italy. The diffuse nature of the current dataset dictates the broad regional and chronological scale of the exercise, which transcends the Middle Republican period. However, this perspective over the *longue durée* is crucial to contextualization of smaller-scale change. It also allows "Roman" developments to be separated from local trajectories and permits comparison with better-documented moments in Italian antiquity. Evidence suggests that prehistoric communities already integrated animal and arable husbandry, irrigated fields, foddered livestock, felled forests, plowed using cattle, and rotated crops – so how, specifically, was Republican farming different from earlier modes of production? As farming regimes scaled with urbanization, specialization, and population growth, was there an inflection point (or points) in the nature of their organization? Was there a moment in Roman history when – as Varro implies – arable farming and pastoral herding became sufficiently different and specialized to be distinguished?[26] Agriculture was the most fundamental form of production in these societies. Its study has huge potential to shape our understanding of social and economic history, but this first requires an appreciation of what ancient farming was, and how, where, when, and why people produced plants and animals – a perspective for which bioarchaeological research is essential.

8.2 An Environmental Dataset: Materials and Methods

Here we focus on the most abundant forms of data that can be aggregated over a broad temporal and geographic scale: presence/absence of charred plant remains and livestock representation expressed by the number of

---

[24] Minniti 2012; De Grossi Mazzorin and Minniti 2017; Trentacoste, Nieto-Espinet, and Valenzuala-Lamas 2018; MacKinnon 2004a. Love 2008.
[25] Not since MacKinnon 2004a; Ikeguchi 2017 uses a similar dataset to address meat consumption, rather than animal production, and not without methodological issues.
[26] Varro *Res Rust.* 3.1.7. Also 1.2.12–16. This following an earlier period when only pastoralism was practiced. See Purcell 2003a on perceptions of change in Republican foodways.

identified specimens (NISP).[27] Although subject to numerous limitations, these data provide an opportunity for quantitative comparison across the peninsula and offer points of departure for further work. This long-term approach is also encouraged by the quantity, quality, and geographic distribution of the data (see Figure 8.1). Given that plant and animal remains are dated primarily by their context, chronological spans are typically assessed in centuries rather than decades. For this synthesis, the material has been divided into three periods: Period 1 – eight to fourth centuries BCE; Period 2 – fourth to second centuries BCE; and Period 3 – second and first centuries BCE. This periodization encompasses major changes in agricultural production, as suggested in previous research. Six main study areas were used to investigate interregional differences (Figure 8.1).

Archaeobotanical data were collected using the BRAIN database[28] of archaeobotanical assemblages from Italy, with the addition of other

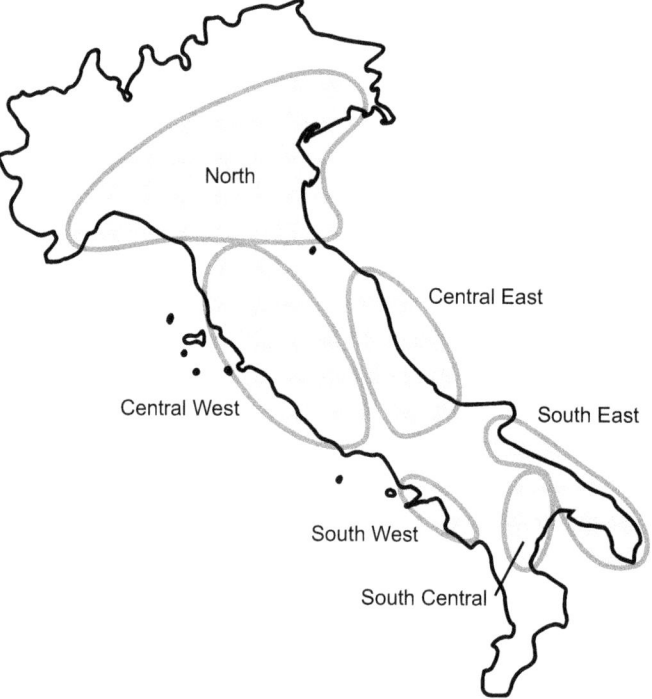

Figure 8.1 Map of the study areas. Drawn by the authors.

---

[27] A comprehensive reinvestigation of more detailed information on crop and animal husbandry is warranted but is beyond the scale of this contribution: for example, evaluation of age, sex, and body-part profiles for livestock; crop choice, husbandry practices and processing for plants.

[28] Mercuri et al. 2015.

published sites.[29] Seventy-seven major site phases were collated. Although not exhaustive, this collection of material can be considered as broadly representative of the Italian Peninsula. Only charred plant remains have been considered, as these are the most common preservation form across the Italian Peninsula. They represent staple crops well – cereals and pulses. However, herbs, vegetables, and fruits are underrepresented;[30] a noteworthy lacuna given the importance of horticultural crops, especially in the Late Republican period.[31] Presence/absence analysis is used here. While this form of analysis gives increased importance to minor crops and is not able to assess relative importance within a site, it is considered the most applicable form of analysis as much of the data come from poor-quality studies, for example those composed of handpicked material, or those with a low sample count and/or small assemblage size. A further consideration is site type – numerous sites in all periods derive from burials or religious sites, hence showing the purposeful selection of plant foods for offerings.[32] These sites are included here, but it is questionable as to what extent they represent the broader agricultural system.

Zooarchaeological data from the first millennium BCE represent 128 site phases.[33] Data from an additional ninety-eight site phases representing the Middle to Late Bronze Age and Iron Age were used as a comparison. Analysis focuses on quantification of livestock representation, which is quantified using NISP. Livestock representation is one of the most cited indicators in broader discussion of cultural and socioeconomic change surrounding the Roman period.[34] However, NISP is not an unproblematic means of assessing changes in exploitation; this is because it can be influenced by many underlying factors.[35] Although NISP alone is not an effective means of investigating *how* or *why* animal exploitation

---

[29] Supplemental tables available online through the Oxford University Research Archive, https://doi.org/10.5287/bodleian:KZq4YqKdO.

[30] Van der Veen 2007.

[31] Cato, *On Agriculture* 156–7. Columella, *On Agriculture* 10. See also Goodchild 2013; Heinrich 2017.

[32] Rottoli and Castiglioni 2011.

[33] Supplemental tables available online through the Oxford University Research Archive, https://doi.org/10.5287/bodleian:KZq4YqKdO.

[34] For example, King's (1999, 2001) well-known comparison of species representation in the western Roman Empire. For changes in livestock size in relation to economic intensification and connectivity, see Kron 2002; Ward-Perkins 2006. More recently Valenzuela-Lamas and Albarella eds. 2017.

[35] Fragmentation, specimen interdependence, and so on. See Lyman 1994 for a full review of the use of NISP as a means of quantifying taxon abundance.

was changing, its sensitivity makes it a useful tool for identifying *when* and *where* particular changes in production and/or consumption occur. NISP data has been plotted using ternary plots, which allow comparison of the relative abundance of cattle, sheep/goats, and pigs in the same figure. Only assemblages with over 100 identified livestock remains were considered, in order to have a statistically robust sample when comparing percentages. Like archaeobotanical data, the assemblages considered here do not constitute an exhaustive list, but they nevertheless provide a broad representation of species frequencies across the peninsula. Animal remains from ritual and cultic deposits are included in this survey but are identified as such. Such assemblages often diverge from general production and consumption trends and therefore warrant separate interpretation.[36]

The assemblages considered here reveal regional and chronological biases in previous research. Records are not evenly distributed by study period or region (Table 8.1). Notably, both plant and animal assemblages become rarer through time. Regional research traditions are also apparent. For instance, Pompeian materials dominate the southwest, with four of nine archaeobotanical assemblages and five of the seven zooarchaeological assemblages from the site.

Table 8.1 *Regional and chronological distribution of assemblages/site phases considered in this study**

	North	Central West	Central East	South East	South Central	South West
Archaeobotanical site phases						
Period 1: 8th–4th c. BCE	9	26	2	3	4	3 (1 Pompeii)
Period 2: 4th–2nd c. BCE	5	4		2	4	3
Period 3: 2nd–1st c. BCE	2	4			2	3 (all Pompeii)
Broad Phase				1		
Zooarchaeological site phases						
Middle-Late Bronze Age	43	16	14	9	6	
Iron Age: 10th–8th c. BCE	4	3	6	1	2	1
Period 1: 8th–4th c. BCE	25	27	4	5	9	
Period 2: 4th–2nd c. BCE	6	14	5	8	5	2 (1 Pompeii)
Period 3: 2nd–1st c. BCE	1	4		1	3	4 (all Pompeii)

Prepared by the authors. * Supplemental tables available online through the Oxford University Research Archive, https://doi.org/10.5287/bodleian:KZq4YqKdO.

---

[36] As by pronounced focus on a particular taxon: Cucinotta, de Grozzi Mazzorin, and Minniti 2010; De Grossi Mazzorin and Minniti 2015; Corbino and Fonzo 2017.

8.3 Setting the Stage: Agriculture in Late Prehistoric Italy

By Republican times, the most common domestic plants and animals – cattle, sheep, pigs, wheat, barley – had been farmed for millennia. Vines and olives had been exploited in various forms since the Neolithic in areas where wild plants were present, and were subject to cultivation from the Bronze Age.[37] Diversification of cereal crops during the Bronze Age allowed for more than one annual harvest, guarding against seasonal variation in temperature and rainfall.[38] The range of staple cultivars was enriched by the widespread introduction of millets (*Panicum miliaceum/Setaria italica*) alongside cultivation of the principle crops: free-threshing wheat (*Triticum durum/aestivum*), emmer (*Triticum dicoccum*), einkorn (*Triticum monococcum*), and barley (*Hordeum vulgare*).[39] Use of other minor cereals like spelt (*Triticum spelta*), rye (*Secale cereale*), and oat (*Avena sativa*) also expanded. Legumes increased in abundance through the Bronze Age and into the Iron Age, including fava bean (*Vicia faba*), pea (*Pisum sativum*), lentil (*Lens culinaris*), chickpea (*Cicer arietinum*), and vetch (*Lathyrus cicero/sativus*). Evidence from Northern Italy suggests an organized division between extensive cereal fields and smaller plots, potentially managed through crop rotation and manuring.[40] Animals were probably moved around the landscape to support crop cultivation, and archaeobotanical remains indicate foddering in winter months.[41] Zooarchaeological studies suggest a mixed-management strategy, with sheep or cattle typically the most abundant species and limited focus on dairying outside of Alpine communities.[42] In some communities, production even appears to be have been geared toward export.[43]

Strategies initially adopted perhaps as a means of diversification and a buffer against failure also provided the tools for increasing surplus production when incentivized by changes in socioeconomic

---

[37] Brun 2004; Fiorentino et al. 2004; Marvelli et al. 2013; Tanasi et al. 2018; Caracuta 2020; Motta and Beydler 2020.
[38] Fiorentino et al. 2004; Primavera et al. 2017.
[39] Fiorentino et al. 2004. For isotopic evidence of millet consumption in Bronze Age Italy see Tafuri et al. 2018 and references therein.
[40] Mercuri et al. 2006b; Perego 2017. Evidence from central Europe suggests a similar strategy: Bogaard 2011.
[41] Perego 2017; Trentacoste et al. 2020.
[42] Riedel and Tecchiati 2002; De Grossi Mazzorin and Minniti 2003; De Grossi Mazzorin 2010; Minniti 2012; De Grossi Mazzorin 2013a, 2013b; Maini and Curci 2013; Stopp 2015; Tecchiati et al. 2019.
[43] Textile tools from Montale near Modena point to village-level textile manufacture for export: Sabatini, Earle, and Cardarelli 2018. For the Bronze Age wool economy see Sabatini and Bergerbrant eds. 2019; Sabatini et al. 2019.

context.[44] From the Late Bronze Age, an intensification of Mediterranean trade and changes in the socioeconomic organization of Italian communities mark the beginning of a period of significant natural-resource exploitation and agricultural development.[45] In southern Italy, shifts in crop choice, greater exploitation of inland areas, and development of storage systems point to a greater surplus production.[46] Increased contact with the Eastern Mediterranean accompanied more widespread evidence for grape and olive cultivation, probably facilitated by the transfer of new technical knowledge and cultivars.[47] With the arrival of donkeys in the Late Bronze Age and chickens in the early Iron Age, new forms of livestock were introduced to the peninsula via Mediterranean trade links.[48] Sheep bones become notably more abundant in Central Italy during the Late Bronze Age, which may also signal investment in wool-producing herds.[49] Uniquely in Western Europe, changes in livestock size are archaeologically visible from as early as the Bronze–Iron Age transition. Cattle and sheep, which had been decreasing in stature for millennia since domestication in the Neolithic, began to increase in size.[50] The pan-regional and incremental nature of increases in size suggests an internally mediated process,[51] rather than one driven by external forces or the wholesale import of new livestock populations.

8.4 Changes and Continuities: Agriculture and Animal Husbandry in First-Millennium-BCE Italy

Following prehistoric introductions and diversification in domestic plant and animal taxa, this agriculture repertoire remained largely stable until into the Late Republic. Rather than changes in the species exploited, bioarchaeological evidence suggests a reorganization in terms of how and for what reason these staples were produced.

---

[44] Primavera et al. 2017.   [45] Bietti Sestieri 2010; Saltini Semerari 2013; Nijboer 2017.
[46] Primavera et al. 2017.
[47] Buxó 2008; Marvelli et al. 2013; Ucchesu et al. 2015; Caracuta 2020; Motta and Beydler 2020.
[48] Chicken: Trentacoste et al. 2020. Donkey: Mitchell 2018.
[49] De Grossi Mazzorin, Riedel, and Tagliacozzo 2004; Minniti 2012.
[50] Trentacoste, Nieto-Espinet, and Valenzuela-Lamas 2018; De Grossi Mazzorin and Minniti 2019.
[51] For example, Gaastra 2014 suggests Greek colonization catalyzed increases in livestock size – a point countered by De Grossi Mazzorin and Minniti 2019. See also Trentacoste, Nieto-Espinet, and Valenzuela-Lamas 2018.

8.4.1 Cereals and Pulses

In cereal and pulse cultivation, the overall impression is one of continuity of crop repertoire throughout the first millennium BCE. Barley and emmer wheat are the most common taxa in all periods, followed by free-threshing wheat. Other cereals include spelt, einkorn, rye, and oat (unclear if cultivated). There is also a continued presence of common millet (*Panicum miliaceum*) and foxtail millet (*Setaria italica*). These results confirm a continuation of crop repertoire from the Bronze Age into the late first millennium BCE.[52] Additionally, they demonstrate the presence of a wide crop spectrum in Central Tyrrhenian Italy before the fifth century BCE, in contrast to a reliance on emmer wheat noted in ancient sources.[53] Results also confirm previous suggestions that millets were consumed much more widely than previously recognized,[54] a conclusion echoed in recent isotopic studies of human diet.[55]

Throughout the first millennium BCE, no change is observed in the ubiquity of barley, emmer, or free-threshing wheat, but a decline is visible in the representation of spelt and einkorn over time (Chart 8.1). The fluctuations are unclear in millets and may be due to sampling taphonomy. The small size of millet grains (c. 1–3 mm) means their recovery is biased by sample collection method and sieve size.

Based on this data, the dramatic expansion of rural sites during the Middle Republic and Roman annexation of the peninsula is not mirrored in the ubiquity of cereals and pulses. On the one hand, the decline in some glume wheats could be seen as a move toward free-threshing wheats, which are easier to process and produce flour more suitable for bread;[56] however, emmer remains more ubiquitous than free-threshing wheat. Spelt has been observed as reasonably abundant in Archaic Rome,[57] while traces of spelt wheat have also been recorded in cremation burials from Northern Italy in the imperial period.[58] Establishing reasons for the decline of einkorn and spelt wheat requires further consideration, including investigation of what part of the plant is present (seed or processing debris) and links with processing centralization, along with considerations of husbandry practices and culinary change.

Regional preferences in cereals crops are also present. Barley and emmer are common in all regions, while free-threshing wheat is less frequent in the Central West, and spelt and einkorn less frequent in the south, where foxtail millet is absent (Chart 8.2). Quantitative studies have noted the abundance of

---

[52] Also previously noted in Lentjes 2013: 126–7; Heinrich 2017: 159.
[53] Goodchild 2013: 203. For example, Ovid, *Fasti* 2.519–510; 6.180; Pliny, *Natural History* 18.62. See Spurr 1986: 11–13.
[54] Murphy 2016.   [55] Killgrove and Tykot 2013; Laffranchi et al. 2016; Tafuri et al. 2018.
[56] Heinrich 2017.   [57] Motta 2002.   [58] Rottoli and Castiglioni 2011.

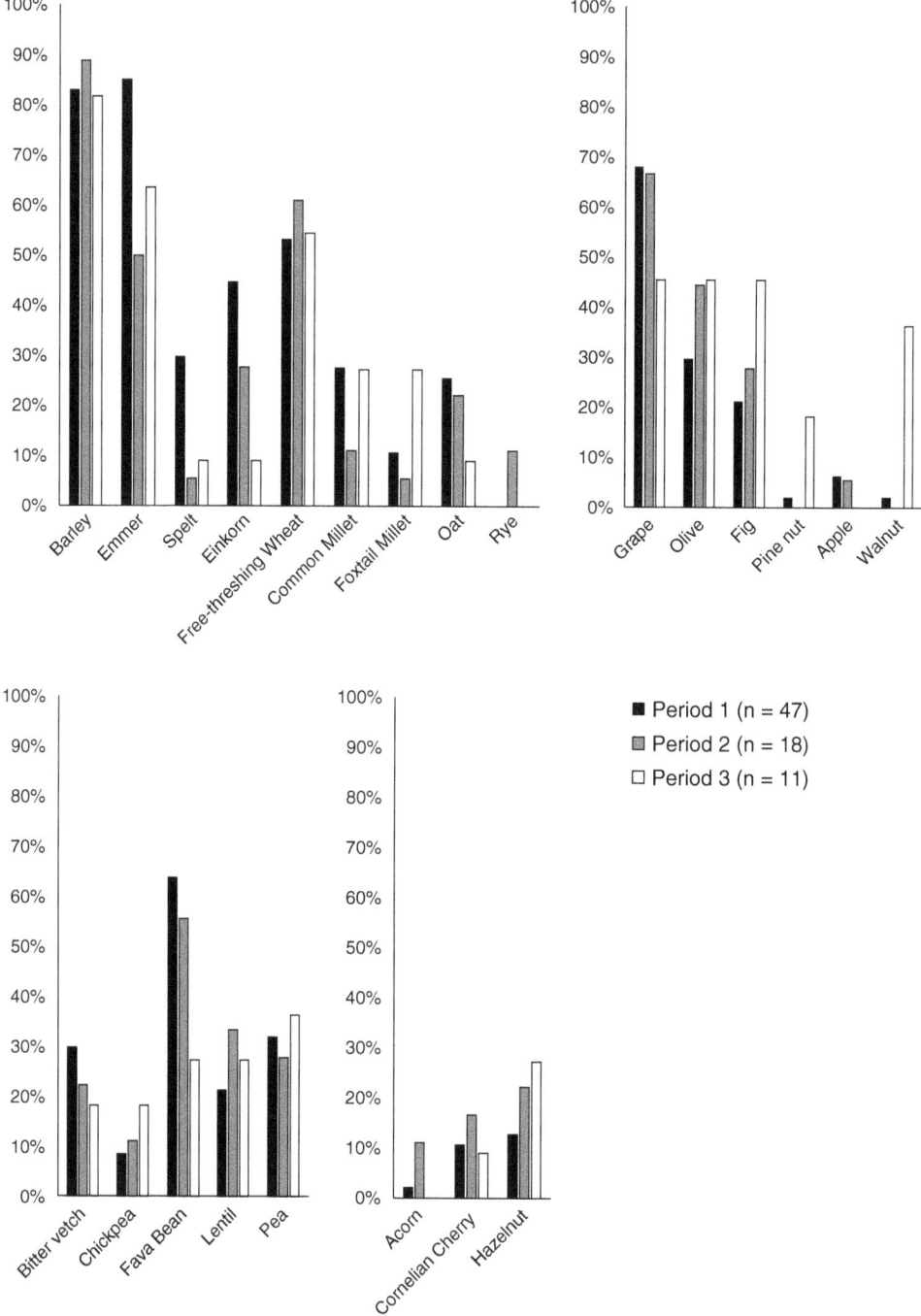

Chart 8.1 Frequency of cereals, pulses, fruits, and wild plant foods throughout first-millennium-BCE Italy, by subperiod.
Prepared by the authors.

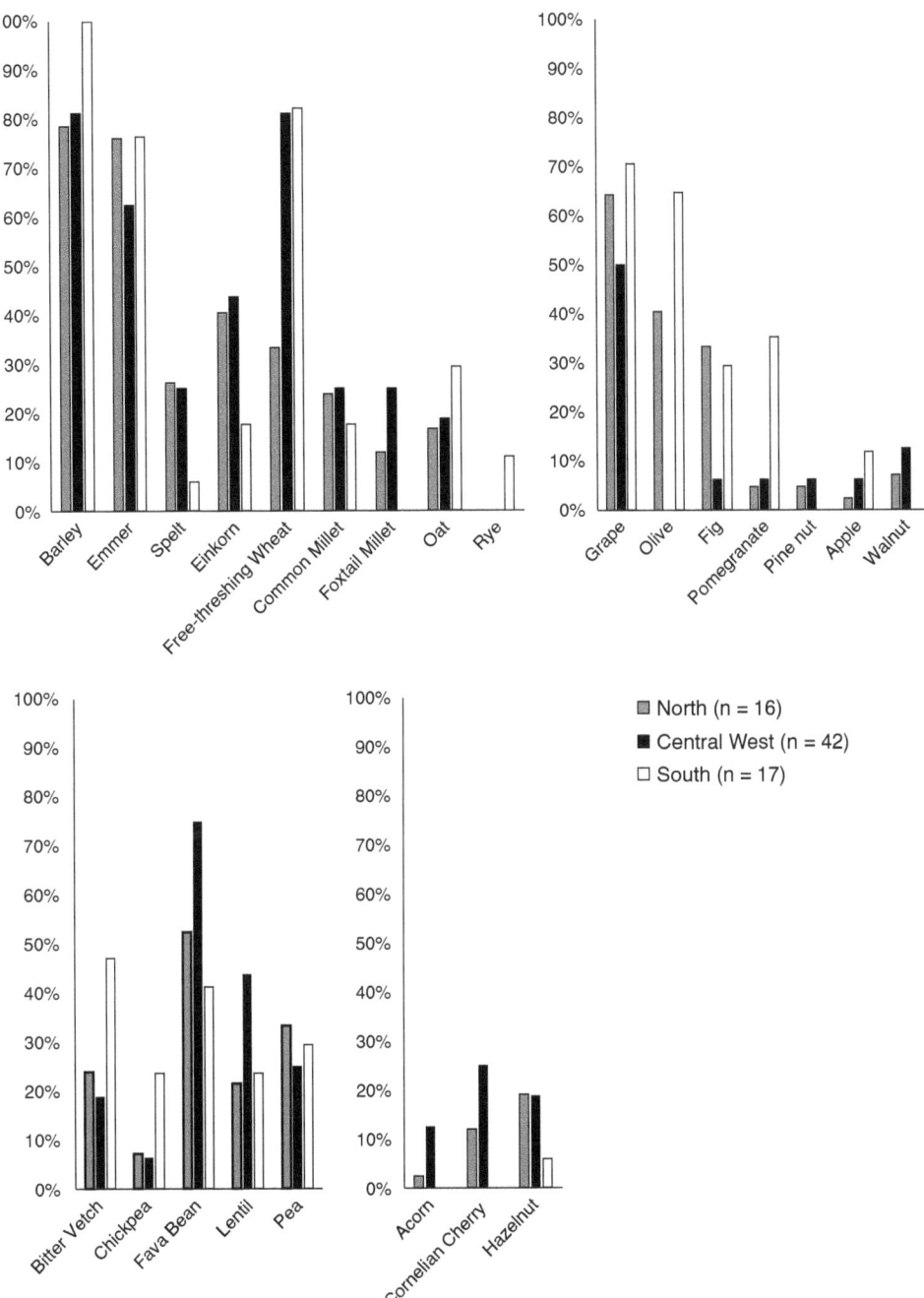

Chart 8.2 Frequency of cereals, pulses, fruits, and wild plant foods throughout first-millennium-BCE Italy, by major region.
Prepared by the authors

barley in southeast Italy, where it is considered most suitable for the soil.[59] Barley, emmer, oats, and pulses could also be sown in spring, allowing a second harvest alongside that of winter-sown wheats. Millet could be sown and harvested in a single season, and isotopic evidence suggests it made a greater contribution to diets, especially in Northern Italy, than previously thought.[60]

As with cereals, there is a continued presence of a range of pulses, with fava bean, pea, lentil, chickpea, and bitter vetch reasonably frequent (Chart 8.1), perhaps with an increase in the ubiquity of lentil through time. Fava bean is the most common pulse, recording at frequencies similar to free-threshing wheat, which mirrors its importance in ancient sources.[61] Regional differences are present in the ubiquity of pulses. In the north, fava bean and lentil are the most commonly identified, while in the south, chickpea and bitter vetch occur at a relatively high frequency.

In general, a broad regional separation can be noted between Northern Italy and the Central West, where spelt and einkorn are more frequent, and the south, where barley, free-threshing wheat, bitter vetch, and chickpea are more frequent. This reflects differences observed in the imperial period, where an emphasis on durum wheat has also been noted.[62] Further consideration of the relative importance of different crops will require quantitative analysis, and establishing to what extent settlements pursued different crop strategies will require further detailed work. Where data currently exist, intriguing patterns can be seen: at Iron Age Gabii, millet and barley are abundant *contra* the regional emphasis on emmer.[63] Overall, there is a wide crop diversity, which has been linked to the environmental variation[64] and a lack of market-orientated cereal production (in the imperial period).[65] However, further clarification is needed on the role of individual crops in the agroecological system before robust conclusions can be drawn: for example, on how different crops were grown, stored, and prepared into different cuisines.

8.4.2 Crop Processing

The limited archaeobotanical evidence provides some suggestion of diachronic changes in the organization of cereal processing. Chaff is present in the Late Orientalizing (late seventh to early sixth centuries BCE) samples from the well-sampled site of Sant'Antonio at Cerveteri,[66] as well in

---

[59] See the detailed report from Pantanello: Costantini and Costantini Biasini 2018.
[60] Killgrove and Tykot 2013; Laffranchi et al. 2016; Tafuri et al. 2018.
[61] For example, Pliny, *Natural History* 18.117–19. Spurr 1986: 105–12.   [62] Ibid.
[63] Evans et al. 2019; Gavériaux et al. 2022.   [64] Spurr 1986: 93–4.   [65] Heinrich 2017.
[66] Izzet 2000.

Archaic samples from the Palatine Hill,[67] indicating the processing of cereals within these settlements. At Pompeii, cereal chaff is present in pre-Roman samples dated to the sixth to second centuries BCE, but virtually absent from Roman phases at the House of Amarantus,[68] a pattern also visible at Regio VI Insula 1.[69] The processing of harvested crops into clean grain is a labor-intensive activity, providing vital insights into the control of cereal harvests and the presence or absence of centralized agricultural practices.[70] The question of whether the shift from domestic to centralized crop processing took place relatively late – after Roman colonization, as in Pompeii – will require future quantitative analysis of samples to resolve. If confirmed, this would suggest a significant reorganization of food production and supply during the Late Republic.

In terms of milling technology, the development and diffusion of new millstone types from the sixth century BCE may provide a line of proxy evidence for a change in the scale of cereal processing, or at least an interest in new tools and techniques.[71] The fourth century BCE saw greater trade in millstones across the Mediterranean and the rapid arrival of Greek hopper-rubber (Olynthus-style) millstones in Southern and Northern Italy.[72] There is also evidence for the production and transport of these new millstone types across Italy,[73] which suggests a greater investment in milling technology as well as a potential change to larger-scale cereal processing well into marginal areas of Northern Italy and the Alps.

8.4.3 Fruits

Finds of olive and grape increase over the periods considered here, although the ubiquity of olive and grape shows no clear diachronic pattern (Chart 8.1). An increase in finds of other fruits and nuts is also important – fig, pomegranate, and walnut all consistently increase in ubiquity throughout the first millennium BCE. Grape occurs in all regions, while olive has only been recorded in the South and Central regions (Chart 8.2), probably reflecting areas of cultivation and the environmental tolerance of these trees. Fig is also more common in these regions than in Northern Italy (Chart 8.2), again likely a reflection of the ubiquity of cultivation and the environmental preferences of these fruit trees.

---

[67] Motta 2011.　[68] Robinson 1999: 101.　[69] Murphy, Thompson, and Fuller 2013.
[70] Fuller and Stevens 2009.　[71] Alonso and Frankel 2017.
[72] Williams-Thorpe and Thorpe 1990; Alonso and Frankel 2017; Francisci 2020.
[73] Renzulli et al. 2002.

The dynamics of this process and associated export of wine and oil amphorae have been discussed extensively elsewhere,[74] but a few points warrant repetition here. Following exploitation over the first half of the first millennium BCE, oil and wine production escalates during the fifth and fourth centuries, before greater expansion in the Late Republic. This trend is visible in a peak in olive pollen at the end of the first millennium BCE,[75] and appearance of wine/oil-processing installations during the fifth–fourth centuries BCE in Central Italy, at the Auditorium site near Rome and the Etruscan farm of Podere Tartuchino north of Saturnia,[76] as well as in Puglia at Oliovitolo near Tarentum.[77] In Puglia, olive remains also expand outside their ecological range on the coast during this period, with a move to surplus olive and wine production on inland indigenous settlements as well as Greek coastal *coloniae*.[78] Central Italy presents a similar timeline of developments, with olives documented in archaeobotanical material from Rome and Cures in the early first millennium BCE, and Tarquinia soon after.[79] Fully domesticated grapes have been documented in Etruscan levels (third–first century BC) from Cetamura near Gaiole in Chianti, based on the morphometric analysis of grape seeds; this is unsurprising in this period considering their long history of exploitation.[80] Genetic evidence obtained from these samples showed long-term continuity in grapevine genetics from the third century BCE through to third-to-fourth century CE,[81] providing archaeological context for Pliny's discussion of local Italian grape varieties.[82] Following Middle Republican developments, production expanded further in the third and second centuries BCE, evidenced by the greater visibility of both processing installations and vine trenches, for example in the *suburbium* of Republican Rome.[83] Like in grain-milling technology, the greater visibility of presses and pressing floors, especially from the fourth century BCE, implies a change in processing style and in the scale of oil and wine production,[84] although how the cultivation of olives, grapes, and cereals was balanced is still an open question.

---

[74] Gras 1985; Hitchner 2002; Perkins 2007; Perkins 2012; Brun 2004; Delpino 2012; Marzano 2013; Lentjes 2013; McGovern et al. 2013; Lentjes and Saltini Semerari 2016; Riva 2017; Caracuta 2020; Motta and Beydler 2020.

[75] Mercuri et al. 2015. [76] Perkins and Attolini 1992; Terrenato 2001.

[77] Alessio 2001; Caracuta 2020. [78] Caracuta 2020.

[79] See online database at https://doi.org/10.5287/bodleian:KZq4YqKdO.

[80] De Grummond 2018; Mariotti Lippi et al. 2020.

[81] Bouby, Ivorra, and Terral 2017; Wales, Ramos-Madrigal, and Gilbert 2017.

[82] Pliny, *Natural History* 14.4.36–39.

[83] Vine trenches: Volpe 2009; Processing installations: De Juliis 1985; Ciancio and Radina 1989: 208; Volpe 1990; Small et al. 1992; Brun 2004; Andreassi 2007.

[84] See Brun 2004 for evidence of these installations.

Beyond grape, olive, and fig, a wider range of fruits and nuts are recorded, including pomegranate, walnut, pine nut, citrus, and mulberry. Numerous studies have addressed the introduction and cultivation of fruit and nut trees.[85] Broad patterns cannot be reassessed on the basis of charred plant remains alone, as the range of taxa is much broader in mineralized and waterlogged assemblages. However, indications are that the import of exotics is more of a gradual process throughout the first millennium BCE, with first appearances of plants like citrus and pomegranate in the sixth century or earlier,[86] facilitated by contacts with the wider Mediterranean.[87] Frequencies of fig, pine nut, walnut, apple, and pomegranate all increase from the second century BCE (Chart 8.1) with the wider integration of trade networks, which lead to further introductions, such as peach in the first century CE.[88]

8.4.4 The Other Triad: Relative Abundance of Livestock

Zooarchaeological assemblages from Central Tyrrhenian Italy show a significant increase in the relative importance of pigs during the first millennium BCE (Chart 8.3). From its origin in around the eighth century

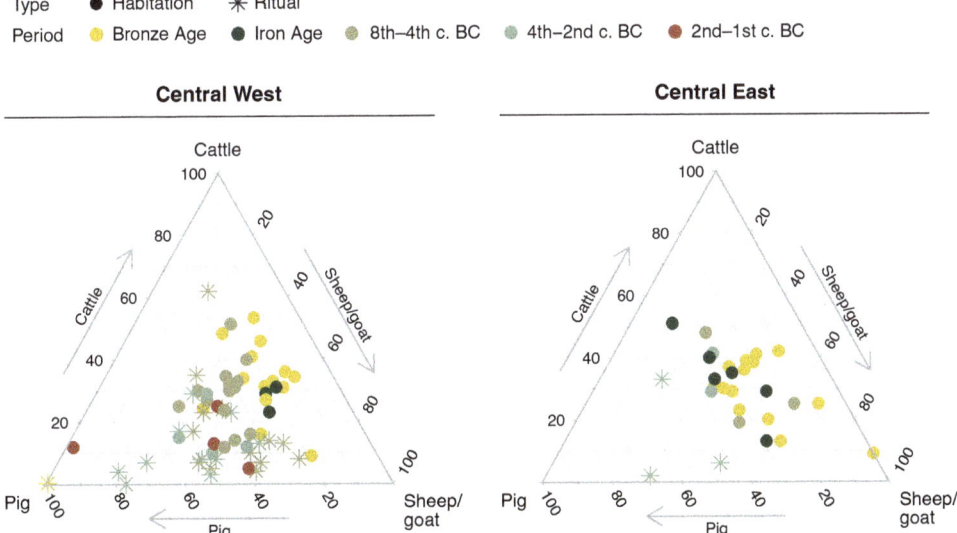

Chart 8.3 Livestock representation on sites in Central Italy. Figures show the relative percentages of the main types of livestock (cattle, sheep/goat, pig) for different sites.
Prepared by the authors.

---

[85] Magri and Sadori 1999; Jacomet et al. 2002; Sadori et al. 2009; Pagnoux et al. 2013.
[86] Jacomet et al. 2002; Pagnoux et al. 2013.
[87] For a Sardinian example see Sabato et al. 2015; Ucchesu et al. 2017. [88] Sadori et al. 2009.

BCE, this increase in pig exploitation is one of the earliest and most lasting developments in protohistoric livestock husbandry, and one of the most recognized in the literature.[89] The increase in pork consumption over this period broadly mirrors trends toward urbanization and demographic growth, and thus has been interpreted as a response to an increased demand for meat in urbanized settings – a task for which pigs are well suited. Additionally, pig bones become increasingly abundant in sanctuaries and ritual deposits over the same period.[90] In these contexts, pigs probably fulfilled a growing demand for meat, but a demand driven as much by changing patterns of surplus production and its use in the construction of social status as by subsistence demands.[91] However, major changes and elevated percentages of pig bones of over 50 percent are not common in the region until the imperial period.[92] Caere and Gabii provide interesting examples of this trend – at both sites the proportion of pigs rises by over 10 percent in the first-century-CE assemblage.[93] Ostia, the site furthest to the bottom left in Chart 8.3, is the only nonritual site to demonstrate what we could consider "imperial-level" percentages of pigs (86 percent) in Republican times (third–first century BCE).[94]

Outside of Ostia, high percentages of pig remains are limited to a few cultic assemblages,[95] while in habitation assemblages the trend is generally one of continuity, variability, and a small increase in the abundance of pigs (Chart 8.4). Ritual assemblages demonstrate a clearer trend, which becomes particularly pronounced from the fourth century BCE, especially in deposits related to the restructuring of urban areas.[96] Multiphase sanctuaries like Poggio Colla and Narce Li Santi also demonstrate a high proportion of pigs in the Middle Republic compared to earlier periods. At least in terms of species representation, these ritual assemblages foreshadow later patterns that become more widely visible across Central Italy site types in the first century CE.

---

[89] Minniti 2012; De Grossi Mazzorin and Minniti 2017; Trentacoste et al. 2020 and references therein.

[90] A practice noted from earlier prehistory: De Grossi Mazzorin and Minniti 2002; Silvestri et al. 2017.

[91] See Rives 2019 for the use of sacrifice to display status and economic potential in the Greek polis. For further discussion see Trentacoste et al. 2020.

[92] See De Grossi Mazzorin and Minniti 2017.   [93] Alhaique 2016; Colivicchi et al. 2016.

[94] See MacKinnon 2014.

[95] Veii: Cucinotta, de Grossi Mazzorin, and Minniti 2010; Rome, Centocelle: De Grossi Mazzorin 2004; Populonia: De Grossi Mazzorin and Minniti 2015.

[96] For example, closing or opening subterranean structures. See examples in previous note and Trentacoste 2021.

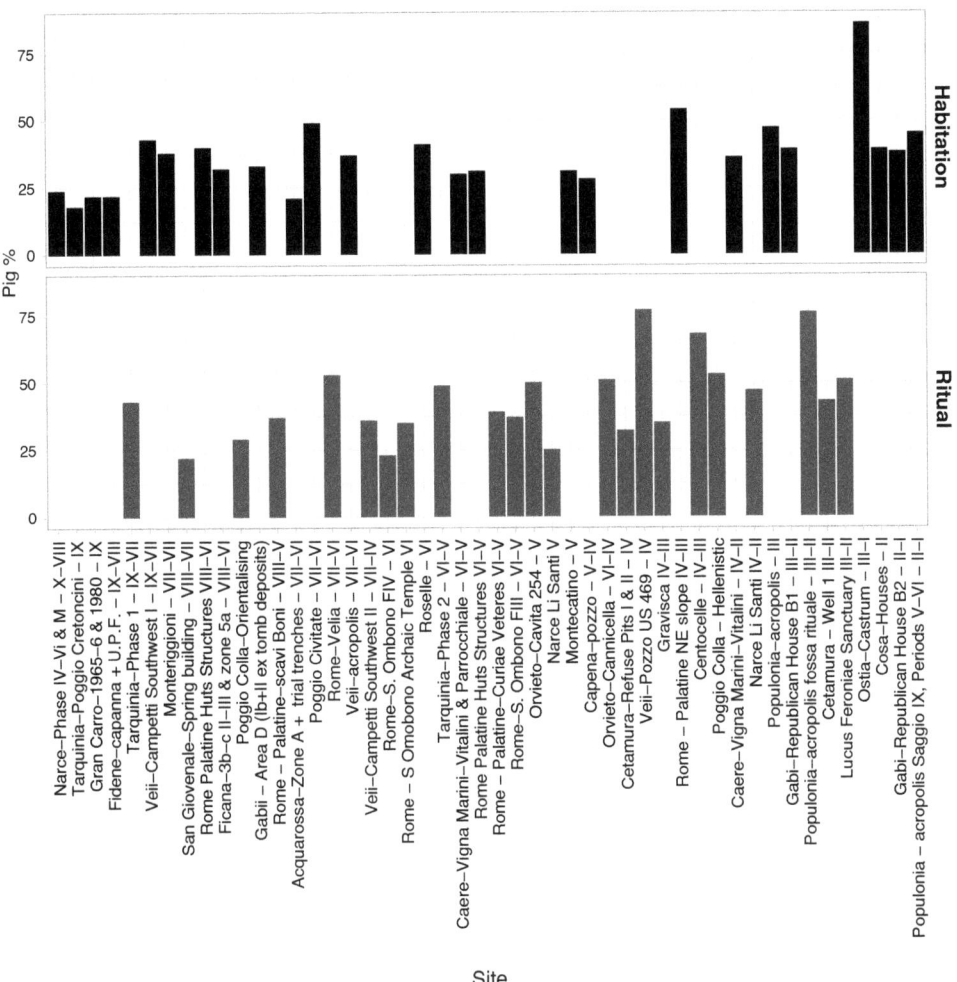

Chart 8.4 Relative percentages of pig bones from sites in Central Tyrrhenian Italy. Ordered chronologically from the tenth to second centuries BCE. Numerals indicate century BCE. Prepared by the authors.

Similar results are visible in the Central East region, where habitation assemblages demonstrate a significant degree of continuity from Bronze Age patterns, albeit with a very slight trend toward increased exploitation of pigs. The Samnite sanctuaries of Campochiaro, Pietrabbondante, and Colle Sparanise diverge notably from habitation assemblages on account of their elevated emphasis on pigs. This tendency was noted by Barker, who argued that these sanctuaries acted as fora for elite display and the distribution of animals and their products.[97] As in the West Central region, these

---

[97] Barker and Clark 1995.

trends in ritual contexts foreshadow pig-focused early imperial patterns visible at the villas of Matrice and Potito, as well as at Monte Pallano.[98]

Southern regions also produced evidence for change over the latter part of the first millennium BCE, although in different directions than those documented in Central Italy (Chart 8.5). The South East region provides evidence for a minor decrease in the relative abundance of cattle, with the exception of an assemblage at Otranto. There, the notable quantity of cattle remains may reflect particular patterns of discard in ditches around

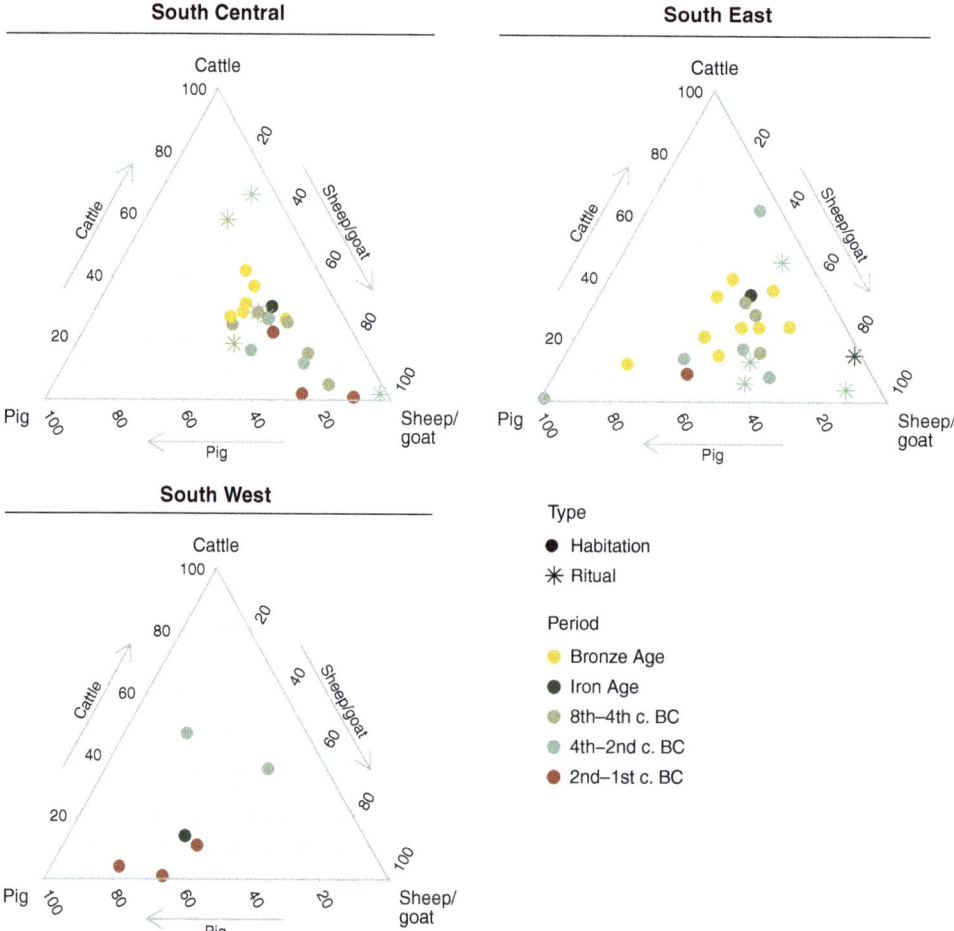

Chart 8.5 Livestock representation on sites in Southern Italy. Figures show the relative percentages of the main types of livestock (cattle, sheep/goat, pig) for different sites.
Prepared by the authors.

[98] See https://doi.org/10.5287/bodleian:KZq4YqKdO for details and references.

the settlement's perimeter, rather than changing food consumption in the town.[99] In assemblages from the South Central area, sheep/goats become increasingly abundant over the time period considered, especially in Republican times. Pompeii (from where all but one of the South West assemblages derive) demonstrates a shift toward pork consumption as in Central Italy, with very high percentages of pig bones present in assemblages from the Middle Republican period (Period 2), before Roman annexation of the town. This diachronic increase is also visible in the assemblages from single properties, like the House of Amarantus[100] and Porta Stabia excavations.[101] In the South East, relatively high percentages of pig remains are found at Valesio from the third century BCE, a change which may suggest a shift to a more Central Italian way of eating; however Bronze Age livestock ratios from the region are very diverse, and as the only example of this shift in region, additional zooarchaeological data would be useful in interpreting the significance of this trend. Like in Central Italy, ritual assemblages from the South East and South Central regions that demonstrate a similar focus on a particular taxon become fairly abundant from the fourth century BCE, but with elevated percentages of sheep/goats and cattle, rather than pig remains.

Northern Italy presents different developments to other areas of the peninsula, with distinct trajectories in the regions divided roughly north and south of the Po River. South of the Po River, in Etruscan Northern Italy – *Etruria Padana* in Italian scholarship – an increase in pork consumption coincides with the rise of cities and is particularly pronounced on urban sites.[102] The increase begins around the eighth century BCE if not earlier, during an important period of settlement nucleation in the southern Po Plain.[103] But rather than continuing progressively into the imperial period, pork consumption peaks with the flourishing of Archaic Etruscan cities, and then declines with the Etruscan urban network.[104] Celtic assemblages from the lowland Cispadane region are lacking, but ancient sources documenting an important livestock and wool market at the Campi Macri near Modena, as well as the high-quality fleeces produced by the region, suggest an agricultural economy in which sheep husbandry had an important role.[105] No wholly Republican assemblages are available for this region,

---

[99] De Grossi Mazzorin and Minniti 2008.   [100] Fulford et al. 1999.   [101] MacKinnon 2016.
[102] Farello 2006; Trentacoste 2016.
[103] Frattesina, an important central place of the late Bronze Age, presents the same trend: De Grossi Mazzorin 2015.
[104] For example at Spina; Briccola, Bertolini, and Thun Hohenstein 2013.
[105] For the Campi Macri see Ortalli and Campi Macri 2012. For fleece quality see Columella 7.2.3–4; Strabo 5.1.12; MacKinnon 2004b.

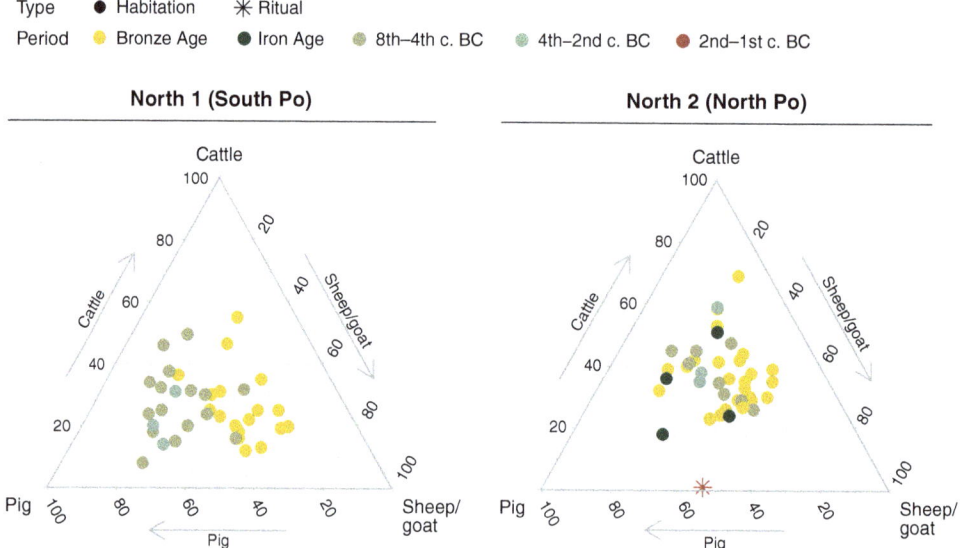

Chart 8.6 Livestock representation on sites in Northern Italy. Figures show the relative percentages of the main types of livestock (cattle, sheep/goat, pig) for different sites.
Prepared by the authors.

but those that span the first century BCE to first century CE have a predominance of sheep/goat or pig, rather than cattle, bones.[106]

North of the River Po in Transpadane Gaul, assemblages display greater continuity in livestock ratios between the Bronze Age and first millennium BCE, perhaps with an indication of high percentages of cattle on Middle Republican Period 2 sites. It is unclear whether divergence of the only culturally Roman material included, from a Late Republican group of pits from Montereale Valcellina in Friuli at the foot of the Alps, reflects broader production strategies or, more probably, the ritual nature of the context.

8.4.5 Livestock Improvement

Trends in livestock body size first documented in late prehistory continued across the first millennium BCE. Counterintuitively, as pigs increased in importance, they decreased in size: a continuation of a trend associated with domestication in the Neolithic.[107] In Northern Italy pigs decline in height but become more robust from the Bronze Age into the Iron Age, including on urban Etruscan sites.[108] Similar trends in size diminution are visible in central

---

[106] Sheep/goat: Spilamberto, Calvatone, Pig: Modena. See https://doi.org/10.5287/bodleian:KZq4YqKdO for details and references.
[107] Albarella et al. 2006.   [108] Trentacoste, Nieto-Espinet, and Valenzuela-Lamas 2018.

Adriatic and Southern Italy;[109] around Rome their size remained stable between the Orientalizing and Republican periods;[110] detailed assessment of earlier trends has yet to be undertaken. Thus, despite their increasing role as a key meat producer, pigs do not show a size increase until imperial times, and in some regions this increase is most notable in Late Antiquity.[111] In contrast, cattle and sheep demonstrate significant size increases from around the Bronze–Iron Age transition that continued across the first millennium BCE.[112] Although most pronounced in urban settlements, these changes were not limited to central places and form part of a general trend across the peninsula.

This increase in the body size of cattle, sheep, and goats implies a significant reorganization in the management of domestic bovids over the first millennium BCE – a reorganization significant enough to break from millennia of size diminution. In contrast, greater continuity in body-size trends in pigs may suggest more conservative development of established management strategies, and potentially a continuation of the free-range extensive systems used in prehistory, at least until the imperial period or even Late Antiquity. What aspect of management strategies changed to support these morphometric developments is still under discussion; these probably resulted from a mixture of factors, for example, changes in herd sex ratios to favor male animals (e.g. oxen, wool-producing wethers[113]), feeding strategies, herding/mobility patterns, genetic diversity, and/or the import of allochthonous breeding stock (particularly individual males). Recent analyses of strontium and oxygen isotopes from Etruscan sheep found greater evidence for mobility in the fifth compared to the seventh century BCE, although these differences may result from site function rather than diachronic change.[114] Cattle, which demonstrate the largest increases, may have experienced these new strategies to a greater degree than sheep or goats as a result of their use in traction; the lack of a size increase in pigs suggests that greater meat content per animal was not the driving concern. The significant investment required to attain and maintain draft cattle, whose working lives could be well over a decade, would also encourage farmers to search more widely for stock. Livestock mortality profiles indicate a continued use of cattle primarily for labor, while sheep/goat profiles suggest greater emphasis on milk, lamb,

---

[109] Love 2008.   [110] De Grossi Mazzorin and Minniti 2017.
[111] MacKinnon 2001; Love 2008; Trentacoste et al. 2020; De Grossi Mazzorin and Minniti 2017.
[112] Trentacoste, Nieto-Espinet, and Valenzuela-Lamas 2018; De Grossi Mazzorin and Minniti 2019.
[113] On the importance of oxen: Columella, *On Agriculture* 6.2; Castrated fine-wooled sheep: Columella, *On Agriculture* 7.4.4.
[114] Trentacoste, Nieto-Espinet, and Valenzuela-Lamas 2018; Trentacoste et al. 2020.

and wool, at least in Central and Northern Italy.[115] Improvements to sheep are demonstrated in wool-fiber quality during this period, resulting in the presence of different fleece types by the Republican period.[116]

8.5 Discussion

Pre- and protohistoric farmers adopted new plants and animals, exploited fodder crops, vines, and olives, practiced different forms of crop rotation, and improved livestock. With the same species of plants and animals, farmers in first-millennium-BCE Italy were able to sustain a major population increase. The environmental data considered here suggest both changes and continuities in agriculture across the first millennium BCE as overall output increased: While *what* was exploited remained fairly stable, *how* these plants and animals were used evolved, particularly from Middle Republican times. Roman sociopolitical annexation appears to have had limited immediate impact, while peninsula-wide changes in production and consumption patterns during the Middle Republican period point to the importance of broader economic developments in mediating agricultural change, with further notable changes from the second century BCE.

In animal husbandry, trends established in earlier periods intensified in Middle Republican times. In Central Italy, pigs grew in importance incrementally, with an acceleration of this trend in ritual assemblages from the fourth–third centuries BCE and then in habitation assemblages a century or so later. Pompeii followed a similar pattern, with a notable intensification of pig exploitation after the fourth century BCE, adopting a "Roman" pork-focused consumption pattern well in advance of Roman hegemony. South Central and South East areas also demonstrate an increasing focus on a single taxon in ritual contexts from this point, a pattern which intensifies on some Republican sites. In contrast, with the decline of Archaic Etruscan cities, Etruria Padana sees a relaxation (although not reversal) of the urban pig-focused pattern.[117] Rather than a radical change in strategy, livestock frequencies suggest an acceleration of – or, in the case of Cispadane Gaul, a de-escalation of – existing patterns, driven by new modes of production rather than new materials. Similar trends are visible

---

[115] De Grossi Mazzorin and Minniti 2017; Minniti 2012; Trentacoste 2015.
[116] Gleba 2012. Also noted by Roman authors, see MacKinnon 2004b.
[117] A similar decrease is noted in Late Antique Rome, which has also been linked to a decline in urban connectivity and intensive production strategies.

in the exploitation of another domestic animal: chickens. After their introduction during the Iron Age, domestic fowl bones are predominantly found across the funerary and religious contexts before becoming common in domestic debris.[118] The recovery of hundreds of chicken bones from a *cunicolo* at Centocelle suggests that poultry farming around Rome had expanded significantly by the early third century BCE,[119] and by the second century BCE, chickens had become a staple in urban diets at Pompeii, where they account for 8 percent of the second–first-century-BCE assemblage from the House of Amarantus.[120] Overall, these changes appear to have been predominantly regional and related to economic organization, rather than driven by culturally defined Roman modes of production.

In terms of crop choice, the Middle Republican period also does not appear to have been a major point of change. The continued cultivation of a diverse crop repertoire was practiced across the peninsula, albeit with varying regional emphasis on crops. Rural infill, so well documented in landscape studies,[121] appears to have little impact on crop ubiquity, and no change in staple cereals and pulses can be correlated with Roman expansion. The only suggestion of change is a decrease in einkorn and spelt, but the unchanged representation of free-threshing wheat does not suggest it replaced the former crops.

However, continuity does not necessarily imply stasis, and the mode of comparison employed here does not permit a detailed analysis. Future analysis of processing and husbandry practices is likely to reveal important developments between species, settlements, landscapes, and through time. The application of weed ecology analysis and crop stable isotope analysis, only starting to be applied to protohistoric or imperial Italy, will be a key area of future research. Based on our limited consideration of reports of cereal chaff, evidence for the centralization of crop processing is not indicated until the Late Republican period – well after changes in milling and pressing technologies had occurred. While biases in area sampled (e.g. ritual versus domestic areas) and the absence of detailed reporting leaves current results open to debate, such patterns may point to intermediate steps between household-level and more centrally controlled forms of production. Further investigation of archaeobotanical evidence for crop processing would provide new insights into the centralization of agricultural labor and the separation of stages of production,[122] as indicated by a

---

[118] Trentacoste et al. 2020. On the introduction, see Corbino et al. 2021.
[119] De Grossi Mazzorin 2004.   [120] Fulford et al. 1999.
[121] De Haas in this volume (Chapter 7); Sewell 2016; Pelgrom 2018; Stoddart et al. 2019.
[122] Fuller and Stevens 2009.

study from Rome.[123] This is a particularly fruitful area for interdisciplinary research, which could shed light on the influence of religious institutions, elite families, and the early state. Zooarchaeological evidence for changes in the ritual sphere suggests surplus animals were preferentially channeled into religious activity. Comparisons with other areas of Italy would also be productive: The early oil press at the Auditorium site suggests elite control over agricultural processing near Rome, but is the diffusion of milling technologies into Northern and Alpine Italy similarly explained?

8.6 Conclusion

Over this *longue durée*, what does this analysis reveal about Middle Republican Italy? Firstly, it suggests that agricultural production was motivated by regional and economic trajectories rather than by cultural "Romanization." Imperial trends toward high levels of pork consumption and increases in livestock size occur well before Roman annexation of different parts of the peninsula, and the crop repertoire points to continuity. Secondly, it demonstrates that rural settlement changes did not have a major immediate impact on the variables considered here. Unlike broader development in processing technologies and landscape organization, NISP and crop uniquity demonstrate continuity based on the evaluated contexts, with the largest change visible in ritual assemblages. The resolution of these units of analysis may miss finer changes; alternatively, Middle Republican production-and-supply systems may have been geared toward supplying surplus animals to priority contexts, like religious institutions, rather than the broader community. Also missing from this picture is bioarchaeological evidence of military supply – the demands of which are highlighted by Rosenstein's contribution to this volume – due to a lack of materials associated with military camps. Finally, the pronounced changes visible in bioarchaeological evidence during the Late Republic caution against uncritical application of agricultural texts to the Middle Republican period. Political and economic unification, especially following the Punic Wars, led to a significant reorganization of rural production,[124] which is visible in bioarchaeological data. It is at this point that clearer patterns emerge in terms of urban patterns of pork and poultry consumption, and crop-processing debris indicates a more pronounced division of labor.

[123] Motta 2011.   [124] Volpe 1990: 72–4; Aldrete and Mattingly 1999; Brun 2004.

While limited shifts appear to take place in the range of cereals and pulses cultivated, shifts in husbandry practices of the same crops would have major implications for crop productivity and labor organization. These are precisely the type of changes visible in animal management: exploitation focused on the same domestic species, but with new husbandry practices. How intensive or extensive cultivation regimes were over this time period remains to be seen. Farming strategies likely varied throughout the Republican period, perhaps even on a generational scale, based on land availability at different moments of history. Landscape evidence for investments like drainage and irrigation works may point to a bottleneck in land supply during the Middle Republic, which was addressed through local land improvements and campaigns for new territory. In other contexts, including Roman Britain, surplus production was achieved through an extensification of cereal cultivation in combination with an increase in the number of small farms across the landscape.[125] Extensification of arable cultivation and animal husbandry would have exacerbated this process, though it is unclear whether the Middle Republican period was a moment of transition or of crystallization of earlier trends. Wealth acquisition and investment – in land, slaves, iron technology, animal power, and processing equipment – during the sixth and fifth centuries BCE would have positioned affluent producers very differently than more modest farmers. However, this Middle Republican bottleneck may have only lasted a few generations, until Late Republican expansion offered new agricultural opportunities: already in the second century BCE, farms in the reclaimed Pontine Plain were beginning to be abandoned.[126]

These proposals are hypothetical, but nonetheless testable. Weed ecology and stable isotope analysis practices would directly address cultivation regimes by assessing key aspects of husbandry intensity – manuring and tillage.[127] A reanalysis of cattle mortality patterns in conjunction with body-size and biometric trends alongside evidence for traction-relation pathologies could investigate evidence for an expansion of traction and greater use of oxen.[128] Contextual and isotopic analysis, as seen for instance in the Neolithic period at Çatalhöyük, the Medieval period in Britain, and

---

[125] Roman Britain: Smith et al. 2016; Allen and Lodwick 2017; Lodwick et al. 2020. Early Mesopotamian cities: Styring et al. 2017b. Iron Age Germany: Styring et al. 2017a.
[126] De Haas 2017b.
[127] Acosta et al. 2019 have suggested elevated $\delta^{15}N$ values in humans at Archaic Gabii indicate increased manuring of crops. However, elevated nitrogen values can derive from numerous processes. See Szpak 2014. This is now contradicted by measurement of crop isotopes, as see Gavériaux et al. 2022.
[128] Thomas 2008.

recently at Gabii, would help to evaluate these hypotheses.[129] Considering the long-term trajectories seen in the development of agriculture from later prehistory, in Italy this evaluation would be most beneficial if conducted over a long period. Rather than linear developments from late prehistory, there were potentially multiple inflection points and solutions to agricultural provision, even within Republican times.

Ultimately, the means of quantification we have applied here are more able to map networks of similarity than details of agricultural economy. Presence/absence and NISP are powerful and comparable modes of analysis, but are ultimately crude tools for measuring changes in agricultural production and consumption. A more specific and integrated discussion, further work, and better data are required in order to redefine these developments. Going forward, a more nuanced vocabulary for discussing ancient agriculture and land use would be helpful, particularly one which distinguishes "intensive" land use from "intensive" cultivation strategies, and that recognizes the full spectrum of farming regimes.[130] Continued investment in the recovery and analysis of bioarchaeological remains is also required.[131] Studies have shown that charred plant remains are often present but in low densities,[132] which require intensive sampling across many contexts as well as financial investment in the labor and materials needed to process and analyze these samples during archaeological fieldwork. Furthermore, an increase in the quality of data reporting is needed. A lack of quantified data and sample-level reporting inhibits the usefulness of datasets for establishing crop husbandry and processing practices;[133] although the situation in zooarchaeological assemblages is better, access to raw data could also be improved. Hopefully this contribution has made some progress toward identifying research themes that would warrant the time and money required for good bioarchaeological analysis and that offer opportunities for collaboration across a far wider range of sources – isotopes, survey, landscape studies, documentary evidence, ceramics, use-wear and residue analysis, and so on. A more nuanced approach is needed, with as much emphasis on *how* materials are exploited as on *what* is exploited all the way from farm to table.

---

[129] Bogaard et al. 2017; Hamerow et al. 2020; Gavériaux et al. 2022.
[130] See especially van der Veen and O'Connor 1998; Halstead 2014: 238–51; Bowes et al. 2017.
[131] See recommendation in Lentjes 2013.   [132] Jones and Sheldon 1985; Bowes et al. 2017.
[133] Lodwick 2019.

PART III

Architecture and Art

9 No Longer Archaic, Not Yet Hellenistic

Urbanism in Transition

DOMENICO PALOMBI

The complexity of the Middle Republican period for Rome's history reveals itself in the constitutional, political, military, socioeconomical, and cultural dynamics that characterized the period between the Gallic Sack and the first war with Carthage. At the end of the Struggle of the Orders and after the constitution of a renewed patrician–plebeian aristocracy, progressive military affirmation on the peninsula led to the formation of Roman Italy – the *terra Italia* celebrated in 268 BCE with the construction of a temple dedicated to Tellus – establishing the foundations for Roman imperialism in the Mediterranean.[1] This transformation of the power of Rome in both quantitative and qualitative terms was accompanied by a growing awareness of its role in an international political context. Among the many signs of profound changes taking place, the period witnessed the metamorphosis of the image of the city in Greek historiography and ethnography, with what sources understood as the "upgrade" of Rome from an "Etruscan city"/*polis tyrrhenis* into a "Greek city"/*polis hellenis*.[2] This "Greek identity" was initially promoted to strengthen Rome's ties with southern Italian *poleis* against the hegemonic aims of Syracuse, allied with the Gauls. It was later supported by the cities of Magna Graecia and Sicily, which were threatened by Italic populations and by Carthage. It was knowingly accepted and valued by Rome itself, which transformed it into an instrument of self-representation, self-promotion, and finally of legitimate affirmation within the Hellenic world. The final "de-Etruscanization" of Rome would have been accomplished with the conquest of Volsinii (265 BCE), the closure of the Etruscan federal sanctuary of Fanum Voltumnae, and the dissolution of the Etruscan dodecapolis. The acceptance of Rome by Greece was recognized in 228 BCE by admission to the Panhellenic Isthmian Games as a result of intense diplomatic activities with Athens and Corinth. To recall the historian Eric

---

[1] The chapters collected in this volume offer a broad overview of materials and themes on the history of Rome in the fourth and third centuries BCE. On Roman ideological construction of *Terra Italia*, see Giardina 1997; Russo 2012a; 2012b.

[2] On the double identity of Rome (Etruscan and Greek) in Greek ethnography between the invasion of the Gauls allied to the tyrants of Syracuse (387 BCE) and the Roman alliance with Alexander the Molossian (in Italy between 333 and 331 BCE), see Fraschetti 1989; Vanotti 1999.

Hobsbawm's famous paradigm of "the invention of tradition," Rome, the *polis hellenis*, was a propagandistic image built mainly by the invention of complex traditions about its mythical origins and by the construction of articulated connections with places and characters of Greek *epos*.[3] This is a particularly sensitive topic within the context we aim to analyze: It probably represents the most complete manifestation of the process of redefining Archaic Rome's identity which, better than any other political or institutional aspect, qualifies the period we generally call Middle Republican.[4]

How and how much the progressive affirmation of this new image influenced the transformation of the Archaic and Late Archaic city remains very difficult to say. In the face of the scarce archaeological documentation we possess, the historical sources emphasize some aspects of the shape and organization of urban space which were destined to characterize the image of the city for centuries to come.[5]

Let us begin with the chaotic aspect of Rome's urban planning, which tradition attributed to hasty reconstruction following the Gallic fire in 387 BCE (Figure 9.1).[6] This historiographical topos still finds no reliable archaeological confirmation, but it highlights a consciously antithetical ideological orientation with respect to the principles of rational urban planning, experimented and applied in the cities of Greece and elsewhere. In contrast to this tradition, three major infrastructural programs created during the fourth century reveal large-scale urban vision and planning with complex economic and social, as well as technical and operational, implications. First, the immense construction site for the (re)building of the city walls (377–353 BCE) which, with its 11-km perimeter enclosing about 427 hectares, reaffirmed and renewed the shape and image of the Archaic city.[7] Then, the construction of the first aqueducts (Aqua Appia 312; Anio Vetus 272) reveals a qualitative leap in the conception of urban amenities, certainly stimulated by the exponential growth of Rome's population, which more than doubled after the Latin War, according to census data. Finally, the construction of the Via Appia (312) joins a general rationalization of the interregional road system which was directly anchored to the layouts of

---

[3] Hobsbawm and Ranger 1983.
[4] For a new periodization of the Roman Republican age on political and legal criteria, see Flower 2010, with the remarks of Yakobson 2011.
[5] For a recent overview of urbanistic evolution of Rome during the Middle and Late Republican periods, see Palombi 2010. See now the updated dossier in D'Alessio, Smith, and Volpe 2021.
[6] On the Gallic Sack of Rome and its archaeological traces, Delfino 2009; Bernard 2018a: 57–62.
[7] On the walls of Rome, Bernard 2012, with the remarks of Ziolkowski 2016 on its Archaic phase. See now D'Alessio, Smith, and Volpe 2021.

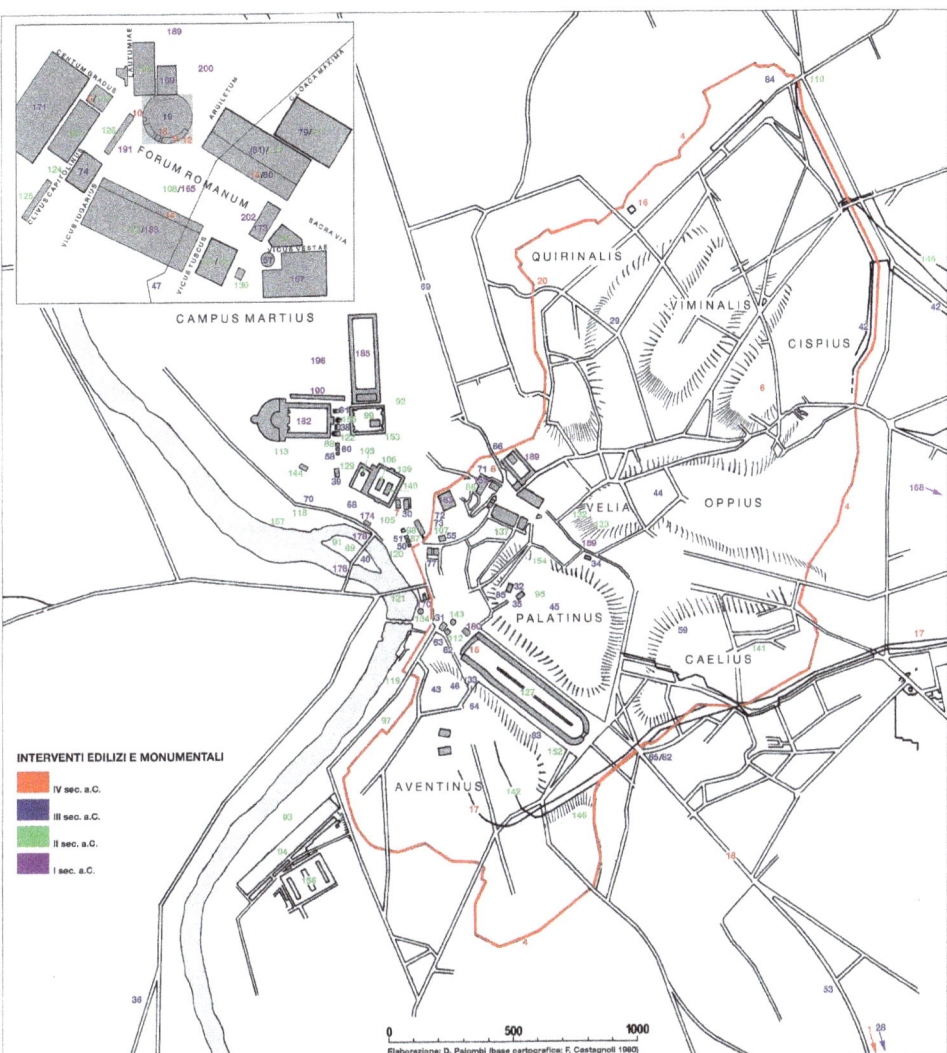

Figure 9.1 Rome, buildings and monuments between fourth and first centuries, after Palombi 2010.

urban roads and constituted a new palimpsest for the organization and exploitation of the *Suburbium*.[8]

Within the city, one can see a tendency toward the functional definition of specific areas: in the significant exclusion of the Aventine from the *pomerium*; in the growing residential occupation of the Palatine; in the

---

[8] For the organization of the Suburb of Rome in the Republican period – roads, aqueducts, settlement – see Pergola, Santangeli Valenzani, and Volpe eds. 2003; Jolivet et al. eds. 2009; Palombi ed. 2019a with previous bibliography.

military and censorial functions reserved for the Campus Martius; in the function of the sacred *arx* assumed by the Capitol which now, following the example of the Greek acropolis model, excluded private residences and obtained an independent fortification.[9] Then, the Forum, after the relocation of traditional craft and commercial activities, acquired the *dignitas* (Varro in Nonius 853L) of a space with not only political and representative, but also economic and financial functions. The Forum, despite the architectural-functional differences detected by Vitruvius (5.1.1–2), expressed the same principles enunciated by Aristotle for the Greek agora (*Politics*, 7.11.2.1331a).[10] Not surprisingly, in the last decades of the fourth century the Comitium – Curia – Carcer complex became a coherent system for the exercise of legislative, executive, and judicial powers. The Comitium, in particular, seems to undergo a series of interventions which, if we still consider Filippo Coarelli's reconstruction valid, transformed the quadrangular, astronomically oriented structure, which had been restored by C. Maenius between 338 and 318 BCE, into a circular building inspired by the *ekklesiasteria* of Greek cities, perhaps during the censorship of Appius Claudius in 312 or, at the latest, during the First Punic War.[11] Also in this updated version, the building complex synthesizes different functions expressing traditional religious values with the sanctuary of *Niger Lapis*, renewed political functions with the tribune of the orators, decorated with the *rostra* of the triumph over the Antiates, and testifies to Rome's recent interests in Mediterranean policy, as revealed by the name *Graecostasis*, assigned to the space of foreign delegations.

[9] For an alternate explanation of the Aventine's continued exclusion from the *pomerium*, see Mignone 2016c. For the different districts of Rome and their urban characters see: Coarelli 1983 and 1985 (*Forum Romanum*); La Rocca 1984 and Coarelli 1997 (*Campus Martius*); Coarelli 1992a (*Forum Boarium*); Palombi 1997 (*Velia, Carinae, Fagutal*); Cecamore 2002 and Coarelli 2012 (*Palatium*); Carandini 2004 and Panella ed. 2013 (northern slopes of *Palatium*); Coarelli 2014 (*Quirinalis, Viminalis*); Palombi 2016 (Republican neighborhoods in the Imperial Forums area); Marcattili 2012; Mignone 2016a; Capodiferro, Mignone, and Quaranta 2017; Prim 2021 (*Aventinum*).

[10] Gros 1996: 450 with recent remarks in Andrews and Bernard 2020, particularly 81.

[11] The shape of the comitium-Curia complex, masterfully reconstructed in Coarelli 1983, is seriously questioned by Carafa 1998: 135–55; Carafa 2005: 135–49; Amici 2004–5; Amici 2007. The functional complexity of this space is discussed, most recently, in Borlenghi 2019; Chillet 2019; and Pina Polo and Rosillo López 2022. The *comitium* of Rome is generally considered the model for comitia of Latin colonies and, necessarily, to be older than their foundation at the end of the fourth and beginning of the third century. See, with different solutions, Coarelli 1998 (263 BCE); Humm 2005: 601–638 (between 338 BCE and the beginning of the third century BCE); Lackner 2008: 260–265 (338 BCE or before); Sewell 2010: 45–7 (Rome is the model of the colonies where it was applied in uncertain chronology). In the broader context of the relationships between urban models in Rome and Latium, see now Palombi 2019b and Cifarelli 2019.

On an urban scale, the making of an imposing network of sanctuaries should be underlined. Especially during the third century, this activity substantially transformed Rome's religious landscape. In fact, after the (approximately) ten sanctuaries founded from the beginning of the Republic to the Gallic Sack, and the seven temples known to have been built throughout the fourth century, forty sacred buildings are known to have been constructed between the beginning of the Third Samnite War and the end of the Second Punic War, an especially impressive tally considering the lacuna of Livy's text, missing for the years 292–219. It is particularly interesting to observe the criteria of distribution, the monumental connections, the theological and ritual contents, and the ceremonial practices of this incredible "explosion of the sacred" that celebrates the military and political affirmation of Rome (and its aristocracy) over Italy and Carthage. All this creates the material and symbolic "web" of the city and represents the most widespread operation of semanticization of the Republican *forma Urbis*.[12]

In these general but not generic indications, one starts to gain the sense of an ongoing transition which continued to recover key elements of the city's Archaic identity (particularly significant is the reconstruction of the fortifications) while introducing forms and functions according to the latest standards common to the most up-to-date urban culture of the Mediterranean (this is particularly visible in the *arx* and Forum). Above all, the sacred dimension dominates: it becomes the most effective locus for the manifestation of the ethical-political values of the new patrician–plebeian aristocracy and for the celebration of the unstoppable military affirmation of Rome.[13] However, as we have seen, the general characteristics of Rome's urban shape are derived, essentially, from the "narration" handed down by ancient literary sources about the city, without proper verification through archaeological data which, for this period, remain punctiform and sporadic, more and more so considering the recent tendency to progressively lower the date of the use of Roman concrete, with direct effects on the relative chronological sequence of buildings of adjacent periods. In this way, considering the fatal attraction of the Archaic period, we risk an "archaeological emptying" of the Middle Republic.[14]

---

[12] Palombi 2021; Padilla Peralta 2020a.
[13] For the cultural paradigms of the Roman nobility: Hölkeskamp 2011 [1987]; Hölkeskamp 2010; Farney 2007.
[14] Mogetta 2015; Davies 2017b. See now the updated dossier on Roman building techniques of the Middle Republican age in Mari 2019.

Ultimately, then, it remains particularly difficult to find the principles of urbanism in terms of planning, zoning, architectural and functional models that define and identify the "idea of the city" developed by Rome at this crucial historical moment.

And yet, Rome in the fourth and third centuries BCE promoted an intense colonization policy, first in Latium and then in the different regions of conquered Italy, with the creation of new cities of great "modernity": *coloniae civium romanorum* and *coloniae latinae*, founded after the fateful events of 338 BCE. Their formal and functional components, also applied to the renewal of existing cities in different cultural contexts on the peninsula, reveal a clear program of urban planning. We are used to considering this extraordinary process, which must be read with the establishment of a widespread infrastructural network and a rational territorial organization, as an expression of "urban models" conceived of and imposed by Rome. In turn, Rome is considered the unique depository, processor, and promoter of a stratified patrimony of urbanistic practices of Etruscan and, above all, Greek origin.[15] On the contrary, it is worth questioning how these practices reflected the Roman experience and how much they expressed the synthesis of wider experimentation involving different Italic cultures, starting from the Archaic period. In fact, the evolution of the urban phenomenon cannot be understood from a unilateral perspective, as in Etruscans *versus* Romans/Greeks *versus* Romans/Romans *versus* Italic; rather, it must be evaluated within the complex relationships of different cultural traditions and in their diversified capacity for dialogue and correlation with the Greek world.[16]

In this perspective, *Latium vetus* represents a special case for consideration: for the precociousness of its urban phenomenon and its cultural contacts with Greece; for its geographical proximity to Rome and common culture; for its early political integration and massive participation in Roman colonization; and for the extraordinary cultural vivacity that Latium displays in every historical era and context. In fact, it appears more and more evident that the urban models of colonization applied by Rome in the fourth and third centuries were largely inspired by the urban experiences of the Latins who, since the Archaic period and in very diverse geographical settings, had developed principles and practices for organizing and structuring a city. With a daring reversal of perspective, then, with respect to what is usually argued, it could be said that Rome did not

---

[15] In this perspective, see also the rich critical synthesis of Sewell 2010.
[16] As well expressed in Lippolis 2016.

"Romanize" Latium but that Rome "Latinized" Italy, assuming from the Latin cities the urbanistic and architectural characteristics with which it founded or refounded new colonies: criteria of settlements, areal organization, architectural models, and the use of materials and construction techniques.

The Middle Republican period was particularly important in the history of the cities of Latium, situated after the Archaic and Late Archaic urban formations, the age of the region's first imposing fortifications in stone and tuff, and before the extraordinary Late Republican monumentalization, the epoch of concrete and of great sacred and public monuments: the relevant urbanistic phase in the fourth and third centuries involved, mainly, city walls and gates, streets and layout, substructions and terraces, and sacred buildings.[17]

Latin cities appear dissimilar in relation to the different geographical contexts of their settlements, as is clearly evident in the distinction between "cities of tuff" and "cities of limestone."[18] By contrast, they do not reveal significant differences with respect to the different political conditions assumed after their annexation into the Roman state. Together, they highlight some common tendencies, which seem to indicate the permanence of traditional urban values and, at the same time, an openness to new experiences, sometimes similar to and at other times significantly divergent from Rome.

The continuity that the cities of Latium, including Rome, manifested with respect to their original shape is very impressive. Certainly, the restoration of essential components of the Archaic urban landscape represents the optimization of urban plans conceived from the beginning as largely predictive, but whose significance in the construction of urban identity and in their value to cultural memory should not be underestimated. This is particularly evident in the case of the city walls, which in fourth- and third-century Latium were restored with the addition of new gates, generally arched, and towers or bastions according to recent tendencies of Hellenistic poliorcetics. Only in Tibur and Ardea were fortifications completely rebuilt during the fourth century.[19] Consequently, the

---

[17] In the last thirty years, our knowledge of the ancient Latium has been enormously increased thanks to the continuous research and documentation activities of many colleagues that would be impossible to mention here; for an updated bibliography on the urbanism of the *Latium vetus*, let me refer the reader to Palombi 2019b.

[18] These effective definitions, owed to Cifarelli, summarize well the double geographical conditions of the cities of the *Latium vetus*, with direct reflections on the shape, consistency, and characteristics of their urban structures; see Cifarelli 2019.

[19] On the city walls in the *Latium vetus*, see Gatti and Palombi 2016 and Quilici and Quilici Gigli 2019.

extension and the network of roads of these Archaic cities were generally confirmed, with very consistent solutions with respect to the positioning of gates and the main functional areas (sanctuaries, Forum, *arx*).

In addition to the "linear" crossing scheme, common in settlements on both tuffaceous and calcareous plateaus from Lavinium to Gabii and Norba, are more complex solutions for sites with conditioning orography, from the steep gradients of Lanuvium and Signia to the original scissor path that climbs Cora's limestone cone (Figure 9.2).

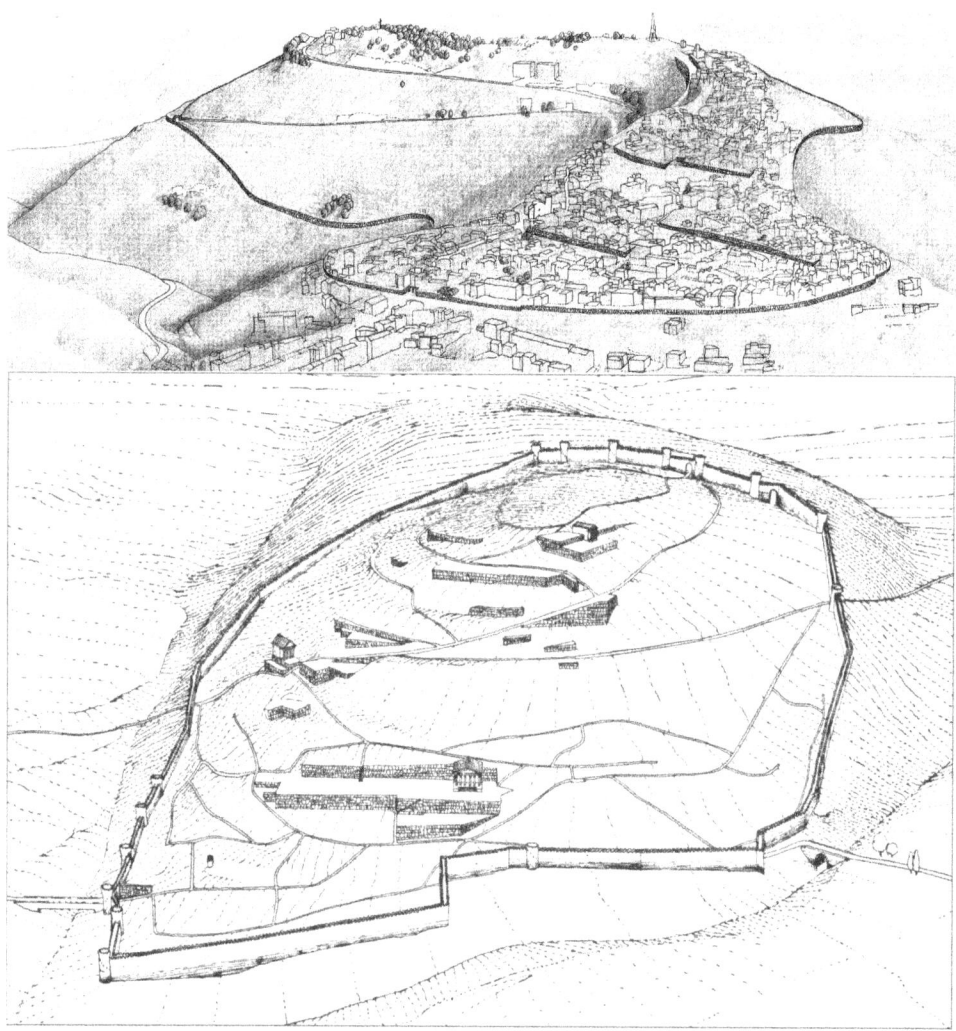

Figure 9.2 Signia and Cora after Cifarelli 2017; Palombi 2003.

Just two cases show significant changes to the extension of Archaic cities: Ardea excluded from its new fortifications a part of the larger ancient settlement, while Aricia and Praeneste extended the inhabited area to include (in the case of the Via Appia) or to connect with (in the case of the Via Praenestina) the interregional road system.

Even the main Archaic components of zoning were generally confirmed and enhanced with demanding architectural interventions. This is the case of the *arces* which, already identified and qualified by important Archaic and Late Archaic sanctuaries, only now obtained wide urban and functional structures that characterized them as fortified citadels, amplifying their representative character and defining their substantial strategic and defensive role. The polygonal terraces, which broadened and regularized the Acropolis of Signia around the Archaic temple of Iuno Moneta, or the complete reconstruction of the Acropolis of Lanuvium around the Archaic sanctuary of Iuno Sospita, are good examples of this trend.

The areas of these cities' *fora* are for the moment elusive subjects. Affected by the reconstructions of the late Hellenistic period, they preserve only scarce evidence of more ancient urban planning, but generally appear to confirm their Archaic position with labor-intensive enlargements and regularization.[20] With regard to continuity, the case of Lavinium is particularly significant. Here, around the Forum, from the sixth century to the imperial period, with an urban arrangement dated right at the beginning of the third century BCE, public buildings were constructed one next to another, with minimal changes of orientation and position. Also emblematic is the case of Cora, where a progressive and rational evolution of the Forum's area is documented: to the Archaic terrace wall of the first type of polygonal masonry, in the Middle-to-Late Republican period builders added a second terrace in polygonal masonry of the third type, which would be further extended at the end of the second century BCE with a huge arched concrete substructure.[21] The Forum of Tusculum also received its trapezoidal shape between the end of the fourth and the first half of the third century thanks to a series of isodomic terrace walls. Around the square there were perhaps residential buildings underneath the theater, sacred structures on the opposite side, and a public building on the southern side. The last, which preceded the basilica constructed in the middle of the first century, was an unusual *porticus* built in the third century with Doric columns and a floor of tuff slabs. The *porticus* of

---

[20] The *fora* of the central Italy cities are analyzed in detail by Etxebarria Akaiturri 2008 and Lackner 2008.

[21] For the types or *maniere* of polygonal masonry, see Lugli 1957 with Gatti and Palombi 2016.

Tusculum's Forum, a real *stoa* in the Greek tradition, contradicts the widespread conviction that this spatial and functional element, especially in *fora*, appeared only in the second century.[22]

The question of the definition of the public square is particularly tricky in relation to urban planning, which characterized the *fora* of new Latin colonies (Figure 9.3). The well-known examples of Fregellae (328 BCE), Alba Fucens (303 BCE), Cosa, and Paestum (273 BCE) display rectangular squares surrounded by buildings and structures for specialized political, religious, commercial, and representative functions. The origin of the "model" of the colonial Forum is for the most part traced back to architectural typologies developed in Rome independent of Greek models.[23] However, while the "Roman model" of the complex Curia-Comitium seems to be contradicted by recent research, there are no comparisons in Latin cities.[24] Certainly, standardization and application in newly founded colonies were promoted by Rome which, by adapting architectural typologies from Magna Graecia (the relationship between circular *comitia* and *ekklesiasteria* is given for certain), created innovative urban-planning solutions. What contribution the urban culture of the cities of Latium made to this process of renewal of the Forum's space between the end of the fourth century and the third century, it is not yet possible to say.

A final observation must be made about the pervasive presence of the sacred which, in Latin cities as well as in Rome, assumed a character of capillary and polycentric diffusion, a "religious landscape" evocative of Livy's famous statement about the presence of religion in the urban space of Rome: "there is no place in it that is not full of religiosity and gods" (Livy 5.52.2).[25] It should be underlined, however, that there is a striking difference between the two contexts relating to the practice of worship and its manifestations: The widespread presence of votive deposits, which characterized the religious landscape of Latium, has no equal at Rome, where the practice and treatment of votive gifts would seem to show significantly different characteristics. It should also be noted that the extraordinary increase of temple building that characterized the *Urbs* in the fourth and above all in the third century was not paralleled in Latin cities, which at the same time appear rather engaged in the restoration of older sanctuaries, as documented from the general reconstruction of fictile decorations. At the moment we know of only one Latin shrine in this period built *ex novo* (probably the temple of Hercules in Lanuvium). Paradoxically, moreover,

---

[22] Sewell 2010: 64–7 speaks of "rejection of the stoa concept."
[23] Sewell 2013 with bibliography. [24] See above, n. 11.
[25] For an overall critical review of the sacred contexts of the *Latium vetus*, see now di Fazio 2019a.

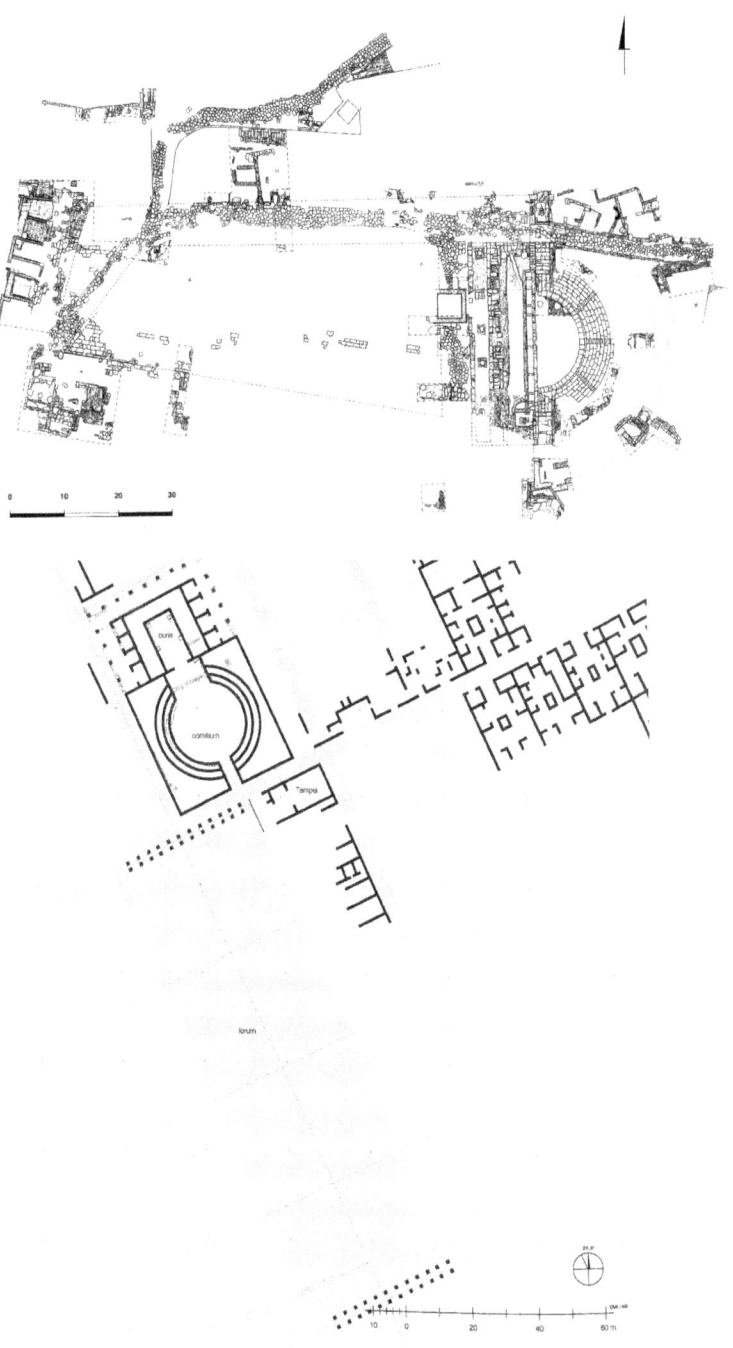

Figure 9.3 The *fora* of Tusculum and Fregellae, after Dupré and Aquilué Abadías 2002; Lackner 2008.

little or nothing is known about the shape of places of worship which would become the great Hellenistic sanctuaries of Latium from the second half of the second century on. Indeed, without literary and epigraphic sources, it remains very difficult to identify the occasions (political, military, social) and promoters (Latins and/or Romans?) in this crucial moment in the urban history of ancient Latium.

On the whole, the innovations of Latin architecture and urbanism manifested on a decidedly larger scale, involving both the shape and the very "idea of the city," which was further developed in the Middle Republic. First of all, we should mention the imposing terraces, which created homogeneous urban sectors on planimetric and altimetric levels. Designed mainly for the monumentalization of *arces* and *fora*, these Middle Republican terraces also supported and regularized roads and neighborhoods of mixed public, sacred, and private functions. The orography of the majority of Latin cities favored the development of these impressive "Italic terraces," long recognized as a basic element of the central Italic urban conception. They expressed already in a very early age the natural scenographic vocation of the cities of Latium, long before their maximum manifestations through contact with the late Hellenistic urban and architectural culture.[26]

Equally innovative, but scarcely valued by scholarship, is a further trend regarding the cities of ancient Latium, which was destined to have important consequences for the urban planning of newly founded colonies. The program of Latin colonization promoted by Rome after 338 BCE applied fully developed principles of regular urban planning, which show an "idea of city" that certainly could not be found in contemporary Rome. In line with what was occurring in the wider Mediterranean, Latin cities show a precocious interest in experimenting with regular urban planning, albeit with different local variations and solutions, based on an ancient Italic *substratum* and completed with reference to the "Hippodamian models" (elongated building blocks) visible in southern Italy.[27] If it is no longer possible to think simplistically of a direct and mechanical adoption of Greek urban schemes by Rome in planning new colonies, it is worth considering a more articulated context for the elaboration and application of this new idea of the city, a context in which to evaluate the possible contribution of Latin urban culture. In fact, a clear tendency toward the application of principles of regular urban planning can also be found in the ancient cities of the *Latium vetus* which, in the same period of the fourth

---

[26] Gullini 1983.   [27] Castagnoli 1971; Sewell 2010: 11–13.

and third centuries, recreated (or planned for the first time?) more or less extensive parts of towns.[28] This clearly happened in Ardea, where the central part of the town assumed an orthogonal layout during the fourth century (or even from the fifth century BCE), in Aricia, perhaps coinciding with the inclusion within the urban boundaries of the new Via Appia, and also in Tibur in the district of Colle San Paolo, with a *terminus ante quem* in the second century.

More generally, it is possible to find a similar tendency toward rational urban planning even in some parts of cities with very complex orography. The area of the Forum of Praeneste shows a regular design around the temple of the cathedral, dated to the fourth century. Also at Cora, the terraces of the Forum are arranged according to a very coherent geometric scheme and orientation. Equally in Signia, the urban terraces have a tendentially regular disposition. At Lanuvium, finally, a regular pattern seems recognizable under the medieval town planning in the area assigned to the Forum of the ancient city.

Among these examples, the anonymous city of Piano della Civita di Artena stands out (Figure 9.4). In the great urban center built at the beginning of the third century, the regular planning of the walls in polygonal masonry and the rational zoning show the full maturity of an urban project strikingly similar to the Latin colonies of that period. Upon closer inspection, even the most ancient cities of the Latium manifest the general principles of regular urban planning as shown today by the "quasi orthogonal" planning of Gabii, dated to the end of the fifth or beginning of the fourth century, where elongated blocks were arranged following the main street, which crosses the inhabited area around the lake. Between Gabii and Civita of Artena in date, the example of Norba seems to represent the largest regular urban-planning laboratory in Latium. The city of Norba, in fact, was characterized by multiple layers, which are testimony to the different phases of urban planning, starting with the foundation of the colony in 492 BCE and developed in the fourth and third centuries (Figure 9.5).[29]

The combination of these examples clearly reveals the participation of Latins in the regular urban-planning experimentation which, with various formal solutions and for a long chronological period, involved the Greek world and different urban cultures of the Mediterranean. In the Latin cities, this trend was accompanied by the renovation of infrastructure and by the

---

[28] Mogetta 2014; Palombi 2019b: 135–42, with documentation and bibliography.
[29] For a recent synthesis on the complex (and still very much debated) urban stratigraphy of Norba, see Quilici Gigli 2019.

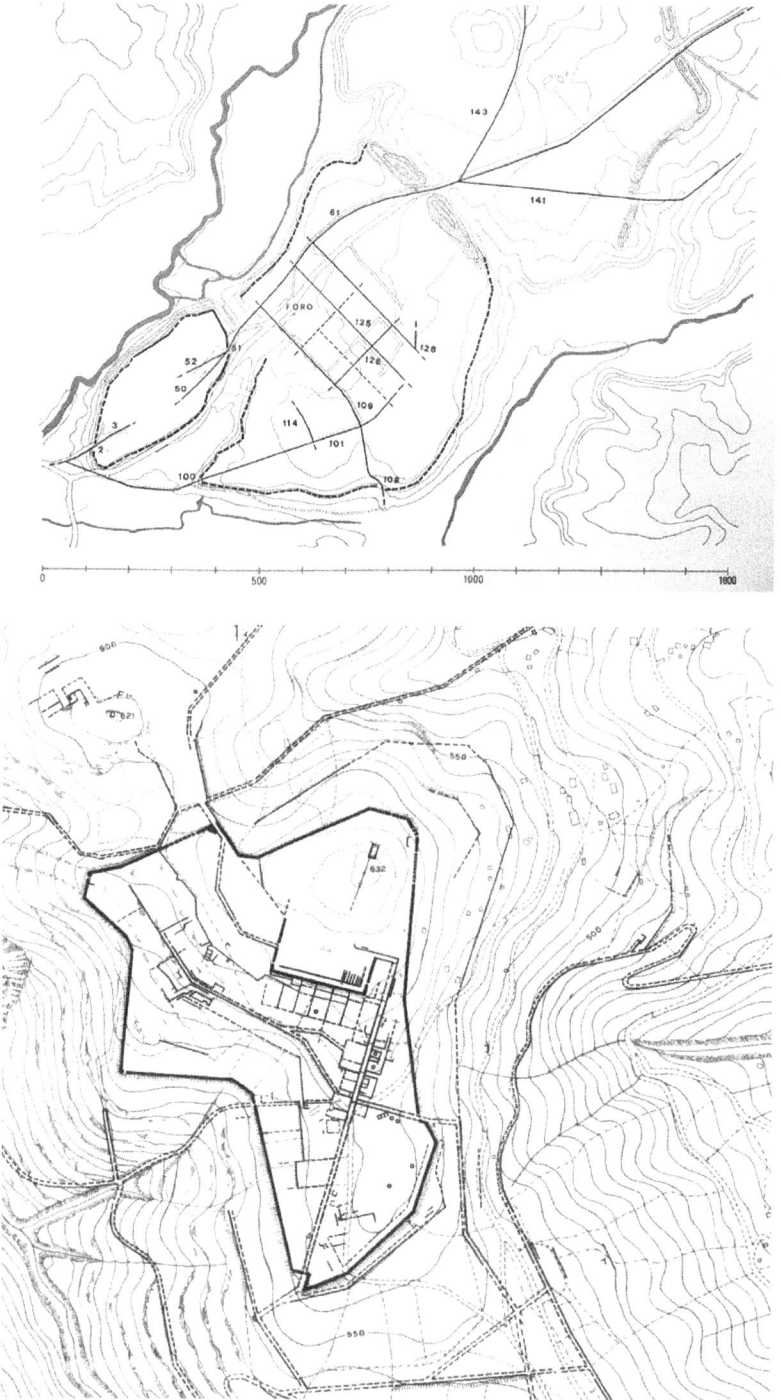

Figure 9.4 Ardea and Civita di Artena after Morselli and Tortorici 1982; Quilici 1982.

9 *Urbanism in Transition* 207

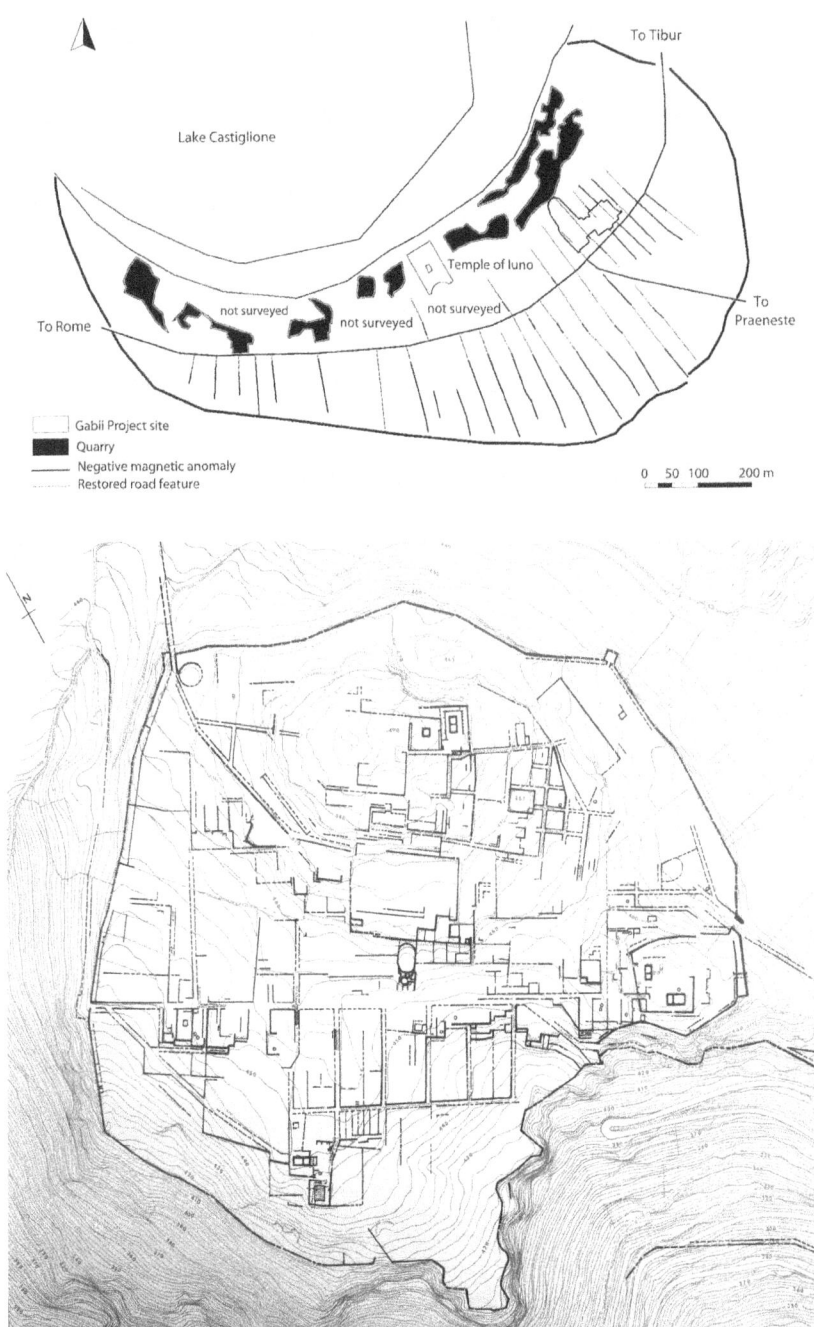

Figure 9.5 Gabii and Norba after Mogetta 2014; Quilici Gigli 2019.

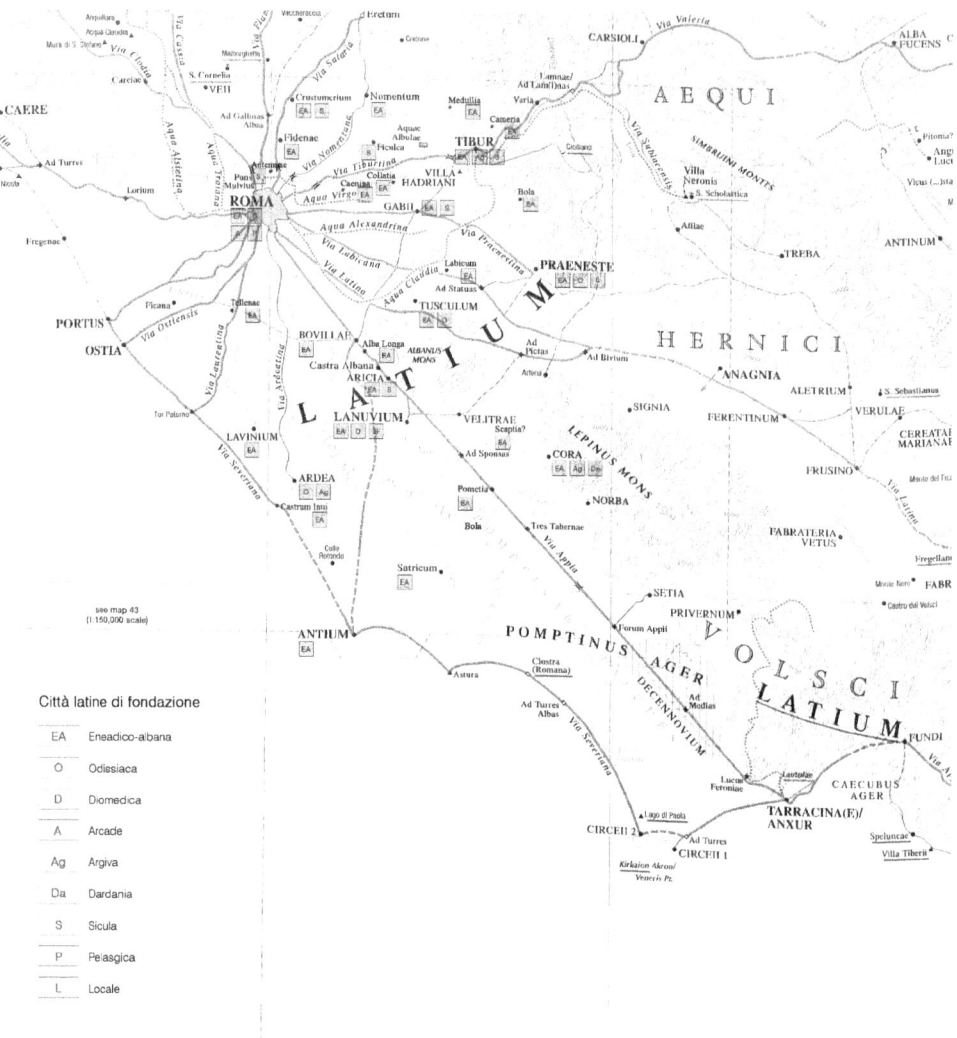

Figure 9.6 Greek mythical origins of the cities of the *Latium vetus*, after Palombi 2019b.

creation of spectacular terraces monumentalizing the main functional areas of the cities. These were signs of a sort of modernity that, however, recovered the shape and basic components of original urban structures, poised between tradition and innovation. These were cities no longer Archaic but not yet Hellenistic, engaged in a significant renewal that expressed the cultural and ideological necessities that matured in this crucial moment in the history of ancient Latium, between the last phases of political independence and the first phase of participation in the construction of Roman Italy.

It is generally assumed that this phenomenon was the direct consequence of Roman conquest, but this is a Roman-centric vision that does not consider the complexity of the role of Latium in the Italian and international political arena: the alliance of some Latin cities with Syracuse and the Gauls against Rome; the centuries-old resistance to Volscian pressure; the defense of Latium's autonomy from Rome until the renewal of the *Foedus Cassianum* (358); the consequences of the second Treaty between Rome and Carthage for the control of Latium (348); the dissolution of the Latin League (338); and the constitutional redefinition of the subject communities and their inclusion in the political, military, and economic dynamics of Rome. At the same time, we must consider the local repercussions of wars against Samnites, the presence in Italy of the armies of Alexander the Molossian and that of Pyrrhus, and the clash with Carthage that brought Hannibal to Latium and the gates of Rome. Evidently, these were particularly favorable circumstances for reconsidering the meaning, function, and organization of cities.

Not by chance, this urbanistic renewal was accompanied by the elaboration of an extraordinary mythological heritage, which linked the cities of *Latium vetus* to the Greek *epos*, as an effective instrument of cultural and political identity within the relationships of the Latin world with Rome and also with the Italic populations and Greek cities of southern Italy and Sicily (Figure 9.6).[30] The Middle Republic, in fact, was the era in which not only Rome upgraded to *polis hellenis* but also Latin cities transformed into *poleis hellenides*, within a material and cultural transition that would have been the base of Rome's urbanism in Italy. The communities of ancient Latium must have held a primary role in the process of conquest and "Romanization" of the peninsula, a process, which, because of its dynamics, manifestations, and outcomes, would be more correctly defined as "Latinization."

---

[30] Palombi 2018.

10 | On Architecture's Agency in Fourth-Century Rome

PENELOPE J. E. DAVIES

At the heart of the construction of history lies the question of periodization: the imposition of chronological matrices on broad swaths of past time. When considering the Roman Republic in its entirety, there are numerous challenges in selecting criteria for this task, challenges that are exacerbated for the fifth and fourth centuries BCE by a poverty of sources, both documentary and archaeological. On the whole, scholars privilege political, legal, and military landmarks, and most designate a break between fifth and fourth centuries (with the so-called Struggle of the Orders, the publication of the Twelve Tables in 451/450 BCE, the Licinio-Sextian Laws of 367/366 BCE, and conflict within Latium) on the one hand, and the end of the fourth century BCE and the beginning of the third on the other (conflict with the Samnites, the emergence of a new *nobilitas* or political elite predicated on personal merit rather than inherited status or specialized religious knowledge; the introduction of plebeians to the major priestly colleges with the *lex Ogulnia* of 300 BCE; and the *lex Hortensia* of 287 BCE).[1] Archaeologists approaching the issue from an urbanistic perspective see a similar break, usually following the censorship of Appius Claudius in 312 BCE, as members of the new political elite turned to the monumental landscape for self-representation.[2] This essay assesses the Middle Republic from an architectural perspective, but rather than characterizing buildings and the broader cityscape as a reflection of political change, as scholars usually do, I explore their agency in effecting such change. Moreover, bearing in mind that time maps, imposed from a chronological distance, are inherently artificial, I question whether Romans were conscious, at the time, of a new era dawning. Circumstantial evidence pertaining to their architecture supports a hypothesis that, at least by the later Republic, they were.

---

[1] Flower 2010: 44–52; Livy 6.15–20, *Per.* 11; Diod. Sic. 15.35.3; Pliny, *Natural History* 16.37; Gellius, *NA* 15.27.4. Also Cornell 1995: 330–40; Brennan 2000; Forsythe 2005: 211–12, 259–69; North 2006: 264; Von Ungern-Sternberg 2005 [1986]; Lintott 1999: 38.

[2] For example, Torelli 2007.

10.1 Object Agency, Object-Scapes

Prevailing anthropocentric views of the world envision society as shaped and reproduced solely through the agency and intentionality of humans, who are themselves formed and constrained by their society. Art and other objects are merely passive products of human agents; designed to exert psychological and physical influence on humans, they may embody diverse intentionalities and mediate social agency, but participate in history only inasmuch as they serve human schemes, whether as instrument or as representation.[3] By contrast, foregrounding object agency entails recognizing that humans (and human agency) are partly formed through their interactions with objects, on both a conscious and an unconscious level. Objects can even constitute new social contexts, universes of their own to which people need to adapt.[4] Taken en masse, objects make up what Miguel John Versluys and others term object-scapes: repertoires of material culture – defined by material and stylistic characteristics and available at certain sites in certain periods – which shape human behavior.[5] People are socialized, Ian Hodder argues, into the object-scapes that pre-exist their birth; they "crystallize out in the interstices between objects, taking up the space allowed them by the object world," to quote Gosden's poetic formulation. Objects that surround them in childhood formulate their attitudes to and assumptions about the world, just as the built environment into which they are born conditions them to internalize a system of spatial and social rules.[6] The impact object-scapes exert is all the more powerful for being unconsciously absorbed rather than formally learned.[7] Objects are also fundamental to change: As Versluys puts it, new styles of object and new materials can challenge the limits of the known, forcing new questions and perspectives, readying the way for new practices.[8] Gosden concludes, "If one is interested in how objects shape people and their social relations, then periods in which objects change their forms and types markedly should be of considerable interest."[9] At the same time, critics caution against reductionism.[10] Somewhere between the humanist and the antihumanist stance, then, exists what Andrew Pickering terms a *post-humanist* option, which posits more complex, mutual dependencies

---

[3] Gell 1998; Hoskins 2006; Van Oyen and Pitts 2017: 12.
[4] Gosden 2005: 193–4; Hoskins 2006; Van Oyen and Pitts 2017: 15; Versluys 2017: 191.
[5] Versluys 2017: 196–7; also Gosden 2005: 208.   [6] Hodder 1979, 1982; also Gosden 2005: 197.
[7] Gosden 2005: 202; also Versluys 2017: 194.   [8] Versluys 2017: 191.   [9] Gosden 2005: 197.
[10] Mol 2017: 170.

between objects and humans, sometimes described as entanglements or the dance of agency.[11]

In Roman architectural history, object agency has played a powerful if underacknowledged role at least since William MacDonald's masterful study of the poetics of form of 1982, which explored how buildings of the Late Republican and imperial periods moved visitors physically and psychologically.[12] Others have furthered his approach, among them Diane Favro, who assesses the urban image of Augustan Rome using Kevin Lynch's model for reading cities, and John Clarke, who explores the influence of decorative ensembles – paintings and mosaics – on human movement inside houses in Roman Italy.[13] Still, in archaeology as a discipline, objects continue to play a secondary role to humans. Their formal aspects are typically understood to chart cultural change rather than effecting it.[14] As Roland Fletcher notes, there is a broad acceptance

> that beyond the basics of description, the proper way to refer to and comprehend the materiality of urbanism is through verbalized meanings that observers and users attach to it. Curiously, materials are treated as an epiphenomenon of what people say about it and claim they do with it, as if the words are more "real" than the actual material.[15]

In Roman archaeology more specifically, built forms in the provinces are often interpreted as markers of "Romanization" or local resistance, but less attention is paid to the sensory and emotional effects that new types of buildings in novel landscapes might have exerted on those who experienced them.[16] And overall, the mass of historical data on the Roman world has allowed focus to linger especially easily on human agency.[17] This focus merits challenging, especially for the Early Republic, when monuments were the principal purveyors of information and narrators of history. Public architecture, I contend, bore heavily on contemporaneous political thought, and had the capacity to establish a climate for human action.

10.2 Rome's Fourth- and Early-Third-Century Object-Scapes

Much remains unknown about Rome's monumental object-scape in the mid-fourth century BCE. Piecing together archaeological and literary evidence, it seems that most construction appears to have dated back to the

---

[11] Pickering 2010; Van Oyen and Pitts 2017: 15.   [12] MacDonald 1982.
[13] Favro 1996; Clarke 1991.   [14] Van Oyen 2017: 134.   [15] Fletcher 2010: 461.
[16] Gosden 2005: 199.   [17] Mol 2017: 170.

late regal or earliest Republican period; new construction was sporadic. Temples were the dominant type of public building, designed in a relatively uniform central Italic style exemplified by the Temple of Castor, vowed in c. 496 BCE (Figure 10.1). Characteristic features included a high podium, frontal steps, and columns on the façade; only the Temple of Jupiter Optimus Maximus, dedicated at the end of the sixth century BCE, is known to have had lateral columns. Columns were likely Tuscan rather than Doric, and arranged in what the Augustan architect Vitruvius would later term an areostyle scheme (with wide intercolumniations, usually measuring over *four* lower-column diameters). A wooden entablature was sheathed with ornamental terracotta revetments; a tympanum wall was recessed, leaving an open pediment, its sloping floor tiled and decorated with antefixes. There were no pedimental sculptures, but terracotta ornaments crowned the building.[18] Temples of this kind graced the principal political, religious, and commercial centers: the Capitoline (e.g. the Temple of Jupiter Optimus Maximus), the Forum (the late-sixth-century-BCE Temple of Saturn and the Temple of Castor), the Forum Boarium (e.g. the Temples of Fortuna and Mater Matuta), and the Aventine zone (the Temples of Diana and Mercury, for instance).[19] The Campus Martius was

Figure 10.1 Temple of Castor, phase I, reconstruction c.496 BCE. Drawn by John Burge.

---

[18] The archaic temple at S. Omobono appears to have had a closed pediment, but this had been destroyed a long time before this period.

[19] On the Temple of Castor: Nielsen and Poulsen eds. 1992. Archaic temples more broadly: Davies 2017a: 9–29, with bibliography.

largely undeveloped, except for the archaic *ovile*, a rectilinear wooden enclosure used for elections, the nearby Altar of Mars, attributed to the regal period, and the Villa Publica of unknown form, established as a headquarters by the first censors in c.435 BCE.[20] On the northwest edge of the Forum was the Comitium, an archaic venue for popular assemblies and for voting, and which had a more-or-less trapezoidal form.[21] On its southern rim was a rectilinear speakers' platform, and on its north side the Curia Hostilia, which Romans attributed to Tullus Hostilius; rectangular in plan, it was used for meetings of the senate. On either long side of the Forum were shops of the archaic period, possibly set into the fronts of houses; just beyond the east end was the Regia, a trapezoidal complex with a courtyard lined with rooms; also originating in the regal period, by the early fifth century BCE it was in its fifth construction phase.[22] In the valley between the Aventine and Palatine hills to the south was the Circus

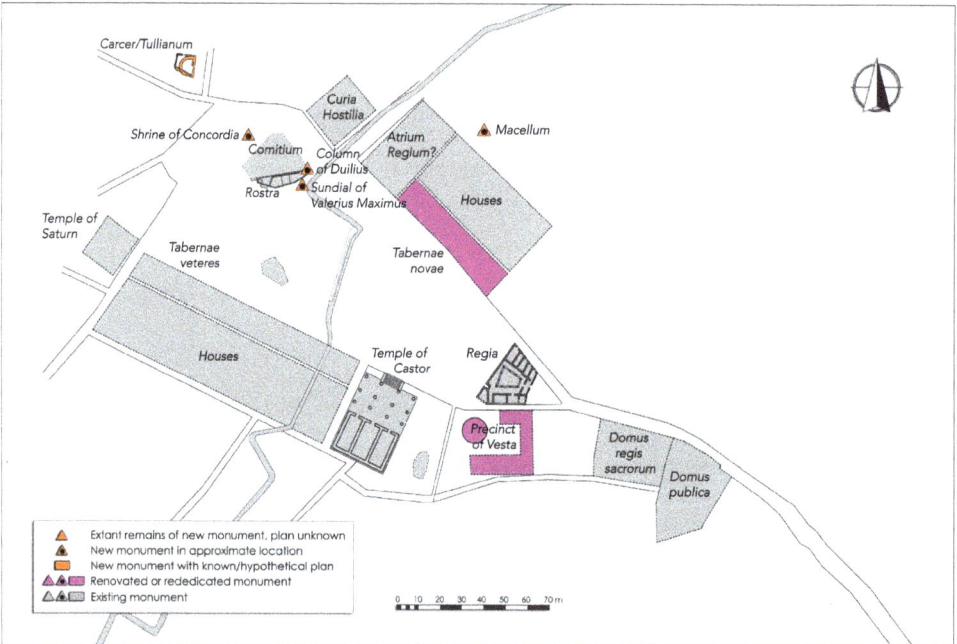

Figure 10.2 Forum Romanum and environs, plan, c.337–218 BCE. Drawn by Penelope J. E. Davies and Onur Öztürk.

[20] Varro *Res Rust*. 3.2; Livy 26.22.11; Castagnoli 1947, 148ff.; Taylor 1966; Richardson 1992: 278; Coarelli 1997: 155–64; Davies 2017a: 35.
[21] Carafa 2005: 139.
[22] Brown 1935: 1967, 1974–5; Downey 1995; *LTUR* 4 189–92, *s. v.* Regia (R. T. Scott); Winter 2009: 350–1, 210; Hopkins 2016: 39–48, 144, with bibliography; Davies 2017a: 9–12. On an adjacent

Maximus, defined in the sixth century by earthworks and wooden seating.[23] From c.378 BCE, massive fortification walls, prompted by the Gallic incursion, surrounded the city.[24] For the most part, buildings were constructed of locally quarried *cappellaccio* (*tufo del Palatino*) and Monteverde (*tufo lionato* from the west bank of the Tiber) until the defeat of Veii in 396 BCE, when Grotta Oscura (*tufo giallo della via Tiberina*) was deployed on a large scale for the walls.[25] As Seth Bernard argues, labor specialization accompanied the importation of this new stone, which was its own form of industrial revolution, but public building was probably still achieved by corvée (labor required of the population as a tax).[26]

By the end of the century, Rome's object-scape looked startlingly different. In incremental changes, established spaces had been reconfigured. Around 338 BCE, a curved *Rostra* replaced the rectilinear speakers' platform (Figures 10.2 and 10.3). Steps adorned its long north side and on the south were mounted battering rams taken from enemy ships in the Battle of Antium.[27] In 318 BCE, perhaps, the butchers' shops on the northeast side of the Forum were relocated further north, and the vacated shops refitted as *tabernae argentariae* for bankers or silversmiths; above them were built wooden galleries, known as *maenianae*. By 308 BCE the shops boasted shields captured in the Second Samnite War for ornament.[28] In the Circus Maximus, starting gates (probably unroofed wooden stalls with mechanisms to improve fairness in races) were installed in 329 BCE.[29] Added to these reconfigurations was a surge of new construction, spread across a broad swath of the city (Figure 10.4, showing monument distribution). In the short space of time from c. 350 to 300 BCE, approximately eight temples and shrines were constructed (to Juno Moneta, c. 345 BCE; Quirinus, c. 325 or 309 BCE; Salus, c. 311 BCE; Victoria, c. 305 BCE; Concordia, 304 BCE; and Portunus, Hora, and Vesta in the late fourth century BCE), and as many as seven more

---

building: Carettoni 1978–80; Coarelli 1983; Carandini 1988: 360–73; Scott 1993a: 11–13, 1993b: 165–6, Scott ed. 2009: 9–11; *LTUR* 2 169–70, *s. v.* Domus Regis sacrorum/sacrificuli (E. Papi); Arvanitis 2004: 58–9, 147–8.

[23] Livy 1.35.8; *De Vir. Illust. 3l.* 6.8; Eutrop. *Brev.* 1.6; Dion. Hal. 4.44.1; Humphrey 1986: 64–7; Marcattili 2009; Bernstein 2011.

[24] Bernard 2018a, with bibliography.

[25] An important exception was the archaic temple beneath Sant' Omobono, where Anio tuff was used for the podium: Brocato et al. 2019.

[26] Bernard 2012: 77–90 and *passim*; 2018.

[27] Amici 2004–5: 354–9; also Coarelli 1985: 11–22; Carafa 1998; Livy 8.14.12; Cornell 1995: 349; Davies 2017a.

[28] Fest. 120 L; Varro, frag. 72 apud Non. 853 L.

[29] Livy 8.20.2; also Enn. in Cic. *Div.* 1.108; Varro, *LL* 5.153; Humphrey 1986: 133, 157–70; Marcattili 2009: 160–1.

Figure 10.3 Rostra, reconstruction with ships' prows, c.338 BCE. Drawn by John Burge.

in the next decade (to Aesculapius, 293–291 BCE; Bellona, 296 BCE; Jupiter Stator, 294 BCE; Fors Fortuna, 293 BCE; Venus Obsequens, 292–291 BCE; Jupiter Fulgur and Temple C, Largo Argentina, between 292 and 217 BCE).[30] And with this construction came new building types: Rome's first monumental road, the Via Appia, and its first aqueduct, the Aqua Appia, both begun in 312 BCE under the sponsorship of censor Appius Claudius (see de Haas in this volume, Chapter 7).[31] Familiar monument types, too, had novel designs, which were evident in details – such as the first *cyma reversa* molding known in Rome, at Temple C in Largo Argentina around the turn of the fourth to the third century BCE (Figure 10.5) – as in broader schemes.[32] The Palatine Temple of Victoria, begun after 305 BCE by L. Postumius Megellus, had a more elongated footprint than earlier temples (approximately 19.35 × - 33.40 m, or roughly 3:5, compared with the Temple of Castor's 27.5 × 37–40 m, or roughly 3:4–4.5), and the first known lateral columns in 200 years (Figure 10.6). More remarkable still, its intercolumniations were dramatically narrowed, to Vitruvius' sistyle (equal to two lower-column diameters) or eustyle (two and a quarter column diameters), a change that was probably effected to support a stone entablature. Found nearby, terracotta sculptural

[30] In general, Davies 2017a; also Padilla Peralta 2020a.
[31] Via Appia: Staveley 1959; MacBain 1980: 361–4; Humm 1996: 704, 716–24, 744–6, 2005: 491–3; Laurence 1999: 15–18. Aqua Appia: Front. *Aq.* 5, also 65.3; Livy 9.29; Diod. Sic. 20.36; Eutr. 2.9.2; *Vir. ill.* 34.6–7; Paul. Fest. 23 L; Van Deman 1934: 23–8; Ashby 1935: 49–54; Evans 1994: 65–74; Hodge 1992: 5–7; De Kleijn 2001: 10–12; Humm 2005: 493.
[32] Shoe Merritt and Edlund-Berry 2000, 1: 23, 146, II: xlv.1.

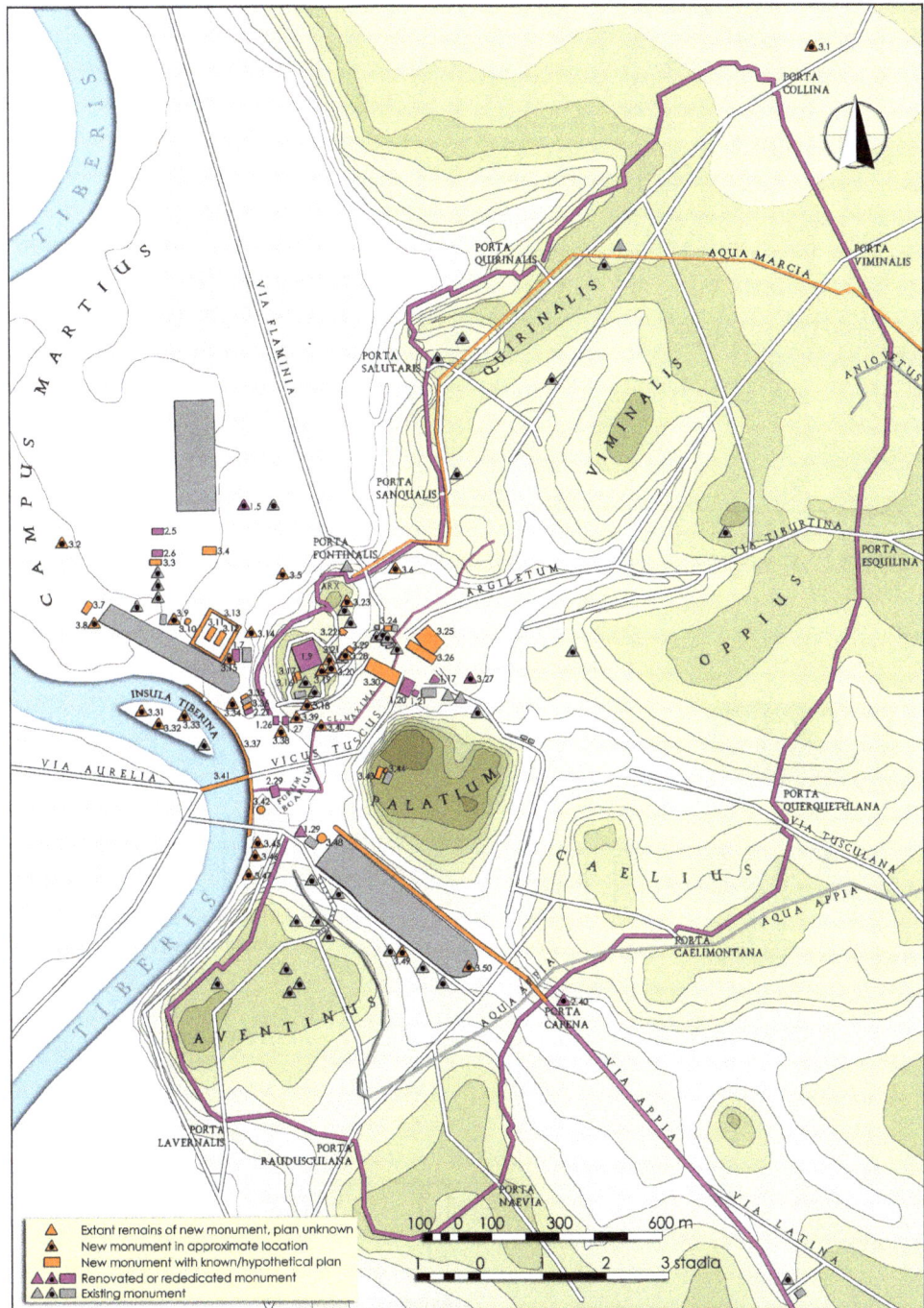

Figure 10.4 Map of Rome, c.337–218 BCE. Drawn by Penelope Davies and Onur Öztürk.

Figure 10.5 Cyma reversa molding, Temple C, Largo Argentina, third century BCE, actual state. Photo by the author.

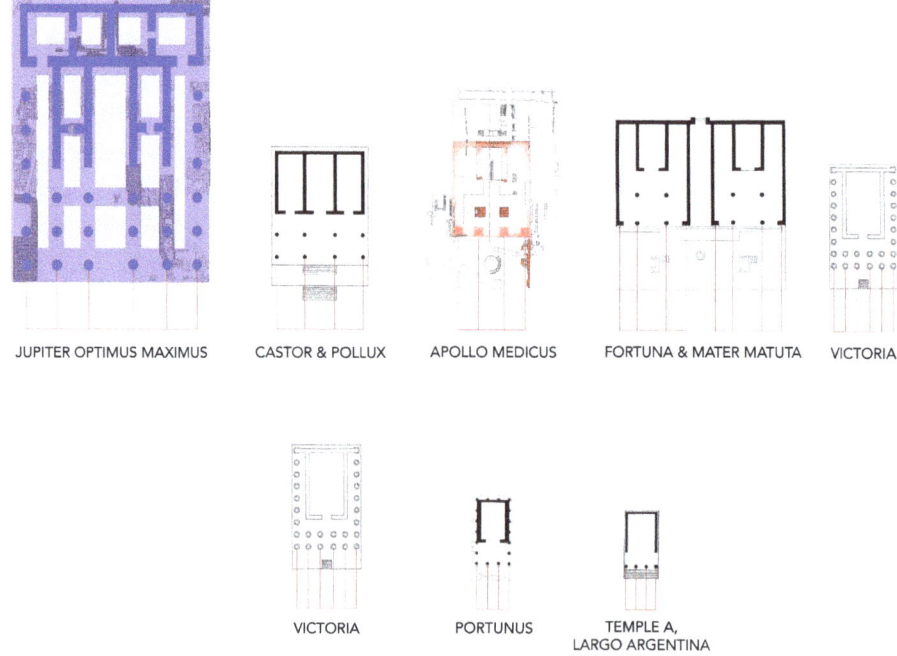

Figure 10.6 Temple plans showing interaxials. Drawn by Penelope Davies and Onur Öztürk.

fragments (two heads, a bearded Jupiter and an unbearded Dionysus) seem to have come from a pediment,[33] which makes them the first known pedimental sculptures from a Republican temple; this, in turn, indicates a closed pediment, another first in 200 years.[34] Moreover, in the foundations for a later phase of the temple were discovered fragments of peperino fluted column shafts, suggesting the possibility that the temple was Ionic, a style attested in Rome by columns carved onto the front of the sarcophagus chest of P. Cornelius Scapula in the second half of the fourth century BCE (Figure 10.7) and, soon after, by Ionic volutes on the lid of the sarcophagus of Scipio Barbatus, c. 280 BCE (Figure 10.8).[35] The Ionic style, in turn, meant attenuated forms and proportions. Where their dimensions are known, temples were also typically smaller than their predecessors of the fifth and earlier fourth century BCE (e.g. the Temple of Portunus of roughly 12 × 20.5 m versus the Temple of Castor of 27.5 × 37–40 m; the

Figure 10.7 Sarcophagus chest, c.350–300 BCE. Rome, Musei Capitolini, Centrale Montemartini. Photo by the author.

---

[33] Pensabene and d'Alessio 2006: 32.
[34] Davies 2012. On the site's identification, Castagnoli 1964: 185–6; Pensabene 1980: 73; Wiseman 1981: 36–40; Ziolkowski 1992: 173. *Contra*: Cecamore 2002: 122–6. In general: Pensabene 1988, 1991: 11, 1998: 26–34; Battistelli 2001; Pensabene and D'Alessio 2006; Coarelli 2012: 226–34.
[35] For the sarcophagi: Pisani Sartorio and Quilici Gigli 1987–8; Coarelli 1972: 17. Fragments of peperino Corinthio-Italic capitals also found in the temple's foundations may indicate that the shaft fragments come from a restoration during the construction of the Temple of Magna Mater, vowed in 205 BCE: Pensabene 1991: 14.

Figure 10.8 Sarcophagus of Scipio Barbatus, c.280 BCE. Vatican Museums. Photo by the author.

façade of the Temple of Apollo Medicus measured approximately 21.45 m, that of the Temple of Saturn something in the range of 15–20 m).[36] And some, according to Pliny, housed a new type of ornament:

> In Rome also honor was fully attained by [the art of painting] at an early date, inasmuch as a very distinguished clan of the Fabii derived from it their surname of Pictor, "Painter," and the first holder of the name, [C. Fabius Pictor], himself painted the Temple of Salus, in the 450th year from the foundation of the City [c. 311 BCE].[37]

Judging by later examples, and by contemporaneous paintings in the Esquiline Tomb and the Tomb of the Scipios, the paintings were probably biographical, and likely mark an enhanced interest in recording history, as Bernard (Chapter 11 in this volume) argues for contemporaneous Campanian paintings.[38] Construction continued in the center, but also occurred on the Quirinal hill (the Temple of Quirinus), Tiber Island (the Temple of Aesculapius), and on the southwest edge of the city (the Via Appia and Aqua Appia). Imported stone – Grotta Oscura – was the norm, and

---

[36] Portunus: Adam 1994. Castor: Nielsen and Poulsen eds. 1992. Apollo Medicus: Viscogliosi 1996. Saturn: Pensabene 1982.

[37] Pliny, *Natural History* 35.7.19 (after Rackham's trans.).

[38] Val. Max. 8.14.6; Dion. Hal. 16.3.6; Livy 9.30.1–2, 9.40.8, 9.40.10–11; Holliday 1980; Bastien 2007: 159.

Bernard concludes that, in a radical shift on process, contracting replaced corvée labor.[39]

10.3 Object and Object-Scape Agency in Rome

To return, then, to Gosden's conjecture. Romans born at different moments in the course of the fourth century BCE absorbed different object-scapes. At mid-century, things were relatively static: New architectural types and styles were few and far between. As the century progressed, at first change was incremental: New construction underlined economic prosperity resulting from the dissolution of the Latin League in 338 BCE, when changes to plunder agreements, taxes, and rent dramatically increased state income.[40] For Varro, with the substitution of bankers for butchers in the Forum, "for the first time the Forum's dignity grew";[41] one might imagine a climate of incipient transformation. Toward the end of the century, vast expenditures of state funds on the Via Appia and the Aqua Appia (so large that Diodorus Siculus, a Greek historian writing between 60 and 30 BCE, claimed that Appius Claudius used state funds on the aqueduct without a senatorial decree, and depleted the treasury on the Via Appia) underscored the availability of resources even as Rome strained under the burden of the Second and Third Samnite Wars.[42] For those born at this time, in fact, a relative glut of building – temples and new types of monument alike – generated a climate of action, and since contracting (which possibly necessitated the bankers' stalls in the Forum) had replaced corvée labor, the act of construction was no longer a performance of the onus of citizenship, but a performance of the state's action on its citizens' behalf.[43] The ubiquity of new buildings, too, throughout the city, encouraged the possibility of increased participation in public affairs by a greater diversity of the populace, and more widespread access to the authority of architecture as a form of political authority. And just as significantly, the innovative building types and styles established a climate in which qualitative change was thinkable: The immutable forms of the Early Republic

---

[39] Bernard 2018a: 108–14.
[40] Pliny, *Natural History* 34.11; Cornell 1995: 345–51; Oakley 2004: 25–6; Forsythe 2005: 292.
[41] Varro, frag. 72 Non. 853. Humm 2009: 124 and others see the influence of Aristotle's vision of an ideal Greek city (Arist. *Pol.* 7.12.4.1331a, 7.12.6.1331b); Coarelli 1985: 142–6; Welch 2003: 18; Filippi 2013: 158.
[42] Diod. Sic. 20.36.1–2.
[43] For an inscription on a fourth-century plate referring to an *argentarios*: Colletti and Pensabene 2017: 585.

proved mutable; norms could change, in urbanism as in politics and religion. Diversity was conceivable.

In temple architecture, a new deployment of materials – stone for entablatures – required more labor at the outset, but promised durability thereafter, imputing durability in turn to the changes they embodied; this new age was solid.[44] Lateral columns, for their part, implied permeability, inviting broad access to the gods as a form of political authority. Gentler, lighter forms are evident: in the *Rostra's* curvature, and, perhaps, in the vegetal ornament and attenuated proportions of the Ionic style. Paintings added human interest, a human dimension, reaching out, simultaneously, to illiterate and foreign visitors. And if these new building types and styles shared a character, it was one of expansiveness: They reached beyond Rome. Conveying an astounding 75,000 m^2 of water a day, the Aqua Appia tapped rich natural resources from a spring 11,190 *passus* (about 16.56 km) away along the Via Praenestina, to supply the city with the kind of water supply enjoyed by Hellenistic metropoleis such as Priene, Magnesia on the Meander, Ephesus, Alexandria, and, closer to hand, Syracuse.[45] Meeting natural and human challenges head-on (the Pontine marches, labor, and engineering issues; see de Haas, Chapter 7 in this volume), the Via Appia extended far into non-Roman and allied territories in southern Latium and Campania, covering a distance of approximately 212 km from the Porta Capena to Capua; for its long linear tracts, engineers may have availed themselves not only of the *groma*, a Roman surveying tool, but also of the geometric theories of Pythagoras of Samos, a Greek mathematician and philosopher who lived in Croton in South Italy from 530 until his death, and Archytas of Tarentum (428–347), a philosopher and mathematician of the Pythagorean school.[46] The ships' prows on the *Rostra*, the first public display of spoils, evoked the liquid sea; together, the *Rostra* and the Samnite shields on the *tabernae argentarii* embodied foreign states. As for temple design, closely set columns supporting stone entablatures and closed pediments were widely employed in the Greek cities of South Italy, as were the peripteral design, the Ionic style, and the *cyma reversa*. The elongated footprint, too, evoked contemporaneous Greek

---

[44] Studying Roman Britain, Gosden 2005: 202 notes that the shift from wooden structures to stone also alters the temporal rhythms of life: Buildings in brick or stone require more labor initially, but have greater durability thereafter. Changes of materials (from wood to stone, brick, and tile, for instance) create a different sensory universe, changing the smells, sounds, and appearance of buildings, helping to create human subjects of new types and attaching unforeseen values to older materials of wood, thatch, and daub.

[45] Front. *Aq.* 5, also 65.3; Humm 2005: 495.

[46] Tibiletti 1972; Humm 1996: 704, 716–24, 744–6; 2005: 489–93.

temple proportions.[47] That the source of the design may have been unknown to many observers mattered not: The Temple of Victoria and its successors represented a new aesthetic in Rome, notable simply for its alterity.

10.4 Rupture and Recasting

When assessing Middle Republican material, scholars are usually working at a disadvantage, from poor physical evidence and from plans rather than reconstructed elevations or 3D models. These, I suspect, underplay the visual magnitude of urban change that took place in this period. The modifications in temple design alone constituted a small revolution, all the more noticeable given the restricted vocabulary of post-and-lintel construction in an age before concrete. An abrupt shift in style of this kind effects a sense of rupture, a sense of then and now. When archaeologists conjecture that the violent destruction of the second temple at S. Omobono at the end of the sixth century BCE, and the apparent ritual burial of its terracottas, signaled a deliberate erasure of monarchy, they are entertaining the notion that Romans might effect rupture through material culture.[48] What I am suggesting for the end of the fourth and beginning of the third century BCE, however, is different: Rather than positing that material culture effected rupture as a result of human intentionality, I am arguing for social rupture through object and object-scape agency.

Rome's object-scape in the late fourth century BCE incorporated the old along with the startlingly new; juxtapositions occurred. These, in turn, provoked comparisons. And comparisons recast existing monuments, redefining their essential qualities, exposing the fact that their forms were not inevitable but the result of earlier design choices. Recasting can, I have argued elsewhere, be conscious and deliberate; this may have been the case in later years with Julius Caesar's response to Pompey's Theater Complex of 61–55 BCE. The first permanent theater of Rome, with a vast accompanying portico framing the city's first public garden, the monument

---

[47] The Ionic style was in use in Sicily (in the late-sixth or early-fifth-century-BCE Ionic Temple at Syracuse), and South Italy (at Temple D, Metaponto, of c.475 BCE, or the early-fifth-century-BCE Ionic Temple at Locri), and by the third century BCE in the Samnite sanctuary at Pietrabbondante (La Regina 1989: 2012). On the Ionic style in Italy and Sicily: Rocco 2003: 97–108, 183–92, who places its introduction between the end of the fourth century and the first century BCE.

[48] Gjerstad 1953–73, III.384; Pisani Sartorio and Virgili 1979: 42; Virgili 1977: 30–1; Ioppolo 1971–2: 14–17.

contained a rich array of artworks, both antique and contemporary, and even Attalid royal tapestries of woven gold. Trees provided welcome shade; flowing water, coolness. On its dedication, Pompey's magnificent manubial monument cast him as the city's glorious benefactor, a man of more-than-mortal stature. Caesar's Forum, begun a year after its dedication, in 54 BCE, and dedicated in 46 BCE, rewrote Pompey's message: The Forum's lean design and decoration, and its use (so Appian, the second-century Greek historian, stated) for strictly business purposes, changed the valency of Pompey's Theater–Portico Complex, recasting it as a place of self-indulgent luxury, its sponsor as a would-be king.[49] Yet recasting is also unforeseen and inevitable, as Pierre Bourdieu recognized:

> [A] position-taking changes, even when the position remains identical, whenever there is change in the universe of options that are simultaneously offered for producers and consumers to choose from. The meaning of a work (artistic, literary, philosophical, etc.) changes automatically with each change in the field within which it is situated for the spectator or reader.[50]

Or, as Astrid Van Oyen and Martin Pitts put it, objects are redefined according to the contexts in which they find themselves.[51] Only with modernism, that is, does what went before become premodern.

Some recasting possibilities emerge. As construction intensified in the here and now, it made the past seem more austere, parsimonious. As architecture grew more ubiquitous, it made architecture of the past seem rarified, confined to controlled places. As form and style became more varied, they cast earlier forms and styles as limited in range. Softer, gentler forms – the *Rostra's* curvature, and, perhaps, the vegetal ornament of Ionic capitals – made previous architecture harder, unyielding. The lighter proportions of the Ionic style made the Tuscan ponderous, as Vitruvius was quick to note.[52] New temples, with their differing configurations, heightened the near-uniformity of earlier sacred architecture; smaller than before, new temples made earlier temples more imposing, daunting; more open, with their lateral colonnades, they rendered earlier temples more closed off, more forbidding; their near-peripteral design exposed the rigid, domineering frontality of their predecessors. Enlivening the cella walls, new paintings made earlier temples drearier; informing the illiterate

---

[49] Appian, *BC* 2.102; Davies 2017b.   [50] Bourdieu 1993: 30–1.
[51] Van Oyen and Pitts 2017: 14.
[52] Vitr. 3.3.5: "The appearance of [araeostyle] temples is splayed and top heavy, low, and sprawling" (trans. Rowland and Howe).

majority, inviting broad curiosity, they exposed the exclusive hold on information implicit in earlier temples, with their written inscriptions. And if new forms reached out, appeared expansive, earlier architecture – the circuit walls, the Villa Publica for the census – became inward-looking, closing the city upon itself, narrowing its horizons. Imported stone – Grotta Oscura *tufo* – distinct for its strength and pale yellow color, underlined the local origin of the darker *cappellaccio* and Monteverde *tufi*, and their friability.[53] Comparison, in short, cast what had gone before as old-fashioned, parochially central Italic, unyielding and exclusive, an architecture tied to an obdurate patrician solidarity at the top of the social and political hierarchy. The new modernism promoted a new age, in which such exclusivity – hereditary authority of patrician families, closed religious access – was left behind, and opportunity was opening up.

10.5 Historical Sense of Rupture/Period

Whether Romans were conscious of this shift at the time is hard to determine. Domenico Palombi (Chapter 9 in this volume) notes that Greek historiographical and ethnographical sources identify a transformation in Rome's power from archaic to Middle Republican Rome; for them, the transformation justifies an "upgrade" in the city's status from an Etruscan city/*polis tyrrhenis* into a Greek city/*polis hellenis*, a characterization Palombi deftly problematizes, noting the diplomatic advantages it offered, and looking to *Latium Vetus* as a whole to understand urbanistic change and to identify its point of origination. It is hard to believe that contemporaneous Romans did not sense a shift. In any case, circumstantial evidence, albeit sparse, does suggest that sometime later, at least, this periodization was apparent. As Karl-Joachim Hölkeskamp notes, the archaic landscape survived visibly into the second and first centuries BCE and later; Gabriele Cifani observes that Mid- and Late Republican historians could survey a wide range of early monuments, which played a powerful role in constructing cultural memory.[54]

The new, more Hellenized style of temple introduced at the end of the fourth century BCE gained extraordinary traction; immediately thereafter, closer intercolumniations and stone entablatures prevailed, as did the Ionic style. By the 140s BCE, imported Greek marble, white and luminous,

---

[53] On the qualities of the stones: Jackson and Marra 2006: 419–20, 427.
[54] Hölkeskamp 2004: 137–68, 2006: 481–92; Cifani 2017: 396.

further enhanced these Hellenizing qualities; so too did the engagement of Hermodorus, a Greek architect from Salamis on Cyprus, to work on Q. Caecilius Metellus' Temple of Jupiter Stator (post-146 BCE), as well as, probably, Mummius' Temple of Hercules Victor (probably the Round Temple by the Tiber, post-146 BCE) and D. Iunius Brutus Callaicus' Temple of Mars (c.135 BCE).[55] And yet, when, in the middle to second half of the second century BCE, the Temple of Castor was overhauled, only a minor concession was made to modernity: though its façade was transformed from tetrastyle to hexastyle, and the addition of a frontal tribunal made it the first *templum rostratum* of Rome, the original terracotta revetments, dating to its archaic phase, were apparently reused (Figure 10.9).[56] Its deliberately Italic appearance, which sat uncomfortably in a modernized cityscape, was a bold expression of ancient traditions, and in the face of the growing activism on the part of tribunes of the plebs and

Figure 10.9 Temple of Castor, reconstruction c. mid-second century BCE. Drawn by John Burge.

---

[55] Jupiter Stator: Vell. Pat. 1.11.2–5; Livy, *Per.* 52.7; Val. Max. 7.5.4; Eutr. 4.14.2; Vitr. 3.2.5, 3.3.8; Gros 1973: 393, 395–7 (where he argues that Hermodorus arrived in Rome after the porticus had been built), 1976; Viscogliosi 1996; Coarelli 1997: 488–92; *LTUR* 3 157–9, *s. v.* Iuppiter Stator, aedes ad circum (A. Viscogliosi). Hercules Victor: Ziolkowski 1988; also Rakob and Heilmeyer 1973; Gros 1973: 158–9. Mars: Prisc. *gramm.* 8.17.4 = Nep. frag. 26 Peter; Gros 1973: 151, 1976; Coarelli 1976: 492–7; Zevi 1976, 1996; Tortorici 1988; *LTUR* 3 226–9, *s. v.* Mars in circo (F. Zevi); La Rocca 2011: 11–14; Kosmopoulos 2012. On the marble: Bernard 2010.

[56] Nielsen and Poulsen eds. 1992: 50, 80–6, 170; Guldager Bilde and Slej in Nielsen and Poulsen eds. 1992: 188–217; Nielsen in Nielsen and Poulsen eds. 1992: 177–80; Grønne in Nielsen and Poulsen eds. 1992: 157–76. Also Ulrich 1994: 87–90; Gorski and Packer 2015: 291–3.

the populace at this time, allowed senatorial conservatives a visible reassertion of control, drawn from access to the gods.⁵⁷

Some decades later, when P. Cornelius Sulla was dictator in 82–81 BCE, his solution to the devastating civil war of the 80s was to enact measures to diminish tribunician powers, and to increase membership of the senate while deploying it mainly as an advisory council for the magistrates and as a source of jurors.⁵⁸ His architectural restorations, meanwhile, focused almost exclusively on regal or Early Republican structures. Chief among them was the Temple of Jupiter Optimus Maximus, icon of the Early Republic, which had burned to the ground as he advanced on Rome on the night of July 6, 83 BCE. Ancient literary sources indicate that the reconstruction begun by Sulla and completed by Q. Lutatius Catulus occupied the vast foundations of the late regal temple and retained its areostyle column scheme and *peripteros sine postico* design (peripteral on three sides with a wall at the rear).⁵⁹ Denarii minted by M. Volteius in 78 BCE, before its completion, give it a Tuscan tetrastyle (not hexastyle) façade;⁶⁰ the finished temple is shown more accurately on denarii issued in 43 BCE by Petillius Capitolinus as hexastyle and Tuscan (or Ionic) (Figure 10.10).⁶¹ As for civic projects, literary sources document an extension of the *pomerium*, established by Romulus and untouched (so Romans

Figure 10.10 Denarii with reverse images of the Temple of Jupiter Optimus Maximus. Left: denarius minted by M. Volteius in 75 BCE. Courtesy of Roma Numismatics Ltd (www.romanumismatics.com). Right: denarius minted by Petillius Capitolinus in 41 BCE. Courtesy of the Classical Numismatic Group (www.cngcoins.com).

---

⁵⁷ Davies 2017a: 102–4. ⁵⁸ Steel 2014. ⁵⁹ Dion. Hal. 4.61.4; Vitr. 3.3.5; Tac. *Hist.* 3.71.4.
⁶⁰ RRC 385 1, pl. 49.3. ⁶¹ RRC 487 1–2; Elkins 2015: 35–6.

claimed) since an extension in Servius Tullius' time.[62] An inscription recording maintenance of the archaic sewers may date to the Sullan period, and meshes well with late phases of work on sewers lining the east–west artery into the Forum on the Velia, and, at either end of the Forum, tracts of *cappellaccio* sewer roofed with a single stone slab, a technique used in and around the Sullan period.[63] Literary sources also document a rebuilding and expansion of the Curia Hostilia, attributed in its earlier form to the legendary third king of Rome, Tullus Hostilius; the structure had been damaged in riots in 100 BCE, and perhaps during civil war conflicts in the 80s BCE.[64] In addition, the archaic Comitium was elevated by about half a meter and paved with creamy travertine slabs; the *Rostra*, too, was raised, the Graecostasis elevated and monumentalized, and the altar at the west end of the *Rostra* paved over in black marble and given the name *Lapis Niger* (Black Stone).[65] The exception is a contract for a Temple of Hercules Custos, perhaps a new vow but more likely a restoration of a temple founded between 293 and 218 on the west side of the Circus Flaminius, attested by Ovid's *Fasti*, which probably dates after Sulla's second march on Rome in 83–82 BCE.[66] Tellingly, perhaps, at some point Pompey, too, restored a temple to Hercules, known thenceforth as the Temple of Hercules Pompeianus; near the Circus Maximus, it may have been associated with the Ara Maxima, and probably dates after his first triumph over resistance fighters in North Africa in 81 (and therefore during Sulla's dictatorship), or after his second triumph in 71 over Sertorius (or, less likely still, after his triumph of 61).[67] The temple challenged Sulla's Temple of Hercules Custos: If it was a reworking of a temple at the Ara Maxima, it trumped Sulla's monument by targeting Hercules' most venerable cult

---

[62] Gellius, *NA* 13.14.1, citing the augur Messalla, consul in 53; Sen. *dial.* 10.13.8; Tac. *Ann.* 12.23; Cass. Dio 43.50.1; Livy 1.44.3; Appian, *BC* 1.59; Sordi 1988; Thein 2002: 348–51; Coarelli 2012: 15–29; Capanna 2013: 71–2.

[63] VI 37043; Gatti 1899; Steinby 2012: 45; Panella 2013: 45–6, who dates the first phase, of concrete, to the first half of the second century BCE; Bianchi and Antognoli 2014: 113–14.

[64] Cic. *Fin.* 5.2; Pliny, *Natural History* 34.21, 34.26; Cass. Dio 40.50.2–3; Amici 2004–5, 2007, refuting Bartoli 1963: 37, and Bonnefond-Coudry 1989: 56–60. Also Coarelli 1985: ch. 2; *LTUR* 1 331–2, *s. v.* Curia Hostilia (F. Coarelli).

[65] Boni 1899, 1900; Gjerstad 1941; Gantz 1974, with a different dating sequence; Amici 2004–5: 360–9; also Coarelli 1983: 161–8, 188–9; *LTUR* 4 295–6, *s. v.* Sepulcrum Romuli (F. Coarelli). Carafa 1998: 75–80, 86–8, 148–51, places this phase in the mid-second century BCE, followed by Morstein-Marx 2004: 47.

[66] Ovid, *Fasti* 6.209–12. Ziolkowski 1992: 50–6; *LTUR* 3 13–14, *s. v.* Hercules Custos, aedes (A. Viscogliosi). *Contra*: Coarelli 1997: 498–503. *LTUR* 3 13–14, *s. v.* Hercules Custos, aedes (A. Viscogliosi); Keaveney 2005: 156–7.

[67] Coarelli 1992a: 77–84; Ziolkowski 1992: 46–50; *LTUR* 3 20–1, *s. v.* Hercules Pompeianus, aedes (F. Coarelli); *LTUR* 3 15–17, *s. v.* Hercules Invictus, ara Maxima (F. Coarelli).

center.⁶⁸ In other words, it seems that when conservatives wanted to impose their ideal of exclusive senatorial authority, they turned to an architectural style and monuments of an age that ended with the fourth century BCE.

Vitruvius' description of the *genera* (styles of architecture) in Books 3 and 4 of *De architectura* makes a tentative addendum to this discussion. While noting that "the Doric was the first to occur and did so in ancient times," with columns that "came to exhibit the proportion, soundness, and attractiveness of the male body," he names not a single Doric building in Rome, and prioritizes the Ionic, both in order of exegesis and by a wide margin in word count.⁶⁹ The Tuscanic style, the dominant style for Roman areostyle temples of the archaic age, he relegates to a quasi-appendix at the end of Book 4, as a remnant of a distant era.⁷⁰

Even if such circumstantial evidence suggests that Romans living two centuries later recognized a change in their cityscape at the turn of the fourth to the third century BCE, it does not, of course, indicate that they consciously perceived it at the time; merely that it is legitimate to attribute to ancient Romans both the perception of stylistic change and the association of a style with a particular era, which not only supports the ideas framed in this chapter, but could have repercussions for the study of Roman art and architecture more broadly.

10.6 Conclusion

I have argued that, rather than being a mere *index* of political transformation in fourth- and early-third-century Rome, architecture was an *agent* of transformation: It helped to effect broader access to power structures and to stabilize and perpetuate such change. Stark shifts in the object-scape cast existing structures as an architecture of the past, and in doing so established a new era in Rome that people may have recognized in real time; at the least, circumstantial evidence suggests that later Romans distinguished archaic architecture from later works, as the architecture of a remote, and politically different, age.

---

[68] On the temple as a restoration: Coarelli 1988: 77–84; Ziolkowski 1992: 46–50; *LTUR* 3 20–1, s. v. Hercules Pompeianus, aedes (F. Coarelli).

[69] Vitr. 4.1.3, 4.1.6, and in general 4.1 and 4.3.

[70] Vitr. 4.7, where his marginalization of the Tuscan style prompts Ingrid Rowland (Rowland, Howe, and Dewar 1999: 229) to comment on the distance he places between the Etruscans and his own time.

11 | Becoming Historical in Oscan Campania

SETH BERNARD

This chapter treats the topic of history before the emergence of Roman historical writing in the later Republic. Recent scholarship stresses the importance of this earlier period when Romans "became historical," to use Purcell's apt phrase, in modes that were not exclusively literary.[1] While I will frequently refer to Roman developments, what interests me is not the prequel to Roman historiography, but rather parallel developments elsewhere in Italy. Scholars thinking about how early Italian events were encoded and transmitted down to our later Republican sources often reach something of an impasse, at least when relying on conventional approaches. For example, in thinking about the sources for the Oscan incursion into Campania in the fifth century, we might posit that Livy, Diodorus, and other historians drew from Cato or Greeks like Timaeus or the so-called Cumaean Chronicle, but the almost complete loss of these writers' works makes such hypotheses impossible to verify.[2] In this situation, it seems beneficial to expand our view of what counts as history and to consider some overlooked evidence, which opens up new perspectives on Campanian engagement with their past in the period before Roman conquest. A number of tomb paintings from the communities of Oscan Campania show remarkable interest in narrative and historical detail. To the extent that these paintings have been studied, focus has been on evaluating their iconographical relationship to events in the known (Roman) historical tradition, largely represented by Livy's narrative of the Samnite Wars. That a positive match remains elusive is perhaps unsurprising considering the very different worlds these cultural products inhabited. Here, I remain agnostic to questions of which scenes these

---

[1] Purcell 2003b; see also now Sandberg and Smith eds. 2018. This chapter forms a preliminary study for a book-length treatment of historical culture in early Italy. Readers will find in that work more extensive discussions of themes such as Etruscan historical painting or other nonliterary modes of historical culture besides painting, which are treated in a cursory manner here for reasons of space and focus. Along with my coeditors and the anonymous readers, I am grateful to Duncan MacRae and Christopher Smith for helpful comments.

[2] Classic in this regard is Cornell 1974, which comes down in favor of Cato but does not venture a strong opinion on Cato's sources. Gallia 2007 urges a cautious assessment of the Cumaean Chronicle, especially as it may have captured information on early Rome.

paintings depict and focus instead on what is implied by the general fact of their commemorative and, in my view, historical content.³

This historical material, for which there is little precedent in the region, forms an important cultural turn for two reasons. First, these paintings inhabit a moment when Romans were also starting to record past events in visual media.⁴ Several parallels between Campanian tomb paintings and what we know about this Roman material can therefore shed light on an important and apparently Italian stage in this broader background. If other chapters in this book have already shown the contribution of non-Romans from Central Italy or from the towns of Latium to what we have often understood as Roman culture and society, then I intend here to show another facet of this scholarly trend. At the same time, this chapter is also motivated by a desire to discover something not Roman: We must admit that the process of Roman conquest will have destroyed many local forms of recording memory and transmitting knowledge.⁵ My assertion is not, then, that Romans adopted Oscan practices in their own historical traditions but rather that we catch a rare glimpse of how trends in history-making played out among the conquered or assimilated peoples of Italy. When compared with the long-run development of Roman history-making, these Campanian tombs appear as a sort of dead end. We possess very little that may be called historiography among the Oscan-speaking peoples of Southern Italy, and even the existence of an autochthonous literary culture is disputed.⁶ But the issue may be that we are projecting what historical culture came to look like into the past and then failing to find it. When we take these local Italian cultures on their own terms and without such teleology, the results are revealing for the sort of cultural possibilities that were lost through, for lack of a better phrase, the Romanization of Italy.

The second reason for looking at these Campanian paintings is for their reflection of the dynamics of elite self-representation at a crucial moment in the history of both Campania and broader Italy. The aristocratic character of early Roman historical writing is often noted. While there were of course various popular forms of historical transmission available to Romans of the Middle Republic, early historians like Fabius Pictor or Cato

---

[3] I prefer the more flexible "historical culture," used in modern scholarship to encompass both material and immaterial as well as both popular and academic historical practice, over narrower terms like history or historiography. For theoretical discussion, see Grever and Adriaansen 2017.

[4] Koortbojian 2002; Holliday 2002.   [5] Padilla Peralta 2020b.

[6] For this reason, I also avoid interpreting these paintings in terms of Hellenistic culture, as is sometimes done; cf. Steingraber 2006: 285. This is not to deny their relationship with wider Mediterranean and specifically Greek artistic trends, but rather the goal here is to understand these paintings on their own terms.

the Elder, themselves members of the *nobilitas*, worked to transform Roman historical consciousness into Roman historiography using material of an often markedly elite nature, from family histories to priestly archives.[7] Because they adorned wealthy tombs, the Oscan paintings discussed here also belong to the world of the ruling elites of their respective communities.[8] I will connect these paintings to other scenes that seem interested in distinguishing individual actors in those same Campanian communities. All of this evidence of Campanian elites takes on great importance when viewed in light of recent work emphasizing the same period as one when Italian aristocracies were binding themselves increasingly to city states.[9] That is, what we find in these tombs are Italian elites turning to historical culture in the midst of an energetic process of state formation. Moreover, these paintings help to reveal the dynamics of this sociopolitical process. Campanian historical paintings do not replace older visual vocabularies of aristocratic behavior but rather exist alongside them, sometimes even within the same tomb. What we sense in this case is that sociopolitical change was taking place even as older forms of aristocratic authority retained value. On the one hand, the act of history-making in Oscan Campanian painting was innovative and broke from earlier artistic and cultural traditions. It finds better parallels in the commemorative practices of later Italian or, more accurately, Roman culture. On the other hand, this moment of significant change comes down to us as intimately connected to an earlier aristocratic past and uninterested in fully dislodging it.

11.1 Central Italian Historical Culture in the Fourth Century

Before turning to the paintings themselves, it is worth noting how little other material there is from early Samnium or Oscan Campania that can be called historical in a traditional sense. The idea that there were local historians of Oscan-speaking peoples, perhaps in their own language, cannot be excluded, of course, but finds little basis in the evidence. There is only the most fragile evidence, for example, to support one assertion that a certain Alfius, whose name seems Oscan in origin and who is cited by Festus for an unusually positive account of the origins of the Mamertines, was himself an indigenous Oscan historian of the third century.[10] Little else

---

[7] From an enormous literature on this expansion of the past, see Badian 1966; Wiseman 1994; Oakley 1997–2005 I.3–108; Sandberg and Smith eds. 2018.

[8] Well recognized by D'Angelo 2017: 80–2. [9] Terrenato 2019.

[10] Dench 1995: 211; the name appears to be Oscan, but Dench's early date before the Hannibalic war is based on the fact that Festus accords him a work on *bellum Carthaginiense*, in the singular

is even this suggestive, and modern scholarship consequently has taken some fairly dim views of Samnites' capacity to transmit historical information. Finding no firm reference to written culture in Samnium other than Livy's reference to a religious text used to initiate the linen legion before the battle of Aquilonia, Salmon thought that Samnites lacked not only anything resembling historiography, but literary culture entirely. He ascribed the famous tradition of Atellane farces (*fabulae Atellanae*) to Oscan speakers' exposure to Greek culture through their incursions into Campania beginning in the fifth century.[11] While recent work on Samnium is generally more sensitive to the potential for indigenous culture, it still admits little evidence of local literary culture.[12]

Whether consciously or not, these views oppose more charitable opinions on Oscan literature from nineteenth-century scholarship. In his 1850 monograph on Italic epigraphy, Mommsen insisted that, since one of Ennius' three native languages was Oscan, the poet must have drawn in part from a now-missing but vibrant Oscan tradition; the problem of Samnite literary culture was the loss of evidence, not one of its existence.[13] This view has found some followers in the debate, which arose in the 1960s between Marta Sordi, Santo Mazzarino, Tim Cornell, and Jacques Heurgon over the extent of lost native traditions of Italian historiography.[14] A variation of the idea appears now in the landmark collection of Oscan epigraphy *Imagines Italicae*, in which the editors claim a broadly diffuse literary culture existed among Oscan-speaking peoples of Italy. However, they base this assertion largely on several long but late inscriptions, many of which show clear interaction with Greek and Latin cultures and are therefore difficult to take as independent witnesses to any local tradition.[15]

In reviewing the absence of evidence for Oscan historical writing, I have deliberately mixed the topic with the broader search for a literary tradition to make a point: If we look for early Oscan historical culture as an offshoot of general literacy or as part of literary culture, we will find nothing. However, we might question whether this is an appropriate way to proceed in the first place, not only as concerns Oscan speakers of the south, but

---

not the plural. For a more circumspect view, see C. J. Smith and T. J. Cornell in Cornell ed. 2013: Alfius, vol. 1.488.

[11] Salmon 1967: 118–19.   [12] Scopacasa 2015: 30.   [13] Mommsen 1850: 116–18.
[14] Sordi 1960: 177–82; Heurgon 1961: 305–9; Cornell 1976; Chassignet 1996: xlv–xlvi; for a more skeptical view, see Poucet 1985: 61–2.
[15] Crawford et al. 2011: 1; cf. Crawford et al. 2011: Paeligni/CORFINIVM 6 and 11, long and possibly metrical inscriptions which they cite dated to c.100 BCE; but as Adams 2003: 141–2 notes, at least one author has close contact with Latin diction. Otherwise, there seems to be in their assertion some slippage between literacy and literature, as I do not otherwise understand how the Iguvine tablets presuppose a literary tradition or what we may make in this direction of a future perfect in an archaic inscription.

many other ethnic and language groups of fourth-century Central Italy. The existence of a robust Etruscan historical tradition, for example, has been contested, as it can only be detected as a *written* tradition in sporadic and often esoteric references in later Roman authors like Varro or the emperor Claudius.[16] However, during the fourth century, Etruscans were certainly invested in the depiction of historical events in visual form, as evinced by those painted scenes of battles between Etruscans and Romans in the famous François tomb from Vulci.[17]

Romans themselves had a very broad view of the processes by which events were commemorated and handed down from generation to generation in the prehistoriographical period. This topic is well studied, but it will serve the point of describing historiography as part of a much wider category of historical culture to review some of the evidence. In telling the development of Roman history, scholarship has sometimes privileged a very close focus on Roman historiography's early development, from the innovations of Fabius Pictor and Cincius Alimentus, to Cato's transformation of this practice from Greek to Latin, to the manipulative middle annalist tradition of Valerius Antias, Licinius Macer, and Claudius Quadrigarius, to the emergence of this tradition in Livy in the form ultimately delivered to us. This process by which events were put down in writing in archival form and then transmitted from author to author was certainly one mode of historical culture in Rome, and one that Romans themselves acknowledged. Livy, likely following the opinion of Quadrigarius, claims at one point that the Gallic fire's destruction of the city's archives (*publicis privatisque ... monumentis*) made the very act of telling prior Roman history impossible (6.1). However, Livy's word for historical material, *monumentum*, is enormously important here, since it apparently held a much wider meaning. The antiquarian lexicon of Festus provides a different definition:

> A monument is both anything built on behalf of someone who has died and anything made in someone's memory such as temples, porticos, writings, and poetry.[18]

This remarkably broad definition, paralleled in other Roman lexicographical works, encompasses written tradition while expanding far beyond it.[19]

---

[16] Cornell 1976; Bourdin 2012: 19–25.

[17] On Etruscan historical painting including the François tomb, see Di Fazio 2019b: 84 with bibliography.

[18] 123L: *Monimentum est, quod et mortui causa aedificatum est et quicquid ob memoriam alicuius factum est, ut fana, porticus, scripta et carmina.*

[19] Sources in Baroin 2010: 33–7.

The basic elements of Festus' *monimentum* are human action and a timespan longer than the life of the actor. We find a similarly wide semantic range in a well-known fragment of Cato's *Origines* describing the heroic actions of a Roman commander during the First Punic War. Cato laments that the Roman hero, whom he does not name, will not receive the same glory as Leonidas of Sparta, not because of the merit of his actions, but because of his lack of *monumenta*: Leonidas received, as Cato lists, "pictures, statues, honorary inscriptions, and other forms of history."[20] Thus, while Livy and probably Quadrigarius use *monumentum* to denote the archival, presumably written, material from which they derive their written histories, the word and implied act of history-making convey much more flexible meanings.

Rather than historiography, it may be better to think of historical culture in this period as a dynamic sociocultural process serving to transmit accomplishments through all forms of media from monumental architecture to written histories, and even to pictures, as Cato explicitly confirms. I have not yet mentioned the fact that Fabius Pictor himself was grandson of C. Fabius Pictor, who painted the walls of the Temple of Salus in 304, built in celebration of C. Junius Bubulcus' victory in war against Samnium. Pictor's career as a painter has been used to interpret surviving Middle Republican paintings from Rome, especially the historical scenes painted in a tomb on the Esquiline, which depict a meeting between a member of the *gens Fabia* and a Fannius, presumably a Samnite peer.[21]

In sum, the end result of the process of becoming historical at Rome should not be applied in isolation in order to understand its beginnings. The development from multivalent historical culture to historical writing seen at Rome was a possible but by no means exclusive outcome. This observation intends to promote the study of historical cultures outside of Rome, where the failure to develop literary history cannot be applied as a fair standard of assessment. We should be studying what historical culture looked like among various Italian peoples not as a way to understand what happened at Rome, but rather for a glimpse of what cultural and intellectual forms were lost through imperial conquest. It seems crucial to understand not only how imperialism affected history but also how it affected the very modes by which past events were transmitted into the present.

---

[20] Cornell 2013: Cato F76 = Gellius, *NA* 3.7: *monumentis: signis, statuis, elogiis, historiis aliisque rebus*. These are thus portrayed as Greek, not Roman, commemorative *monumenta*, but Cato's complex view toward the two cultures is well known, and anyway we possess plenty of evidence contemporary to his career for Roman equivalents.

[21] Coarelli 1990, and consider also the so-called Arieti tomb from the Esquiline, whose date is disputed. The Tomb of the Scipios had a painted façade in the third century, but preservation prevents its reconstruction; see Volpe et al. 2014.

11.2 Historical Paintings in Campania

In the hope, then, of recovering a glimpse of what the past meant in a non-Roman context, let us turn to Campania. The tradition of adorning tombs with painted figural scenes flourished in Oscan Campania starting in the early fourth century and continued into the early third, crossing through the period during which Campania's elites were incorporated into the Roman state. In his monumental 1909 study, Weege grouped together tombs from various communities in Campania under the rubric of Oscan culture.[22] Considering this, it is worth noting that tomb painting was not a common feature of Samnium itself, although there was an earlier Italic tradition of tomb painting beginning in the very late sixth century in Apulia and Campania. The identification of fourth- and early-third-century Campanian tombs as culturally Oscan is largely a product of their chronological overlap with the occupation, starting in the mid-fifth century, of a number of cities in the region by peoples allegedly of Samnite origin.[23]

The extant source tradition, whatever its ultimate derivation, portrays the Oscan takeover of Campania as a series of invasions and seditions, often violent, which disrupted Etruscan or Greek settlements in the region's cities and installed elites from Samnium.[24] This narrative forms part of a larger tradition of great mobility and demographic instability across fifth-century Italy, one that is starting to be reassessed as some alleged migrations find less-than-clear archaeological confirmation.[25] For Campania in particular, the arrival of Rome in the last decades of the fourth century complicates matters further, as it is not always clear how much the cultural record is being affected by Samnite incursions and how much may be owed to progressive Roman realignment or even Greek influence.[26] There was cultural change in the region's material record over this time period, but it is normally layered and complex. Take for example the proliferation of Oscan epigraphy in Campania, clearly speaking to a major change in the cultural orientation of the region's elites, but the use of a Greek alphabet and more profound linguistic borrowings from Greek characterize this Oscan epigraphic corpus.[27] The tombs should be seen as similarly complex in cultural orientation, as earlier traditions

---

[22] Major studies since include Corrigan 1979; Pontrandolfo and Rouveret 1992; Benassai 2001.
[23] Cf. Scopacasa 2015: 125–9.   [24] Cornell 1974.
[25] See now Acconcia ed. 2020; Di Fazio 2020 on the Volsci.
[26] Pontrandolfo and D'Agostino 1991 for the material culture; D'Angelo 2017 for paintings as response to this highly complex political scenario.
[27] For the arrival of Oscan into Campania, see Crawford et al. 2011, vol. 1.16–24; for Greek and Oscan, see McDonald 2015.

of Campanian painting were revived and adapted through new imagery and motifs to fit the tastes of different elite groups.

Several stock scenes feature in these Oscan painted tombs from the earliest examples. The majority of depictions of male figures show a returning warrior, which appears already on some of the earliest Oscan tombs (Figure 11.1).[28] There are numerous variations on this theme, sometimes growing to multifigure processions, or depicting warriors in armor on horseback attended by other figures on foot. These scenes all

Figure 11.1 Andriuolo necropolis, Paestum, Tomb 12A. The return of the warrior, 380–370 BCE. Image © Parco Archeologico di Paestum e Velia/Ministero della Cultura.

---

[28] Nicolet 1963; Corrigan 1979: 365–90; Pontrandolfo and Rouveret 1992: 44.

belong to a broader genre, general in nature, of depictions of aristocratic display. They find parallels in scenes of women sitting at their toilet, mourners, or iconography related to elite activities such as banqueting, or athletic contests and chariot races. Such generic depictions of aristocratic behavior appear in the earlier tombs but persist into the third century.

From this background, three tombs distinguish themselves for very different subject matter. The first is a tomb painting from Cumae. Cumae does not present extensive evidence of painted tombs in this period, with few other examples, the best known of which is a traditional scene of a woman at her toilet.[29] In 1996, Valenza Mele published a painted limestone block from a different tomb, which had been discovered in the storerooms to which it had presumably been taken from the city's extensive northern necropolis (Figure 11.2).[30] Despite the challenges posed by the

Figure 11.2 Cumae, painted slab from a tomb, Benassai 2001 no. Cu.13, c.300 BCE. Drawing by author modified from Benassai 2001.

---

[29] Weege 1909: 100–1. Valenza Mele 1996: 351–5; Benassai 2001: 260 suggests Cumae's elite intentionally rejected painted tombs as an expression of political differentiation; *contra* D'Angelo 2017: 80.

[30] Valenza Mele 1996; Caputo 2000; Benassai 2001: 215–18; D'Ippolito 2004, all largely in agreement. The block's dimensions find architectural parallels with ashlar construction in the other Cumaean painted tomb, Weege 1909 no. 1; cf. Benassai 2001: 80.

small size of the surviving painted surface (24 × 21 cm) and the fact that we have no information about context, there remains enough visible of the scene to discern immediately that we are viewing something considerably different from the generic aristocratic scenes of other Oscan tombs. The fragmentary scene depicts figures arranged either in at least two registers, or in foreground and background perspective.[31] Four pairs of legs are visible along the upper margin of the block; notably only one of each pair is fitted with a greave. An arm, larger in scale and in the foreground, frames the scene's right side with its hand closed around what appears to be a lit torch. At the lower-left margin is another hand, belonging to a figure whose togate shoulder may perhaps be seen along the block's leftmost edge. His hand holds something sprouting, perhaps a clump of grass or leaves. The ground beneath the legs is painted an ochre color. The space defined by that color is delimited on the right side by a dark line, while the background further to the right is lighter in color. The interaction of these figures thus appears to be taking place within an architecturally defined space of some sort, and also probably at night, as suggested by the torch.

In her initial publication of this fragment, Valenza Mele suggested that this assembly of armed men and priests in an enclosed space at night depicts the ritual of the Samnite linen legion, vividly described by Livy, on the eve of the Samnite defeat to the Romans at the Battle of Aquilonia in 293 (10.38). It is in the context of this ritualistic levy of the linen legion according to a practice allegedly employed for the Samnite coup of Capua that we find reference to an old priestly book on linen (*libro vetere linteo*), the only reference to writing used by Samnites that Salmon could locate in extant literature.[32]

Some elements may be seen to support her identification. We have in the Cumaean fresco an assembled group of warriors inside a structure and in the presence of a priest. Single greaves are featured in Samnite military depictions and even in later Samnite gladiatorial equipment, but may also be seen as a sign of monosandalism, often indicative in ancient culture of transitional moments in the lives of recruits binding themselves to military service.[33] It is very unclear just what the hand at the left of the scene is clutching, but Valenza Mele suggests this may be the clump of turf carried by the *fetiales*.

---

[31] Valenza Mele 1996: 216 saw the scene as arranged in registers similar to the Esquiline tomb painting, but Benassai 2001: 216 rightly observes that we more likely see figures depicted in three-dimensional space.
[32] Salmon 1967: 118–19.   [33] Cf. Vidal Naquet 1981; Rouveret 1986.

A significant obstacle to Valenza Mele's reconstruction, however, is that Livy's account of the levy of the linen legion is notoriously fraught and forms a poor guide for iconographic interpretation.[34] The passage is replete with redundant and illogical details. Livy's repeated use of linen to etymologize the linen legion from both the tent and the ritual book seems overwrought, considering he elsewhere notes that Samnite legions typically wore linen armor. The troops, unusually, swear two oaths, not a single oath, while it is unclear why a vow of secrecy was even necessary when each initiate was subsequently tasked with recruiting up to 16,000 soldiers.

Moreover, one wonders what relevance this scene had at Cumae at all. Where the assembly of the Samnite legion took place is not precisely known. Some identify it with the sanctuary at Pietrabbondante, but in any case, these events happened in Samnium, rather than Campania. As the painting's style suggests a date around 300, we may also note an apparent celebration of Rome's enemies at a time when Cumaeans held *civitas sine suffragio* and were allied with Rome.[35] To get around such issues, Valenza Mele proposes this painting came from the tomb of a *philoromaios*, with a style directly influenced by painters in Rome itself, while lost parts of the tomb at Cumae might have shown Roman triumphs over Samnites. All of this is highly imaginative and leaves little room for agency or innovation on the part of the Cumaean workshop, while formal parallels between the Cumaean fragment and Roman paintings are less close than Valenza Mele suggests.[36]

Perhaps the tomb's reference is to the Samnite coupe at Capua in the fifth century, which Livy cites as the origin of the secretive ceremony performed before Aquilonia. Tradition held that the Oscan elites of Capua, having seized control of that city, turned a few years later to conquer Cumae, providing a plausible link to that city. Secrecy in the case of the Capuan coupe was obviously necessary, and Altheim first suggested that Livy mistakenly inserted irrelevant antiquarian information about the Samnites' entrance into Campania into his account of the leadup to Aquilonia.[37] However, this interpretation, too, only imperfectly fits our written sources. It is not clear, for example, why the participants of the Capuan coupe are portrayed as armed warriors. In any case, and

---

[34] Cornell 1974: 200; Oakley 1997–2005: 4.392–406.
[35] For the connection between Pietrabbondante and this passage, see Coarelli 1996.
[36] Valenza Mele 1996; Benassai 2001: 218; I have noted the disposition of figures in perspective at Cumae rather than in registers at Rome, the latter arrangement possibly reflecting the Roman *tabula triumphalis*, as see Coarelli 1990: 175.
[37] Altheim 1961: 201–7; expanded upon by Cornell 1974: 201–2; Coarelli 1996: 10–11.

considering the very fragmentary state of the scene, it seems safest to reserve judgment to more cautious conclusions: Given what appear to be specific and unparalleled details in the scene, the impulse to interpret it using otherwise known historical data is understandable, even if we cannot reach any certainty. This is a narrative or historical tomb painting.

Painted tombs from Poseidonia-Paestum (here, Paestum for convenience) present a similar impulse to connect their imagery with the historical record.[38] Paestum has a long and rich history of tomb painting extending back to the Greek settlement of the early fifth century with the famous Tomb of the Diver. As the enigmatic iconography of the diving scene in that tomb suggests, workshops in the city were not bound to stock images of aristocratic behavior, although the diving scene was painted on that tomb's lid, while its interior walls were decorated by more standard scenes of banqueting. It is a similar combination of expected and unexpected that draws our attention to fourth-century painted tombs from the city's Lucanian necropolis at Andriuolo.

The first, Tomb 114, is better preserved. The tomb sits at the margin of the Italic burials in the Andriuolo necropolis and is one of the latest, dated by its contents to 330–320 (Figure 11.3).[39] The atelier that painted it also painted more traditional tombs, and here, too, they fill three walls of the rectangular structure with generic images of returning warriors and a scene of youth and

Figure 11.3 Andriuolo necropolis, Paestum, Tomb 114, north wall. Battle scene, 330–320 BCE. Image © Parco Archeologico di Paestum e Velia/Ministero della Cultura.

---

[38] Pontrandolfo and Rouveret 1992: 67 connect these Paestan tombs with Hellenistic painting traditions, Fabius Pictor, and the Esquiline.
[39] Pontrandolfo 2003.

women bearing vases.[40] The long north wall visually divided the scene in two with an Ionic column. To the left, we find a youth who belongs to the adjacent slab's depiction of a returning warrior. To the right of the column is a more unusual and elaborate scene of battle, which occupies the major portion of the south wall. We see two armies facing each other in hoplite formation, with tall, pointed helmets and spear tips peeking out from overlapping shields. Above the left army is a large rock formation or mountain range, with the head and shoulders of four oxen to the left and above the slope. Between the two armies is a nude figure, facing left, who wears a shield and a crested and plumed helmet of gold, and raises his arm as if to throw a javelin at the hoplites facing him on the left. Behind him, the five hoplites are not uniform, but the fourth figure's head emerges entirely above his shield and he wears an Attic-style helmet without plumes or crest, in contrast to his adjacent soldiers, who wear peaked helmets like those of the warriors on the left.[41]

There is too much specific detail in this scene to think this is a casual depiction of war that did not intend to recall some particular event. Attempts to fix it to particular battles largely focus on the profile of the rocky hill, which has been related to a peak near Caudium or another nearer Paestum itself.[42] Briquel offers an extended reading of the painting as a depiction of the Samnites' ambush of the Romans led by C. Junius Bubulcus in a mountain pass at Bovianum in 311. As an aside, I note it was in the course of this campaign that Bubulcus vowed the Temple of Salus, which hosted paintings by the grandfather of Fabius Pictor. Livy mentions cattle among the spoils taken by victorious Romans (9.31), but interestingly Zonaras' epitome of Cassius Dio calls the encounter a Roman defeat and suggests the Samnites used cattle to disguise their path and set the ambush (8.1). Briquel thus sees the tomb painting as reflecting the true outcome of a battle later manipulated by the Junian *gens* into a Roman victory. The nude figure is Mars, in his view, leading the victorious Samnites. It is an ingenious proposition, but it is not clear why a scene of warfare against Pentrian Samnites was celebrated in the burial of a Lucanian elite in Campania. Briquel is compelled to point to an alliance between some Lucanian elites and the Samnites made in 326 BCE, but this agreement

---

[40] Pontrandolfo 2003; Pontrandolfo, Rouveret, and Cipriani 2004: 30.

[41] Zuchtriegel 2020 suggests the two fighting forces' armor are differentiated such that the group on the right appears more Greek and that on the left more barbarian, in line with what he sees as a wider influence of barbarian imagery in Lucanian painting; in this case, the episode, while still historical, becomes even less associable with the Roman historical traditions in which it has sometimes been interpreted, as see Briquel 2001 and discussion in this chapter.

[42] For sources, see Briquel 2001: 138, n. 8.

came about only after the major portion of Lucanians had aligned themselves with Rome, while no specific evidence mentions Lucanians at Bovianum. Again, I will set aside the very difficult question of what episode in particular this scene depicts and instead return to emphasize the basic fact that it appears historical.

Andriuolo Tomb 114 is perhaps not the only tomb painting in that necropolis to exhibit specific or historical information, although the second possibility's very poor state of preservation hinders our reading. The long northern wall of Tomb 104a also shows a battle scene with multiple individuals advancing against each other; similar to Tomb 114, the other sides of the tomb show more traditional fare, including a return of the warrior.[43] The scene consists of two groups of three fighters, each paratactically disposed in the upper margin of the slab. The rightmost figure appears to be wearing a tunic rather than armor and shooting a bow, while between the two groups is a bounding white dog, perhaps on a lead. As fragmentary as it is, we can at least state that the scene is uncanonical as its details find little comparison.

I have thus far described these scenes as historical rather than generic, and it is worth parsing in more detail why this is so and what it means in this context. In the Cumaean fresco and that from Andriuolo 114, the tomb painters break with formal aspects of earlier tomb paintings. Both scenes stand out for the inclusion of multiple, sometimes numerous figures, and for the spatial arrangement of certain figures to draw attention either to collective (repetitive hoplites at Andriuolo, repetitive soldiers' legs at Cumae) or individual (centrally placed nude figure at Andriuolo, foregrounded priests at Cumae) status. Otherwise, size, dress, and particular attributes also serve to distinguish figures and grant them individuality, which we assume was recognizable to their original viewers. These formal aspects all deviate from the formal layout and figural presentations of generic aristocratic images, while this developed method of inserting particularism into these paintings implies that we are dealing with a more established phenomenon than the small number of examples might otherwise suggest.

While I have resisted identifying which events in particular these images relate to their viewer, these formal traits confirm that they did intend to transmit a specific past into the present of the burial ritual. Importantly, these paintings are not deprived of context but, as decorations on the interior of tombs, belong with the other objects used in the funeral ritual.

---

[43] Pontrandolfo and Rouveret 1992: 66–7.

Unlike the grand tumuli of Etruria or the Tomb of the Scipios at Rome, which contain multiple burials deposited over long periods of time, Campanian burials were architecturally relatively small and were usually intended to house only one or two individuals, while postdepositional rituals concentrated on the area surrounding, rather than inside, closed tombs.[44] Campanian tomb paintings were thus performatively linked to the funeral in the sense that their primary display formed part of the rites that accompanied the burial of the deceased, akin to the deposition of grave goods or mortuary banqueting.[45] It seems obvious enough how stock aristocratic scenes might serve during burial to reinforce a deceased's status, and this makes the rise of historical consciousness in this same context all the more interesting. The stories told visually at these tombs, anchored by detail and arrangement to particular past moments in time, functioned as what Zerubavel calls mnemonic infrastructure.[46] The viewing of these historical paintings in the context of highly structured ritual action saw the past used for socialization and within the community-affirming practices linked with burial.

This communal context makes it interesting that all the Campanian scenes with historical content have to do in some way with corporate warfare, either initiation into a fighting force or the act of fighting itself. While there are several scenes of monomachy from Campanian tombs, these belong to the aristocratic genre, and there is little to suggest they show particularized individuals. Notably, it is possible that other multifigure and more complex scenes of battle in Oscan culture may also reveal historical specificity. A series of polychromatic painted vases from Arpi and Canosa of roughly the same date as our tombs show very detailed combat scenes which have been suggested to reflect historically specific episodes.[47] We might include in this discussion those monumental red-figure Apulian vases from sites in North Apulia by the Darius painter and his circle, active 340–320 BCE and known for portrayals of historical scenes from the wars of Alexander the Great. This workshop's depiction of recognizably historical scenes on vases was facilitated by the greater popularity of large-format vases, particularly volute kraters, in elite tombs from several Daunian centers. These showy kraters are found in burials accompanied by other vases and also frequently by armor and weaponry, affirming the continuing importance of military leadership to aristocratic status.[48] As an aristocratic

---

[44] Bérard 2017: 56.   [45] For grave goods and associated ritual, see Benassai 2001: 243–56.
[46] Zerubavel 2003: 11–12.   [47] Mazzei 1987.
[48] Massa-Pairault 1996; for the Darius painter's vases and their context in Daunian tombs, see Ciancio 2014.

activity, participating in war or leading an army into battle appears to have presented particularly attractive material in these Italian communities for commemorating specific events.

11.3 Campanian Elites and Fourth-Century State Formation

I stress this intersection between group combat and historical narrative in Oscan tomb paintings because the act of fighting on behalf of a political community seems to have been a relatively new phenomenon in Italy in the fifth and fourth centuries, as the smaller-scale raiding and war bands more characteristic of Iron Age warfare started gradually to diminish in importance.[49] This transition to proper Italian armies forms part of a larger and radical transformation of Italian political culture, now well described by Terrenato, who traces how Iron Age clans converged into territorially ambitious city states over the course of the fourth century. This process happened at Rome but was widespread across the western Mediterranean, from Syracuse to Tarquinia, Massilia, Carthage, and beyond.[50] The implication of the overlap between Campanian historical paintings and corporate warfare, then, would be that historical culture played a role in the wider process of Italian state formation. This connection makes a certain amount of sense if we think in turn that new forms of community will have required new cultural modes of self-representation and authority.

Before pursuing these intriguing possibilities, however, let me add one further ingredient of Campanian tomb iconography, which distinguishes itself from traditional displays of aristocratic fare in ways parallel to the historical paintings just examined. Several tombs at Capua, Paestum, and possibly also Nola contain paintings depicting magistrates.[51] The trend appears repeatedly in later, possibly even early-colonial tombs from the Paestan necropolis at Spinazzo, where it can be seen developing out of earlier aristocratic images, as motifs from earlier scenes of the returning warrior give way to portrayals of individualized members of the civic elite.[52] The faces of some of the magistrates depicted in these Campanian

---

[49] Armstrong 2016.   [50] Terrenato 2019.
[51] Benassai 2001: 210–15; also Nola Tomb 7, which shows a procession of togate figures. I refer to these male individuals as magistrates following scholarly convention, although I intend this only to mean holders of civic, that is, nonmilitary, power. The implication is not that they were elected as in the Roman Republican system.
[52] Pontrandolfo, Rouveret, and Cipriani 2004: 70; for the date, see Horsnaes 2015.

tombs are accurately called portraits as they show significant artistic attention to detail, well above that of earlier scenes of returning warriors or aristocratic duels. Some individuals are older, including a bald and bearded male figure in a toga from Capua.[53] Another individual from Spinazzo Tomb 1 wears a cloak and tunic as well as a jeweled ring, all signs of high civic rank, and displays highly individualized facial features, with gray hair, a wrinkled forehead, round eyes, and a snub nose (Figure 11.4). He is painted in a style reminiscent of the veristic Republican portraiture familiar

Figure 11.4 Spinazzo necropolis, Paestum, Tomb 1, back wall. Older male individual, c.320–300 BCE. Image © Parco Archeologico di Paestum e Velia/Ministero della Cultura.

[53] Weege 1909, no. 25 = Benassai 2001: no. C.5.

from Middle Republican Rome.[54] While we can go no further in identifying these figures, these are surely not generic images. Rather, they intend to portray specific high-ranking individuals of the community.

This trend finds wider, if somewhat earlier, parallels elsewhere in Italian painting, above all in Etruria, where depictions of magistrates become common starting in the early fourth century. There, painted magistrates appear as an outgrowth of the traditional depictions in tombs of elite behavior, but also show novel conceptions of what constituted aristocracy.[55] A good example is found in the Tomb of the Shields at Tarquinia, where several couples are depicted in tunics on curule seats, banqueting. The male figures are magistrates, as epigraphic labels tell us, and we also in this case know their names.[56] Returning to the Campanian material, we are unfortunately not aided by epigraphy in identifying any of the magistrates depicted in tombs. Nonetheless, it is hard to resist the idea that these highly individualized figures held a close relationship to the deceased, if they were not in fact portraits of the deceased themselves. That is, while not historical narrative per se, it is possible to connect the depiction of these individuals with the wider mnemonic infrastructure of the tomb and with rising interest in the context of burial in commemorating specific figures and their civic accomplishments.

Both fighting in or leading an army and holding office were spheres of activity which prioritized aristocrats' role with respect to the city state, and it is plausible therefore to think that these novel themes in Campanian tomb paintings reflect new political forms. In fleshing out the details of this relationship between historical culture and state formation in Italy, we can turn momentarily to sketch out the better-attested situation at Rome, where we are fully aware of history's importance to the Middle Republican *nobilitas*. Over the course of the fourth century, a number of laws promoted senatorial membership as the prime qualification for political power, and this meant career achievements started to matter in combination with inherited social rank, rather than merely the latter, as had been the case during the previous century of patrician domination.[57] Achievements on behalf of the Roman state thus formed vital material for inter-elite competition. Following this, in their jockeying for political

---

[54] Pontrandolfo, Rouveret, and Cipriani 2004: 70; D'Angelo 2017: 82 raises the intriguing idea that some of the Spinazzo painted tombs in fact postdate the implantation of the Roman colony at Paestum in 273; epigraphic labels are not uncommon in Italian, including Roman, painting in this period, as see Padilla Peralta 2019: 85 n. 30, but for whatever reason do not seem to feature in South Italy.

[55] Menzel and Naso 2007; Roth 2013b; Tagliamonte 2015: 133–4; Di Fazio 2019b: 83–4.

[56] Morandi 1987. [57] The classic account is Hölkeskamp 2011 [1987].

pre-eminence, members of leading *gentes* sought to articulate past achievements by themselves and their ancestors as individually guided but carried out for the benefit of the Republic. In this context, historical commemoration became a crucial tool for political ambitions, as is clear from any number of pieces of evidence, from Middle Republican *elogia* to Polybius' famous account of the use of ancestor masks at the funeral of a Roman nobleman.[58]

As Terrenato's work now stresses, older aristocratic groups were not canceled out by the rise of city states like Rome, but rather we find numerous signs of the continuity even into the later Republic of old aristocratic families using the city state as a platform to their own advantage. In terms of cultural production, the result of this tension between family agendas and those of the state was the coexistence of old with new practices, as it were, as aristocrats sought success in both family-based and state-based arenas.

The way historically specific detail appears in the painted tombs of Oscan Campania appears to speak to just this scenario of a transitional aristocracy, which was invested in traditional forms of authority as well as in new state-based collective interaction. On the one hand, scenes from the banquet or of the return of the warrior show the persistent importance of a traditional aristocratic ethos; on the other hand, historically specific scenes of corporate battle or office-holding speak to newfound desires to promote individual accomplishments on behalf of the broader community. We sometimes find traditional and novel scenes together in the same tomb, as at Paestum's Andriuolo tombs 104a and 114, where returning warriors are depicted in the same tomb as historically specific battle narratives. Otherwise, we have seen cases like the Spinazzo tomb at Paestum, where images of magistrates seem from their poses to grow out of the iconography of traditional scenes of the return of the warrior. I do not think this juxtaposition of old and new would have been jarring to its intended viewer; rather, it speaks to a Campanian aristocracy still existing to some extent in both worlds.

What is clear is that historical culture mattered in the dynamic social situation in Campania in this period as, we might add, it did at contemporary Middle Republican Rome. Narrative or individualized portrayals presented a usefulness for those interested in portraying themselves or their family members as invested in collective or community-based modes of aristocratic behavior. In other words, becoming historical was one way for Campanian elites to promote their participation in the state.

---

[58] Bernard 2018c: 234–5.

11.4 Conclusions: Roman Imperialism and Italian Historical Cultures

This chapter has endorsed the Middle Republic not only as a consequential point for the development of Rome, but also for Italian city states and their own leading actors, as visible in Campanian historical culture. The ongoing process of state formation saw aristocratic communities in transition, and such changes motivated the rise of new modes of accessing and maintaining authority. These geopolitical circumstances provided an impulse for Italian elites to become historical.

The foregoing discussion of Campanian tombs has shown multiple parallels with Rome, where historical culture in the Middle Republic was often instrumental to the construction of a new ruling elite, the senatorial *nobilitas*. It has, moreover, been useful to draw from better-known Roman circumstances in interpreting Campanian tombs, if not so much to explicate their historical content as to unlock the sociopolitical pressures behind them. However, I want to conclude by reasserting that the material at the core of this analysis is decidedly not Roman. It is interesting that both the Cumaean tomb and Andriuolo 114 at Paestum have prompted scholarly readings as depictions of moments of Roman conflict with, or even disaster at the hands of, the Samnites. I have questioned the particular interpretations of both scenes, but there remains in this scholarship a valiant desire to discover in these paintings a sort of alternative or even subaltern source, writing back against the conquerors in the final moments when that may have been possible. While we do possess considerable details about some Campanian families of this era, we must admit that this pertains as a rule to families like the Decii or the Plautii, who rose from Campanian origins to become major players in Roman politics and whose histories were therefore picked up by Roman commemorative processes. The tomb paintings from Cumae and Lucanian Paestum form tantalizing windows into the lives of elite Campanian families who did not follow identical paths and so were not similarly remembered. Nonetheless, the material presented here confirms that these elites, while anonymous to us, retained considerable interest in their history. The tomb paintings from Oscan Campania remind us that Rome was not alone in its process of becoming historical, and it is time we gave Italian historical culture its own place in this story.

Conclusion

12 | Becoming Political

Middle Republican Quandaries

CHRISTOPHER SMITH

12.1 Introduction

Occasional moments of doubt and disagreement notwithstanding, this volume is a gathering of true believers. There is an increasing sense that we can identify the direction of travel which the Romans were taking in the aftermath of the victory over Veii and the sack by the Gauls. The very fact that we can argue about Middle Republican politics in English is a step forward.[1] Yet it has to be acknowledged that one can imagine a different group of people taking a different view. Oakley's vast commentary on Livy has done a very good job of suppressing a lot of doubt and anxiety – it is a massive comfort blanket in the dark nights of the philologico-historical soul – but at least for the early period, it does not go without challenge.[2] Doubts persist over the content of legislation, the nature of magistracies, the transmission of information, and social structure.[3] There is a lot of confidence that something exciting is happening; the problem is isolating the "what it is that happened."

Two potential watershed moments have been identified in the politics of the Middle Republic: the Licinio-Sextian Laws of 367 BCE, and the late-fourth-century reforms of Appius Claudius Caecus. Both have been challenged. The annalistic account of the former contains what appear to be

---

[1] Scholarship has been rather more vigorous in other languages, with notable contributions by Hölkeskamp 2011 [1987], Loreto 1993, Humm 2005. It is striking how much more attention was paid in the past by Anglophone scholars to subjects such as the consular tribunate or the constitution of the assemblies, topics which have subsequently rather languished. Recent work on *imperium*, for instance Vervaet 2014 or Drogula 2015, may suggest that there is something of a renaissance of institutional history, at the same time as Terrenato's synthesis (2019) revives Münzer's more elite-driven account (1920); cf. also Gelzer 1912 and an important demonstration of the linkages between him and Münzer by Ridley 1986.

[2] Oakley 1997–2005.

[3] For a more skeptical take see for instance Wiseman 2018; Richardson 2012 is based on an argument over the importance of family characteristics in shaping ancient historical accounts, which reduces much of the historiography of the early and Middle Republic to the illustration of Late Republican concerns. Other skepticism is to be inferred from the relative avoidance of this period except in surveys.

anachronisms and inaccuracies, which has given rise to substantial skepticism. This has made it difficult to assess with confidence the nature of the reforms and specifically what kind of innovations the laws reflect.[4] Similarly, Michel Humm's long and radical interpretation of Appius Claudius Caecus' intellectual revolution at Rome has not convinced all his readers, with its highly imaginative development of the tenuous evidence.[5]

Part of the reason for skepticism about the period before the Punic Wars arises from the direction from which one approaches the evidence. Those who look backward from the Late Republic are tempted to see retrojection, and to underestimate the early capacity for sophisticated political thought. Those who look from the early history of Rome forward are perhaps more tempted to allow for development. The obvious danger of teleology lurks here; not everyone has the same picture of archaic Rome; and the fifth century remains a problem. It is not difficult to reconceptualize a long fourth century as the awakening of a hitherto relatively underdeveloped state, into a new elite-driven focus, a focus which might include the wholesale invention of a suitable past.

In this chapter, by way of concluding this volume, I would like to try to run the clock both forward and backward. We will end up framing a relatively positive background to the Middle Republican period, though we can also see some reasons why later periods were consciously and unconsciously constructing this period as somehow pivotal. The critical issue here is identifying the level of detail one can genuinely utilize, and to what end.

12.2 Paths to Confidence

Much of this volume is rooted in this sense of confidence in one or other way. One can believe the sources preserve genuine information and correctly contextualize it, or that the information is correct but the contextualization is wrong but open to correction. So Tan (Chapter 3) and Rosenstein (Chapter 4) take seriously the evidence we have for *tributum-stipendium* and *tribuni aerarii* and army development, which has the

---

[4] See von Fritz 1950; Billows 1989; Wiseman 1991, an early statement of the argument that would become Wiseman 1995; Cornell 1995: 333–40; various contributions to Beck et al. 2011; Pellam 2014. See also below for debates over the Licinio-Sextian legislation on land.

[5] Humm 2005, reviewed by, for instance, Bispham (*The Journal of Roman Studies* 98, 2008: 188–9) and Raepsaet-Charlier (*L'Antiquité classique* 76, 2007: 533–5).

consequence of making us take Roman military capacity in the fourth century rather seriously, and therefore bolster confidence in ancient accounts of Roman imperialism. Bernard looks to recover a widespread notion of historical culture. Terrenato and Wright (Chapter 2) do not quite believe the contextual presentation of the Roman elite, but they can arrive at their version by accepting the lists of magistrates.

This confidence is important precisely because it gives space for other arguments from material culture to find their correct place in notions of scale and complexity. And, naturally, one can derive a degree of confirmation from our increasing knowledge of the archaeology of the period. So at one level, one is more inclined to believe Palombi (Chapter 9) and Davies' (Chapter 10) rich contextual readings of the architectural developments of Rome and the influence of Hellenistic models because our social and political models for Rome presuppose a society of significant scale and complexity, and equally those who lay emphasis on the rather extraordinary developments in urbanism at Rome may expect to see parallel sophistication in other areas of thinking, including thinking about politics. It then becomes natural to test evidence for metallurgy, as Yarrow does in Chapter 6, or agricultural growth, as Trentacoste, Lodwick, and de Haas do in Chapters 7–8, to find similar confirmatory evidence. Scheidel's chapter (Chapter 5) setting Central Italian slavery practices against those of sub-Saharan large-scale social systems offers a benchmark of progress; comparative history presumes sufficiently settled parameters to allow the definition of *comparanda*.

One might imagine a couple of challenges to this. The first is the "mirage" argument; the Romans could not imagine their Early Republican condition to be significantly weaker than it was to become. They located primitivism in the very earliest years of the city, under Romulus, and only knew how to write a history of rapid growth; we should be more skeptical. In particular, we should not be tempted to overstate the institutional development of Rome. The second is the "miracle" argument; Rome explodes into prominence by some combination of factors which lifts the city from small-scale player to world power in a very short period of time. Arguably, some ancient historians such as Polybius saw an acceleration after the Gallic Sack. In what follows, I want to use Rome's fifth-century law code, the Twelve Tables, as a way into an argument that would offer less mirage and less miracle, and more development and more determination.

Most scholars have a good deal of confidence about the sophistication of later-fourth-century Rome, and the excavations of Clementina Panella near the Arch of Constantine in particular have put paid to many lingering doubts.[6] But it is precisely because of the messy transition to the early fourth century that the tendency has been to assume that Rome reaches this level of sophistication by accelerating quickly from a standing start. Livy's confession, however it was motivated, at the beginning of Book 6 about the unreliability of his own first five books due to the destruction of records in the Gallic Sack reinforces that perception, which then opens the door to a number of arguments: no dual consulship until the fourth century, radical doubts about the content of the Licinio-Sextian Laws, no magistrates' lists – or no coherent lists – until the later fourth century, assumptions about the social structures of the period. Bluntly, if Rome is a mess in the fifth century and maybe for a while after that, then the period of its subsequent development can become very short. This is to linger on a rather foolish periodization which bears no relationship to ancient conceptions, but the skeptics' line is rather more like a very long dark fifth century before a very long brighter third century, with the break coming sometime after the Latin Wars and the *leges Publiliae*. The interim period largely disappears.

It is worth saying that the archaeological evidence is mostly in line with this, in that until we have revised chronologies for the pottery sequences, there is much more to be said for the later fourth century and third century than there is for the earlier period.[7] It is also true that when we say things like "the Middle Republic is a critical phase," we commit all sorts of errors of anachronism. This is why Harriet Flower's notion of periodizing Rome through a series of successive Republics was such a good idea; it was so precisely because it avoids laying an entirely alien and irrelevant conception of time across the past.[8] Ultimately, this chapter and this volume take us forward in attempts not only to understand what ancient authors were reading back into the development of Rome, but also to preserve and enhance our understanding of the sociopolitical shifts across the 300 years after the fall of kingship at Rome.

12.3 Becoming Political: The Twelve Tables

As an alternative to periodization, this chapter, whose title contains an obvious reference to Nicholas Purcell's argument for Rome "becoming historical"[9] seeks to draw attention to processes whereby citizenship,

---

[6] Panella and Saguì 2013–17. [7] This is evident from Cifarelli, Gatti, and Palombi eds. 2019.
[8] Flower 2010. [9] Purcell 2003b.

community, and the *res publica* gain definition, and to identify the extent to which we can trace a political process in motion. My case studies are the Twelve Tables (the code of laws passed in the mid-fifth century) and private law, land ownership, and early relations with the Latins. In so doing, this paper operates like other arguments in the volume, for instance that of James Tan, to establish the existence of preconditions which underpin the potential for discussing the period between the Gallic Sack and the First Punic War. In so doing, we necessarily also identify the preconditions for the production of history, memory, and invention, which Bernard tackles (Chapter 11), and reflect also the *longue durée* archaeological treatments of De Haas and Trentacoste and Lodwick.

I want to start with what is arguably the most important and reliable pieces of evidence for Early Republican Rome, including the fourth century, the Twelve Tables. After the publication of a new text in *Roman Statutes* in 1996, and an important edited volume by Michel Humbert, we now have two new and massive studies. Humbert has returned to the subject with a 1,000-page edition and commentary, and an Italian team led by Maria Floriana Cursi has produced a two-volume set of essays.[10] We seem to have come a long way from the late Alan Watson's little book of 1975, *Rome of the Twelve Tables*, although for all that, he said a great deal in a short compass.

Bruce Frier, in a largely positive account of Watson's book, gave a superb summary of its argument:

> Rome of 449 BC was a grim world: its isolated farms ringing a small residential core, with commerce only marginally important – a State in the throes of economic crisis, seeking both to protect itself against the squabbles of adjacent landowners and to encourage maximum utilization of the precious resource they controlled. Rome shared with its Latin neighbors an inherited and largely unwritten legal system; yet only Rome is known to have moved towards codification. . . . The Twelve Tables were a crude "code" of selected traditional rules of law, especially in debated areas; but many details of law "remained a mystery". There was little innovation. . . . The code was conservative, also, in what it avoided: public magistracies and state religion. By restricting themselves largely to private law, the codifiers effectively gave a permanent cast to Roman legal science.[11]

This points to the challenge of the Twelve Tables as a text. We have just a few fragments which have to be unearthed from the mass of subsequent

---

[10] Crawford 1996; Humbert 2005, 2018; Cursi 2018.   [11] Frier 1977: 379.

commentary, and the original text may not be recoverable in many instances.

For my clock-running-backward metaphor, the key issue is the pervasive commitment on the part of the jurists of the late second and first centuries BCE onward to anchor their enterprise of codification and commentary in the existence of an antecedent tradition; but it is also important to recognize the persisting significance of this codification, or the belief in it, in embedding a notion of Rome as a law-based community, and one in which history was critically important in giving authority to the present. One reason that it is important that the Romans had a notion of laws even predating the Twelve Tables, the *leges regiae*, is that the implication that there was something previously in existence supports a notion that the Twelve Tables were fundamentally conservative, codifying existing custom.[12]

Unlike Watson, the recent editions have been reluctant to set out clearly what historical reconstruction of fifth-century-BCE Rome can be inferred from the fragments. However, there is a general agreement between the two editions that one of the absolutely clear intentions and outcomes of the law is to control the power of the magistrate. The magistrate was put under rules, and this is the really distinctive feature; indeed Humbert presents the Twelve Tables much more as a manual for a magistrate. The question immediately arising is under whose power is the magistrate then? And the answer seems to be the *populus*. One of the key passages is *de capite civis iniussu populi ne roganto* as Pomponius puts it. The *populus* is the *comitia centuriata*, and there is a strong presumption that in the case of capital punishment, the people are sovereign, as Polybius says (6.11.2).

It is possible of course to think that this actually comes from much later thinking, and that Pomponius is wrong (again), but an early abstraction is entirely consonant with the clear notion of constraining the magistrate, and in addition the very notion of the magistrate is itself dependent on the process of election, which is itself dependent on the abstraction of popular choice, however defined.

There is of course a certain circularity here, and it can either be seen as reinforcement or more of the mirage effect, but at the least the tendency of the other chapters in this volume which stress a significant military capacity (Tan, Rosenstein), the possibility of slave ownership from an early point (Scheidel), and evidence for agricultural intensification (de Haas,

---

[12] On the *leges regiae*, see Mantovani 2012; Laurendi 2013; and the volume of essays edited by Bell and Du Plessis 2020, which includes arguments by both myself and Nicola Terrenato with Matthew Naglak.

Trentacoste and Lodwick) sit in interesting counterpoint to the "small Rome" picture which Watson presents. They are not necessarily incompatible, but we might see the Twelve Tables as reflecting a moment in time in a society that was beginning to accelerate. The question arises as to the vectors of that acceleration, to which we now turn.

12.4 Becoming Political: The Problem of Property

I want to take a side step into the Greek world and think about a brilliant article by Emily Mackil in Ando and Richardson's book *Ancient States and Infrastructural Power: Europe, Asia, and America*.[13] Mackil argues that jurisgeneration in archaic Greece played a crucial role in the formation of Greek states. One of her key points is that regulations in the field of private law necessarily affect the infrastructural power of the state, and nowhere more so than in regulations over property. As Mackil puts it, the juridical formation of property is a necessary condition for the formation of state power. But that is not all, because in both the Greek and the early Roman formulations, the concentration on usufruct takes one past simple territorial definitions to the relationship between the owner and other people in relation to the object owned.

Her main case study, the Gortyn code, offers striking parallels to some of the concerns of the Twelve Tables – it established procedures for the resolution of boundary disputes, worried about trespassing, and set down penalties for water damage due to negligence to a neighbor's property. I think this is plausibly the same sort of conceptual world as we find in early Rome and the Twelve Tables; the same areas of interest, the same mix of innovation and conservatism, the same foundational significance. But Mackil's conclusion (drawing heavily on Michael Mann's theories of institutional power) is then striking:

> I have suggested that the concern with property reflected in inscribed laws of the Archaic period was both a response to the needs of individual possessors for the maintenance of the existing social order and a mechanism by which the emergent state could begin to establish and enforce its territorial jurisdiction, a crucial component of infrastructural state power.[14]

The emergence of *ager publicus* seems to me to be centrally in this nexus of state autonomy and abstraction. This is really tricky – Capogrossi Colognesi's

[13] Mackil 2017.   [14] Mackil 2017: 80.

suggestion that we can trace a move from *ager gentilicius* to *ager publicus* has been highly influential, but my own view is that it is better to think in terms of complex regimes of resolving common pool resource issues; and I also think we may be better thinking about regulations which relate to the relationships between people and property rather than neatly distinguished definitions of property.[15]

Let us take an early and controversial example. Lisa Mignone has recently tackled the extremely difficult evidence for the *lex Icilia* and the *publicatio* of the Aventine.[16] It seems hard to argue the *lex Icilia* away altogether, even if we do not believe that the original text was available quite as Dionysius claimed. Dionysius talks about "fractioning" and Livy about making public, whatever that exactly means, and Mignone has developed good reasons for thinking that it is primarily about confiscation. In the terminology proposed here, the Aventine is put into a certain relationship with a certain group of people (or definition of the people/state) for certain functions, and therefore is taken from, retrospectively and prospectively, any other relationship. Mignone is surely right that this does not have to be about plebeians as such.

This, then, seems to require two sides of a coin – the power of an autonomous state to make such a definitive declaration and a spectrum of complex notions of property from common pool resources to private ownership. The fact that we cannot quite work out how this plebiscite was passed so that it could have the effect it did is, to my mind, interesting evidence for the contested nature of the state which is being created through the constant battle over property. As Mackil says, if we stop thinking with Locke that property is a natural and innocent thing, but is rather the product of legal intervention in an area of constant dispute, we are on better grounds.

Running my clock backward, it is reasonably clear that there were good reasons for antedating plebeian interventions in a unitary history of *ager publicus* as a defined juridical concept. And for that reason we are of course right to be skeptical all the way through about the *lex Icilia* and about the later legislation.

But running the clock forward, this seems entirely compatible with the sort of story which John Rich and Saskia Roselaar are telling in which private property is part of the story alongside what comes to be known as *ager publicus*.[17] In other words, again it is the relational aspect to land that is important. If Rich is right that the *lex Licinia* bundled all forms of land

---

[15] Capogrossi Colognesi 1980; I draw the notion of common pool resources from the work of Elinor Ostrom, for example Ostrom 2018.
[16] Mignone 2016a: esp. 48–76; Dion. Hal. 10.32; Livy 3.31–2. [17] Rich 2008; Roselaar 2013b.

together and concentrated instead on the just relationship between an individual, the community, and land, then it seems to me we might locate that in the same nexus that Mackil is talking about. That is to say that the concern with private property is critical (alongside other forms of property) but that the creation of laws reinforces the autonomy of the state, and that that forces the argument about the nature of the state.

So we can see both why the historians and lawyers in the later Republic did what they did with the fourth-century rules and the even earlier *lex Icilia*, but we can also see that these were genuine problems which we can set into a rather different historical and legal story. I think this story is compatible with Terrenato's elite clans, referred to here *in nuce* by his and Wright's chapter, as long as one sets these ideas into the context of a legal framework which is in the process of persistently redefining the community (and largely against narrow definitions of privilege).

There is more to be drawn from this volume which supports thinking hard about property regimes. Tan argues that taxes on the revenues of small farmers were critical to sustaining the army but also challenged ownership by exacerbating debt, and Rosenstein in this volume and throughout his work has worried about the precarity of the small farmer in a time of continual war. Both de Haas and Scheidel open the possibility of substantial low-level familial slave ownership. It is at least arguable that we are seeing the awkward and contested evolution of regimes of private ownership alongside state obligations and the transformation of common pool resources, all seeking uneasy balances alongside an expansionist external agenda and a fractious internal politics, in all of which the notion of the commons is in tension with private ambition. These processes are not fully worked out even by the Late Republic, but that does not mean they were not in play earlier.

One might venture to suggest that we are edging toward a better synthesis of the earlier period, which then makes more sense of the fourth century and situates both private property and state autonomy as critical elements at an early stage. I actually think we need something like this to sustain Bernard's convincing arguments on Middle Republican debt, and how the Romans escaped from it. Bernard argues that the massive building works and forced labor of the early fourth century placed pressure on Rome's economic structures, and created debt; later in the fourth century, the economics of labor, payment, and extraction circumvented the problem. Bernard questions whether the Romans thought in terms of conscious economic policy, but we might get to the right sort of thinking through shifts in the relationships between individual, community, and land. The consequences of an over-commitment to central need without communal support were redressed through a distribution of land but also a relocation of burden away from the citizenry. This back and forth would characterize the history of the Republic.[18]

12.5 The Politics of Exchange

From ownership, the next step is to look at transfer of ownership of movable and of landed property. What I want to argue in this section is that a key battleground over the nature and sophistication of Early Republican society is the debate over the regulation of exchange. Moreover, this is located precisely in relations with property and the notion of social evolution. We have suggested that the Twelve Tables offers an opportunity to understand the working out of relative power relations between individual, magistrate, and community. We then suggested that emergent regimes of private ownership were part of the development of the infrastructure of the state. Now I want to argue that the notion of exchange exemplifies these same trends of political evolution, reinforcing our notion of the sophistication of the political and economic issues at stake. Here the key issue is *commercium*, or the right to trade and enter into legal contracts, a topic which has been overlooked in recent work on the Twelve Tables, but benefits from Saskia Roselaar's important article on this subject.[19] Humbert has taken the more traditional view that *commercium* is assumed to be possible between Romans and non-Romans (*peregrini*) in the Twelve Tables, whereas Roselaar argued that it was conspicuously absent and not to be inferred here, or in the Rome–Carthage treaty of 509 BCE.

If we assume that Roselaar is correct, something rather interesting seems to happen. The logic runs something like this: The absence of possession of *commercium* was no strong barrier to commercial links. But the Latins are said to lose *commercium* in 338 BCE. It cannot be proven to exist by any of the earliest evidence; therefore it must at best come into existence over the period, as a transformation of rights to engage in *mancipatio*, which clearly did exist in the Twelve Tables (critically this relates to those items which are most closely related to and which include land). So the question we have to answer is either, why and when did the Latins get *commercium*? Or, why did Livy think they lost it in 338 BC? And this is made all the sharper by Roselaar's parallel contention that exactly the same argument can be used

[18] Bernard 2018a. [19] Roselaar 2013a.

for *conubium*.[20] Conversely, the privileges seem to continue for Latin colonists.

The tide has been turning in this direction for some time, with important additional arguments by Broadhead and Coşkun, with Kremer and Humbert defending the more traditional view. The right to gain citizenship by magistracy has long been downdated, and Coşkun in particular has argued for a downdating to the second century BCE of the *ius migrandi*.[21] In short, there is little evidence that Latins and other non-Romans had legal rights to engage in formal contractual relations with Romans, including over land and its products.

From one point of view, even if correct, this might be seen to be of limited import. Both Coşkun and Roselaar argue that trade was significant and substantial regardless of whether it was governed by *commercium* or not. Intermarriage is unlikely to have stopped. There clearly were possibilities for Latins to move into citizenship in Rome and therefore gain such rights, as Terrenato has shown in his discussion of the Plautii, for instance, and more generally in his and Wright's chapter in this volume.[22]

If the negative argument is correct, when Livy wrote in 8.14.10 *ceteris Latinis populis conubia commerciaque et concilia inter se ademerunt* (the rest of the Latins [i.e. apart from those not given citizenship, those who had been deported, the Tiburtines and Praenestines, or others who were punished with the imposition of a colony] were deprived of their rights of mutual trade and intermarriage and of holding common councils) he may well have been reflecting the retrojection of a much later situation. It is interesting that at some point it made sense to tell a story in which the relationship between Rome and the Latins was closer than it was, and there seems every reason to connect this to the very complex interrelationship between Romans, Latins, and colonists which are discussed by de Haas and Palombi and which are by no means adequately defined by the unidirectional power of Rome. If mutual trade, intermarriage, and political action were the rights which were at some stage given to Latin colonists, that presumably was a relevant consideration. Was the claim that these were rights of long standing a justification in the argument for their presence in colonies, or was the fact of Latin colonists having this right regarded as evidence that it was a broader right which must have been removed?

This kind of argument might be taken as another support for the idea that part of what is presented as true about earlier periods is in fact the

---

[20] Roselaar 2013a.   [21] Broadhead 2001; Coşkun 2016; Kremer 2007, 2014; Humbert 2014.
[22] Terrenato 2014.

product of retrojection. Is there anything that can be rescued for the actual conditions of early Rome? One way of telling this story, which is highly compatible with Terrenato's version of the grand bargain between Central Italian elites, is to emphasize that this is all an elite game.[23] After all, the Twelve Tables did not help a poor individual gain access to jurisdiction, since the procedures were not published until the fourth century. If we do away with a picture of legal relationships clearly established between communities after the *Foedus Cassianum* for instance, and choose a model of more ad hoc recognition which is of particular relevance to elite individuals, and one stresses social mobility between communities at an elite level which circumvented lack of formal legal capacity, it would be easy to come to the sort of elite interaction which Terrenato describes so convincingly, and at operational level I am sure that must be partly right. That said, even the Twelve Tables is aware of less formal mechanisms of property exchange.[24] It is not hard to imagine different levels of legitimacy and litigable or nonlitigable contracts, which is compatible with our suggestion made in this chapter that forms of property ownership and consequent indications of power were being worked out alongside the redefinitions of community and state.

12.6 Building the Community

This emphasis on the way that later authors have made the situation in the Early Republic more neat and formal than it actually was might be thought to leave my attempt to stress community-wide models somewhat in difficulty. But I do not think that we should rush to deduce the absence of formal communal actions, decisions, and enterprises even from the beginning of our period. On the three key areas of trade, intermarriage, and access to Roman political office, we could perhaps read the situation forward as follows:

On trade, the critical distinction which Roselaar draws is between *res mancipi* and *res nec mancipi*, and if there was a concern over non-Roman access to Roman land, that is fairly comprehensible, and interestingly mirrors distinctions made in the Rome–Carthage treaties between land and other possessions.[25] It is also part of the previous discussion – the issue is about the relationship between individuals and property. The same concern may have operated with regard to marriage, since in a legitimate

---

[23] Terrenato 2019. [24] Bernard 2016: 329. [25] Nörr 2005.

cum manu marriage, property could transfer out of one city to another, which was a matter again of legitimate concern. However, elite marriages clearly had taken place in the past, part of the famous horizontal social mobility, although there are hints that one could not entirely be assimilated (Tarquinius Priscus' alleged inability to rise to the highest office in Tarquinia despite his Etruscan mother and wife would be an example).[26] The curiate assembly's concerns over maintenance of *sacra* and property, the evident concern over property and marriage in the Twelve Tables, the concerns over patricio-plebeian marriage are all recognizably part of the same world. Notice though that these are all community restrictions on elite behavior, and it would be reasonable to think that the undoubted individual grants of citizenship which occurred were granted at an assembly level.

The formal role of the community in establishing status and rights touches directly on the problem of Latins in office, such as, but not only, the Plautii, and therefore on themes emergent in the chapters by Wright and Terrenato and Palombi, and implicitly running through several others that tackle the shifting relationship between Rome and its wider region. It is clear that the legal relationships between Romans and Latins were more distant than we may have thought, though the effect is felt not on normal commerce, which probably continued regardless, but in specifically the area where Mackil sees the operation of an autonomous state, that is, ownership of land and protection of property. There were no automatic rights which brought someone into the Roman citizenship, even from the most favored neighbors, and when citizenship was granted, for instance to Tusculum, it came without the vote. It is unsurprising that only the most ambitious and conspicuous may have circumvented this, but the barrier was high, and unless we can conjure up a different mechanism, it must have been a state grant. It is very important to remember that when we look at the supposed entry of non-Romans into Roman citizenship before and during the long fourth century, we must recognize that, first, we have almost no information about what happened before 509 BCE; second, the first appearance of a family in the *fasti* does not imply that this was close to the moment when they arrived in Rome; third, we have to be wary of arguments about the ethnic identity of names. So even granting that some plebeians are indeed non-Romans, as Wright and Terrenato do here, implies community choices, perhaps spread over some 200 years. Again this is very close to the arguments Coşkun made in suggesting that we

---

[26] Livy 1.34.1.

should not overdo Roman generosity over citizenship, but also implies that whatever benefits may have accrued from any such act, a good deal must have been conspicuously acquired or expected to be acquired by the Roman state or *populus*. This position is close to James Tan's arguments about Roman rationality over the extraction of maximum benefit from its neighbors.

It is possible to believe that this system of access to *mancipatio*, restrictive access to citizenship and a predisposition against a general extension of unregulated intermarriage, all of which sustained a certain level of trade but was also highly defensive of the community, was what one would have found elsewhere in Latium. In other words, in casting back the later principles of *commercium* and *conubium* to a world that pre-existed 338 BCE, Livy not only technically misdescribed Rome's position with regard to other Latin states, but also the position of other Latin states with regard to Rome. There was a principle of autonomy and a mechanism of interaction. A very significant change then took place as a result of the Latin War of 340–338 BCE, which as John Rich pointed out to me, probably led to a citizen-to-ally ratio which would only be surpassed in 212 CE. The tension between the various views of what this actually felt like and how it was resolved can only be distantly heard in our sources.

12.7 Bringing in the Gods

Another area of innovation and change was surely in religion, which is an acknowledged lacuna in this book. Both Champion and Padilla Peralta have in rather different ways identified this as a period in which the relationship between religion as an increasingly identifiable sphere of action and the state as an increasingly visible arena was productive of social, economic, and political transformation.[27] In one way or another both emphasize noninstrumental and society-wide entwinements of the gods and the community.

John Scheid has argued that there is a deep connection between law and religion at the level of the authority and space within which law was made. Two potential laws relate to calendrical and cultic activity in the fifth century BCE.[28] The *lex Licinia Sextia de Xviris sacris faciundis* in 367 BCE is specifically about changing the personnel of Roman religion, and

---

[27] Champion 2017; Padilla Peralta 2020a.
[28] Scheid 2012; the laws are the *lex Pinaria Furia de mense intercalari* (472 BCE) and *lex de clavo pandendi* (463 BCE).

half the priestly laws we know are plebiscites. There is no real reason why the Twelve Tables should include these sorts of areas given that other mechanisms existed, and at the same time, many of the *leges regiae* include the necessary *sanctio* which brings law back to the gods.[29] We touch here on the substantial argument about the laicization represented by the Twelve Tables, and whether this was overturned or not in subsequent decades. By this we mean specifically the extent to which law placed relationships on a different humanized footing, thereby undermining the previous obscure and potentially arbitrary power of priests. The sources give us hints of tense debates, which may not be far from the kinds of arguments that underlie Penelope Davies's account of temple building from the fourth to third centuries,[30] and specifically the transforming conceptualizations of religious authority.

However, laicization does not seem quite the right way to position this argument, not least because it artificially divides religion from law in a rather modern way. Instead, in common with other parts of our argument, I suggest that the implication of the gods in everybody's lives through temple building, festivals, pilgrimage, and the rituals of war, alongside the decentered and personal capacity of individuals, mirrors precisely the symbiotic emergence of sharper notions of personal agency and of community definition – and indeed and crucially of the relationships across this spectrum.

It is extremely difficult, I think, to argue that this is new in the fourth century BCE.[31] Rather, we again see the transformation and acceleration of previous interactions. We suspect that the fifth century was less empty than we used to think. I have suggested that the Twelve Tables and arguments around the processes of legal exchange and, here, the teasing out and

---

[29] However, there is perhaps another way of looking at this, which both complicates and makes rather exciting the aftermath of the Twelve Tables in all the fields we have been discussing. Aldo Schiavone suggested that we should see the Twelve Tables as a striking and revolutionary step forward toward a classificatory model of Roman law, but one which then ground to a halt, became monumentalized and was subjected to the interpretation of the priests through their profound interaction with law. Breaking into the priesthood then became the crucial goal of the plebeians, but this was not necessarily going to continue the move toward a radical solution. Thus, Schiavone's argument is that the reason the Twelve Tables is so central to our and the Romans' reading is that it was not updated; but while the tendency from antiquity on has been to see continuity, in fact we should see a profound rupture (Schiavone 2012). However, the history of plebiscitary legislation, with all the problems that surround it, indicates that the patrician control of law was persistently resisted, though less in the area of private law.

[30] Davies in this volume (Chapter 10) and 2017a.

[31] Just some examples of pre-existing religious sophistication include the calendar, as well as the emergence of major temples and of an artistic and artisanal economy closely tied to the religious sphere. Rüpke 2018: 55–108 is a convenient summary.

monitoring of personal and community agency in religion, are deep-seated vectors of change, which we see accelerating across this period. The reasons for that may lie in the steady growth of the military, as Tan and Rosenstein illustrate; the kinds of ideological influences which shaped, are shaped by, and made visible in architectural choices, in the ways that Palombi and Davies describe; by the consequences of the sorts of changes wrought by slave ownership, mobility, agricultural change, and possibly even some climatic features, and by the emergence of a historical culture, as Bernard argues; and, as I have argued here, a political culture.

12.8 Conclusion

I will close by using Frier's summary of Watson as a negative picture of Roman sophistication, which this volume and my contribution challenges at every point.

> Rome of 449 BC was a grim world: its isolated farms ringing a small residential core, with commerce only marginally important – a State in the throes of economic crisis, seeking both to protect itself against the squabbles of adjacent landowners and to encourage maximum utilization of the precious resource they controlled.[32]

It is certainly true that the depredations of inland peoples made life tougher in the fifth century. Commerce only marginally important? That is not so clear, and at any rate the mechanisms were there. And one can read protection of land as desperate, and/or as the clear expression of the role of the autonomous state.

> Rome shared with its Latin neighbors an inherited and largely unwritten legal system; yet only Rome is known to have moved towards codification.

Part of this is simply an argument from silence. However another way of looking at this is that if we see both Romans and Latins developing concepts around *mancipatio*, this could be a more dynamic process.

> The Twelve Tables were a crude "code" of selected traditional rules of law, especially in debated areas; but many details of law "remained a mystery." There was little innovation.

This seems to me an example of reading back. And it also is worth saying that the Twelve Tables were no obstacle to innovation; rather, perhaps, we

---

[32] This extract and the following quotes are all from Frier 1977: 379.

see flexible mechanisms of dispute resolution and agile defense of what was perceived as community interest. The Romans did not rewrite the Twelve Tables, but added and constructed an apparatus of statutory law to drive innovation forward. And lastly,

> The code was conservative, also, in what it avoided: public magistracies and state religion. By restricting themselves largely to private law, the codifiers effectively gave a permanent cast to Roman legal science.

Perhaps. But I have suggested that in the area of land ownership, capital punishment, and foreign relations, principles surrounding the notion of community and its abstract form exist in and around the Twelve Tables that would evolve in the course of subsequent years.

This volume argues that the transformations of society and economy after the defeat of Veii and the sack of Rome by the Gauls were remarkable, significant, and constitutive of the Rome which was then able to rise rapidly to global dominance. This is not teleological; Romans, individually and collectively, had to make difficult and complex decisions to reorganize their behaviors, relationships, and institutions. The period is often seen through the lens of the Struggle of the Orders, or the glimpses of military adaptations, but we are hampered by lack of evidence. In this volume, however, the evidence we do have has been deployed to show what a remarkable achievement the Roman state that entered the Punic Wars was. My argument here is to circumvent any artificial chronological boundaries and to insist on the extraordinary capacity of ancient society to solve problems of immense complexity through argument and experiment.

There is absolutely no question that the Romans' "read back" their later history and that this causes us genuine problems, not least with the Twelve Tables, but with much more of the fourth-century material too. They attributed later developments to an earlier period. But the attempt made here of reading forward, looking in an earlier period for the antecedents of social, economic, and political change, while it will always be controversial, seems to suggest, at least to me, that by the time the critical transformations of the Middle Republic began, the intellectual lights had already been burning brightly and for some time.

Bibliography

Ancient sources and modern corpora are cited according to the *Oxford Classical Dictionary*.

Abrams, E., and T. Bolland. 1999. "Architectural energetics, ancient monuments, and operations management." *Journal of Archaeological Method and Theory* 6: 263–91.

Acconcia, V. ed. 2020. *L'età delle trasformazioni: l'Italia medio-adriatica tra il V e il IV secolo a.C. Nuovi modelli di autorappresentazione delle comunità a confronto e temi di cultura materiale*. Rome.

Acosta, A. N., K. Killgrove, V. C. Moses, and B. L. Turner. 2019. "Nourishing urban development: A palaeodietary study of Archaic Gabii, Italy (6th–5th c BCE)." *Journal of Archaeological Science: Reports* 27: 1019–62.

Adam, J.-P. 1994. *Le Temple du Portunus au Forum Boarium*. Rome.

Adams, J. N. 2003. *Bilingualism and the Latin Language*. Cambridge, UK.

Afzelius, A. 1942. *Die römische Eroberung Italien (340–264 v. Chr.)*. Aarhus.

Albarella, U., A. Tagliacozzo, K. Dobney, and P. Rowley-Conwy. 2006. "Pig hunting and husbandry in prehistoric Italy: A contribution to the domestication debate." *Proceedings of the Prehistoric Society* 72: 193–227.

Aldrete, G. S., and D. J. Mattingly. 1999. "Feeding the city: The organization, operation, and scale of the supply system for Rome." In D. Potter and D. Mattingly, eds., *Life, Death, and Entertainment in the Roman Empire*, 171–204. Ann Arbor, MI.

Alessio, A. 2001. "Grottaglie (Taranto), Oliovitolo, F. 202 I N.E." *Taras. Rivista di Archeologia* 21: 102–3.

Alhaique, F. 2016. "Zooarchaeological remains from the Tincu House at Gabii." In R. Opitz, M. Mogetta, and N. Terrenato, eds., *A Mid-Republican House from Gabii*, 137–60. Ann Arbor, MI.

Allen, M., and L. Lodwick. 2017. "Agricultural strategies in Roman Britain." In M. Allen, L. Lodwick, T. Brindle, M. Fulford, and A. Smith, eds., *The Rural Economy of Roman Britain. Britannia Monograph Series* Vol. 30, 142–77. London.

Alonso, N., and R. Frankel. 2017. "A survey of ancient grain milling systems in the Mediterranean." *Revue archéologique de l'Est Supplément* 43: 461–78.

Altheim, F. 1961. *Einzeluntersuchungen zur altitalischen Geschichte : Anfänge römischer Geschichtsschreibung*. Frankfurt am Main.

Ambrosini, L., and L. M. Michetti. 2013. "L'ultima frequentazione del santuario meridionale: Testimonianze dai contesti." In M. P. Baglione and M. D. Gentili, eds., *Riflessioni su Pyrgi: Scavi e ricerche nelle aree del santuario*, Supplementi e Monografie, *Archeologia Classica* 11: 123–66.

Amici, C. M. 2004–5. "Evoluzione architettonica del comizio a Roma." *Rendiconti della Pontificia Accademia Romana di Archeologia* 77: 351–79.

Amici, C. M. 2007. "Problemi topografici dell'area retrostante la Curia dall'età arcaica all'epoca tardo-repubblicana." In C. M. Amici, P. Dell'Amico, M. C. Leotta, F. Pallarés, M. Ricci, and I. Sciortino, eds., *Lo scavo didattico della zona retrostante la Curia (Foro di Cesare): Campagne di scavo 1961-1970*, 161–8. Rome.

Ampolo, C. 1976–7. "Demarato: Osservazioni sulla mobilità sociale arcaica." *Dialoghi di Archeologia* 9–10: 333–45.

Andreassi, G. 2007. "L'attività archeologica in Puglia nel 2006." In aa.vv. *Passato e futuro dei convegni di Taranto : Atti del quarantaseiesimo Convegno di studi sulla Magna Grecia, Taranto 29 settembre–1 ottobre 2006*, 503–28. Taranto.

Andrews, M., and S. Bernard. 2020. "Spaces of economic exchange." In M. L. Caldelli and C. Ricci, eds., *City of Encounters, Public Spaces and Social Interaction in Ancient Rome*, 69–112. Rome.

Antonio, M. L., Z. Gao, H. M. Moots et al. 2019. "Ancient Rome: A genetic crossroads of Europe and the Mediterranean." *Science* 366: 708.

Appleton, C. 1919. "Contribution à l'histoire du prêt à intérêt à Rome." *Revue historique de droit français et étranger* 43: 467–543.

Arco, L., and E. Abrams. 2006. "An essay on energetics: The construction of the Aztec chinampa system." *Antiquity* 80: 906–18.

Armstrong, J. 2016. *War and Society in Early Rome: From Warlords to Generals*. Cambridge, UK.

Armstrong, J. 2020. "Organized chaos: Manipuli, socii, and the Roman army c. 300." In M. Fronda and J. Armstrong, eds., *Romans at War: Soldiers, Citizens, and Society in the Roman Republic*, 76–98. London.

Arobba, D., R. Caramiello, and A. Del Lucchese, 2003. "Archaeobotanical investigations in Liguria: preliminary data on the early Iron Age at Monte Trabocchetto (Pietra Ligure, Italy)." *Vegetation History and Archaeobotany* 12.4: 253–62.

Arvanitis, N. 2004. "La Casa delle Vestali d'età arcaica." *Workshop di Archeologia Classica* 1: 145–53.

Ashby, T. 1935. *The Aqueducts of Ancient Rome*. Oxford.

Attema, P. 1993. "An archaeological survey in the Pontine Region: A contribution to the settlement history of south Lazio 900–100." (Unpublished PhD thesis, Rijksuniversiteit Groningen)

Attema, P. 2000. "Landscape archaeology and Livy: Warfare, colonial expansion and town and country in Central Italy of the 7th to 4th c." *Babesch* 75: 115–26.

Attema, P. 2017. "Landscape archaeology in Italy: Past questions, current state and future directions." In T. De Haas and G. Tol, eds., *The Economic Integration of Roman Italy: Rural Communities in a Globalizing World*, 426–35.Leiden.

Attema, P., G. J. Burgers, and M. Van Leusen. 2010. *Regional Pathways to Complexity*. Amsterdam.

Attema, P., W. Carafa, C. J. Jongman et al. 2022. "The Roman hinterland project: Integrating archaeological field surveys around Rome and beyond." *European Journal of Archaeology* 25.2: 238–58.

Attema, P., T. de Haas, J. Seubers, and G. Tol. 2017. "In search of the archaic countryside: Different scenarios for the ruralisation of Satricum and Crustumerium." In P. Lulof and C. Smith, eds., *The Age of Tarquinius Superbus: Central Italy in the Late 6th Century*, 195–204. Leuven.

Attema, P., T. de Haas, G. Tol, and J. Seubers. 2018. "Towards an integrated database for the study of long-term settlement dynamics, economic performance and demography in the Pontine Region and the hinterland of Rome." Conference paper presented in P. A. J. Attema and G. Schörner, eds., *The Rural Foundations of the Roman Economy: 19th International Congress of Classical Archaeology, Archaeology and Economy in the Ancient World, Cologne/Bonn, 22-26 May 2018*, 35–53. Heidelberg.

Attema, P., and G. Schoerner, eds. 2012. "Comparative issues in the archaeology of the Roman rural landscape, site classification between survey, excavation and historical categories." Supplement Series Vol. 88. *Journal of Roman Archaeology*.

Averill, S. 1990. "Local elites and communist revolution in the Jiangxi hill country." In P. J. Esherick and M. B. Rankin, eds., *Chinese Local Elites and Patterns of Dominance*, 282–304. Berkeley.

Badian, E. 1966. "The early Roman historians." In T. A. Dorey, ed., *Latin Historians*, 1–38. London.

Baglione, M. P., B. B. Marchesini, C. Carlucci, M. D. Gentili, and L. M. Michetti. 2015. "Pyrgi: A sanctuary in the middle of the Mediterranean sea." In E. Kistler, B. Öhlinger, M. Mohr, and M. Hoernes, eds., *Sanctuaries and the Power of Consumption: Networking and the Formation of Elites in the Archaic Western Mediterranean World*, 221–37. Wiesbaden.

Bailey, G. 2007. "Time perspectives, palimpsests and the archaeology of time." *Journal of Anthropological Archaeology* 26: 198–223.

Baker, A., J. C. Hellstrom, B. F. J. Kelly, G. Mariethoz, and V. Trouet. 2015. "A composite annual-resolution stalagmite record of North Atlantic climate over the last three millennia." *Scientific Reports* 5: 10307.

Baldassarri, M., G. Cristoforetti, I. Fantozzi et al. 2007. "Analisi LIBS di esemplari di AES Rude proveniente dall'abitato etrusco di Ghiaccio Forte (Scansano – GR)." In M. Baldassarri, G. Cristoforetti, I. Fantozzi et al., eds., *Atti del IV Congresso di Archeometria, Scienza e Beni Culturali, Pisa 2006*, 561–74. Bologna.

Barker, G. 1988. "Archaeology and the Etruscan countryside." *Antiquity* 62: 722–85.

Barker, G., and G. Clark. 1995. "The faunal data." In G. Barker, ed., *The Biferno Valley Survey*, 143–76. Leicester.

Barker, G., A. Grant, P. Beavitt et al. 1991. "Ancient and modern pastoralism in central Italy: An interdisciplinary study in the Cicolano mountains." *Papers of the British School at Rome* 59: 15–88.

Baroin, C. 2010. *Se souvenirà Rome: Formes, représentations et pratiques de la mémoire*. Paris.

Bartoli, A. 1963. *Curia Senatus, lo scavo e il restauro*. Rome.

Bastien, J.-L. 2007. *Le triomphe romain et son utilisation politique, á Rome aux trois derniers siècles de la république*. Rome.

Battistelli, P. 2001. "L'area sud-occidentale del Palatino tra il VI e il IV secolo a.C." In P. Pensabene and S. Falzone, eds., *Scavi del Palatino* 1: 79ff. Rome.

Beard, M. 2007. *The Roman Triumph*. Cambridge, MA.

Beck, H. 2005. *Karriere und Hierarchie: Die römische Aristokratie und die Anfänge des* cursus honorum *in der mittleren Republik*. Berlin.

Beck, H., A. Duplá, M. Jehne, and F. P. Polo, eds. 2011. *Consuls and Res Publica: Holding High Office in the Roman Republic*. Cambridge, UK.

Beck, H., and U. Walter. 2001. *Die frühen römischen Historiker*. 2 vols. Darmstadt.

Becker, J. A. 2013. "Villas and agriculture in Republican Italy." In J. DeRose Evans, ed., *A Companion to the Archaeology of the Roman Republic*, 309–22. Oxford.

Becker, J., and N. Terrenato, eds. 2012. *Roman Republican Villas: Architecture, Context, and Ideology*. Ann Arbor, MI.

Bell, S., and P. Du Plessis, eds. 2020. *Roman Law Before the Twelve Tables: An Interdisciplinary Approach*. Edinburgh.

Bellotti, P., G. Calderoni, P. L. Dall'Aglio, et al. 2016. "Middle-to late-Holocene environmental changes in the Garigliano delta plain (Central Italy): Which landscape witnessed the development of the Minturnae Roman colony?" *The Holocene* 26.9: 1457–71.

Beloch, K. J. 1926. *Römische Geschichte bis zum Beginn der punischen Kriege*. Berlin and Leipzig.

Benassai, R. 2001. *La pittura dei Campani e dei Sanniti*. Rome.

Benelli, E. 1994. *Le iscrizioni bilingui etrusco-latine*. Florence.

Bérard, R-M. 2017. "Paleoantropologia e archeotanatologia: nuovi metodi e approcci per lo studio delle necropoli magno-greche." In M. Niola and G. Zuchtriegel, eds., *Action Painting: rito e arte nelle tombe di Paestum*, 45–58. Naples.

Berechman, J. 2003. "Transportation – economic aspects of Roman highway development: The case of the Via Appia." *Transportation Research Part A: Policy and Practice* 37: 453–78.

Bernard, S. 2010. "Pentelic marble in architecture at Rome and the Republican marble trade." *Journal of Roman Archaeology* 23: 35–54.

Bernard, S. 2012. "Continuing the debate on Rome's earliest circuit walls." *Papers of the British School at Rome* 80: 1–44.

Bernard, S. 2016. "Debt, land, and labor in the Early Republican economy." *Phoenix* 70: 317–38.

Bernard, S. 2017. "The quadrigatus and Rome's monetary economy in the third century." *Numismatic Chronicle* 177: 501–13.

Bernard, S. 2018a. *Building Mid-Republican Rome: Labor, Architecture, and the Urban Economy*. New York.

Bernard, S. 2018b. "The social history of early Roman coinage." *Journal of Roman Studies* 108: 1–26.

Bernard, S. 2018c. "Political competition and economic exchange in Mid-Republican Rome." In C. Damon and C. Pieper, eds., *Eris v. Aemulatio: Competition in Classical Antiquity*, 230–50. Leiden.

Bernard, S. 2022. "Food, energy, and architectural production in the Roman world." In D. Maschek and M. Trümper, eds., *Architecture and the Ancient Economy*, 35–57. Rome.

Bernardi, A. 1973. *Nomen Latinum*. Pavia.

Bernstein, F. 2011. "Complex rituals: Games and processions in republican Rome." In J. Rüpke, ed., *A Companion to Roman Religion*, 222–34. Oxford.

Bertol, A., and K. Farac. 2012. "Aes Rude and Aes Formatum: A new typology based on the revised Mazin hoard." *Vjesnik Arheološkog muzeja u Zagrebu* 45: 93–113.

Bevan, A. 2020. "A stored-products revolution in the 1st millennium BC." *Archaeology International* 22.1: 127–44.

Bianchi, E., and L. Antognoli. 2014. "La Cloaca Massima dal Foro Romano al Velabro dagli studi di Heinrich Bauer alle nuove indagini." In E. Bianchi, ed., *La Cloaca Maxima e i sistemi fognari di Roma dall'antichità ad oggi*, 108–55. Rome.

Bielenstein, H. 1986. "Wang Mang, the restoration of the Han Dynasty, and later Han." In D. Twitchett and M. Loewe, eds., *The Cambridge History of China: Volume 1: The Ch'in and Han Empires, 221 BC–AD 220*, 223–90. Cambridge, UK.

Bietti Sestieri, A. M. 2010. *L' Italia nell'età del bronzo e del ferro. Dalle palafitte a Romolo (2200–700 a.C.)*. Rome.

Billeter, G. 1898. *Geschichte des Zinsfusses im griechisch-römischen Altertum bis auf Justinian, Volume 1*. Leipzig.

Billows, R. 1989. "Legal fiction and political reform at Rome in the early second century BC." *Phoenix* 43: 112–33.

Bleckmann, B. 2002. *Die römische Nobilität im ersten punischen Krieg: Untersuchungen zur aristokratischen Konkurrenz in der Republik*. Berlin.

Bleicken, J. 1955. *Das Volkstribunat der klassischen Republik: Studien zu seiner Entwicklung zwischen 287 und 133 v. Chr.* Munich.

Bleicken, J. 1995. *Cicero und die Ritter*. Göttingen.

Boehm, R. 2018. *City and Empire in the Age of the Successors: Urbanization and Social Response in the Making of the Hellenistic Kingdoms*. Berkeley.

Bogaard, A. 2011. "Farming practice and society in the central European Neolithic and Bronze Age: An archaeobotanical response to the secondary products revolution model." In A. Hadjikoumis, E. Robinson, S. Viner, eds., *The Dynamics of Neolithisation in Europe: Studies in Honour of Andrew Sherratt*, 266–83. Oxford.

Bogaard, A., D. Filipović, A. Fairbairn et al. 2017. "Agricultural innovation and resilience in a long-lived early farming community: The 1,500-year sequence at Neolithic to early Chalcolithic Çatalhöyük, Central Anatolia." *Anatolian Studies* 67: 1–28.

Bogaard, A., M. Fochesato, and S. Bowles. 2019. "The farming-inequality nexus: New insights from ancient Western Eurasia." *Antiquity* 371: 1129–43.

Bolder-Boos, M. 2019. "Adorning the city: urbanistic trends in Republican Central Italy." in K.-J. Hölkeskamp, S. Karataş, R. Roth, eds., *Empire, Hegemony or Anarchy? Rome and Italy, 201–31 BCE*, 107–29. Stuttgart.

Boni, G. 1899. "Notizie degli Scavi." Notizie degli scavi di antichità 5: 151–8.

Boni, G. 1900. "Esplorazioni nel Comizio." *Notizie degli scavi di antichità* 6: 295–340.

Bonnefond-Coudry, M. 1989. *Le sénat de la république romaine: De la guerre d'Hannibal à Auguste: pratiques délibératives et prise de décision*. Rome.

Borgers, B., G. Tol, and T. De Haas. 2018. "Reconstructing production technology and distribution, using thin section petrography: A pilot study of Roman pottery production in the Pontine region, Central Italy." *Journal of Archaeological Science: Reports* 21: 1064–72.

Borlenghi, A. 2019. "Les installation de vote dans les villes d'Italie. État de la question sur les assemblées électorales dans l'aire du forum." In A. Borlenghi, C. Chillet, V. Holland, L. Lopez, and J.-C. Moretti, eds., *Voter dans l'antiquité: Pratiques, lieux et finalités en Grèce, à Rome et en Gaule*, 297–332. Lyons.

Bosi, G., E. Castiglioni, R. Rinaldi, M. Mazzanti, M. Marchesini, and M. Rottoli. 2020. "Archaeobotanical evidence of food plants in Northern Italy during the Roman period." *Vegetation History and Archaeobotany* 29: 681–97.

Bouby, L., S. Ivorra, J.-F. Terral. 2017. "Morphometric analysis of vitis seeds from Well # 1 at Cetamura del Chianti: First results." In N. T. de Grummond, ed., *Wells of Wonders: New Discoveries at Cetamura del Chianti*, 289–93. Florence.

Bouma, J. 1996. *Religio Votiva: The archaeology of latial votive religion. The 5th–3rd century votive deposit south west of the main temple at 'Satricum' Borgo le Ferriere*. Groningen.

Bourdieu, P. 1993. *The Field of Cultural Production*. New York.

Bourdin, S. 2012. *Les peuples de l'Italie préromaine*, BEFAR 350. Rome.

Bowes, K., A. M. Mercuri, E. Rattigheri et al. 2017. "Peasant agricultural strategies in Southern Tuscany: Convertible agriculture and the importance of pasture." In T. C. A. de Haas and G. W. Tol, eds., *The Economic Integration of Roman Italy. Rural Communities in a Globalizing World*, 170–99. Leiden.

Bradley, G. J. 2001. *Ancient Umbria: State, Culture, and Identity in Central Italy from the Iron Age to the Augustan Era*. Oxford.

Bradley, G. J. 2008. "The Roman republic: Political history." In E. Bispham, ed., *Roman Europe*, 32–68. Oxford.

Bradley, G. J. 2014. "The nature of Roman strategy in Mid-Republican colonization and road building." In T. Stek and J. Pelgrom, eds., *Roman Republican Colonization: New Perspectives from Archaeology and Ancient History*, 60–72. Rome.

Bradley, G. J. 2015. "Investigating aristocracy in archaic Rome and central Italy: Social mobility, ideology and cultural influences." In N. R. E. Fisher and H. van Wees, eds., *"Aristocracy" in Antiquity: Redefining Greek and Roman Elites*, 85–124. Swansea.

Bradley, G. J. 2020. *Early Rome to 290 BC: The Beginnings of the City and the Rise of the Republic*. Edinburgh.

Bradley, K. 1984. "The Vicesima Libertatis: Its history and significance." *Klio* 66: 175–82.

Bradley, K. 1985. "The early development of slavery at Rome." *Historical Reflections/Réflexions Historiques* 12: 1–8.

Bradley, K. 1994. *Slavery and society at Rome*. Cambridge, UK.

Bradley, K. 2011. "Slavery in the Roman republic." In Bradley and Cartledge, eds., 241–64.

Bradley, K., and P. Cartledge, eds. 2011. *The Cambridge World History of Slavery, Vol. I: The Ancient Mediterranean World*. Cambridge, UK.

Bransbourg, G. 2011. "'Fides Et Pecunia Numerata': Chartalism and metallism in the Roman world Part 1: The republic." *American Journal of Numismatics* 23: 87–152.

Braund, D. 2011. "The slave supply in classical Greece." In Bradley and Cartledge, eds., 112–33.

Brennan, T. C. 2000. *The Praetorship in the Roman Republic: Volume 1: Origins to 122 BC*. Oxford.

Bresson, A. 2019. "Slaves, fairs and fears: Western Greek sanctuaries as hubs of social interaction." In K. Freitag and M. Haake, eds., *Griechische Heiligtümer als Handlungsorte: zur Multifunktionalität supralokaler Heiligtümer von der frühen Archaik bis in die römische Kaiserzeit*, 251–77. Stuttgart.

Briccola, N., M. Bertolini, and U. Thun Hohenstein, 2013. "Gestione e sfruttamento delle risorse animali nell'abitato di Spina: Analisi archeozoologica dei reperti faunistici." In C. C. Cassai, S. Giannini, and L. Malnati, eds., *Spina. Scavi nell'abitato della città etrusca, 2007–2009*, 178–87. Florence.

Bridgman, T. P. 2003. "The 'Gallic disaster': Did Dionysius I of Syracuse order it?" *Proceedings of the Harvard Celtic Colloquium* 23: 40–51.

Briggs, C. 2009. *Credit and Village Society in Fourteenth-Century England*. Oxford.

Briquel, D. 2001. "La tombe Andriuolo 114 de Paestum (IX, 31)." In D. Briquel and J.-P. Thuillier, eds., *Le censeur et les samnites: Sur Tite-Live, livre IX*, 135–46. Paris.

Broadhead, W. 2001. "Rome's migration policy and the so-called 'ius migrandi.'" *Cahiers du Centre Gustave-Glotz* 12: 69–89.

Brocato, P., D. P. Diffendale, D. Di Giuliomaria, M. Gaeta, F. Marra, and N. Terrenato. 2019. "A previously unidentified Tuff in the archaic temple podium at Sant' Omobono, Rome and its broader implications." *Journal of Mediterranean Archaeology* 32.1: 114–36.

Broughton, T. R. S. 1951–86. *The Magistrates of the Roman Republic*. 3 vols. New York.

Brown, F. E. 1935. "The Regia." *Memoirs of the American Academy in Rome* 12: 67–88.

Brun, J.-P. 2004. *Archéologie du vin et de l'huile de la préhistoire à l'époque hellénistique Collection des Hespérides*. Paris.

Brunt, P. A. 1971. *Italian Manpower, 225 BC.–AD. 14*. Oxford.

Bruun, C. 2000. "'What every man in the street used to know': M. Furius Camillus, Italic legends and Roman historiography." In C. Bruun, ed., *The Roman Middle Republic: Politics, Religion, and Historiography, c. 400–133 BC*, 41–68. Rome.

Bruun, C. ed. 2000. *The Roman Middle Republic: Politics, Religion, and Historiography, c. 400–133 BC*. Rome.

Burnett, A. M. 1989. "The beginnings of Roman coinage." *Annali dell'Istituto Italiano di Numismatica* 36: 33–64.

Burnett, A. M., P. T. Craddock, and N. Meeks. 1986. "Italian currency bars." In J. Swadling, ed., *Italian Iron Age Artefacts in the British Museum: Papers of the Sixth British Museum Classical Colloquium*, 127–30. London.

Burnett, A. M., and M. H. Crawford. 2014. "Coinage, money and mid-republican Rome: reflections on a recent book by Filippo Coarelli." *Annali dell'Istituto Italiano di Numismatica* 60: 231–65.

Burns, M. T. 2003. "The homogenisation of military equipment under the Roman Republic." *"Romanization"? Digressus* Supplement 1: 60–85.

Bussi, R., and V. Vandelli. 1985. *Misurare la terra: Centuriazione e coloni nel mondo romano. Città, agricoltura, commercio: materiali da Roma e dal suburbio*. Modena.

Buxó, R. 2008. "The agricultural consequences of colonial contacts on the Iberian Peninsula in the first millennium BC." *Vegetation History and Archaeobotany* 17: 145–54.

Cadoux, T. J. 1948. "The Athenian archons from Kreon to Hypsichides." *Journal of Hellenic Studies* 86: 70–123.

Calderini, G., G. Calderoni, G. P. Cavinato, E. Gliozzi, and P. Paccara. 1998. "The upper Quaternary sedimentary sequence at the Rieti Basin (central Italy): A record of sedimentation response to climatic changes." *Palaeogeography, Palaeoclimatology, Palaeoecology* 140: 97–111.

Camerieri, P. 2013. "La centuriazione dell'ager Nursinus." In S. Sisani, ed., *Nursia e l'ager Nursinus. Un distretto sabino dalla praefectura al municipium*, 25–34. Rome.

Camerieri, P., A. De Santis, and T. Matteoli. 2009. "La Limitatio dell'Ager Reatinus. Paradigma del rapporto tra agrimensura e pastorizia, viabilità e assetto idrogeologico del territorio." *Agri Centuriati* 6: 325–45.

Campbell, B. 2000. *The Writings of the Roman Land Surveyors: Introduction, Text, Translation and Commentary*. London.

Cancellieri, M. 1983. "Lo sbocco meridionale della Valle interna dei Lepini: Privernum e il suo territorio." *Bollettino dell'Istituto di Storia e di Arte del Lazio Meridionale*, 11: 35–41.

Cancellieri, M. 1990. "Il territorio pontino e la Via Appia." *Archeologia Laziale* 10.1: 61–71.

Candotti, M. 2010. "The Hausa textile industry: origins and development in the precolonial period." In A. Haour and B. Rossi, eds., *Being and Becoming Hausa: Interdisciplinary Perspectives*, 187–211. Leiden.

Capanna, M. C. 2013. "I *pomeria*, il dazio e il miglio." In A. Carandini and P. Carafa, eds., *Atlante di Roma*, vol. 1: 71–3. Milan.

Capodiferro, A., L. M. Mignone, and P. Quaranta, eds., 2017. *Studi e scavi sull'Aventino. 2003–2015*. Rome.

Capogrossi Colognesi, L. 1980. "Alcuni problemi di storia romana arcaica. Ager publicus, gentes e clienti." *Bullettino dell'Istituto di Diritto romano* 83: 29–65.

Capogrossi Colognesi, L. 1990. *Dalla tribù allo stato: Le istituzioni dello stato cittadino*. Rome.

Capogrossi Colognesi, L. 2012. *Padroni e contadini nell'Italia repubblicana*. Rome.

Caputo, P. 2000. "Su un frammento di pittura funeraria di Cuma." In R. Cappelli, ed., *Studi sull'Italia dei Sanniti*, 74–6. Rome.

Caracuta, V. 2020. "Olive growing in Puglia (southeastern Italy): A review of the evidence from the Mesolithic to the Middle Ages." *Vegetation History and Archaeobotany* 29: 595–620.

Carafa, P. 1998. *Il Comizio di Roma dalle origini all'età di Augusto*. Rome.

Carafa, P. 2005. "Il Volcanal e il comizio." *Workshop di archeologia classica* 2: 135–49.

Carafa, P., and M. Capanna. 2009. "Il progetto 'Archeologia del Suburbio di Roma' per la ricostruzione dei paesaggi agrari antichi." In V. Jolivet, C. Pavolini, M. A. Tomei, and R. Volpe eds., *Suburbium II. Il suburbio di Roma dalla fine dell'età monarchica alla nascita del sistema delle ville (V–II secolo d.C.). Atti delle giornate di studio sul suburbio romano tenute a Roma il 16 ottobre e i 3 novembre 2004, 17 e 18 febbraio 2005*, 27–39. Rome.

Carafa, P., and M. Capanna. 2019. "I Paesaggi Rurali tra il Suburbio di Roma e il Latium Vetus." In A. Fischetti and P. Attema, eds., *Alle pendici dei Colli Albani. Dinamiche insediative e cultura materiale ai confini con Roma*, 15–27. Groningen.

Carandini, A. 1988. *Schiavi in Italia: gli strumenti pensanti dei Romani fra tarda Repubblica e medio impero.* Rome.

Carandini, A. 2004. *Palatino, Velia e Sacra via: paesaggi urbani attraverso il tempo.* Rome.

Carandini, A., M. D'Alessio, and H. Di Giuseppe. 2006. *La fattoria e la villa dell'auditorium nel quartiere Flaminio di Roma.* Rome.

Carettoni, G. 1978–1980. "La Domus Virginum Vestalium e la Domus Publica del periodo repubblicano." *Rendiconti della Pontificia Accademia Romana di Archeologia* 51–2: 325–55.

Carlà, F. 2014. "Ein Sklavenaufstand in Syrakus (414 v. Chr.)." *Incidenza dell'antico: Dialoghi di storia greca* 12: 61–89.

Carpenter, T. H., K. M. Lynch, and E. G. D. Robinson, eds. 2014. *The Italic People of Ancient Apulia: New Evidence from Pottery for Workshops, Markets, and Customs.* Cambridge, UK.

Carra, M., L. Cattani, P. Luciani, M. Rizzi, and J. Wiethold. 2005. "Derrate alimentari nell'economia della comunità etrusco-celtica di Monte Bibele. Studio archeobotanico della Casa 2." *Ocnus* 13: 147–70.

Carrer, F. 2016. "Secondary products exploitation: Preliminary ethnoarchaeological insights from Alpine cases study." In S. Biagetti and F. Lugli, eds., *The Intangible Elements of Culture in Ethnoarchaeological Research*, 115–24. Cham.

Carrer, F., and M. Migliavacca, 2019. "Prehistoric transhumance in the Northern Mediterranean." In S. Sabatini and S. Bergerbrant, eds., *The Textile Revolution in Bronze Age Europe: Production, Specialisation, Consumption*, 217–38. Cambridge, UK.

Carroll, M. 2019. "Mater Matuta, 'fertility cults' and the integration of women in religious life in Italy in the fourth to first centuries BC." *Papers of the British School at Rome* 87: 1–45.

Casarotto, A., J. Pelgrom, and T. Stek. 2016. "Testing settlement models in the early Roman colonial landscapes of Venusia (291 BC), Cosa (273 BC) and Aesernia (263 BC)." *Journal of Field Archaeology* 41.5: 568–86.

Càssola, F., 1988. "Aspetti sociali e politici della colonizzazione." *Dialoghi di Archeologia* 6.2: 5–17.

Castagnoli, F. 1947. "Il Campo Marzio nell'antichità." *Memorie: Atti dell'Accademia nazionale dei Lincei, Classe di scienze morali, storiche e filologiche* 1.4: 93–193.

Castagnoli, F. 1964. "Note sulla topografia del Palatino e del Foro Boario." *Archeologia Classica* 16: 173–99.

Castagnoli, F. 1971. *Orthogonal Town Planning in Antiquity.* Cambridge, UK.

Cavazzuti, C., A. Cardarelli, F. Quondam et al. 2019a. "Mobile elites at Frattesina: Flows of people in a Late Bronze Age 'port of trade' in northern Italy." *Antiquity* 93: 624–44.

Cavazzuti, C., R. Skeates, A. R. Millard et al. 2019b. "Flows of people in villages and large centres in Bronze Age Italy through strontium and oxygen isotopes." *PLOS ONE* 14.1, e0209693.

Cébeillac-Gervasoni, M, ed. 1983. *Les "bourgeoisies" municipales italiennes aux IIe et Ier siècles av. J.-C.* Paris.

Cecamore, C. 2002. *Palatium: Topografia storica del Palatino tra III sec. a.C. e I sec. d.C.* Rome.

Champion, C. B. 2017. *The Peace of the Gods: Elite Religious Practices in the Middle Roman Republic.* Princeton, NJ.

Chassignet, M. 1996. *L'annalistique romaine. Tome I. Les annales des pontifes et l'annalistique ancienne (fragments).* Paris.

Chillet, C. 2019. "Le *comitium* comme lieu de vote à Rome: une relecture." In A. Borlenghi, C. Chillet, V. Holland, L. Lopez, and J.-C. Moretti, eds., *Voter dans l'antiquité. Pratiques, lieux et finalités en Grèce, à Rome et en Gaule*, 277–9. Lyons.

Chouquer, G., M. Clavel-Leveque, F. Favory, and J. P. Vallat. 1987. *Structures agraires en Italie centro-meridionale. Cadastres et paysage rureaux.* Rome.

Ciacci, A., and A. Zifferero. 2010. "Per un'archeologia dell'olivo in Etruria: verso il 'Progetto Eleiva.'" In G. Barbieri, A. Ciacci, and A. Zifferero, eds., *Eleiva, Oleum, Olio. Le origini dell'olivicoltura in Toscana: nuovi percorsi di ricerca tra archeologia, botanica e biologia molecolare*, 107–20. San Quirico D'Orcia.

Ciancio, A. 2014. "The diffusion of Middle and Late Apulian vases in Peucetian funerary contexts: A comparison of several necropoleis." In T. H. Carpenter, K. M. Lynch, and E. G. D. Robinson, eds., *The Italic People of Ancient Apulia: New Evidence from Pottery for Workshops, Markets, and Customs*, 152–67. Cambridge, UK.

Ciancio, A., and F. Radina. 1989. *Monte Sannace: Gli scavi dell'acropoli 1978–1983.* Galatina.

Cibecchini, F., and J. Principal. 2002. "Alcune considerazioni sulla presenza commerciale romano-italica nella penisola iberica prima della seconda guerra punica." In M. Khanoussi, P. Ruggeri, and C. Vismara, eds., *L´Africa romana. Lo spazio marittimo del Mediterraneo occidentale: Geografia storica ed economia*, 653–63. Rome.

Cifani, G. 1998. "Caratteri degli insediamenti rurali nell'Ager Romanus tra VI e III secolo a. C." In M. Pearce and M. Tosi, eds., *Papers from the EAA Third Annual Meeting at Ravenna 1997, vol. II: Classical and Medieval*, 53–64. Oxford.

Cifani, G. 2002. "Notes on the rural landscape of central Tyrrhenian Italy in the 6th–5th c. BC and its social significance." *Journal of Roman Archaeology* 15: 247–60.

Cifani, G. 2008. *Architettura romana arcaica. Edilizia e società tra Monarchia e Repubblica.* Rome.

Cifani, G. 2009. "Indicazioni sulla proprietà agraria nella Roma arcaica in base all'evidenza archeologica." In V. Jolivet, C. Pavolini, M. A. Tomei, and R. Volpe, eds., *Suburbium II: il suburbio di Roma dalla fine dell'età monarchica alla nascita del sistema delle ville (V–II secolo a.C.)*, 312–24. Rome.

Cifani, G. 2017. "Visibility matters: Notes on Archaic monuments and collective memory in Mid-Republican Rome." In K. Sandberg and C. J. Smith, eds., *Omnium Annalium Monumenta: Historical Evidence and Historical Writing in Republican Rome*, 390–8. Leiden.

Cifani, G. 2021. *The Origins of the Roman Economy: From the Iron Age to the Early Republic in a Mediterranean Perspective*. Cambridge, UK.

Cifarelli, F. M. 2017. "Sulle tracce della Signia medio repubblicana : problemi storici e archeologici." In L. M. Caliò, J. Des Courtils, and F. Leoni, eds., *L'architettura greca in Occidente nel III secolo a.C. Atti del convegno di studi, Pompei-Napoli, 20-22 maggio 2015*, 285–300. Rome.

Cifarelli, F. M., A. D'Alessio, S. Gatti, D. Palombi, C. J. Smith, and R. Volpe, eds. 2021. *Roma e Lazio Medio Repubblicano: Dalla conquista di Veio alla battaglia di Zama (Atti del Convegno Internazionale, Roma 2017)*. Rome.

Cifarelli, F. M., S. Gatti, and D. Palombi, eds. 2019. *Oltre "Roma medio repubblicana": Il Lazio tra i Galli e la battaglia di Zama (Atti del Convegno Internazionale, Roma 2017)*. Rome.

Cifarelli, F. M. 2019. "Forma e cultura della città nel *Latium vetus* in età medio repubblicana." In F. M. Cifarelli, S. Gatti, and D. Palombi, eds., 149–70. Rome.

Clark, E. 1981. "Debt litigation in a late medieval Essex village." In J. A. Raftis, ed., *Pathways to the Medieval Peasant*, 247–79. Toronto.

Clarke, J. R. 1991. *The Houses of Roman Italy, 100 B.C.–A.D. 250: Ritual, Space, and Decoration*. Berkeley, CA.

Clarke, K. 2008. *Making Time for the Past: Local History and the* Polis. Oxford.

Coarelli, F. 1972. "Il Sepolcro degli Scipioni." *Dialoghi di Archeologia* 6: 36–106.

Coarelli, F. 1976. "Architettura e arti figurative in Roma: 150–50 a. C." In P. Zanker, ed., *Hellenismus in Mittelitalien I*, 20–51. Göttingen.

Coarelli, F. 1983. *Il Foro Romano. Periodo arcaico*. Rome.

Coarelli, F. 1985. *Il Foro Romano. Periodo repubblicano e augusteo*. Rome.

Coarelli, F. 1988. "Colonizzazione romana e viabilità." *Dialoghi d'Archeologia* 2: 35–48.

Coarelli, F. 1990. "Cultura artistica e società." In A. Schiavone, ed., *Storia di Roma*, vol. 2.1: 159–85. Turin.

Coarelli, F. 1992a. *Il Foro Boario dalle origini alla fine della Repubblica*. Rome.

Coarelli, F. 1992b. "Colonizzazione e municipalizzazione: Tempi e modi." *Dialoghi di Archeologia* 10: 21–30.

Coarelli, F. 1996. "Legio linteata: l'iniziazione militare nel Sannio." In L. del Tutto del Palma, ed., *La Tavola di Agnone in contesto italico: Convegno di studi: Agnone, 13-15 aprile 1994*, 3–45. Florence.

Coarelli, F. 1997. *Il Campo Marzio. Dalle origini alla fine della Repubblica*. Rome.

Coarelli, F. 1998. "Comitium e comitia: l'assemblea e il voto a Roma in età repubblicana." In E. Greco and L. Canfora, eds., *Venticinque secoli dopo l'invenzione della democrazia, Atti del Convegno (Paestum 1994)*, 133–43. Paestum.

Coarelli, F. 2012. *Palatium: il Palatino dalle origini all'impero*. Rome.

Coarelli, F. 2013. *Argentum signatum: le origini della moneta d'argento a Roma*. Rome.

Coarelli, F. 2014. *Collis. Il Quirinale e il Viminale nell'antichità*, Rome.

Coccia, S., and D. Mattingly. 1995. "Settlement history, environment and human exploitation of an intermontane basin in the central Apennines: The Rieti Survey 1988–1991, Part II. Land use patterns and gazetteer." *Papers of the British School at Rome* 50: 105–58.

Coffee, N. 2017. *Gift and Gain: How Money Transformed Ancient Rome*. New York.

Colivicchi, F. ed. 2011. *Local Cultures of South Italy and Sicily in the Late Republican Period: Between Hellenism and Rome*. Portsmouth, RI.

Colivicchi, F., G. L. Gregori, M. Lanza et al. 2016. "New excavations in the urban area of Caere." *Mouseion* 13: 359–450.

Colletti, F., and P. Pensabene. 2017. "Le forme rituali dell'area sacra sud-ovest del Palatino." *Scienze dell'Antiquità* 23.2: 573–91.

Corbino, C., J. De Grossi Mazzorin, C. Minniti, and U. Albarella. 2021. "The earliest evidence of chicken in Italy." *Quaternary International* 626-7:80–6.

Corbino, C., and O. Fonzo. 2017. "The use of animals in Etruscan and Roman rituals at Cetamura del Chianti (SI)." In N. T. De Grummond, ed., *Wells of Wonders: New Discoveries at Cetamura del Chianti*, 323–35. Florence.

Cornell, T. J. 1974. "Notes on the sources for Campanian history in the fifth century BC." *Museum Helveticum* 31.4: 193–207.

Cornell, T. J. 1976. "Etruscan historiography." *AnnaliPisa* 3.6: 411–39.

Cornell, T. J. 1978. "Principes of Tarquinia." *Journal of Roman Studies* 68: 167–73.

Cornell, T. J. 1983. "The failure of the plebs." In E. Gabba, ed. *Tria Corda: Scritti in onore di Arnaldo Momigliano*, 101–20. Como.

Cornell, T. J. 1995. *The Beginnings of Rome. Italy and Rome from the Bronze Age to the Punic Wars (c. 1000–264 BC)*. London.

Cornell, T. J. 2004. "Deconstructing the Samnite Wars: An essay in historiography." In H. Jones, ed., *Samnium: Settlement and Cultural Change. Proceedings of the Third E. Togo Salmon Conference on Roman Studies*, 115–31. Providence.

Cornell, T. J. 2008. "The conquest of Italy." In. F. Walbank et al. eds., *Cambridge Ancient History Volume 7-2: The Rise of Rome to 220*, 351–41. Cambridge, UK.

Cornell, T. J. 2009. "Cato the Elder and the origins of Roman autobiography." In C. Smith and A. Powell, eds., *The lost memoirs of Augustus and the development of Roman autobiography*, 15–40. Swansea.

Cornell, T. J. ed. 2013. *The Fragments of the Roman Historians*. 3 vols. Oxford.

Corrigan, E. H. 1979. "Lucanian tomb paintings excavated at Paaestum 1969–1972: An iconographic study." (Unpublished PhD diss., Columbia University)

Coşkun, A. 2016. "The Latins and their legal status in the context of the cultural and political integration of pre- and early Roman Italy." *Klio* 98.2: 526–69.

Costantini, L., and L. Costantini Biasini. 2018. "Archaeobotanical investigations at Pantanello." In J. C. Carter and K. Swift, eds., *The Chora of Metaponto 7: The Greek Sanctuary at Pantanello*, 371–428. New York.

Costello, E., and E. Svensson, 2018. "Transhumant pastoralism in historic landscapes: Beginning a European perspective." In E. Costello and E. Svensson, eds., *Historical Archaeologies of Transhumance across Europe. Themes in Contemporary Archaeology* 6: 1–14. London.

Crawford, M. H. 1974. *Roman Republican Coinage: 2 Volumes*. Cambridge, UK.

Crawford, M. H. 1977. "Republican denarii in Romania: The suppression of piracy and the slave-trade." *Journal of Roman Studies* 67: 117–24.

Crawford, M. H. 1983. "Coins." In T. F. C. Blagg, ed., *Mysteries of Diana: The Antiquities from Nemi in Nottingham Museums*. Nottingham.

Crawford, M. H. 1985. *Coinage and Money under the Roman Republic: Italy and the Mediterranean Economy*. London.

Crawford, M. H. 1995. "La storia della colonizzazione romana secondo i Romani." In A. Storchi Marino, ed., *L'incidenza dell'antico. Studi in memoria di Ettore Lepore*, vol. I 187–92. Naples.

Crawford, M. H. 1996. *Roman Statutes: 2 Volumes*. London.

Crawford, M. H. 2006. "From Poseidonia to Paestum via the Lucanians." In J.-P. Wilson and G. Bradley, eds., *Greek and Roman Colonization: Origins, Ideologies and Interactions*, 59–72. Swansea.

Crawford, M. H. 2009. "From 'aes signare' to 'aes signatum.'" *Revue Suisse de Numismatique* 88: 195–7.

Crawford, M. H., W. M. Broadhead, J. P. T. Clackson, F. Santangelo, S. Thompson, and M. Watmough, 2011. *Imagines italicae: A Corpus of Italic Inscriptions*. 3 vols. London.

Cremaschi, M., A. M. Mercuri, P. Torri, A. Florenzano, C. Pizzi, M. Marchesini, and A. Zerboni, 2016. "Climate change versus land management in the Po Plain (Northern Italy) during the Bronze Age: New insights from the VP/VG sequence of the Terramara Santa Rosa di Poviglio." *Quaternary Science Reviews* 136: 153–72.

Cristofani, M. 1987. "Duo sunt liquores." In G. Barbieri, ed., *L'Alimentazione nel mondo antico: Gli Etruschi*, 37–40. Rome.

Cucinotta, C., J. de Grossi Mazzorin, and C. Minniti. 2010. "La città etrusca di Veio: Analisi archeozoologiche del pozzo US 469." In A. Tagliacozzo, I. Fiore, S. Marconi, and U. Tecchiati, eds., *Atti del 5° Convengo Nazionale di Archeozoologia, Rovereto, 10–12 novembre 2006*, 235–8. Rovereto.

Cursi, M. F. 2018. *XII Tabulae: Testo e commento*. Naples.

D'Alessio, A., C. J. Smith, and R. Volpe, eds. 2021. *Roma medio repubblicana: Dalla conquista di Veio alla battaglia di Zama (Atti del Convegno Internazionale, Roma 2017)*. Rome.

D'Angelo, T. 2017. "La pittura funeraria pestana tra Magna Grecia e Roma." In M. Niola and G. Zuchtriegel, eds., *Action Painting: rito e arte nelle tombe di Paestum*, 75–92. Naples.

D'Ippolito, F. M. 2004. "Leges obscatae." *Parola del Passato* 59: 81–91.

Davenport, C. 2019. *A History of the Roman Equestrian Order*. Cambridge, UK.

Davies, P. J. E. 2012. "On the introduction of stone architraves in Republican temples in Rome." In M. Thomas and G. Meyers, eds., *Monumentality in Etruscan and Early Roman Architecture: Ideology and Innovation*, 139–65. Austin, TX.

Davies, P. J. E. 2017a. *Architecture and Politics in Republican Rome*. Cambridge, UK.

Davies, P. J. E. 2017b. "Constructing, deconstructing and reconstructing civic memory in Late Republican Rome." In K. Sandberg and C. J. Smith, eds., *Omnium Annalium Monumenta: Historical Evidence and Historical Writing in Republican Rome*, 477–511. Leiden.

De Caro, T., G. M. Ingo, and D. Salvi. 2005. "Indagine microchimica e microstrutturale di masse metalliche ascrivibili alla categoria dell'aes rude." *Rivista italiana di numismatica e scienze affini* 106: 23–38.

De Grossi Mazzorin, J. 2004. "I resti animali della struttura ipogea di Centocelle: una testimonianza di pratiche cultuali?" In P. Gioia and R. Volpe, eds., *Centocelle I. Roma S.D.O., le indagini archeologiche*, 323–9. Soveria Mannelli.

De Grossi Mazzorin, J. 2005. "Introduzione e diffusione del pollame in Italia ed evoluzione delle sue forme di allevamento fino al Medioevo." In I. Fiore, G. Malerba, and S. Chilardi, eds., *Atti del 3º Convengo Nazionale di Archeozoologia. Siracusa, 3–5 novembre 2000. Studi di Paletnologia II, Collana del Bullettino di Paletnologia italiana*, 351–60. Rome.

De Grossi Mazzorin, J. 2009. "Fauna ed economia animale." In M. Bernabò Brea and M. Cremaschi, eds., *Acqua e civiltà nelle terramare. La vasca votiva di Noceto*, 170–1. Milan.

De Grossi Mazzorin, J. 2010. "L'utilizzazione degli animali nella documentazione archeozoologica dell'età del Bronzo in Puglia." In F. Radina and G. Recchia, eds., *Ambra per Agamennone: Indigeni e Micenei tra Adriatico, Ionio ed Egeo*, 69–72. Bari.

De Grossi Mazzorin, J. 2013a. "Considerazioni sullo sfruttamento animale in ambito terramaricolo." In J. De Grossi Mazzorin, A. Curci, and G. Giacobini, eds., *Economia e ambiente nell'Italia padana nell'età del Bronzo. Le indagini bioarcheologiche. Beni Archeologici - Conoscenza e Tecnologie Quaderno*, vol. 11: 257–63. Bari.

De Grossi Mazzorin, J. 2013b. "Considerazioni sullo sfruttamento animale nell'area delle palafitte." In J. De Grossi Mazzorin, A. Curci, and G. Giacobini, eds., *Economia e ambiente nell'Italia padana nell'età del Bronzo. Le indagini bioarcheologiche. Beni Archeologici – Conoscenza e Tecnologie Quaderno* 11, 155–60. Bari.

De Grossi Mazzorin, J. 2015. "Fondo Paviani e Frattesina: Economia animale di due *central places* della tarda Età del bronzo veneta." In G. Leonardi and V. Tiné, eds, *Preistoria e Protostoria del Veneto. Studi di Preistoria e Protostoria* 2, 389–400. Florence.

De Grossi Mazzorin, J., and C. Minniti. 2002. "Testimonianze di pratiche cultuali nella Grotta 10 di Sorgenti della Nova: recenti analisi sul materiale osteologico." In N. Negroni Catacchio, ed., *Preistoria e Protostoria in Etruria. Atti del Quinto Incontro di Studi: Paesaggi d'acque. Ricerche e Scavi, vol. II*. 627–36. Milan.

De Grossi Mazzorin, J., and C. Minniti. 2003. "Il quadro zooarcheologico dell'Abruzzo alla luce delle recenti acquisizioni." In *Atti XXXVI Riunione Scientifica dell'Istituto Italiano di Preistoria e Protostoria, Chieti-Celano 27–30 settembre 2001*, 431–48. Florence.

De Grossi Mazzorin, J., and C. Minniti. 2008. "Nota sui resti faunistici provenienti da Otranto – Cantiere Mitello." *Studi di Antichità* 12: 146–9.

De Grossi Mazzorin, J., and C. Minniti. 2009. "L'Utilizzazione degli animal nella documentazione archeozoologica a Roma e nel Lazio dalla preistoria recente all'età classica." In L. Drago Troccoli, ed., *Il Lazio dai Colli Albani ai Monti Lepini tra preistoria ed età moderna*, 39–67. Rome.

De Grossi Mazzorin, J., and C. Minniti. 2015. "Le hostiae animales dalla fossa rituale del saggio IV." In V. Di Cola and F. Pitzalis, eds., *Materiali per Populonia* 11, 139–58. Pisa.

De Grossi Mazzorin, J., and C. Minniti. 2017. "Changes in lifestyle in ancient Rome (Italy) across the Iron Age/Roman transition." In U. Albarella, M. Rizzetto, H. Russ, K. Vickers, and S. Viner-Daniels, eds., *The Oxford Handbook of Zooarchaeology*, 127–46. Oxford.

De Grossi Mazzorin, J., and C. Minniti. 2019. "Variabilità dimensionale e sviluppo dei caprovini in Italia durante l'età del Ferro." In J. De Grossi Mazzorin, I. Fiore, C. and Minniti, eds., *Atti 8° Convegno Nazionale di Archeozoologia (Lecce, 2015)*, 127–38. Lecce.

De Grossi Mazzorin, J., Riedel, A., and A. Tagliacozzo. 2004. "L'Evoluzione delle popolazioni animali e l'economia nell'età del bronzo recente." In D. Cocchi Genic, ed., *L'età del bronzo recente in Italia. Atti del Congresso nazionale di Lido di Camaiore, 26–29 ottobre 2000*, 227–32. Viareggio.

De Grummond, N. T. 2018. "Grape pips from Etruscan and Roman Cetamura del Chianti: On stratigraphy, literary sources and pruning hooks." *Etruscan Studies* 21.1–2: 27–57.

De Grummond, N.T., ed. 2017. *Wells of Wonders: New Discoveries at Cetamura del Chianti. Catalog of the exhibition, June 9–September 30, 2017, Florence, National Archaeological Museum, MAF, Museo archeologico nazionale di Firenze*. Florence.

De Guio, A. 2012. "Interfacce di bronzo per una vita da pecora. Il fenomeno della pastorizia nell'area prealpina veneto-trentina in età preromana: Archeologia ed etnoarcheologia." In M. S. Busana, P. Basso, A. R. Tricomi, and

S. Pesavento Mattioli, eds., *La lana nella cisalpina romana: Economia e società. Studi in onore di Stefania Pesavento Mattioli.* Antenor Quaderni Vol. 27, 43–67. Padua.

De Haas, T. 2011. *Fields, farms and colonists: Intensive field survey and early Roman colonization in the Pontine region, central Italy.* Groningen.

De Haas, T. 2012. "Beyond dots on the map: Intensive survey data and the interpretation of small sites and off-site distributions." In P. A. J. Attema and G. Schoerner, eds., *Comparative Issues in the Archaeology of the Roman Rural Landscape. Site Classification between Survey, Excavation and Historical Categories (Journal of Roman Archaeology)* supplementary series 88: 55–79.

De Haas, T. 2017a. "The geography of Roman Italy and its implications for the development of rural economies." In T. De Haas and G. Tol, eds., *The Economic Integration of Roman Italy. Rural Communities in a Globalizing World*, 51–82. Leiden.

De Haas, T. 2017b. "Managing the marshes: An integrated study of the centuriated landscape of the Pontine plain." *Journal of Archaeological Science: Reports* 15: 470–81.

De Haas, T., P. Attema, and G. Tol. 2012. "Platform sites along the Lepine mountains: A review of the data gathered by the Pontine Region Project." *Palaeohistoria* 53/54: 195–282.

De Haas, T., and G. Tol., eds. 2017. *The Economic Integration of Roman Italy: Rural Communities in a Globalizing World.* Leiden.

De Haas, T., G. Tol, and P. Attema. 2011. "Investing in the colonia and ager of Antium." *Facta* 5: 111–44.

De Haas, T. C. A., and G. W. Tol. In press. "The analytical potential of intensive field survey data: Developments in the collection, analysis and interpretation of surface ceramics within the Pontine Region Project." In A. Meens, M. Naou, and W. van de Put, eds., *Fields, Sherds and Scholars: Recording and Interpreting Survey Ceramics.* Leiden.

De Juliis, E. M. 1985. "Un quindicennio di ricerche archeologiche in Puglia: 1970–1984. Parte II: 1978–84." *Taras. Rivista di Archeologia* 5: 177–228.

De Kleijn, G. 2001. *The Water Supply of Ancient Rome: City Area, Water, and Population.* Amsterdam.

De Ligt, L. 2012. *Peasants, Citizens and Soldiers: Studies in the Demographic History of Roman Italy 225 BC–AD 100.* Cambridge, UK.

De Sanctis, G. 1965. *Storia dei Romani, vol. 2: La conquista del primato in Italia.* Rome.

DeLaine, J. 1997. *The Baths of Caracalla: A Study in the Design, Construction, and Economics of Large-Scale Building Projects in Imperial Rome.* Portsmouth, RI.

Delfino, A. 2009. "L'incendio gallico: Tra mito storiografico e realtà storica." *Mediterraneo Antico* 12.1–2: 339–60.

Delpino, F. 2012. "Viticoltura, produzione e consumo del vino nell'Etruria proto-storico." In A. Ciacci, P. Rendini, and A. Zifferero, eds., *Archeologia della vite e del vino in Toscana e nel Lazio. Dalle tecniche dell'indagine archeologica alle prospettive della biologia molecolare*, 189–99. Borgo San Lorenzo.

Dench, E. 1995. *From Barbarians to New Men: Greek, Roman, and Modern Perceptions of Peoples from the Central Apennines*. Oxford.

Dench, E. 2003. "Beyond Greeks and barbarians: Italy and Sicily in the Hellenistic Age." In A. Erskine, ed., *A Companion to the Hellenistic World*, 294–310. Malden.

Dench, E. 2005. *Romulus' Asylum: Roman Identities from the Age of Alexander to the Age of Hadrian*. Oxford.

Dench, E. 2018. *Empire and Political Cultures in the Roman World*. Cambridge, UK.

Develin, R. 1985. *The Practice of Politics at Rome, 366–167 BC*. Brussels.

Di Fazio, M. 2019a. *Latinorum Sacra. Il sistema religioso delle città latine: luoghi, culti, pratiche*. Rome.

Di Fazio, M. 2019b. "Religioni e memoria della *gens*." In M. Di Fazio and S. Paltinieri, eds., *La società gentilizia nell'Italia antica tra realtà e mito storiografico*, 73–95. Bari.

Di Fazio, M. 2020. *I Volsci. Un populo "liquido" nel Lazio antico*. Rome.

Di Fazio, M., and S. Paltinieri, eds. 2019. *La società gentilizia nell'Italia antica tra realtà e mito storiografico*. Bari.

Di Giuseppe, H. 2005. "Villae, villulae e fattorie nella Media Valle del Tevere." In B. Santillo Frizzel and A. Klynne, eds., *Roman Villas around the Urbs: Interaction with Landscape and Environment. Proceedings of the Conference at the Swedish Institute in Rome, September 17–18, 2004*, 1–19. Rome.

Di Giuseppe, H. 2009. "Assetti territoriali nella media valle del Tevere all'epoca orientalizzante a quella Repubblicana." In F. Coarelli and H. Patterson, eds., *Mercator Placidissimus: The Tiber Valley in Antiquity. New Research in the Upper and Middle River Valley*, 431–65. Rome.

Di Guiseppe, H. 2012. *Black-Gloss Ware in Italy: Production Management and Local Histories*. Oxford.

Di Giuseppe, H. 2018. *Lungo il Tevere scorreva lento il tempo dei paesaggi tra XV e I secolo a.C.* Rome.

Di Rita, F., and D. Magri. 2012. "An overview of the Holocene vegetation history from the central Mediterranean coasts." *Journal of Mediterranean Earth Sciences* 4: 35–52.

Di Rita, F., F. Molisso, and M. Sacchi. 2018. "Late Holocene environmental dynamics, vegetation history, human impact, and climate change in the ancient Literna Palus (Lago Patria; Campania, Italy)." *Review of Palaeobotany and Palynology* 258: 48–61.

Dilke, O. 1972. *The Roman Land Surveyors: An Introduction to the Agrimensores*. Newton Abbott.

Dobson, M. 2008. *The Army of the Roman Republic: The Second Century BC, Polybius, and the Camps at Numantia, Spain*. Oxford.

Downey, S. B. 1995. *Architectural Terracottas from the Regia*. Ann Arbor, MI.

Drago Troccoli, L. 2013. "Le offerte in metallo: riflessioni preliminari sugli aspetti formali, ponderali ed economici." In M. P. Baglione and M. D. Gentili, eds., *Riflessioni su Pyrgi: Scavi e ricerche nelle aree del santuario*, 167–92. Rome.

Driediger-Murphy, L. G. 2019. *Roman republican augury: Freedom and control.* Oxford.

Drogula, F. 2017. "Plebeian tribunes and the government of early Rome." *Antichthon* 51: 101–23.

Drogula, F. 2020. "The institutionalization of warfare in early Rome." In M. Fronda and J. Armstrong, eds., *Romans at War: Soldiers, Citizens, and Society in the Roman Republic*, 17–34. Routledge.

Drogula, F. K., and M. Project. 2015. *Commanders and Command in the Roman Republic and Early Empire.* Chapel Hill, NC.

Drummond, A. 1990. "Appendix." In F. W. Walbank, A. E. Astin, M. W. Frederiksen, and R. M. Ogilvie, eds., *The Cambridge Ancient History*, 2nd ed., 7, 625–44.

Dupré, X., and J. Aquilué Abadías. 2002. *Excavaciones arqueológicas en Tusculum: informe de las campañas de 2000 y 2001.* Rome.

Duval, C., and B. Clavel. 2018. "Bœufs gaulois et bœufs français: morphologies animales et dynamiques économiques au cours de La Tène et des périodes historiques." *Gallia* 75: 141–71.

Eckstein, A. 1987. *Senate and General: Individual Decision-Making and Roman Foreign Relations, 264–194 B.C.* Berkeley, CA.

Eckstein, A., 2006. *Mediterranean Anarchy, Interstate War, and the Rise of Rome.* Berkeley, CA.

Eder, W. 1990. "Der Bürger und sein Staat- Der Staat und seine Bürger." In W. Eder, ed., *Staat und Staatlichkeit in Der Frühen Römischen Republik: Akten Eines Symposiums, 12.–15. Juli 1988, Freie Universität Berlin*, 12–32. Stuttgart.

Eder, W. ed. 1990. *Staat und Staatlichkeit in der frühen römischen Republik*, 494–510. Stuttgart.

Ehrman, D. 2011. *The New Testament: A Historical Introduction to the Early Christian Writings.* Oxford.

Elkins, N. 2015. *Monuments in Miniature: Architecture on Roman Coinage.* New York.

Enei, F. 2001. *Progetto Ager Caeretanus. Il litorale di Alsium. Ricognizioni archeologiche nel territorio dei comuni di Ladispoli, Cerveteri e Fiumicino (Alsium, Caere, Ad Turres, Ceri).* Ladispoli.

Erdkamp, P. 1998. *Hunger and the Sword: Warfare and Food Supply in Roman Republican Wars (264–30 BC).* Leiden.

Erdkamp, P. ed. 2010. *A Companion to the Roman Army.* London.

Erdkamp, P. 2010. "Army and society." In N. Rosenstein and R. Morstein Marx, eds., *A Companion to the Roman Republic*, 278–96. Malden, MA.

Erdkamp, P. 2011. "Soldiers, Roman citizens, and Latin colonists in mid-Republican Italy." *Ancient Society* 41: 108–46.

Etxebarria Akaiturri, A. 2008. *Los foros romanos republicanos en la Italia centro-meridional tirrena: origen y evolución formal.* Madrid.

Evans, H. B. 1994. *Water Distribution in Ancient Rome.* Ann Arbor, MI.

Evans, J. M., J. T. Samuels, L. Motta, M. Naglak, and M. D'Acri, 2019. "An Iron Age settlement at Gabii: An interim report of the Gabii Project Excavations in Area D, 2012–2015." *Etruscan Studies* 70: 1–33.

Farello, P. 2006. "Caccia, pesca e allevamento nell'Etruria padana dall'VIII al IV secolo a.C." In A. Curci and D. Vitali, eds., *Animali tra uomini e dei: Archeozoologia del mondo preromano. Atti del Convegno internazionale 8–9 novembre 2002. Studi e Scavi, Nuova serie*, Vol. 14, 97–109. Bologna.

Farney, G. D. 2007. *Ethnic Identity and Aristocratic Competition in Republican Rome.* Cambridge, UK.

Farney, G. D. 2019. "Forum Novum and the limits of Roman colonization in Italy." In A. De Giorgi, ed., *Cosa and the Colonial Landscape of Republican Italy (Third and Second Centuries BCE)*, 159–81. Ann Arbor, MI.

Farney, G. D., and G. Bradley, eds. 2017. *The Peoples of Ancient Italy.* New York.

Favro, D. 1996. *The Urban Image of Augustan Rome.* Cambridge, UK.

Feeney, D. 2007. *Caesar's Calendar: Ancient Time and the Beginnings of History*, Berkeley, CA.

Feeney, D. 2016. *Beyond Greek: The Beginnings of Latin Literature.* Cambridge, MA.

Feig Vishnia, R. 1996. *State, Society and Popular Leaders in Mid-Republican Rome, 241–167 BC.* London.

Feiken, H. 2014. *Dealing with Biases. Three Geo-archaeological Approaches to the Hidden Landscapes of Italy.* Eelde/Groningen.

Fernique, E. 1878. "Les dernières fouilles de Préneste." *Revue Archéologique* 35: 233–42.

Ferrandes, A. 2006. "Produzioni stampigliate e figurate in area etrusco-laziale tra fine IV e III secolo A.C. Nuove riflessioni alle luce di vecchi contesti." *Archeologia Classica* 57: 115–74.

Filippi, D. 2013. "Regione VIII. Forum Romanum Magnum." In A. Carandini and P. Carafa, eds., *Atlante di Roma*, 1: 143–206. Milan.

Finley, M. I. 1964. "Between slavery and freedom." *Comparative Studies in Society and History* 6: 233–49.

Finley, M. I. 1980. *Ancient Slavery and Modern Ideology.* London.

Finley, M. I. 1981. *Economy and Society in Ancient Greece.* Ed. Brent D. Shaw and Richard P. Saller. London.

Finley, M. I. 1998. *Ancient Slavery and Modern Ideology.* Expanded ed. by Brent D. Shaw. Princeton, NJ.

Finley, M. I. 1999. *The Ancient Economy.* Updated ed. Berkeley, CA.

Fiorentino, G., Castiglioni, E., Rottoli, M., and R. Nisbet. 2004. "Le colture agricole in Italia nel corso dell'età del Bronzo: Sintesi dei dati e linee di tendenza." In D. Cocchi Genick, ed., *L'età del Bronzo Recente in Italia. Atti del Congresso nazionale di Lido di Camaiore, 26–29 ottobre 2000*, 219–26. Viareggio.

Fisher, N., and H. van Wees, eds. 2015. *Aristocracy in Antiquity: Redefining Greek and Roman Elites*. Swansea.

Flach, D. 1994. *Die Gesetze der frühen römischen Republik: Text und Kommentar*. Darmstadt.

Flaig, E. 1995. "Die *pompa funebris*. Adlige Konkurrenz und annalistische Erinnerung in der Römischen Republik." In O. Oexle, ed., *Memoria als Kultur*, 115–48. Göttingen.

Flaig, E. 2009. *Weltgeschichte der Sklaverei*. Munich.

Fletcher, R. 2010. "Urban materialities: Meaning, magnitude, friction, and outcomes." In D. Hicks and M. C. Beaudry, eds., *Oxford Handbook of Material Culture Studies*, 459–83. Oxford.

Flower, H. I. 1996. *Ancestor Masks and Aristocratic Power in Roman Culture*. Oxford.

Flower, H. I. 1998. "The significance of an inscribed breastplate captured at Falerii in 241 BC." *Journal of Roman Archaeology* 11: 224–32.

Flower, H. I. 2010. *Roman Republics*. Princeton, NJ.

Flower, H. I. 2017. *The Dancing Lares and the Serpent in the Garden: Religion at the Roman Street Corner*. Oxford.

Flower, H. I. 2022. "Veni, vidi, vici: When did Roman politicians use the first person singular?" In K. Kingsley, G. Monti, and T. Rood, eds., *The Authoritative Historian: Tradition and Innovation in Ancient Historiography*, 224–40. Cambridge, UK.

Forsythe, G. 2005. *A Critical History of Early Rome*. Berkeley, CA.

Forsythe, G. 2007. "The army and centuriate organization in early Rome." In P. Erdkamp, ed., *A Companion to the Roman Army*, 24–41. Malden.

Foxhall, L. 2000. "The running sands of time: Archaeology and the short-term." *World Archaeology* 31.3: 484–98.

Foxhall, L., H.-J. Gehrke, and N. Luraghi, eds. 2010. *Intentional History: Spinning Time in Ancient Greece*. Stuttgart.

Fraccaro, P. 1956. *Opuscula*, 1. Pavia.

France, J. 2021. *Tribut: une histoire fiscale de la conquête romaine*. Paris.

Franceschelli, C. 2015. "Riflessioni sulla centuriazione romana: paradigmi interpretativi, valenza paesaggistica, significato storico." *Agri Centuriati* 12: 175–211.

Francisci, D. 2020. "The Olynthus mill in the Alps: New hypotheses from two unidentified millstones discovered in Veneto region (Italy)." *Journal of Lithic Studies* 7.3: 1–20.

Fraschetti, A. 1989. "Eraclide Pontico e Roma città greca." In A. C. Cassio and D. Musti, eds., *Tra Sicilia e Magna Graecia. Aspetti di interazione culturale nel IV secolo a.C. Annali dell'Istituto Universitario Orientale di Napoli, Dipartimento di Studi del Mondo Classico e del Mediterraneo Antico, Sezione filologico-letteraria* Vol. 11, 81–95. Rome.

Frayn, J. M. 1979. *Subsistence Farming in Roman Italy*. Fontwell.

Frayn, J. M. 1984. *Sheep-Rearing and the Wool Trade in Italy during the Roman Period*. Liverpool.

Frederiksen, M. 1985. *Campania*. Ed. N. Purcell. London.

Frémondeau, D., M.-P. Horard-Herbin, O. Buchsenschutz, J. Ughetto-Monfrin, and M. Balasse. 2015. "Standardized pork production at the Celtic village of Levroux Les Arènes (France, 2nd c. BC): Evidence from kill-off patterns and birth seasonality inferred from enamel δ18O analysis." *Journal of Archaeological Science: Reports* 2: 215–26.

Frey-Kupper, S. 2014. "Coins and their use in the Punic Mediterranean: Case studies from Carthage to Italy from the fourth to the first century BCE." In J. C. Quinn and N. C. Vella, eds., *The Punic Mediterranean: Identities and Identification from Phoenician Settlement to Roman Rule*, 76–108. Cambridge, UK.

Frier, B. W. 1977. Untitled review of A. Watson. *Rome of the Twelve Tables: Persons and property*. *The Classical Journal* 72.4: 379–80.

Fronda, Michael. 2010. *Between Rome and Carthage: Southern Italy during the Second Punic War*. Cambridge, UK.

Fulford, M., A. Wallace-Hadrill, G. Clark et al. 1999. "Towards a history of Pre-Roman Pompeii: Excavations beneath the House of Amarantus (I.9.11–12), 1995–8." *Papers of the British School at Rome* 67: 37–144.

Fuller, D., and C. Stevens. 2009. "Agriculture and the development of complex societies: An archaeobotanical agenda." In A. Fairbairn and E. Weiss, eds., *From Foragers to Farmers: Papers in Honour of Gordon C. Hillman*, 37–57. Oxford.

Fulminante, F. 2014. *The Urbanisation of Rome and Latium Vetus from the Bronze Age to the Archaic Era*. Cambridge, UK.

Gaastra, J. S. 2014. "Shipping sheep or creating cattle: Domesticate size changes with Greek colonisation in Magna Graecia." *Journal of Archaeological Science* 52: 483–96.

Gabba, E. 1977. "Esercito e fiscalità a Roma in età repubblicana." In A. Chastagnol, C. Nicolet, and H. Van Effenterre, eds., *Armées et fiscalité dans le monde antique*, 13–27. Paris.

Gabba, E. 1988. "Aspetti militari e agrari." *Dialoghi di Archeologia* 6.2: 19–22.

Gabba, E. 1989. "Rome and Italy in the second century BC." In A. E. Astin, F. W. Walbank, M. W. Frederiksen, and R. M. Ogilvie, eds., *Cambridge Ancient History*, 2nd ed., vol. 8, 197–243. Cambridge, UK.

Gabba, E. 1990. "Dallo stato-città allo stato municipale." In A. Schiavone, ed., *Storia di Roma*, vol. 2.1: *L'impero mediterraneo*, 697–714. Turin.

Gabba, E. 1993. "Problemi di metodo per la storia di Roma arcaica." In aa.vv. *Bilancio critico su Roma arcaica fra monarchia e repubblica in memoria di Ferdinando Castagnoli, Roma, 3-4 giugno 1991*, 13–24. Rome.

Gabba, E., and M. Pasquinucci. 1979. *Strutture agrarie e allevamento transumante nell'Italia romana*. Pisa.

Gabrielli, C. 2003. *Contributi alla storia economica di Roma repubblicana: Difficoltà politico-sociali, crisi finanziaria e debiti fra 5. e 3. sec. a.C.* Como.

Gallia, A. 2007. "Reassessing the 'Cumaean Chronicle': Greek Chronology and Roman History in Dionysius of Halicarnassus." *Journal of Roman Studies* 97: 50–67.

Gallini, C. 1973. "Che cosa intendere per ellenizzazione. Problemi di metodo." *Dialoghi di Archeologia* 7: 175–91.

Galsterer, H. 1976. *Herrschaft und Verwaltung im republikanischen Italien. Die Beziehungen Roms zu den italischen Gemeinden vom Latinerfreuden 338 v. Chr. bis zum Bundesgenossenkrieg 91 v. Chr.* Munich.

Gantz, T. N. 1974. "Lapis Niger: The tomb of Romulus." *Parola del Passato* 29: 350–60.

Gargola, D. 2017. *The Shape of the Roman Order: The Republic and Its Spaces.* Chapel Hill, NC.

Garlan, Y. 1987. "War, piracy and slavery in the Greek world." In M. I. Finley, ed., *Classical Slavery*, 7–21. London.

Garrucci, R. 1885. *Le monete dell'Italia antica.* Rome.

Gatti, G. 1899. "Nuove scoperte nella città e nel suburbio." *Notizie degli Scavi*: 10–14.

Gatti, S., and D. Palombi. 2016. "Le città del Lazio con mura poligonali: questioni di cronologia e urbanistica." In P. Fontaine and S. Helas, ed., *Fortificazioni arcaiche del Latium vetus e dell'Etruria meridionale (IX–VI sec. a.C.). Stratigrafia, cronologia, urbanizzazione*, 233–49. Brussels.

Gatti, S. 2009. "La necropoli di Praeneste. Nuovi contesti e corredi." *Lazio e Sabina* 5: 159–71.

Gavériaux, F., L. Motta, P. Bailey, M. Brilli and L. Sadori (2022). "Crop Husbandry at Gabii During the Iron Age and Archaic Period: The Archaeobotanical and Stable Isotope Evidence." Environmental Archaeology: 1–14.

Gell, A. 1998. *Art and Agency: A New Anthropological Theory.* Oxford.

Gelzer, M. 1912. *Die nobilität der römischen Republik.* Berlin.

Genis, N. 2018. "Les annales politiques dans l'espace public: une nouveauté du IVe siècle av. J.-C.?" In S. Montel and A. Pollini, eds., *La question de l'espace au IVe siècle avant J.-C. dans les mondes grec et étrusco-italique: Continuités, ruptures, reprises*, 115–32. Besançon.

Giardina, A. 1997. *L'Italia romana. Storie di un'identità incompiuta.* Rome and Bari.

Gjerstad, E. 1941. "Il comizio romano dell'età repubblicana." *Opuscula Archeologica* 2: 97–158.

Gjerstad, E. 1953–1973. *Early Rome.* Lund.

Gleba, M. 2008. *Textile Production in Pre-Roman Italy.* Oxford.

Gleba, M. 2012. "From textiles to sheep: investigating wool fibre development in pre-Roman Italy using scanning electron microscopy (SEM)." *Journal of Archaeological Science* 39.12: 3643–61.

Gleba, M. 2017. "Tracing textile cultures of Italy and Greece in the early first millennium BC." Antiquity 91.359: 1205–22.

Gomez, M. A. 2018. *African Dominion: A New History of Empire in Early and Medieval West Africa*. Princeton, NJ.

Goodchild, H. 2013. "Agriculture and the environment of Republican Italy." In J. D. Evans, ed., *Companion to Roman Republican Archaeology*, 198–213. Malden.

Gorski, G. J., and J. E. Packer. 2015. *The Roman Forum: A Reconstruction and Architectural Guide*. Cambridge, UK.

Gosden, C. 2005. "What do objects want?" *Journal of Archaeological Method and Theory* 12: 193–211.

Govi, E. ed. 2014. *Il mondo etrusco e il mondo italico di ambito settentrionale prima dell'impatto con Roma (IV-II secolo a.C.), atti del Convegno Bologna 28 febbraio–1 marzo 2013*. Rome.

Graeber, D. 2011. *Debt: The First 5,000 Years*. Brooklyn, NY.

Graf, F. 1995. "Bemerkungen zur bürgerlichen Religiosität im Zeitalter des Hellenismus." In M. Wörrle and P. Zanker, eds., *Stadtbild und Bürgerbild im Hellenismus. Kolloquium, München, 24. bis 26. Juni 1993*, 103–14. Munich.

Gras, M. 1985. *Trafics tyrrheniens archaïques*. Rome.

Grever, M., and R.-J. Adriaansen. 2017. "Historical culture: A concept revisited." In M. Carretero, S. Berger, and M. Grever, eds., *Palgrave Handbook of Research in Historical Culture and Education*, 73–89.

Griffeth, R. 2000. "The Hausa city-states from 1450 to 1804." In M. H. Hansen, ed., *A Comparative Study of Thirty City-State Cultures: An Investigation Conducted by the Copenhagen Polis Centre*, 482–506. Copenhagen.

Griffith, G. T. 1968 [1935]. *The Mercenaries of the Hellenistic World*. Groningen.

Grillo, L. 2018. "Speeches in the *Commentarii*." In Grillo and Krebs, eds., 131–43.

Grillo. L., and C. Krebs, eds. 2018. *The Cambridge Companion to the Writings of Julius Caesar*. Cambridge, UK.

Gros, P. 1973. "Hermodoros et Vitruve." *Mélanges de ls'École française de Rome. Antiquité* 85: 137–61.

Gros, P. 1976. "Les premiers génerations d'architectes hellènistiques à Rome." In *L'Italie préromaine et la Rome républicaine. Mélanges offerts à Jacques Heurgon I*, 387–410. Rome.

Gros, P. 1996. *L'Architecture romaine: Du début du IIIe siècle av. J.-C. à la fin du Haut-Empire. 1. Les monuments publics*. Paris.

Gullini, G. 1983. "Terrazza, edificio, uso dello spazio. Note su architettura e società nel periodo medio e tardo repubblicano." In *Architecture et societé. De l'archaïsme grec à la fin de la République romaine (CEFR 66)*, 119–89. Rome.

Haake, M., and Harders, A.-C., eds. 2017. *Politische Kultur und soziale Struktur der Römischen Republik. Bilanzen und Perspektiven*. Stuttgart.

Habinek, T. 1998. *The Politics of Latin Literature: Writing, Identity, and Empire in Ancient Rome*. Princeton, NJ.

Haeberlin, E. J. 1910. *Aes Grave: Das Schwergeld Roms und Mittelitaliens*. Frankfurt.

Hall, J. F. 1996. "From Tarquins to Caesars: Etruscan governance at Rome." In J. F. Hall, ed., *Etruscan Italy: Etruscan Influences on the Civilizations of Italy from Antiquity to the Modern Era*, 149–90. Provo, UT.

Halstead, P. 1996. "Pastoralism or household herding? Problems of scale and specialisation in early Greek animal husbandry." *World Archaeology* 28: 20–42.

Halstead, P. 2014. *Two Oxen Ahead: Pre-Mechanized Farming in the Mediterranean*. Chichester.

Hamerow, H., A. Bogaard, M. Charles et al. 2020. "An integrated bioarchaeological approach to the Medieval Agricultural revolution: The case study of Stafford, England." *European Journal of Archaeology* 23.4: 585–609.

Hanell, K. 1946. *Das altrömische eponyme Amt*. Lund.

Hansen, M. H. 1991. *The Athenian Democracy in the Age of Demosthenes: Structure, Principles, and Ideology*. Trans. J. Crook. Norman, OK.

Harper, K. 2011. *Slavery in the Late Roman World, AD 275–425*. Cambridge, UK.

Harper, K., and M. McCormick. 2018. "Reconstructing the Roman climate." In W. Scheidel, ed., *The Science of Roman History: Biology, Climate, and the Future of the Roman Past*, 11–52. Princeton, NJ.

Harper, K., and W. Scheidel. 2018. "Roman slavery and the idea of 'slave society.'" In Lenski and Cameron, eds., 86–105.

Harris, E. M. 2012. "Homer, Hesiod, and the 'origins' of Greek slavery." *Revue des Etudes Anciennes* 114: 345–66.

Harris, J. 2018. "Continuity through rupture: Space, time, and politics in the mass migrations of Dionysius the Elder." In S. Montel and A. Pollini, eds., *La question de l'espace au IVe siècle avant J.-C. dans les mondes grec et étrusco-italique: Continuités, ruptures, reprises*, 135–57. Besançon.

Harris, W. V. 1979. *War and Imperialism in Republican Rome, 327–70 BC*. Oxford.

Harris, W. V. 1990. "Roman warfare in the economic and social context of the fourth century BC." In W. Eder, ed. *Staat und Staatlichkeit in der frühen römischen Republik*, 494–510. Stuttgart.

Harris, W. V. 2007. "Quando e come l'Italia divenne per la prima volta Italia?" *Studi Storici* 48: 301–22.

Harris, W. V. 2017. "Rome at sea: The beginnings of Roman naval power." *Greece and Rome* 64: 14–26.

Haverfield, F. 1906. *The Romanization of Roman Britain*. Oxford.

Haverfield, F. 1913. *Ancient Town-Planning*. Oxford.

Heinrich, F. 2017. "Modelling crop-selection in Roman Italy: The economics of agricultural decision making in a globalizing economy." In T. de Haas and G. Tol, eds., *The Economic Integration of Roman Italy: Rural Communities in a Globalising World. Mnemosyne, Supplements* 404, 141–69. Leiden.

Helm, M. 2021. *Kampf um Mittelitalien: Roms ungerader Weg zur Großmacht*. Stuttgart.

Heurgon, J. 1961. *La vie quotidienne chez les Étrusques*. Paris.
Hill, H. 1946. "The history of Pignoriscapio." *The American Journal of Philology* 67: 60–6.
Hitchner, R. B. 2002. "Olive production and the Roman economy: The case for intensive growth in the Roman Empire." In W. Scheidel and S. von Reden, eds., *The Ancient Economy*, 71–83. Edinburgh.
Hobsbawm, E. 1962. *The Age of Revolution, 1789–1848*. New York.
Hobsbawm, E., and T. Ranger, eds. 1983. *The Invention of Tradition*. Cambridge, UK.
Hodder, I. 1979. "Economic stress and material culture patterning." *American Antiquity* 44: 446–54.
Hodder, I. 1982. *Symbols in Action*. Cambridge, UK.
Hodge, T. 1992. *Roman Aqueducts and Water Supply*. London.
Hölkeskamp, K.-J. 1993. "Conquest, competition and consensus: Roman expansion in Italy and the rise of the *nobilitas*." *Historia* 42.1: 12–39.
Hölkeskamp, K-J. 2001. "Fact(ions) or fiction? Friedrich Münzer and the aristocracy of the Roman Republic: Then and now. Review of: *Roman Aristocratic Parties and Families* by Friedrich Münzer and Thérèse Ridley." *International Journal of the Classical Tradition* 8.1: 92–105.
Hölkeskamp, K.-J. 2004. *SENATVS POPVLVSQVE ROMANVS. Die politische Kultur der Republik – Dimensionen und Deutungen*. Stuttgart.
Hölkeskamp, K.-J. 2006. "History and collective memory in the Middle Republic." In N. Rosenstein and R. Morstein Marx, eds. *A Companion to the Roman Republic*, 478–95. Oxford.
Hölkeskamp, K.-J. 2010. *Reconstructing the Roman Republic: An Ancient Political Culture and Modern Research*. Trans. H. Heitmann-Gordon. Princeton, NJ.
Hölkeskamp, K.-J. 2011. "Self-serving sermons: oratory and self-construction of the republican aristocrat." In C.J. Smith and R. Covino, eds., *Praise and Blame in Roman Republican Rhetoric*, 17–34. Swansea.
Hölkeskamp, K.-J. 2011 [1987]. *Die Entstehung der Nobilität: Studien zur sozialen und politischen Geschichte der Römischen Republik im 4. Jhdt. v. Chr.* Stuttgart.
Hölkeskamp, K.-J. 2013. "Friends, Romans, countrymen: Addressing the Roman people and the rhetoric of inclusion." In C. J. Steel and H. van der Blom, eds., *Community and Communication: Oratory and Politics in Republican Rome*, 11–28. Oxford.
Hölkeskamp, K.-J. 2019. "'Cultural turn' oder Paradigmenwechsel in der Althistorie? Die politische Kultur der römischen Republik in der neueren Forschung." *Historische Zeitschrift* 309: 1–35.
Hölkeskamp, K.-J. 2020. "The politics of elitism." In *Roman Republican Reflections: Studies in Politics, Power, and Pageantry*, 13–29. Stuttgart.
Hollander, D. B. 2007. *Money in the Late Roman Republic*. Netherlands.
Holliday, P. J. 1980. "*Ad Triumphum Excolendum*: The political significance of Roman historical painting." *Oxford Art Journal* 3.2: 3–8.

Holliday, P. J. 2002. *The Origins of Roman Historical Commemoration in the Visual Arts*. Cambridge, UK.

Holloway, R. R. 2008. "Who were the Tribuni Militum Consulari Potestate?" *L'antiquité Classique* 77: 107–25.

Holzer, A. C. 2013. *Rehabilitationen Roms: Die römische Antike in der deutschen Kultur zwischen Winckelmann und Niebuhr*. Heidelberg.

Holmén, T. 2014. "Authenticity criteria." In C. A. Evans, ed., *The Routledge Encyclopedia of the Historical Jesus*, 43–54. New York.

Hopkins, J. N. 2016. *The Genesis of Roman Architecture*. New Haven, CT.

Hopkins, K. 1978. *Conquerors and Slaves: Sociological Studies in Roman History*, vol. 1. Cambridge, UK.

Horden, P., and N. Purcell. 2000. *The Corrupting Sea: A Study of Mediterranean History*. London.

Horky, P. 2011. "Herennius Pontius: The construction of a Samnite philosopher." *Classical Antiquity* 30.1: 119–47.

Hornblower, S., and A. Spawforth, eds. 2005. *The Oxford Classical Dictionary*. Oxford.

Horsnaes, H. 2015. "Romanization at Paestum in the 3rd c. BC: A note on the chronology of the ΠΑΙΣΤΑΝΟ coins and the interpretation of the wall-paintings from the Spinazzo cemetery." *Journal of Roman Archaeology* 17: 305–11.

Hoskins, J. 2006. "Agency, biography and objects." In C. Tilley, K. Webb, S. Küchler, M. Rowlands, and P. Spyer, eds., *Handbook of Material Culture*, 74–84. London.

Howley, J. 2018. *Aulus Gellius and Roman Reading Culture: Text, Presence, and Imperial Knowledge in the* Noctes Atticae. Cambridge, UK.

Humbert, M. 1978. *Municipium et civitas sine suffragio: L'organisation de la conquête jusqu'à la guerre sociale*. Rome.

Humbert, M. 2005. *Le dodici tavole: Dai decemviri agli umanisti*. Pavia.

Humbert, M. 2014. *La loi des XII tables: Édition et commentaire*. Rome.

Humbert, M. 2018. *La loi des XII tables*. Rome.

Humm, M. 1996. "Appius Claudius Caecus et la construction de la via Appia." *Mélanges de l'École française de Rome. Antiquité* 108: 693–749.

Humm, M. 2005. *Appius Claudius Caecus: la Republique accomplie*. Rome.

Humm, M. 2006. "Tribus et citoyenneté: Extension de la citoyenneté romaine et expansion territoriale." In M. Jehne and R. Pfeilschifter, eds., *Herrschaft ohne Integration? Rom und Italien in republikanischer Zeit*, 9–64. Frankfurt.

Humm, M. 2009. "Exhibition et 'monumentalisation' du butin dans la Rome médio-républicaine." In M. Coudry and M. Humm, eds., *Praeda: Butin de guerre et société dans la Rome républicaine/Kriegsbeute und Gesellschaft im republikanischen Rom*, 117–52. Stuttgart.

Humm, M. 2016. "Timée de Tauromenium et la 'découverte de Rome' par l'historiographie grecque des IVe et IIIe siècles." In B. Mineo and T. Piel, eds., *Les premiers temps de Rome, VIe–IIIe siècle: La fabrique d'une histoire*, 87–110, Rennes.

Humphrey, J. H. 1986. *Roman Circuses: Arenas for Chariot Racing.* Berkeley, CA.

Ialongo, N., A. Vacca, and L. Peyronel. 2018. "Breaking down the bullion: The compliance of bullion-currencies with official weight systems in a case study from the ancient Near East." *Journal of Archaeological Science* 91: 20–32.

Ikeguchi, M. 2017. "Beef in Roman Italy." *Journal of Roman Archaeology* 30: 7–37.

Ingo, G., de Caro, T., Riccucci, C. et al. 2006. "Large scale investigation of chemical composition, structure and corrosion mechanism of bronze archeological artefacts from Mediterranean basin." *Applied Physics A* 83: 513–20.

Ioppolo, G. 1971–2. "I reperti ossei animali nell'area archeologica di S. Omobono." *Rendiconti della Pontificia Accademia Romana di Archeologia* 44: 3–19.

Isayev, E. 2007. *Inside Ancient Lucania: Dialogues in History and Archaeology.* London.

Isayev, E. 2017. *Migration, Mobility and Place in Ancient Italy.* Cambridge, UK.

Izzet, V. 2000. "The Etruscan sanctuary at Cerveteri, Sant'Antonio: Preliminary report of excavations 1995–1998." *Papers of the British School at Rome* 68: 321–35.

Jackson, M., and F. Marra. 2006. "Roman stone masonry: Volcanic foundations of the ancient city." *American Journal of Archaeology* 110.3: 403–36.

Jacomet, S., Kucan, D., Ritter, A., Suter, G., and A. Hagendorn. 2002. "Punica granatum L. (pomegranates) from early Roman contexts in Vindonissa (Switzerland)." *Vegetation History and Archaeobotany* 11: 79–92.

Jaia, A. M., 2013. "Le colonie di diritto romano: Considerazioni sul sistema difensivo costiero tra IV e III secolo a.C." *Scienze dell'antichità: Storia, archeologia, antropologia* 19.2–3: 475–89.

Jaia, A. M., and M. C. Molinari. 2011. "Two deposits of aes grave from the sanctuary of Sol Indiges (Torvaianica/Rome): The dating and function of the Roman libral series." *Numismatic Chronicle* 171: 87–97.

Jaia, A. M. and M. C. Molinari. 2012. "Il santuario di *Sol Indiges* e il sistema di controllo della costa laziale nel III sec. a.C." In G. Ghini and Z. Mari, eds., *Lazio e Sabina* vol. 8, 373–83. Rome.

Jaspers, K. 1953. *The Origin and Goal of History.* New Haven, CT.

Jewell, E. 2019. "(Re)moving the masses: Colonisation as domestic displacement in the Roman Republic." *Humanities* 8.66: doi: 10.3390/h8020066.

Johnston, A. C., and M. Mogetta. 2020. "Debating early Republican urbanism in Latium Vetus: The town planning of Gabii, between archaeology and history." *Journal of Roman Studies* 110: 91–121.

Jolivet, V., and E. Lovergne. 2014. "La tomba rupestre monumentale di Grotta Scalina (Viterbo)." In L. Mercuri and R. Zaccagnini, eds., *Etruria in Progress: La ricerca archeologica in Etruria meridionale*, 165–70. Rome.

Jolivet, V., Pavolini, C., Tomei, M. A., and R. Volpe, eds. 2009. *Suburbium II. Il suburbio di Roma dalla fine dell'età monarchica alla nascita del sistema delle ville (V–II secolo a.C.)*. Rome.

Jones, M. K., and J. Sheldon. 1985. "I resti vegetali." In A. Carandini and M. Rossella Filippi, eds., *Settefinestre una villa schiavistica nell'etruria Romana*, 306–9. Modena.

Jongman, W. 2014. "Re-constructing the Roman economy." In L. Neal and J. Williamson, eds., *The Cambridge History of Capitalism*, 75–100. Cambridge.

Kahrstedt, U. 1959. "Ager publicus und Selbstverwaltung in Lukanien und Bruttium." *Historia* 8: 174–206.

Kaser, M. 1953. "Vom Begriff des commercium." In *Studi in onore di V. Arangio-Ruiz nel XLV anno del suo insegnamento II*, 131–67. Naples.

Kay, P. 2014. *Rome's Economic Revolution*. Oxford.

Keaveney, A. 2005. *Sulla: The Last Republican*. London.

Kent, P. 2012. "Reconsidering *socii* in Roman Armies before the Punic Wars." In S. T. Roselaar, ed. *Process of Integration and Identity Formation in the Roman Republic*, 71–83. Leiden.

Killgrove, K., and R. H. Tykot. 2013. "Food for Rome: A stable isotope investigation of diet in the Imperial period (1st–3rd centuries AD)." *Journal of Anthropological Archaeology* 32.1: 28–38.

Kindt, J. 2015. "Personal religion: A productive category for the study of ancient Greek religion." *The Journal of Hellenic Studies* 135: 35–50.

King, A. C. 1999. "Diet in the Roman world: A regional inter-site comparison of the mammal bones." *Journal of Roman Archaeology* 12.1: 168–202.

King, A. C. 2001. "The Romanization of diet in the western Empire: Comparative archaeozoological studies." In S. Keay and N. Terrenato, eds., *Italy and the West: Comparative Issues in Romanization*, 210–23. Oxford.

Koestermann, E. ed. 1971. *C. Sallustius Crispus: Bellum Iugurthinum*. Heidelberg.

Kondratieff, E. 2004. "The column and coinage of C. Duilius: Innovations in iconography in large and small media in the Middle Republic." *Scripta Classica Israelica* 23: 1–39.

Koortbojian, M. 2002. "A painted *exemplum* at Rome's Temple of Liberty." *Journal of Roman Studies* 92: 33–48.

Kosmopoulos, D. 2012. "Il tempio presso S. Salvatore in Campo: Lo stato della questione." *Bullettino della Commissione Archeologica Comunale di Roma* 113: 7–41.

Kremer, D. 2007. *Ius Latinum: Le concept de droit latin sous la République et l'Empire*. Paris.

Kremer, D. 2014. "À propos d'une tentative récente de déconstruction des privilèges latins et en particulier du *ius migrandi*." *Athenaeum* 102: 226–38.

Kroll, J. H. 2008. "The monetary use of weighed bullion in Archaic Greece." In W. V. Harris, ed., *The Monetary Systems of the Greeks and Romans*, 12–37. Oxford.

Kron, G. 2002. "Archaeozoological evidence for the productivity of Roman livestock farming." *Münstersche Beiträge zur Antiken Handelsgeschichte* 21.2: 53–73.

Kron, G. 2017. "The diversification and intensification of Italian agriculture: The complementary roles of the small and wealthy farmer." In T. de Haas and G. Tol, eds., *The Economic Integration of Roman Italy*, 112–40. Leiden.

La Regina, A. 1989. "I sanniti." In G. Pugliese Caratelli, ed., *Italia Omnium Terrarum Parens. La civiltà degli Enotri, Choni, Ausoni, Sanniti, Lucani, Brettii, Sicani, Elimi*, 301–432. Milan.

La Rocca, E. 1984. *La riva a mezzaluna: Culti, agoni, monumenti funerari presso il Tevere del Campo Marzio occidentale*. Rome.

La Rocca, E. 2011. "La forza della tradizione: l'architettura sacra a Roma tra II e I secolo a. C." In E. La Rocca and A. D'Alessio, eds., *Tradizione e innovazione. L'elaborazione del linguaggio ellenistico nell'architettura romana e italica di età tardo-repubblicana*, 1–24. Rome.

Lackner, E.-M. 2008. *Republikanische Fora*. Munich.

Laffi, U. 1966. *Adtributio e contributio: Problemi del sistema politico-amministrativa dello stato romano*. Pisa.

Laffi, U. 1995. "Sull'esegesi di alcuni passi di Livio relativi ai rapporti tra Roma e gli alleati Latini e Italici nel primo quarto del II sec. a. C." In A. Calbi and G. Susini, eds., *Pro poplo arimenese*, 43–77. Faenza.

Laffranchi, Z., A. D.Huertas, S. A. Jiménez Brobeil, A. G. Torres, and J. A. Riquelme Cantal. 2016. "Stable C and N isotopes in 2100 Year-BP human bone collagen indicate rare dietary dominance of C4 plants in NE-Italy." *Scientific Reports* 6.1: 38817.

Lahiri, N. 2015. *Ashoka in Ancient India*. Cambridge, MA.

Lambrugo, C., L. Heinze, and S. Amicone. 2019. "Back to Manfria: Continuity or disruption in the countryside of Gela in the fourth century BC." In E. Perego, R. Scopacasa, and S. Amicone, eds., *Collapse or Survival: Micro-Dynamics of Crisis and Endurance in the Ancient Central Mediterranean*, 57–80. Philadelphia.

Lanfranchi, T. 2015. *Les tribuns de la plèbe et la formation de la République romaine, 494–287 avant J.-C.* Rome.

Lanfranchi, T. 2021. "Le développement des magistratures à Rome dans son contexte italien." *Mélanges de l'École française de Rome – Antiquité* 133.2: 321–46.

Lange, M. 2013. *Comparative-historical methods*. Los Angeles.

Langgut, D., R. Cheddadi, J. S. Carrión et al. 2019. "The origin and spread of olive cultivation in the Mediterranean Basin: The fossil pollen evidence." *The Holocene* 29.5: 902–22.

Langslow, D. 2013. "Archaic Latin inscriptions and Greek and Roman authors." In P. Liddel and P. Low, eds., *Inscriptions and Their Uses in Greek and Latin Literature*, 167–95. Oxford.

Launaro, A. 2011. *Peasants and Slaves: The Rural Population of Roman Italy (200 BC to AD 100)*. Cambridge, UK.

Launaro, A., and N. Leone. 2018. "A view from the margin? Roman commonwares and patterns of distribution and consumption at Interamna Lirenas (Lazio)." *Journal of Roman Archaeology* 31: 323–38.

Laurence, R. 1999. *The Roads of Roman Italy: Mobility and Cultural Change*. New York.

Laurendi, R. 2013. *Leges Regiae e Ius Papirianum: Tradizione e storicità di un Corpus normativo*. Rome.

Le Goff, J. 2015. *Must We Divide History into Periods?* Trans. M. DeBevoise. New York.

Leigh, M. 2010. "Early Roman epic and the maritime movement." *Classical Philology* 105: 265–80.

Lejars, T. 2020. "Les Celtes et les populations étrusques et italiques entre les VIe et IIIe siècles av. J.-C." *Mélanges de l'École française de Rome – Antiquité* 132.1: 67–80.

Lendon, J. E. 2007. "The Hellenistic world and the Roman Republic: War and society." In P. Sabin, M. Whitby, and H. van Wees, eds., *The Cambridge History of Greek and Roman Warfare*, Vol. 1, *Greece, the Hellenistic World, and the Rise of Rome*, 498–516. Cambridge, UK.

Lengle, J. 1936. "Tribunus Aerarius." *Paulys Realencyclopädie der klassischen Altertumswissenschaft* 6: 2432–5.

Lenski, N. 2018a. "What is a slave society?" In Lenski and Cameron, eds., 15–57.

Lenski, N. 2018b. "Ancient slaveries and modern ideology." In Lenski and Cameron, eds. 106–47.

Lenski, N., and C. M. Cameron, eds. 2018. *What Is a Slave Society? The Practice of Slavery in Global Perspective*. Cambridge, UK.

Lentjes, D. 2013. "From subsistence to market exchange: The development of an agricultural economy in 1st-millennium BC Southeast Italy." In M. Groot, D. Lentjes, and J. Zeiler, eds., *Barely Surviving or More than Enough: The Environmental Archaeology of Subsistence, Specialization and Surplus Food Production*, 101–30. Leiden.

Lentjes, D. 2016. *Planting the Seeds of Change: Landscape and Land Use in First Millennium BC Southeast Italy*. Amsterdam Archaeological Studies. Amsterdam.

Lentjes, D., and G. Saltini Semerari. 2016. "Big debates over small fruits: Wine and oil production in Protohistoric Southern Italy (ca 1350–750 BC)." *Babesch* 91: 1–16.

Lewis, D. M. 2018. *Greek Slave Systems in Their Eastern Mediterranean Context, c. 800–146 BC*. Oxford.

Lewis, D. M. In press. "The local slave systems of ancient Greece." In D. W. Tandy and S. D. Gartland, eds., *Voiceless, Invisible, and Countless: The Experience of Subordinates in Greece, 800–300 BC*. Oxford.

Libertini, G. 2018. Liber Colonarivm *(Libro Delle Colonie): Dai* Gromatici Veteres *(Gli Antichi Agrimensori) nella ricognizione di Karl Lachmann (Berlino 1848), con traduzione in italiano e figure concernenti la persistenza di tracce delle antiche limitationes nei luoghi moderni*. Frattamaggiore.

Licordari, A. 1982. "Italia: Regio I (Latium)." In S. Panciera, ed., *Epigrafia e ordine senatorio*, vol. 4–5, 9–57. Rome.

Linderski, J. 2013. "Lily Ross Taylor and the Roman tribes." In *The Voting Districts of the Roman Republic*, rev. edition, 355–94. Ann Arbor, MI.

Lintott, A. 1999. *The Constitution of the Roman Republic*. Oxford.

Lippolis, E. 2016. "La città in Italia tra modelli ellenistici e politica romana." In M. Aberson, M. C. Biella, M. Di Fazio, P. Sánchez, and M. Wullschleger, eds., *L'Italia centrale e la creazione di una koiné culturale? I percorsi della "romanizzazione.*" E pluribus unum? Italy from the Pre-Roman Fragmentation to the Augustan Unity, vol. 2, 201–48. Bern.

Liverani, P. 2019. "Rusellae between crisis and revival: The evidence for colonial status." In A. De Giorgi, ed., *Cosa and the Colonial Landscape of Republican Italy (Third and Second Centuries BCE)*, 139–58. Ann Arbor, MI.

Loar, M., C. MacDonald, and D. Padilla Peralta, eds. 2017. *Rome, Empire of Plunder: The Dynamics of Cultural Appropriation*. Cambridge, UK.

Lodwick, L. 2019. "Sowing the seeds of future research: Data sharing, citation and reuse in archaeobotany." *Open Quaternary* 5: 7.

Lodwick, L., Campbell, G., Crosby, V., and G. Müldner. 2020. "Isotopic evidence for changes in cereal production strategies in Iron Age and Roman Britain." *Environmental Archaeology* 26.1: 13–28.

Loman, P. 2005. "Mercenaries, their women, and colonisation." *Klio* 87.2: 346–65.

Lomas, K. 2004. "Italy during the Roman Republic, 338–31 BC." In H. I. Flower, ed., *The Cambridge Companion to the Roman Republic*, 199–224. Cambridge, UK.

Long, L., L.-F. Gantès, and M. Rival. 2006. "L'épave Grand Ribaud F. Un chargement de produits étrusques du début du Ve siècle avant J.-C." In S. Gori and M. C. Bettini, eds., *Gli Etruschi da Genova ad Ampurias : Atti del XXIV convegno di studi etruschi ed italici, Marseille – Lattes, 26 settembre–1 ottobre 2002)*, 455–95. Pisa.

Loreto, L. 1993. *Un' epoca di buon senso : Decisione, consenso e stato a Roma tra il 326 e il 264 a.C.* Amsterdam.

Lott, J. B. 2004. *The Neighborhoods of Augustan Rome*. Pisa.

Love, E. 2008. "The evolution of animal husbandry and society in the backcountry of Ancient Italy." (Unpublished MSc dissertation, University of Sheffield)

Lovejoy, P. E. 2005. *Slavery, Commerce and Production in the Sokoto Caliphate of West Africa*. Trenton, NJ.

Lovejoy, P. E. 2012. *Transformations in Slavery: A History of Slavery in Africa*. 3rd ed. Cambridge, UK.

Lovejoy, P. E. 2016. *Jihad in West Africa during the Age of Revolutions*. Athens, OH.

Lovejoy, P. E. 2018. "Slavery in societies on the frontiers of centralized states in West Africa." In Lenski and Cameron, eds., 220–47.

Lugli, G. 1957. *La tecnica edilizia Romana*, 2 vols. Rome.

Lulof, P., and Smith, C. J. eds. 2017. *The Age of Tarquinius Superbus: Central Italy in the Late 6th Century*. Leuven.

Lyman, R. L. 1994. *Vertebrate Taphonomy*. Cambridge, UK.

Ma, J. 2013. "Hellenistic empires." In W. Scheidel and P. Bang, eds., *The Oxford Handbook of the State in the Ancient Near East and Mediterranean*, 324–57. Oxford.

MacBain, B. 1980. "Appius Claudius Caecus and the Via Appia." *Classical Quarterly* 30: 356–72.

MacDonald, W. L. 1982. *The Architecture of the Roman Empire, Volume 1: An Introductory Study*. New Haven, CT.

MacKay, C. S. 2000. "Sulla and the monuments: Studies in his public persona." *Historia* 99.2: 161–210.

Mackil, E. 2004. "Wandering cities: Alternatives to catastrophe in the Greek *polis*." *AJA* 108.4: 493–516.

Mackil, E. 2017. "Property claims and state formation in the Archaic Greek world." In C. Ando and S. Richardson, eds., *Ancient States and Infrastructural Power: Europe, Asia, and America*, 63–90. Pennsylvania.

MacKinnon, M. 2001. "High on the hog: Linking zooarchaeological, literary, and artistic data for pig breeds in Roman Italy." *American Journal of Archaeology* 105.4: 649–73.

MacKinnon, M. 2004a. *Production and Consumption of Animals in Roman Italy: Integrating the Zooarchaeological and Textual Evidence. Journal of Roman Archaeology* supplementary series, vol. 54. Portsmouth, RI.

MacKinnon, M. 2004b. "The role of caprines in Roman Italy: idealized and realistic reconstructions using ancient textual and zooarchaeological data." In B. Santillo Frizell, ed., *PECUS: Man and Animal in Antiquity. Proceedings of the conference at the Swedish Institute in Rome, September 9–12, 2002*, 54–60. Rome.

MacKinnon, M. 2014. "Animals in the urban fabric of Ostia: initiating a comparative zooarchaeological synthesis." *Journal of Roman Archaeology* 27: 175–201.

MacKinnon, M. 2016. "PARP-PS zooarchaeological report." (Unpublished archaeological report)

MacLean, R. 2018. *Freed Slaves and Roman Imperial Culture: Social Integration and the Transformation of Values*. Cambridge, UK.

MacMullen, R. 2011. *The Earliest Romans: A Character Sketch*. Ann Arbor, MI.

Maddox, G. 1983. "The economic causes of the Lex Hortensia." *Latomus* 42: 277–86.

Magri, D., and L. Sadori. 1999. "Late Pleistocene and Holocene pollen stratigraphy at Lago di Vico, central Italy." *Vegetation History and Archaeobotany* 8: 247–60.

Maini, E., and A. Curci. 2013. "Considerazioni sull'economia di allevamento nella Romagna durante l'età del bronzo." In J. De Grossi Mazzorin, A. Curci, and G. Giacobini, eds., *Economia e ambiente nell'Italia padana nell'età del Bronzo. Le indagini bioarcheologiche. Beni Archeologici - Conoscenza e Tecnologie Quaderno* 11: 357–76.

Malone, C., S. Stoddart, L. Ceccarelli et al. 2014. "Beyond feasting: Consumption and life style amongst the invisible Etruscans." In K. Boyle, R. J. Rabett, and C. O. Hunt, eds., *Living in the Landscape: Essays in Honour of Graeme Barker*, 257–66. Cambridge, UK.

Manfredi, A. M., and L. Malnati, eds. 2003. *Gli Etruschi in Val Padana*. Milan.

Manning, J. G., F. Ludlow, A. R., Stine et al. "Volcanic suppression of Nile summer flooding triggers revolt and constrains interstate conflict in ancient Egypt." *Nature Communications* 18: 900.

Mantovani, D. 2012. "Le due serie di leges regiae." In J.-L. Ferrary, ed., *Leges publicae: la legge nell'esperienza giuridica romana / a cura di Jean-Louis Ferrary*, Vol. 8, 283–92. Pavia.

Marcattili, F. 2009. *Circo Massimo: Architetture, funzioni, culti, ideologia*. Rome.

Marcattili, F. 2012. "Per un'archeologia dell'Aventino: i culti della media repubblica." *Mélanges de l'École française de Rome – Antiquité* 124: n.p.

Marchesini, S. 2007. *Prosopographia Etrusca II, 1: Studia: Gentium Mobilitas*. Rome.

Marchetti, P. 1977. "À propos du tributum romain: Impôt de quotité ou de répartition?" In A. Chastagnol, C. Nicolet, and H. Van Effentere, eds., *Armées et fiscalité dans le monde antique. Actes du Colloque national du CNRS*, 107–31. Paris.

Marcone, A. 2016. "Il rapporto tra agricoltura e pastorizia nel mondo romano nella storiografia recente." *Mélanges de l'École française de Rome – Antiquité* 128.2: 2–12.

Mari, Z. 2019. "Materiali e tecniche costruttive nel *Latium vetus* in età medio repubblicana." In F. M. Cifarelli, S. Gatti, and D. Palombi, eds., 195–212.

Marincola, J. 1997. *Authority and Tradition in Ancient Historiography*. Cambridge, UK.

Marinovic, L. 1988. *Le mercenariat grec au IV siecle avant notre ere et la crise de la Polis*. Paris.

Mariotti Lippi, M., M. Mori Secci, G. Giachi et al. 2020. "Plant remains in an Etruscan-Roman well at Cetamura del Chianti, Italy." *Archaeological and Anthropological Sciences* 12.1: 35.

Martin, I., A. Mehrotra, and M. Prasad 2009. "The thunder of history: The origins and Development of the new fiscal sociology." In I. Martin, A. Mehrotra, and M. Prasad, eds., *The New Fiscal Sociology: Taxation in Comparative and Historical Perspective*, 1–28. Cambridge, UK.

Martin, J. 1990. "Aspekte antiker Staatlichkeit." In W. Eder, ed., *Staat und Staatlichkeit in Der Frühen Römischen Republik: Akten Eines Symposiums, 12.–15. Juli 1988, Freie Universität Berlin*, 220–32. Berlin.

Marvelli, S., S. D. Siena, E. Rizzoli, and M. Marchesini. 2013. "The origin of grapevine cultivation in Italy: The archaeobotanical evidence." *Annali di Botanica* 3: 155–63.

Marzano, A. 2007. *Roman Villas in Central Italy: A Social and Economic History*. Leiden.

Marzano, A. 2013. "Agricultural production in the hinterland of Rome: Wine and olive oil." In A. K. Bowman and A. I. Wilson, eds., *The Roman Agricultural Economy: Organisation, Investment and Production*. Oxford Studies on the Roman Economy, Vol. 3, 85–106. Oxford.

Massa-Pairault, F. H. 1986. "Notes sur le problème du citoyen en armes: Cité romaine et cité étrusque." In A.-M. Adam and A. Rouveret, eds., *Guerre et sociétés en Italie (Ve-IVe siècles av. J.-C.)*, 29–50.

Massa-Pairault, F.-H. 2001. "Relations d'Appius Claudius Caecus avec l'Étrurie et la Campanie." In D. Briquel and J.-P. Thuillier, eds., *Le censeur et les Samnites: Sur Tite-Live, livre IX*, 97–116. Paris.

Massa-Pairault, F.-H. 2011. "Romulus et Remus: réexamen du miroir de l'Antiquarium Communal." *Mélanges de l'École française de Rome – Antiquité* 123.2: 505–25.

Massa-Pairault, F. H. 1996. "Le peintre de Darius et l'actualité: De la Macédoine à la Grande Grèce." In L. Breglia Pulci Doria, ed., *L'incidenza dell'antico: Studi in memoria di Ettore Lepore*, Vol. 2, 235–62. Naples.

Mazzei, M. 1987. "Nota su un gruppo di vasi policromi decorati con scene di combattimento, da Arpi (FG)." *Aion* 9: 167–88.

McCabe, A. 2013. "The anonymous struck bronze of the Roman Republic: A provisional arrangement." In P. van Alfen and R. B. Witschonke, eds., *Essays in Honour of Roberto Russo*, 101–274. Zürich.

McCoskey, D. E. 2012. *Race: Antiquity and Its Legacy*. Ancients and Moderns. Oxford.

McCurdy, L., and E. M. Abrams, eds. 2019. *Architectural Energetics in Archaeology*. Analytical Expansions and Global Explorations. London.

McDonald, K. 2015. *Oscan in Southern Italy and Sicily: Evaluating Language Contact in a Fragmentary Corpus*. Cambridge, UK.

McDonald, K. 2019. "Education and literacy in ancient Italy: Evidence from the dedications to the goddess Reitia." *Journal of Roman Studies* 109: 131–59.

McGovern, P. E., B. P. Luley, N. Rovira, A. Mirzoian, M. P. Callahan, K. E. Smith, G. R. Hall, T. Davidson, J. M. Henkin. 2013. "Beginning of viniculture in France." *Proceedings of the National Academy of Sciences* 110.25: 10147.

Méniel, P. 1996. "Importation de grands animaux romains et amélioration du cheptel à la fin de l'Âge du Fer en Gaule Belgique." *Revue archéologique de Picardie* 3-4: 113–22.

Menzel, M., and A. Naso. 2007. "Raffigurazioni di cortei magistratuali in Etruria: Viaggi nell'aldilà o precessioni reali?" *Ostraka* 16: 23–43.

Mercuri, A. M. 2014. "Genesis and evolution of the cultural landscape in central Mediterranean: The 'where, when and how' through the palynological approach." *Landscape Ecology* 29.10: 1799–1810.

Mercuri, A.M., C. A. Accorsi, M. B. Mazzanti et al. 2006a. "Economy and environment of Bronze Age settlements – Terramaras – on the Po Plain (Northern Italy): First results from the archaeobotanical research at the Terramara di Montale." *Vegetation History and Archaeobotany* 16: 23–60.

Mercuri, A. M., E. Allevato, D. Arobba et al. 2015. "Pollen and macroremains from Holocene archaeological sites: A dataset for the understanding of the bio-cultural diversity of the Italian landscape." *Review of Palaeobotany and Palynology* 218: 250–66.

Mercuri, A. M., M. Bandini Mazzanti, A. Florenzano, M. C. Montecchi, and E. Rattighieri. 2013. "Olea, Juglans and Castanea: The OJC group as pollen evidence of the development of human-induced environments in the Italian peninsula." *Quaternary International* 303.25: 24–42.

Mercuri, A. M., M. Mazzanti, G. Bosi, A. Cardarelli, L. Olmi, and P. Torri. 2006b. "Cereal fields from the Middle-Recent Bronze Age, as found inthe Terramara di Montale, in the Po Plain (Emilia Romagna, Northern Italy), based on pollen, seeds/fruits and microcharcoals." In J.-P. Morel, J. J. Tresserras, and J. C. Matamala, eds., *The Archaeology of Crop Fields and Gardens*, 251–70. Bari.

Mersing, K. M. 2007. "The war-tax (tributum) of the Roman Republic: A reconsideration." *Classica et Mediaevalia* 58: 215–35.

Meunier, N. 2011. "*Tribuni plebis* ou *tribuni militum*? Le tribunat originel dans la Haute République de Rome (Ve-IVe s. av. J.-C.)." *Les Etudes Classiques* 79: 347–60.

Meunier, N. 2014. "The tribunes and the federal army of the Latin League." *Les Etudes Classiques* 82: 271–88.

Mignone, L. M. 2016a. *The Republican Aventine and Rome's Social Order*. Ann Arbor, MI.

Mignone, L. M. 2016b. "The augural contest at Rome: The view from the Aventine."*Classical Philology* 111: 391–405.

Mignone, L. M. 2016c. "Rome's *Pomerium* and the Aventine Hill: From *auguraculum* to *imperium sine fine*." *Historia* 65.4: 427–49.

Mignone, L. M. In press. *Rome's Juno: Religious Imperialism and Self-Preservation*.

Millar, F. 1989. "Political power in Mid-Republican Rome: Curia or comitium?" *Journal of Roman Studies* 79: 138–50.

Miller, J. C. 2012. *The Problem of Slavery as History: A Global Approach*. New Haven, CT.

Millett, M. 1991. "Pottery: population or supply patterns? The ager tarraconensis approach." In G. Barker and J. Lloyd, eds., *Roman Landscapes: Archaeological Survey in the Mediterranean Region*. London.

Mineo, B., and T. Piel, eds. 2014. "Les premiers temps de Rome : VIe-IIIe siècles av. J.-C.: la fabrique d'une histoire." Rennes.

Minniti, C. 2012. *Ambiente, sussistenza e l'articolazione sociale nell'Italia centrale tra Bronzo medio e Primo Ferro*. British Archaeological Reports International Series 2394. Oxford.

Minniti, C., S. Valenzuela-Lamas, J. Evans, and U. Albarella. 2014. "Widening the market: Strontium isotope analysis on cattle teeth from Owslebury (Hampshire, UK) highlights changes in livestock supply between the Iron Age and the Roman period." *Journal of Archaeological Science* 42: 305-14.

Mirnik, I. 2009. "Nacrt numizmatičke topografije Like." *Identitet Like: korijeni i razvitak* 2: 442-92.

Mitchell, P. 2018. *The Donkey in Human History: An Archaeological Perspective*. Oxford.

Mitchell, R. E. 1990. *Patricians and Plebeians: The Origin of the Roman State*. Cornell, NY.

Moatti, C., ed. 2004. *La mobilité des personnes en Méditerranée de l'antiquité à l'époque moderne: Procédures de contrôle et documents d'identification*. Rome.

Mogetta, M. 2014. "From Latin planned urbanism to Roman colonial layouts: The town-planning of Gabii and its cultural implications." In E. C. Robinson, ed., *Papers on Italian Urbanism in the First Millennium BC (JRA, suppl. series 97)*, 145-74. Portsmouth, RI.

Mogetta, M. 2015. "A new date for concrete in Rome." *Journal of Roman Studies* 105: 1-40.

Mol, E. 2017. "Object ontology and cultural taxonomies: Examining the agency of style, material and objects in classification through Egyptian material culture in Pompeii and Rome." In A. Van Oyen and M. Pitts, eds., *Materializing Roman Histories*, 169-89. Oxford.

Molinari, M. C. 2014. "The two Roman types with two-faced gods on third century BC coinage." In N. T. Elkins and S. Krmnicek, eds., *"Art in the Round": New Approaches to Ancient Coin Iconography*, 89-96. Rahden.

Mommsen, T. 1850. *Die unteritalischen Dialekte*. Leipzig.

Monson, A. 2015. "Hellenistic empires." In A. Monson and W. Scheidel, eds., *Fiscal Regimes and the Political Economy of Premodern States*, 169-207. Oxford.

Mora, F. 1999. *Fasti e schemi cronologici: La riorganizzazione annalistica del passato remoto romano*.

Morandi, A. 1987. "La Tomba degli Scudi di Tarquinia. Contributo epigrafico per l'esegesi dei soggetti." *Mélanges de l'École française de Rome - Antiquité* 99.1: 95-110.

Morandi Tarabella, M. 2004. *Prosopographia etrusca, I, Corpus, 1: Etruria meridionale*. Rome.

Morel, J. P. 1969. "Etudes de céramique campanienne, I: L'atelier des petites estampilles." *Mélanges de l'ecole Française de Rome* 81: 59-117.

Morel, J. P. 2007. "Early Rome and Italy." In W. Scheidel, I. Morris, and R. Saller, eds., *The Cambridge Economic History of the Greco-Roman World*. Cambridge, UK.

Morley, N. 2006. "Social structure and demography." In N. Rosenstein and R. Morstein-Marx, eds., *A Companion to the Roman Republic*, 299–323. Oxford.

Morris, I. 2003. "Mediterraneanization." *Mediterranean Historical Review* 18.2: 30–55.

Morselli, C., and E. Tortorici. 1982. *Ardea: Forma Italiae XVI*. Florence.

Morstein-Marx, R. 2004. *Mass Oratory and Political Power in the Late Roman Republic*. Cambridge, UK.

Moser, C. 2019. *The Altars of Republican Rome: Sacrifice and the Materiality of Roman Religion*. Cambridge, UK.

Motta, L. 2002. "Planting the seed of Rome." *Vegetation History and Archaeobotany* 11: 71–8.

Motta, L. 2011. "Seeds and the city: Archaeobotany and state formation in early Rome." In N. Terrenato and D. C. Haggis, eds., *State Formation in Italy and Greece: Questioning the Neoevolutionist Paradigm*, 245–55. Oxford.

Motta, L. 2016. "Archaeobiology at Gabii: Sampling and recovery strategies in an urban context." In R. S. Opitz, M. Mogetta, and N. Terrenato, eds., *A Mid-Republican House from Gabii*. Ann Arbor, MI.

Motta, L., and K. Beydler. 2020. "Agriculture in Iron Age and Archaic Italy." In D. Hollander and T. Howe, eds. *A Companion to Ancient Agriculture*, 399–415. Hoboken, NJ.

Mouritsen, H. 2007. "The *Civitas sine Suffragio*: Ancient Concepts and Modern Ideology." *Historia* 56: 141–58.

Mouritsen, H. 2011. *The Freedman in the Roman World*. Cambridge, UK.

Muñiz Coello, J. 2011. El stipendium, el cuestor y qui aes tribuebat (Gai. Inst. IV 26). El abono de la paga al soldado en la República. *Klio* 93: 131–48.

Münzer, F. 1891. *De gente Valeria*. Oppeln.

Münzer, F. 1920. *Römische Adelsparteien und Adelsfamilien*. Stuttgart.

Münzer, F. 1999. *Roman Aristocratic Parties and Families*. Trans T. Ridley. Baltimore, MD.

Murphy, C. 2016. "Finding millet in the Roman world." *Archaeological and Anthropological Sciences* 81: 65–78.

Murphy, C., G. Thompson, and D. Fuller. 2013. "Roman food refuse: Urban archaeobotany in Pompeii, Regio VI, Insula 1." *Vegetation History and Archaeobotany* 22: 409–19.

Muzzioli, M. 1985. "Cures Sabini, Capena e Lucus Feroniae." In R. Bussi and V. Vandelli, eds., *Misurare la terra: Centuriazione e coloni nel mondo romano. Città, agricoltura, commercio: materiali da Roma e dal suburbio*, 48–58. Modena.

Ñaco del Hoyo, T. 2011. "Roman economy, finance, and politics in the Second Punic War." In D. Hoyos, ed., *A Companion to the Punic Wars*, 376–92. London.

Naglak, M., and N. Terrenato. 2019. "A house society in Iron Age Latium? Kinship and state formation in the context of new discoveries at Gabii." In M. Di Fazio and S. Paltineri, eds., 99–119.

Nash Briggs, D. 2003. "Metals, salt, and slaves: Economic links between Gaul and Italy from the eighth to the late sixth centuries BC." *Oxford Journal of Archaeology* 22: 243–59.

Natali, E., and V. Forgia. 2018. "The beginning of the Neolithic in Southern Italy and Sicily." *Quaternary International* 470: 253–69.

Nenci, G. 1982. "ΚΟΛΑΒΡΙΖΕΣΘΑΙ (*Vet. Test.*, Job, 5, 4." *Annali della Scuola Normale Superiore di Pisa. Classe di Lettere e Filosofia* Ser. III. 12: 1–6.

Neudecker, R. ed. 2011. *Krise und Wandel: Süditalien im 4. und 3. Jahrhundert v. Chr.: internationaler Kongress anlässlich des 65. Geburtstages von Dieter Mertens, Rom 26. bis 28. Juni 2006. Palilia*, vol. 23. Wiesbaden.

Nicolet, C. 1963. "Les 'equites campani' et leurs représentations figurées." *Mélanges de l'École française de Rome – Antiquité* 74: 463–517.

Nicolet, C. 1966. *L'Ordre équestre à l'époque républicaine (312–43 av. J.-C.) . . .* Rome.

Nicolet, C. 1976. *Tributum: Recherches Sur La Fiscalité Directe Sous La République Romaine*. Rome.

Nicolet, C. 1980. *The World of the Citizen in Republican Rome*. Berkeley and Los Angeles.

Nicolet, C. 2000. *Censeurs et publicains: Économie et fiscalité dans le Rome antique*. Rome.

Nielsen, I., and B. Poulsen, eds. 1992. *The Temple of Castor and Pollux I*. Rome.

Nielsen, M. 2013. "The last Etruscans: Family tombs in northern Etruria." In J. MacIntosh Turfa, ed., *The Etruscan World*, 180–93. London.

Nieto-Espinet, A., S. Valenzuela-Lamas, D. Bosch, and A. Gardeisen. 2020. "Livestock production, politics and trade: A glimpse from Iron Age and Roman Languedoc." *Journal of Archaeological Science: Reports* 30: 102077.

Nijboer, A. 2017. "Economy, 10th cent.–730 BCE." In A. Naso, ed., *Etruscology*, 795–810. Berlin.

Nörr, D. 2005. "Osservazioni in tema di terminologia giuridica predecemvirale e di ius mercatorum mediterraneo: il primo trattato cartaginese-romano." In M. Humbert, ed., *Le Dodici Tavole*, 147–90. Pavia.

North, J. A. 2006. "The Constitution of the Roman Republic." In N. Rosenstein and R. Morstein Marx, eds. *A Companion to the Roman Republic*, 256–77. London.

Northwood, S. J. 2008 "Census and *tributum*." In L. de Ligt and S.J. Northwood, eds., *People, Land, and Politics: Demographic Developments and the Transformation of Roman Italy, 300 BC–AD 14*, 257–70. Leiden.

Oakley, S. P. 1997–2005. *A Commentary on Livy, Books VI–X*. 4 vols. Oxford.

Oakley, S. P. 2002. "The Roman conquest of Italy." In J. Rich and G. Shipley, eds., *War and Society in the Roman World*, 9–37. London.

Oakley, S. P. 2004. "The early Republic." In H. I. Flower, ed. *The Cambridge Companion the Roman Republic*, 15–30. Cambridge, UK.

Olcese, G. 2017. "Wine and amphorae in Campania in the Hellenistic age: The case of Ischia." In T. De Haas and G. Tol, eds., *The Economic Integration of Roman Italy. Rural Communities in a Globalizing World*, 299–321. Leiden.

Orlin, E. 1997. *Temples, Religion, and Politics in the Roman Republic*. Leiden.

Orlin, E. 2010. *Foreign Cults in Rome: Creating a Roman Empire*. Oxford.

Ortalli, J., and I Campi Macri. 2012. "Un mercato panitalico sulla via della lana." In M. S. Busana, P. Basso, and A. R. Tricomi, eds., *Economia e Società. Studi in onore di Stefania Pesavento Mattioli*. Atti del Convegno (Padova-Verona, 18–20 maggio 2011). Antenor Quaderni 27 (Padova) 195–211. Padua.

Ostrom, E. 2018. *Governing the Commons: The Evolution of Institutions for Collective Action*. Cambridge, UK.

Padilla Peralta, D. 2017. "Slave religiosity in the Roman Middle Republic." *Classical Antiquity* 36.2: 317–69.

Padilla Peralta, D. 2018. "Hammer time: The Publicii Malleoli between cult and cultural history." *Classical Antiquity* 37.2: 267–320.

Padilla Peralta, D. 2019. "Monument men: Buildings, inscriptions, and lexicographers in the creation of Augustan Rome." In M. Loar, S. C. Murray, and S. Rebeggiani, eds., *The Cultural History of Augustan Rome: Texts, Monuments, and Topography*, 80–102. Cambridge, UK.

Padilla Peralta, D. 2020a. *Divine Institutions: Religion and State Formation in Mid-Republican Rome*. Princeton, NJ.

Padilla Peralta, D. 2020b. "Epistemicide: The Roman case." *Classica. Revista Brasileira de Estudos Clássicos* 33.2: 151–86.

Padilla Peralta, D., and S. Bernard. 2022. "Middle Republican Connectivities." *Journal of Roman Studies* 112: doi:10.1017/S0075435821000915.

Pagnoux, C., A. Celant, S. Coubray, G. Fiorentino, and V. Zech-Matterne. 2013. "The introduction of citrus to Italy, with reference to the identification problems of seed remains." *Vegetation History and Archaeobotany* 22: 421–38.

Palombi, D. 1997. *Tra Palatino ed Esquilino: Velia Carinae Fagutal. Storia urbana di tre quartieri di Roma antica*. Rome.

Palombi, D. 2003. "Cora: Bilancio storico e archeologico." *Archeologia Classica* 54: 197–252.

Palombi, D. 2010. "Roma tardo-repubblicana: Verso la città ellenistica." In E. La Rocca, ed., *I giorni di Roma: L'età della conquista*, 65–82. Milan.

Palombi, D. 2016. *I Fori prima dei Fori. Storia urbana dei quartieri di Roma antica cancellati per la realizzazione dei Fori Imperiali*. Rome.

Palombi, D. 2018. "Eroi greci fondatori di città latine." In H. Bernier-Farella, R. Carboni, M. P. Castiglioni, and M. Giuman. eds., *Héros fondateurs et identités communautaires dans l'Antiquité, entre mythe, rite et politique*, 555–89. Perugia.

Palombi, D. ed. 2019a. *La "Villa dei Gordiani" al III miglio della Via Praenestina: La memoria e il contesto.* Rome.

Palombi, D. 2019b. "Forma e cultura della città nel Latium vetus in età medio repubblicana." In F. M. Cifarelli, S. Gatti, and D. Palombi, eds., 113–47.

Palombi, D. 2021. "Il 'paesaggio religioso' di Roma medio repubblicana: Luoghi, tempi, pratiche." In A. D'Alessio, C. Smith, and R. Volpe, eds., 315–37.

Panella, C. 2010. "Roma, il suburbio e l'Italia in età medio- e tardo-repubblicana: Cultura materiale, territori, economie." *Facta* 4: 11–123.

Panella, C., and L. Saguì. 2013–17. *Valle del Colosseo e pendici nord-orientali del Palatino.* Rome.

Panella, C., ed. 2013. *Scavare nel centro di Roma. Storie uomini paesaggi.* Rome.

Parkin, T. G. 1992. *Demography and Roman Society.* Baltimore, MD.

Patterson, H., H. Di Giuseppe, and R. Witcher. 2004. "Three South Etrurian crises: First results of the Tiber Valley Project." *Papers of the British School at Rome* 72: 1–37.

Patterson, H., H. Di Giuseppe, and R. Witcher. 2020. *The Changing Landscapes of Rome's Northern Hinterland: The British School at Rome's Tiber Valley Project.* Oxford.

Patterson, J. R. 2006. "Colonization and historiography: The Roman Republic." In J.-P. Wilson and G. Bradley eds., *Greek and Roman Colonization: Origins, Ideologies and Interactions*, 189–218. Swansea.

Patterson, O. 1982. *Slavery and Social Death: A Comparative Study.* Cambridge, MA.

Pearce, M. 2016. "Hard cheese: Upland pastoralism in the Italian Bronze and Iron Ages." In J. Collis, M. Pearce, and F. Nicolis, eds., *Summer Farms: Seasonal Exploitation of the Uplands from Prehistory to the Present.* Sheffield Archaeological Monographs vol. 16, 47–56. Sheffield.

Pelgrom, J. 2018. "The Roman rural exceptionality thesis revisited." *Mélanges de l'École française de Rome - Antiquité*: 130–1. doi: https://doi.org/10.4000/mefra.4770

Pelgrom, J., and T. D. Stek. 2014. "Roman colonization under the Republic: historiographical contextualisation of a paradigm." In T. D. Stek and J. Pelgrom, eds., *Roman Colonization under the Republic: Historiographical Contextualisation of a Paradigm*, 11–41. Rome.

Pellam, G. 2014. "A peculiar episode from the 'struggle of the orders'? Livy and the Licinio-Sextian rogations." *Classical Quarterly, New Series* 64.1: 280–92.

Pelling, C. 2013. "Xenophon's and Caesar's third-person narratives – or are they?" In A. Marmodoro and J. Hill, eds., *The Author's Voice in Classical and Late Antiquity*, 39–75. Oxford.

Pensabene, P. 1980. "La zona sud-occidentale del Palatino." *Archeologia Laziale* 3: 65–81.

Pensabene, P. 1982. *Tempio di Saturno. Architettura e decorazione.* Rome.

Pensabene, P. 1988. "Scavi nell'area del Tempio della Vittoria e del santuario della Magna Mater sul Palatino." *Archeologia Laziale* 9: 54–67.

Pensabene, P. 1991. "Il Tempio della Vittoria sul Palatino." *Bollettino di archeologia* 11–12: 11–51.

Pensabene, P. 1998. "Vent'anni di studi e scavi dell'Università di Roma 'La Sapienza' nell'area Sud Ovest del Palatino." In C. Giavarini, ed., *Il Palatino: Area Sacra sud-ovest e Domus Tiberiana*. Rome.

Pensabene, P., and A. D'Alessio. 2006. "L'immaginario urbano. Spazio sacro sul Palatino tardo-repubblicano." In L. Haselberger and J. Humphrey, eds., *Imaging Ancient Rome. Documentation, Visualization, Imagination. Proceedings of the Third Williams Symposium on Classical Architecture Held at the American Academy in Rome, the British School at Rome and the Deutsches Archäologisches Institut, Rome, on May 20–23, 2004*, 30–50. Portsmouth.

Perego, E. 2017. "Contribution to the development of the Bronze Age plant economy in the surrounding of the Alps: An archaeobotanical case study of two Early and Middle Bronze Age sites in northern Italy (Lake Garda region)." (Phd thesis, University of Basel)

Pergola, P., R. Santangeli Valenzani, and R. Volpe, eds. 2003. *Suburbium: Il suburbio di Roma dalla crisi del sistema delle ville a Gregorio Magno*. Rome.

Perkins, P. 2007. "Production and distribution of wine in the Etruscan Albegna Valley." In A. Ciacci, P. Rendini, and A. Zifferero, eds., *Archeologia della vite e del vino in Etruria. Atti del convegno internazionale di studi, Scansano, Teatro Castagnoli, 9–10 settembre 2005*, 185–90. Siena.

Perkins, P. 2012. "Production and commercialization of Etruscan wine in the Albegna Valley." In A. Ciacci, P. Rendini, and A. Zifferero, eds., *Archeologia della vite e del vino in Toscana e nel Lazio: Dalle tecniche dell'indagine archeologia alle prospettive della biologia molecolare*, 413–26. Borgo San Lorenzo.

Perkins, P., and I. Attolini. 1992. "An Etruscan farm at Podere Tartuchino." *Papers of the British School at Rome* 60: 71–134.

Perkins, P. 2021. "The Etruscan pithos revolution." In M. Gleba, B. Marín-Aguilera, and B. Dimova, eds., *Making Cities: Economies of Production and Urbanization in Mediterranean Europe, 1000–500 BC*, 231–58. Cambridge, UK.

Pickering, A. 2010. "Material culture and the dance of agency." In D. Hicks and M. C. Beaudry, eds., *Oxford Handbook of Material Culture Studies*, 191–208. Oxford.

Pieraccini, L. C. 2014. "The ever elusive Etruscan Egg." *Etruscan Studies* 17.2: 267–92.

Pina Polo, F. 2011. *The Consul at Rome: The Civil Functions of the Consuls in the Roman Republic*. Cambridge, UK.

Pina Polo, F., and A. Díaz Fernández. 2019. *The Quaestorship in the Roman Republic*. Berlin.

Pina Polo, F., and C. Rosillo López. 2022. "Lugares de participacion politica del pueblo y frente al pueblo en Roma." In C. Courrier, J.-P.Guilhembet, N. Laubry, and D. Palombi, eds., *Rome, archéologie et histoire urbaine: Trente ans après l'Urbs 1987*, 305–20. Rome.

Pisani Sartorio, G., and S. Quilici Gigli. 1987–88. "A proposito della Tomba dei Cornelii." *Bullettino della Commissione archeologica Comunale di Roma* 92: 247–64.

Pisani Sartorio, G., and P. Virgili. 1979. "Area sacra di San Omobono." *Archeologia Laziale* 2: 41–7.

Platteau, J. 1995. "An Indian model of aristocratic patronage." *Oxford Economic Papers*, 47.4, new series: 636–62.

Pontrandolfo, A. 2003. "L'elogio della *virtus*. La scena di battaglia della tomba 114 di Paestum." *Incidenza dell'Antico* 1: 97–119.

Pontrandolfo, A., and B. D'Agostino. 1991. "Greci, Etruschi e Italici nella Campania e nella Lucania tirrenica." In *Crise et transformation des sociétés archaïques de l'Italie antique au Ve siècle av. J.- C.: Actes de la table ronde organisée par l'École française de Rome et l'Unité de recherches étrusco-italiques associée au CNRS (Rome, 19–21 novembre 1987)*, 101–16. Rome.

Pontrandolfo, A., and A. Rouveret. 1992. *Le tombe dipinte di Paestum*. Modena.

Pontrandolfo, A., A. Rouveret, and M. Cipriani 2004. *The Painted Tombs of Paestum*. Naples.

Potter, T. 1979. *The Changing Landscape of South Etruria*. New York.

Poucet, J. 1985. *Les origines de Rome: Tradition et histoire*. Brussels.

Prachner, G. 1995. "Untersuchungen zum Verhältnis von Lösegeld-Forderungen für Kriegsgefangene im 4. und 3. Jahrhundert v.Chr., zu den Verkaufserlösen bei einer Auktion im Jahre 293 v.Chr. und Sklavenpreisen im italisch-sizilischen und griechischen Raum sowie in Ägypten." *Laverna* 6: 1–40.

Prag, J., and J. Crawley Quinn, eds. 2013. *The Hellenistic West: Rethinking the Ancient Mediterranean*. Cambridge, UK.

Prag, J. R. W. 2010. "Siculo Punic Coinage and Siculo Punic Interactions." In M. Della Riva, ed. *Meetings between Cultures in the Ancient Mediterranean. Proceedings of the 17th International Congress of Classical Archaeology, Rome 22–26 sept. 2008*. Rome.

Prim, J. 2021. *Aventinus mons. Limites, fonctions urbaines et représentations politiques d'une colline de la Rome antique*. Rome.

Primavera, M., C. D'Oronzo, I. M. Muntoni, F. Radina, and G. Fiorentino. 2017. "Environment, crops and harvesting strategies during the II millennium BC: Resilience and adaptation in socio-economic systems of Bronze Age communities in Apulia (SE Italy)." *Quaternary International* 436: 83–95.

Pulcinelli, L. 2015. "Monete e circolazione monetaria in Etruria Meridionale nel III sec. a.C.." *Archeologia Classica* 66: 481–92.

Pulcinelli, L. 2016. *L'Etruria meridionale e Roma : insediamenti e territorio tra IV e III secolo a.C*. Rome.

Purcell, N. 1994. "South Italy in the fourth century BC." In D. M. Lewis, S. Hornblower, and M. Ostwald, eds., *Cambridge Ancient History* VI^2: 381–403. Cambridge, UK.

Purcell, N. 2003a. "The way we used to eat: Diet, community, and history at Rome." *American Journal of Philology* 124.3: 329–58.

Purcell, N. 2003b. "Becoming historical: The Roman case." In D. Braund and C. Gill, eds., *Myth, History and Culture in Republican Rome: Studies in Honour of T. P. Wiseman*, 12–40. Exeter.

Quilici, L. 1982. *La Civita di Artena*. Rome.

Quilici, L. 1991. "La Via Latina e l'organizzazione del territorio attorno alla Civita di Artena." In J. Mertens, R. Lambrechts, and R. Mertens, eds., *Comunità indigene e problemi della romanizzazione nell'Italia centro-meridionale (IV-III sec. av. C.): Actes du colloque international organisé à l'occasion du 50e anniversaire de l'Academia Belgica et du 40e anniversaire des fouilles belges en Italie (Rome, Academia Belgica, 1er–3 février 1990)*, 195–216. Brussels.

Quilici, L. 1994. "Centuriazione e paesaggio agrario nell'Italia central." In J. Carlsen, P. Orsted, and J. Skydsgaard, eds., *Land Use in the Roman Empire*, 127–33. Rome.

Quilici, L. and S. Quilici Gigli. 1993. *Ficulea, Latium Vetus V*. Rome.

Quilici, L., and S. Quilici Gigli. 2019. "Le fortificazioni tra ristrutturazioni, adeguamenti, nuove costruzioni." In F. M. Cifarelli, S. Gatti, and D. Palombi eds., *Oltre "Roma medio repubblicana". Il Lazio tra i Galli e la battaglia di Zama (Atti del Convegno Internazionale, Roma 2017)*, 171–84. Rome.

Quilici Gigli, S. 2019. "Between colonial echoes and urban transformations: The case of Norba." In A. U. De Giorgi, ed., *Cosa and the Colonial Landscape of Republican Italy (Third and Second Centuries BCE)*, 102–18. Ann Arbor, MI.

Raaflaub, K. A. 1996. "Born to be wolves? Origins of Roman imperialism." In R. W. Wallace and E. M. Harris, eds., *Transitions to Empire: Essays in Greco-Roman History, 360–146 BC, in Honor of E. Badian*, 272–314. Norman, OK.

Raaflaub, K. A. ed. 2005 [1986]. *Social Struggles in Archaic Rome: New Perspectives on the Conflict of the Orders*, 2nd ed. Malden, MA.

Raaflaub, K. 2010. "Between myth and history: Rome's rise from Village to Empire (the eighth century to 264)." In N. Rosenstein and R. Morstein Marx, eds., *A Companion to the Roman Republic*, 125–46. Malden, MA.

Rakob, F., and E. D. Heilmeyer. 1973. *Der Rundtempel am Tiber in Rom*. Mainz.

Ranouil, P. C. 1975. *Recherches sur le patriciat, 509–366 avant J.-C.* Rome.

Rathmann, H., B. Kyle, E. Nikita, K. Harvati, and G. Saltini Semerari. 2019. "Population history of southern Italy during Greek colonization inferred from dental remains." *American Journal of Physical Anthropology* 170.4: 519–34.

Rawlings, L. 2007. "Army and battle during the conquest of Italy (350–264 BC)." In P. Erdkamp, ed., *A Companion to the Roman Army*, 45–62. Oxford.

Rawson, E. 1971. "Literary sources for the Pre-Marian army." *Papers of the British School at Rome* 39: 13–31.

Renzulli, A., P. Santi, G. Nappi, M. Luni, and D. Vitali. 2002. "Provenance and trade of volcanic rock millstones from Etruscan-Celtic and Roman archaeological sites in Central Italy." *European Journal of Mineralogy* 14.1: 175–83.

Rich, J. 2007. "Warfare and the army in Early Rome." In P. Erdkamp, ed., *A Companion to the Roman Army*, 7–23. London.

Rich, J. 2008. "Lex Licinia, Lex Sempronia: B. G. Niebuhr and the limitation of landholding in the Roman Republic." In L. de Ligt and S. Northwood, eds., *People, Land and Politics: Demographic Developments and the Transformation of Roman Italy, 300 BC–AD 14*, 519–72. Leiden.

Richardson, J. 2007. "On the location of the Urbs and Tribus Scaptia." *Hermes* 135: 166–73.

Richardson, J. 2012. *The Fabii and the Gauls: Studies in Historical Thought and Historiography in Republican Rome.* Stuttgart.

Richardson, J. 2017. "The Roman nobility, the Early Consular Fasti, and the Consular tribunate." *Antichthon* 51: 77–100.

Richardson, L. Jr. 1992. *A New Topographical Dictionary of Rome.* Baltimore, MD.

Richlin, A. 2021. "The woman in the street: Becoming visible in Mid-Republican Rome." In R. Ancona and G. Tsouvala, eds., *New Directions in the Study of Women in the Greco-Roman World*, 213–30. Oxford.

Ridley, R. T. 1980. "Fastenkritik: A stocktaking." *Athenaeum* 58: 264–98.

Ridley, R. T. 1983. "Falsi Triumphi, Plures Consulatus." *Latomus* 42: 372–82.

Ridley, R. T. 1986. "The genesis of a turning-point: Gelzer's 'Nobilität.'" *Historia: Zeitschrift für Alte Geschichte* 35.4: 474–502.

Riedel, A., and U. Tecchiati. 2002. "Insediamenti ed economia nell'età del Bronzo e del Ferro in Trentino Alto Adige: Appunti per un modello archeozoologico." In *Atti della XXXIII Riunione Scientifica dell'Istituto Italiano di Preistoria e Protostoria, Preistoria e Protostoria del Trentino Alto Adige. In ricordo di Bernardino Bagolini, Trento, 21–24 ottobre 1997*, 117–30. Florence.

Riggsby, A. 2019. *Mosaics of Knowledge: Representing Information in the Roman World.* Oxford.

Riva, C. 2017. "Wine production and exchange and the value of wine consumption in sixth-century BC Etruria." *Journal of Mediterranean Archaeology* 30.2: 237–61.

Rives, J. B. 2019. "Animal sacrifice and euergetism in the Hellenistic and Roman polis." *Religion in the Roman Empire* 5.1: 83–102.

Robinson, E. C. ed. 2014. *Papers on Italian Urbanism in the First Millennium BC.* JRA, suppl. series 97. Portsmouth, RI.

Robinson, M. 1999. "Macroscopic plant remains from the pre-Roman phases of Houses 11 and 12 of Regio I, Insula 9, Pompeii." In M. Fulford and A. Wallace-Hadrill, eds., "Towards a history of pre-Roman Pompeii: Excavations beneath the House of Amarantus (I.9.11–12) 1995–8." *Papers of the British School at Rome* 67: 95–102.

Robinson, M. 2002. "Domestic burnt offerings and sacrifices at Roman and pre-Roman Pompeii, Italy." *Vegetation History and Archaeobotany* 11: 93–9.

Rocco, G. 2003. *Guida alla lettura degli ordini architettonici antichi. II. Lo ionico.* Naples.

Roma tra oligarchia e democrazia : Classi sociali e formazione del diritto in epoca medio-repubblicana : Atti del convegno di diritto romano, Copanello, 28–31 maggio. 1986. Naples.

Roncaglia, C. E. 2018. *Northern Italy in the Roman World: From the Bronze Age to Late Antiquity.* Baltimore, MD.

Roselaar, S. T. 2010. *Public Land in the Roman Republic: A Social and Economic History of Ager publicus in Italy, 396–89 BC.* Oxford.

Roselaar, S. T. 2011. "Colonies and processes of integration in the Roman Republic." *Mélanges de l'École française de Rome, Antiquité* 123: 527–55.

Roselaar, S. T. 2013a. "The concept of commercium in the Roman Republic." *Phoenix* 66: 381–413.

Roselaar, S. T., 2013b. "The concept of conubium in the Roman Republic." In P. Du Plessis, ed., *New Frontiers: Law and Society in the Roman World,* 102–22. Edinburgh.

Roselaar, S. T. 2019. *Italy's Economic Revolution: Economic Relations and the Integration of Republican Italy.* Oxford.

Rosenberg, A. 1913. *Der Staat der alten Italiker: Untersuchungen über die ursprüngliche Verfassung der Latiner, Osker, und Etrusker.* Berlin.

Rosenstein, N. 1999. "Republican Rome." In K. A. Raaflaub and N. Rosenstein, eds., *War and Society in the Ancient and Medieval Worlds: Asia, the Mediterranean, Europe, and Mesoamerica,* 193–235. Washington, DC.

Rosenstein, N. 2002. "Marriage and manpower in the Hannibalic war: *Assidui, Proletarii,* and Livy 24.18.7–8." *Historia. Zeitschrift für Alte Geschichte* 51: 163–91.

Rosenstein, N. 2004. *Rome at War: Farms, Families, and Death in the Middle Republic.* Chapel Hill, NC.

Rosenstein, N. 2008. "Aristocrats and agriculture in the Middle and Late Republic." *Journal of Roman Studies* 98: 1–26.

Rosenstein, N. 2010a. "War, state formation, and the evolution of military institutions in ancient China and Rome." In W. Scheidel, ed. *Rome and China: Comparative Perspectives on Ancient Empires,* 24–51. Oxford.

Rosenstein, N. 2010b. "Phalanges in Rome?" In G. Fagan and M. Trundle, eds., *New Perspectives on Ancient Warfare,* 289–303. Leiden.

Rosenstein, N. 2012. *Rome and the Mediterranean 290 to 146 BC: The Imperial Republic.* Edinburgh.

Rosenstein, N. 2016a. "*Bellum se ipsum alet?* Financing Mid-Republican imperialism." In H. Beck and J. Serrati, eds., *Money and Power in the Roman Republic,* 114–30. Brussels.

Rosenstein, N. 2016b. "*Tributum* in the Middle Republic." In J. Armstrong, ed. *Circum Mare: Themes in Ancient Warfare,* 80–97. Leiden.

Rosenstein, N. 2017. Untitled review: N. Coffee, Gift and Gain: *How money transformed Ancient Rome. Bryn Mawr Classical Review* 11.04.

Rosivach, V. J. 1989. "The 'Miles' Inpransus of Plaut. Aul 528." *Latomus* 48: 344–5.
Roth, J. 2012. *The Logistics of the Roman Army at War (264 BC–AD 235)*. Leiden.
Roth, R. E. 2013a. "The internal frontier: An African model for culture change in south central Italy (fourth-third centuries BC)." In A. Bokern, M. Bolder-Boss, S. Krmnicek, D. Maschek, and S. Page, eds., *TRAC 2012: Proceedings of the Twenty-Second Annual Theoretical Roman Archaeology Conference, Frankfurt 2012*, 49–60. Oxford.
Roth, R. E. 2013b. "Fragmented images: The last tomb paintings of Tarquinia." *Oxford Journal of Archaeology* 32.2: 187–201.
Rottoli, M., and E. Castiglioni. 2011. "Plant offerings from Roman cremations in northern Italy: A review." *Vegetation History and Archaeobotany* 20: 496–506.
Rottoli, M., and A. Pessina. 2016. "Neolithic agriculture in Italy: An update of archaeobotanical data with particular emphasis on northern settlements." In S. Colledge and J. Conolly, eds., *The Origins and Spread of Domestic Plants in Southwest Asia and Europe*, 157–70. New York.
Rouveret, A. 1986. "Tite-Live, Histoire Romaine IX, 40: la description des armées Samnites ou les pièges de la symétrie." In A.-M. Adam and A. Rouveret, eds., *Guerre et societies en Italie (Ve–IVe s. avant J.-C.)*, 91–128. Paris.
Rowan, E. 2014. *Roman Diet and Nutrition in the Vesuvian Region: A Study of the Bioarchaeological Remains from the Cardo V Sewer at Herculaneum*. Oxford.
Rowan, E. 2015. "Olive oil pressing waste as a fuel source in antiquity." *American Journal of Archaeology* 119.4: 465–82.
Rowland, I., T. Howe, and M. Dewar. 1999. *Vitruvius: Ten Books on Architecture*. Cambridge, UK.
Rüpke, J. 1990. Domi militia: *Die religiöse Konstruktion des Krieges in Rom*. Stuttgart.
Rüpke, J. 2018. *Pantheon: A New History of Roman Religion*. Princeton, NJ.
Russell, A. 2015. "The tribunate of the plebs as a magistracy of crisis." In V. Gouščhin and P. J. Rhodes, eds., *Deformations and Crises of Ancient Civil Communities*, 127–39. Stuttgart.
Russell, A. 2019. "The Augustan senate and the reconfiguration of time on the *Fasti Capitolini*." In I. Gildenhard, U. Gotter, W. Havener, and L. Hodgson, eds., *Augustus and the Destruction of History: The Politics of the Past in Early Imperial Rome*, 157–81. Cambridge, UK.
Russo, F. 2012a. "The beginning of the first Punic War and the concept of Italia." In S. Roselaar, ed., *Processes of Integration and Identity Formation in the Roman Republic*, 35–50. Leiden.
Russo, F. 2012b. "L'Italia nella prospettiva romana (III secolo a.C.)." *Sudi Classici e Orientali* 58: 11–186.
Sabatini, S., and S. Bergerbrant, eds. 2019. *The Textile Revolution in Bronze Age Europe: Production, Specialisation, Consumption*. Cambridge, UK.

Sabatini, S., S. Bergerbrant, L. Ø. Brandt, A. Margaryan, and M. E. Allentoft. 2019. "Approaching sheep herds origins and the emergence of the wool economy in continental Europe during the Bronze Age." *Archaeological and Anthropological Sciences* 11.9: 4909–25.

Sabatini, S., T. Earle, and A. Cardarelli. 2018. "Bronze Age textile and wool economy: The case of the Terramare site of Montale, Italy." *Proceedings of the Prehistoric Society* 84: 359–85.

Sabato, D., A. Masi, C. Pepe et al. 2015. "Archaeobotanical analysis of a Bronze Age well from Sardinia: A wealth of knowledge." *Plant Biosystems–An International Journal Dealing with all Aspects of Plant Biology* 149.1: 205–15.

Sadori, L., E. Allevato, G. Bosi et al. 2009. "The introduction and diffusion of peach in ancient Italy." In J. P. Morel and A. M. Mercuri, eds. *Plants and Culture: Seeds of the Cultural Heritage of Europe*, 45–61. Bari.

Salau, M. B. 2018. *Plantation Slavery in the Sokoto Caliphate: A Historical and Comparative Study*. Rochester, NY.

Saller, R. P. 1994. *Patriarchy, Property and Death in the Roman Family*. Cambridge, UK.

Salmon, E. T. 1953a. "Rome and the Latins: I." *Phoenix* 7.3: 93–104.

Salmon, E. T. 1953b. "Rome and the Latins: II." *Phoenix* 7.4: 123–35.

Salmon, E. T. 1967. *Samnium and the Samnites*. Cambridge, UK.

Salmon, E. T. 1969. *Roman Colonization under the Republic*. London.

Saltini Semerari, G. 2013. "Taranto before Magna Graecia: Long term interactions between Italy and Greece and their consequences." In R. P. Preston and K. Schörle, eds., *Mobility, Transition and Change in Prehistory and Classical Antiquity*. BAR International Series 2534, 131–45. Oxford.

Salway, B. 1994. "What's in a name? A survey of Roman onomastic practice from c. 700 BC to AD 700." *Journal of Roman Studies* 84: 124–45.

Sandberg, K., and C. J. Smith, eds. 2018. Omnium annalium monumenta: *Historical Writing and Historical Evidence in Republican Rome*. Leiden.

Sanz, A.-M. 2011. "The Roman Republic and mercenaries in the age of the Punic Wars: An ideological approximation." *Mélanges de La Casa de Velázquez* 41: 163–79.

Sarao, K. T. S. 2014. "Janapadas, Mahajanapadas, kingdoms, and republics." In D. K. Chakrabarti and M. Lal, eds., *History of Ancient India*, Vol. III: *The Texts, Political History and Administration, till c. 200 BC*, 183–204. New Delhi.

Savunen, L. 1993. "Debt legislation in the fourth century BC." In U. Paananen, K. Sandberg, and K. Heikkilä, eds., *Senatus populusque romanus: Studies in Roman Republican Legislation*, 143–59. Helsinki.

Sblendorio-Cugusi, M. T. 1982. *Catonis Censorii orationum reliquiae*. Turin.

Scheeres, M., C. Knipper, M. Hauschild et al. 2013. "Evidence for 'Celtic migrations'? Strontium isotope analysis at the early La Tène (LT B) cemeteries of Nebringen (Germany) and Monte Bibele (Italy)." *Journal of Archaeological Science* 40: 3614–25.

Scheid, J. 2012. "Leggi e religione." In J.-L. Ferrary, ed., *Leges Publicae: La legge nell'esperienza giuridica romana*, 219–38. Pavia.

Scheidel, W. 2005. "Human mobility in Roman Italy, II: The slave population." *Journal of Roman Studies* 95: 64–79.

Scheidel, W. 2006. "The demography of Roman state formation in Italy." In M. Jehne and R. Pfeilschifter, eds., *Herrschaft ohne Integration? Rom und Italien in republikanischer Zeit*, 207–26. Frankfurt.

Scheidel, W. 2007. "Demography." In W. Scheidel, I. Morris, and R. Saller, eds. *The Cambridge Economic History of the Greek and Roman Worlds*, 38–86. Cambridge, UK.

Scheidel, W. 2008. "The comparative economics of slavery in the Greco-Roman world." In E. Dal Lago and C. Katsari, eds., *Slave Systems, Ancient and Modern*, 105–26. Cambridge, UK.

Scheidel, W. 2010. "The monetary systems of the Han and Roman Empires." In W. Scheidel, ed., *Rome and China: Comparative Perspectives on Ancient Empires*, 137–207. Oxford.

Scheidel, W. 2011. "The Roman slave supply." In Bradley and Cartledge, eds., 287–310.

Scheidel, W. 2012. "Slavery." In W. Scheidel, ed., *The Cambridge Companion to the Roma Economy*, 89–113. Cambridge, UK.

Scheidel, W. 2013. "Studying the state." In P. F. Bang and W. Scheidel, eds., *The Oxford Handbook of the State in the Ancient Near East and Mediterranean*, 5–58. Oxford.

Scheidel, W. 2018. "Comparing comparisons." In G. E. Lloyd and J. J. Zhao, eds., *Ancient Greece and China Compared: Interdisciplinary and Cross-Cultural Perspectives*, 40–58. Cambridge, UK.

Scheidel, W. 2019. *Escape from Rome: The Failure of Empire and the Road to Prosperity*, Princeton, NJ.

Scheidel, W. 2020. "Roman wealth and wealth inequality in comparative perspective." *Journal of Roman Archaeology* 33: 341–53.

Scheidel, W. ed. 2010. *Rome and China: Comparative Perspectives on Ancient Empires*. Oxford.

Scheidel, W. ed. 2015. *State Power in Rome and China*. Oxford.

Schiavone, A. 2012. "Dodici Tavole e 'ortodossia' repubblicana." In J.-L. Ferrary, ed., *Leges publicae: la legge nell'esperienza giuridica romana*, Vol. 8, 293–305. Pavia.

Schmitt, H. H. 1957. *Rom und Rhodos*. Munich.

Schulman, B. J. 2021. "Islands in time, or how I learned to stop worrying and love the decade." *Reviews in American History* 49.2: 322–37.

Schultz, C. E. 2006. *Women's Religious Activity in the Roman Republic*. Chapel Hill, NC.

Sciarrino, E. 2011. *Cato the Censor and the Beginnings of Latin Prose: From Poetic Translation to Elite Transcription*. Columbus, OH.

Scopacasa, R. 2015. *Ancient Samnium: Settlement, Culture, and Identity between History and Archaeology*. Oxford.

Scott, J. 1972. "Patron-client politics and political change in Southeast Asia." *The American Political Science Review* 66.1: 91–113.

Scott, R. T. 1993a. "Lavori e ricerche nell'Area Sacra di Vesta." *Archeologia Laziale* 11: 11–17.

Scott, R. T. 1993b. "Excavations in the area sacra of Vesta, 1987–1989." In F. E. Brown, R. T. Scott, and A. R. Scott, eds., *Eius Virtutis Studiosi: Classical and Postclassical Studies in Memory of Frank Edward Brown 1908–1988*, 161–82. Washington, DC.

Scott, R. T. ed. 2009. *Excavations in the Area Sacra of Vesta 1987–1996*. Rome.

Sevink, J., J. van der Plicht, H. Feiken, M. Van Leusen, and C. Bakels. 2013. "The Holocene of the Agro Pontino graben: Recent advances in its palaeogeography, palaeoecology, and tephrostratigraphy." *Quaternary International* 303: 153–62.

Sewell, J. 2010. *The Formation of Roman Urbanism, 338–200 BC: Between Contemporary Foreign Influence and Roman Tradition* (JRA suppl. s. 97). Ann Arbor, MI.

Sewell, J. 2013. "New observations on the planning of Fora in the Latin colonies." In C. P. Dickenson and O. M. van Nijf, eds., *Public Space in the Post-Classical City* (*Caeculus* 7), 76–112. Leuven.

Sewell, J. 2016. "Higher-order settlements in Early Hellenistic Italy: A quantitative analysis of a new archaeological database." *American Journal of Archaeology* 120.4: 603–30.

Sherk, R. K. 1990. "The eponymous officials of Greek cities: Mainland Greece and the adjacent islands." *Zeitschrift für Papyrologie und Epigraphik* 84: 231–95.

Sherwin-White, A. N. 1973. *The Roman Citizenship*. Oxford.

Shoe Merritt, L., and I. E. M. Edlund-Berry. 2000. *Etruscan and Republican Roman Mouldings*. Austin, TX.

Silvestri, L., K. F. Achino, M. Gatta, and M. F. Rolfo. 2017. "Bioarchaeological remains as indicators of costly signalling: Two case studies from the Middle Bronze Age of Central Italy." *World Archaeology* 49.4: 491–505.

Sisani, S. 2007. *Fenomenologia della conquista: la romanizzazione dell'Umbria tra il IV sec. a.C. e la guerra sociale*. Rome.

Skard, E. 1956. "Sallust und seine Vorgänger: Eine sprachliche Untersuchung." *Symbolae Osloenses* Supplement 15.

Smaldone, J. P. 1977. *Warfare in the Sokoto Caliphate: Historical and Sociological Perspectives*. Cambridge, UK.

Small, A. M., S. G. Moncton, R. J. Buck, and C. J. Simpson. 1992. "Excavations at Gravina di Puglia, 1991: Interim report." *Echos du monde classique/Classical Views* 36.2: 189–99.

Smith, A., Allen, M., Brindle, T., and M. Fulford. 2016. *The Rural Settlement of Roman Britain*. London.

Smith, C. J. 2019. "Revisiting the Roman clan." In M. Di Fazio and S. Paltineri, eds., *La società gentilizia nell'Italia antica tra realtà e mito storiografico*, 25–45. Rome.

Smith, C. J. 2006. *The Roman Clan: The Gens from Ancient Ideology to Modern Anthropology*. Cambridge, UK.

Smith, C. J. 2011. "The magistrates of the Early Roman Republic." In H. Beck, A. Duplá, F. Pina Polo, and M. Jehne, eds., *Consuls and Res Publica: Holding High Office in the Roman Republic*, 19–40. Cambridge, UK.

Smith, C. J. 2017. "Ager Romanus antiquus." *Archeologia Classica* 68: 1–26.

Smith, C. J. 2012. "The origins of the tribunate of the *plebs*." *Antichthon* 46: 101–25.

Smith, M. 1992. "Braudel's temporal rhythms and chronology theory in archaeology." In A. Knapp, ed., *Archaeology, Annales and Ethnohistory*. Cambridge, UK.

Sole, L. 2014. "Mercenari italici in viaggio verso l'entroterra della Sicilia? Il contributo delle evidenze numismatiche e archeologiche." In M. Congiu, C. Micciché, and S. Modeo, eds., *Viaggio in Sicilia: Racconti segni e città ritrovate*, Caltanisetta. 201–13.

Sommella, P. 1988. *Italia antica: L'urbanistica romana*. Rome.

Sordi, M. 1960. *I rapporti romano-ceriti e l'origine della Civitas sine suffragio*. Rome.

Sordi, M. 1988. "Silla e lo *ius pomerii proferendi*." In *Il confine nel mondo classico*, 200–11. Cremona.

Sorrentino, R., E. Bortolini, G. Lugli et al. 2018. "Unravelling biocultural population structure in 4th/3rd century BC Monterenzio Vecchio (Bologna, Italy) through a comparative analysis of strontium isotopes, non-metric dental evidence, and funerary practices." *PLoS ONE* 13.3: 0193796.

Spannagel, M. 2000. "Zur Vergegenwärtigung abstrakter Wertbegriffe in Kult und Kunst der römischen Republik." In M. Braun and A. Halt, eds., Moribus antiquis res stat Romana: *Römische Werte und römische Literatur im 3. und 2. Jh. v. Chr*, 237–69. Leipzig.

Spielberg, L. 2015. "The rhetoric of documentary quotation in Roman historiography." (PhD thesis, University of Pennsylvania)

Spurr, M. S. 1986. *Arable Cultivation in Roman Italy, c. 200 B.C.–c. A.D. 100*. London.

Squatriti, P. 2002. "Digging ditches in early Medieval Europe." *Past and Present* 176: 11–65.

Stan, M. G. 2014. "The phenomenon of Roman republican coinage in pre-Roman Dacia: A reexamination of the evidence." *Journal of Ancient History and Archaeology* 1.4: 44–67.

Stanco, E. A. 2009. "La seriazione cronologica della ceramica a vernice nera etrusco laziale nell'ambito dell III sec. a.c." In V. Jolivet, ed., *Suburbium II: il suburbio di Roma dalla fine dell'età monarchica alla nascita del sistema delle ville : (V-II secolo a.C.)*, 157–93. Rome.

Staveley, E. S. 1959. "The political aims of Appius Claudius Caecus." *Historia* 8: 410–33.

Steel, C. 2014. "Rethinking Sulla: The case of the Roman senate." *Classical Quarterly* 64.2: 657–68.

Stein-Hölkeskamp, E., and K.-J. Hölkeskamp. 2018. *Ethos-Ehre-Exzellenz: Antiken Eliten im Vergleich*. Göttingen.

Steinby, E. M. 2012. *Edilizia pubblica e potere politico nella Roma repubblicana*. Rome.

Steingraber, S. 2006. *Etruskische Wandmalerei: von der geometrischen Periode bis zum Hellenismus*. Mosel.

Stek, T. D. 2017. "The impact of Roman expansion and colonization on ancient Italy in the Republican period: From diffusionism to networks of opportunity." In G. D. Farney and G. Bradley, eds., *The Peoples of Ancient Italy*, 269–94. Berlin.

Stek, T. D. 2018. "Early Roman colonisation beyond the Romanising agrotown: Village patterns of settlement and highland exploitation in the Abruzzi mountains." In B. S. Düring and T. D. Stek, eds. *The Archaeology of Imperial Landscapes: A Comparative Study of Empires in the Ancient Near East and Mediterranean World*, 145–72. Cambridge, UK.

Stek, T. D. 2009. *Cult Places and Cultural Change in Republican Italy: A Contextual Approach to Religious Aspects of Rural Society after the Roman Conquest*. Amsterdam.

Stek, T. D., and J. Pelgrom, eds. 2014. *Roman Republican Colonization: New Perspectives from Archaeology and Ancient History*. Rome.

Stewart, J. R. M., R. B. Allen, A. K. G. Jones, K. E. H. Penkman, and M. J. Collins. 2013. "ZooMS: making eggshell visible in the archaeological record." *Journal of Archaeological Science* 40.4: 1797–1804.

Stewart, O. 2017. "Citizenship as a reward or punishment? Factoring language into the Latin settlement." *Antichthon* 51: 186–201.

Stillwell, R. et al. 1976. *The Princeton Encyclopedia of Classical Sites*. Princeton, NJ.

Stilwell, S. 2000. "Power, honour and shame: The ideology of royal slavery in the Sokoto caliphate." *Africa* 70: 394–421.

Stoddart, S. 2010. "The physical geography and environment of Republican Italy." In N. Rosenstein and R. Morstein-Marx, eds., *A Companion to the Roman Republic* Chichester.

Stoddart, S. J., A. Woodbridge, A. M. Palmisano et al. 2019. "Tyrrhenian central Italy: Holocene population and landscape ecology." *The Holocene* 29.5: 761–75.

Stopp, B. 2015. "Animal husbandry and hunting activities in the Late Bronze Age Circum-Alpine region." In F. Menotti, ed., *The End of the Lake-Dwellings in the Circum-Alpine Region*, 179–210. Oxford.

Styring, A. K., M. Charles, F. Fantone et al. 2017a. "Isotope evidence for agricultural extensification reveals how the world's first cities were fed." *Nature Plants* 3: 17076.

Styring, A., M. Rösch, E. Stephan et al. 2017b. "Centralisation and long-term change in farming regimes: Comparing agricultural practices in Neolithic and

Iron Age south-west Germany." *Proceedings of the Prehistoric Society* 83: 357–81.
Szpak, P. 2014. "Complexities of nitrogen isotope biogeochemistry in plant-soil systems: implications for the study of ancient agricultural and animal management practices." *Frontiers in Plant Science* 5: 288.
Tafuri, M. A., M. Rottoli, M. Cupitò et al. 2018. "Estimating C4 plant consumption in Bronze Age Northeastern Italy through stable carbon and nitrogen isotopes in bone collagen." *International Journal of Osteoarchaeology* 28.2: 131–42.
Tagliamonte, G. 2015. "Political organization and magistrates." In A. Naso, ed., *Etruscology*, 133–4. Berlin.
Tagliamonte, G. L. 1994. *I figli di Marte: Mobilità, mercenari e mercenariato italici in Magna Grecia e Sicilia*. Rome.
Tagliamonte, G. L. 2002. "Mercenari italici ad Agrigento." In N. Bonacasa, L. Braccesi, and E. De Miro, eds., *La Sicilia dei due Dionisi*, 501–18. Rome.
Talbert, R. J. A. 1975. *Timoleon and the Revival of Greek Sicily, 344–317 BC*. Cambridge, UK.
Tan, J. 2017. *Power and Public Finance at Rome, 264–49 BCE*. Oxford.
Tan, J. 2020. "The *Dilectus-Tributum* system and the settlement of fourth century Italy." In J. Armstrong and M. Fronda, eds., *Romans at War: Soldiers, Citizens, and Society in the Roman Republic*, 52–75. London.
Tanasi, D., E. Greco, R. E. Noor et al. 2018. "1H NMR, 1H–1H 2D TOCSY and GC-MS analyses for the identification of olive oil in Early Bronze Age pottery from Castelluccio (Noto, Italy)." *Analytical Methods* 10.23: 2756–63.
Tarpin, M. 2003. *Vici et pagi dans l'Occident romain*. Rome.
Tarpin, M. 2014. "Strangers in paradise: Latins (and some other non-Romans) in colonial context – A short story of territorial complexity." In T. D. Stek and J. Pelgrom, eds., *Roman Republican Colonization. New Perspectives from Archaeology and Ancient History*, 160–91. Rome.
Taylor, L. R. 1960. *The Voting Districts of the Roman Republic*. Rome.
Taylor, L. R. 1966. *Roman Voting Assemblies*. Ann Arbor, MI.
Taylor, M. 2017. "State finance in the Middle Roman Republic: A reevaluation." *American Journal of Philology* 138: 143–80.
Taylor, M. 2018. "The election of centurions in the Republican period." *Ancient Society* 48: 147–67.
Taylor, M. 2020a. "The evolution of the manipular region in the Early Republic." *Historia* 69: 38–56.
Taylor, M. 2020b. *Soldiers and Silver: Mobilizing Resources in the Age of Roman Conquest*. Austin, TX.
Taylor, T. 2001. "Believing the ancients: Quantitative and qualitative dimensions of slavery and the slave trade in later prehistoric Europe." *World Archaeology* 33: 27–43.

Tecchiati, U., L. Salvagno, A. Amato et al. 2019. "Zooarchaeological evidence of functional and social differentiation in northern Italy between the Neolithic and Bronze ages." *Quaternary International* 539: 105–21.

Teichmann, M. 2017. *Mensch und Landschaft im südwestlichen Latium in der römischen Antike*. Vienna.

Terrenato, N. 2001. "The Auditorium site in Rome and the origins of the villa." *Journal of Roman Archaeology* 14: 5–32.

Terrenato, N. 2007. "The clans and the peasants: reflections on social structure and change in Hellenistic Italy." In P. Van Dommelen and N. Terrenato, eds., *Articulating Local Cultures: Power and Identity under the Expanding Roman Republic*, 13–22. Portsmouth, RI.

Terrenato, N. 2011. "The versatile clans: Archaic Rome and the nature of the early city-states in central Italy." In N. Terrenato and D. Haggis, eds., *State Formation in Italy and Greece: Questioning the Neoevolutionist Paradigm*, 231–44. Oxford.

Terrenato, N. 2012. "The enigma of 'Catonian' villas: The *De agricultura* in the context of second-century BC Italian architecture." In J. A. Becker and N. Terrenato, eds., *Roman Republican Villas: Architecture, Context, and Ideology*, 69–93. Ann Arbor, MI.

Terrenato, N. 2014. "Private *vis*, public *virtus*: Family agendas during the early Roman expansion." In T. D. Stek and J. Pelgrom, eds., *Roman Republican Colonization: New Perspectives from Archaeology and Ancient History*, 45–59. Rome.

Terrenato, N. 2019. *The Early Roman Expansion into Italy: Elite Negotiation and Family Agendas*. Cambridge, UK.

Thein, A. G. 2002. "Sulla's public image and the politics of civic renewal." (PhD dissertation, University of Pennsylvania)

Thomas, N. 1991. *Entangled Objects: Exchange, Material Culture and Colonialism in the Pacific*. Cambridge, MA.

Thomas, R. 2008. "Diachronic trends in lower limb pathologies in later medieval and post-medieval cattle from Britain." In G. Grupe, G. McGlynn, and J. Peters, eds., *Limping Together Through the Ages: Joint Afflictions and Bone Infections*. Documenta Archaeobiologiae, Vol. 6, 187–201. Rahden.

Thomsen, R. 1957–61. *Early Roman Coinage: A Study of the Chronology*. Copenhagen:

Thonemann, P. 2016. *The Hellenistic World: Using Coins as Sources*. Cambridge, UK.

Thornton, M., and R. Thornton. 1989. *Julio-Claudian Building Programs: A Quantitative Study in Political Management*.

Thurlow, B. K., and I. G. Vecchi. 1979. *Italian Cast Coinage: Italian aes grave*. London.

Tibiletti, G. 1972. "Problemi gromatici e storici." *Rivista storica dell'antichità* 2: 87–96.

Till, R. 1968 [1935]. *Die Sprache Catos*, Philologus Supplementband 28.2 = *La lingua di Catone*, translated by C. de Meo. Rome.

Tilly, C. 1993. *Coercion, Capital and European States: AD 990–1992*. Cambridge, MA.

Tilly, C. 2010. *Regimes and Repertoires*. Chicago.

Tilly, C., and S. G. Tarrow. 2015. *Contentious Politics*. Oxford.

Timpe, D. 1972. "Fabius Pictor und die Anfänge der römischen Historiographie." *Aufstieg und Niedergang der römischen Welt* 1.2: 928–69.

Tocci, L. M. 1967–8. "Monete della stipe di Vicarello nel Medagliere Vaticano." *Atti della Pontificia Accademia Romana di archeologia* 40: 75–81.

Tol, G., and B. Borgers. 2016. "An integrated approach to the study of local production and exchange in the lower Pontine Plain." *Journal of Roman Archaeology* 29: 349–70.

Tol, G. 2012. *A Fragmented History: A Methodological and Artefactual Approach to the Study of Ancient Settlement in the Territories of Satricum and Antium*. Groningen.

Tol, G. 2017. "From surface find to consumption trend: A ceramic perspective on the economic history of the Pontine region (Lazio, central Italy) in the Roman period." In T. De Haas and G. Tol, eds., *The Economic Integration of Roman Italy. Rural Communities in a Globalizing World*, 367–87. Leiden.

Tol, G., and T. De Haas. 2016. "The role of minor centres in local economies: new insights from recent archaeological fieldwork in the lower plain." *The Amphora Issue* 44–2: 33–61.

Tol, G., T. De Haas, K. Armstrong, and P. Attema. 2014. "Minor centres in the Pontine plain: The cases of Forum Appii and Ad Medias." *Papers of the British School at Rome* 82: 109–34.

Toohey, P. 2005. "Periodization and didactic poetry." In M. Horster and C. Reitz, eds., *Wissensvermittlung in dichterischer Gestalt*, 15–26. Stuttgart.

Tol, G., T. de Haas, J. Sevink et al. 2020. "'There's more than meets the eye': Developing an integrated archaeological approach to reconstruct human–environment dynamics in the Pontine marshes (Lazio, Central Italy)." *Geoarchaeology* 36.1: 109–29.

Torelli, M. 1975. *Elogia Tarquiniensia*. Florence.

Torelli, M. 1982. "Italia: Regio VII (Etruria)." In S. Panciera, ed., *Epigrafia e ordine senatorio*, Vol. 4–5, 275–99. Rome.

Torelli, M. 1988. "Aspetti ideologici della colonizzazione romana più antica." *Dialoghi di Archeologia* 6.2: 65–72.

Torelli, M. 1995. *Studies in the Romanization of Italy*. Edmonton.

Torelli, M. 2007. "L'urbanistica di Roma regia e repubblicana." In P. Gros and M. Torelli, eds., *Storia dell'urbanistica. Il mondo romano 4*, 81–157. Rome.

Torelli, M. 2012. "The early villa: Roman contributions to the development of a Greek prototype." In J. Becker and N. Terrenato, eds., *The Roman Republican Villa: Architecture, Context and Ideology*. Ann Arbor, MI.

Tortorici, E. 1988. "Il tempio presso San Salvatore in Campo: V. Vespignani e Ermodoro di Salamina." *Quaderni di Topografia* 10: 59–75.

Toynbee, A. M. 1965. *Hannibal's Legacy: The Hannibalic War's Effects on Roman Life.* New York.

Trentacoste, A. 2015. "Distinguere le pecore dalle capre: le evidenze archeozoologiche sulla produzione della lana nell'Italia centrale e settentrionale pre-romana." *Forma Urbis* 20.9: 37–9.

Trentacoste, A. 2016. "Etruscan foodways and demographic demands: Contextualizing protohistoric livestock husbandry in Northern Italy." *European Journal of Archaeology* 19.2: 279–315.

Trentacoste, A. 2020. "Fodder for change: Animals, urbanisation, and socio-economic transformation in protohistoric Italy." *Theoretical Roman Archaeology Journal.* doi: https://doi.org/10.16995/traj.414

Trentacoste, A. 2021. "In the belly of the earth: Bones and the closing of subterranean space in central Italy." In S. Deschler-Erb, U. Albarella, and S. Valenzuela-Lamas, eds., *Roman Animals in Ritual and Funerary Contexts,* 217–36. Frankfurt.

Trentacoste, A., E. Lightfoot, P. Le Roux et al. 2020. "Heading for the hills? A multi-isotope study of sheep management in first-millennium BC Italy." *Journal of Archaeological Science: Reports* 29: 102–36.

Trentacoste, A., A. Nieto-Espinet, and S. Valenzuela-Lamas. 2018. "Pre-Roman improvements to agricultural production: Evidence from livestock husbandry in late prehistoric Italy." *PLOS One* 13.12: E0208109.

Trentacoste, A., A. Nieto-Espinet, and S. Valenzuela-Lamas. In press. "Divergent trajectories or accelerating change? Roman transformation of animal husbandry in Cisalpine Gaul." *Journal of Anthropological and Archaeological Science.*

Trundle, M. 2004. *Greek Mercenaries: From the Late Archaic Period to Alexander.* London.

Tucci, P. L. 2018. "A funerary monument on the Capitoline: Architecture and painting in mid-Republican Rome, between Etruria and Greece." *Journal of Roman Archaeology* 31.1: 31–52.

Turner, D. 2018. "Comparative labour rates in cross-cultural contexts." In A. Brysbaert, V. Klinkenberg, M. Gutiérrez Garcia, and I. Vaikatou, eds., *Constructing Monuments, Perceiving Monumentality and the Economics of Building: Theoretical and Methodological Approaches to the Built Environment.* Leiden.

Ucchesu, M., M. Sarigu, C. D. Vais et al. 2017. "First finds of Prunus domestica L. in Italy from the Phoenician and Punic periods (6th–2nd centuries bc)." *Vegetation History and Archaeobotany* 26.5: 539–49.

Ucchesu, M., M. Orrù, O. Grillo et al. 2015, "Earliest evidence of a primitive cultivar of Vitis vinifera L. during the Bronze Age in Sardinia (Italy)." *Vegetation History and Archaeobotany* 24.5: 587–600.

Ulrich, R. B. 1994. *The Roman Orator and the Sacred Stage: The Roman "Templum Rostratum."* Brussels.

Vaglieri, D. 1907. "Palestrina." *Notizie degli scavi di antichità* 4: 19–26.

Valamoti, S. M., E. Gkatzogia, and M. Ntinou. 2018. "Did Greek colonisation bring olive growing to the north? An integrated archaeobotanical investigation of the spread of Olea europaea in Greece from the 7th to the 1st millennium BC." *Vegetation History and Archaeobotany* 27.1: 177–95.

Valentini, A. 2012. Matronae *tra* novitas *e mos maiorum: Spazi e modalità dell'azione pubblica femminile nella Roma medio repubblicana*. Venice.

Valenza Mele, N. 1996. "Una nuova tomba dipinta a Cuma e la Legio Linteata." In L. Breglia Pulci Doria, ed. *L'incidenza dell'antico. Studi in memoria di Ettore Lepore. Vol. II.* Naples: 325–60.

Valenzuela-Lamas, S., and U. Albarella, eds. 2017. "Animal husbandry in the Western Roman empire: A zooarchaeological perspective." *European Journal of Archaeology* 20.3: 402–15.

Valenzuela-Lamas, S., H. A. Orengo, D. Bosch et al. 2018. "Shipping amphorae and shipping sheep? Livestock mobility in the north-east Iberian peninsula during the Iron Age based on strontium isotopic analyses of sheep and goat tooth enamel." *PLOS One* 13.10: E0205283.

Van Deman, E. B. 1934. *The Building of the Roman Aqueducts*. Washington, DC.

Van Der Blom, H. 2010. *Cicero's Role Models: The Political Strategy of a Newcomer.* Oxford Classical monographs Series. Oxford.

Van der Veen, M. 2007. "Formation processes of desiccated and carbonized plant remains – the identification of routine practice." *Journal of Archaeological Science* 34: 968–90.

Van der Veen, M., and T. O'Connor. 1998. "The expansion of agricultural production in late Iron Age and Roman Britain." In J. Bayley, ed., *Science in Archaeology: An Agenda for the Future*, 127–43. London.

Van Leusen, M., and H. Feiken. 2002. "Kapen op de kust. Aanvullend en voorbereidend veldwerk in de Pontijnse regio, juli/augustus 2001." *Paleoaktueel*, 13: 53–8.

Van Leusen, P. M., T. C. A. De Haas, S. Pomicino, P. A. J. Attema. 2003–2004. "Protohistoric to Roman settlement on the Lepine margins near Ninfa (south Lazio, Italy)." *Palaeohistoria* 45/46: 301–47.

Van Oyen, A. 2017. "Finding the material in 'material culture.'" In A. Van Oyen and M. Pitts, eds. *Materializing Roman Histories*, 133–52. Oxford.

Van Oyen, A., and M. Pitts. 2017. "What did objects do in the Roman world?" In A. Van Oyen and M. Pitts, eds. *Materializing Roman Histories*, 3–19. Oxford.

van Sickle, J. 1987. "The *elogia* of the Cornelii Scipiones and the origin of epigram at Rome." *American Journal of Philology* 108: 41–105.

Vandermersch, C. 2001. "Au source du vin romain, dans le Latium et la Campania à l'époque médio-républicaine." *Ostraka* 10: 157–206.

Vanotti, G. 1999. "*Roma polis hellenis, Roma polis tyrrhenis.* Riflessioni sul tema." *MEFRA* 111: 217–55.

Vanzetti, A. 2002. "Results and problems of some current approaches to protohistoric centralization and urbanization in Italy." In P. A. J. Attema, G.-J. Burgers, E. van Joolen, M. van Leusen, and B. Mater, eds., *New Developments in Italian Landscape Archaeology. BAR International Series* 1091, 36–51. Oxford.

Vecchi, I. 2014. *Italian Cast Coinage a Descriptive Catalogue of the Cast Bronze Coinage and Its Struck Counterparts in Ancient Italy from the 7th to 3rd Centuries BC.* London.

Vermeulen, F. 2017. *From the Mountains to the Sea: The Roman Colonisation and Urbanisation of Central Adriatic Italy.* Leuven.

Versluys, M. J. 2017. "Discussion: Object-scapes: Towards a material constitution of Romanness?" In A. Van Oyen and M. Pitts, eds., *Materializing Roman Histories.* 191–200, Oxford.

Vervaet, F. 2014. *The High Command in the Roman Republic: The Principle of the* summum imperium auspiciumque *from 509 to 19 BCE.* Stuttgart.

Vidal Naquet, P. 1981. *Le chasseur noir: Formes de pensée et formes de société dans le monde grec.* Paris.

Villa, E. 1952-3. "Attualità e tradizione nell'ideale politico e sociale del *vir bonus* in Catone." *Rivista di studi classici* 1: 96–115.

Virgili, P. 1977. "Scavo stratigrafico (1974–1975." *Parola del Passato* 32: 20–34.

Viscogliosi, A. 1996. *Il Tempio di Apollo in Circo e la formazione del linguaggio architettonico augusteo.* Rome.

Visonà, P. 2018. "Rethinking early Carthaginian coinage." *Journal of Roman Archaeology* 31: 7–29.

Vlassopoulos, Ks. 2016. "Finley's slavery." In D. Jew, R. Osborne and M. Scott, eds., *M. I. Finley: An Ancient Historian and His Impact,* 76–99. Cambridge, UK.

Volkmann, H. 1990. *Die Massenversklavungen der Einwohner eroberter Städte in der hellenistisch-römischen Zeit,* edited by G. Horsmann. 2nd ed. Stuttgart.

Volpe, G. 1990. *La Daunia nell'eta della romanizzazione: paesaggio agrario, produzione, scambi.* Bari.

Volpe, R. 2009. "Vino, vigneti ed anfore in roma repubblicana." In V. Jolivet, C. Pavolini, and M. A. Tomei, eds., *Suburbium II: Il Suburbio di Roma dalla fine dell'età monarchica alla nascita del sistema delle ville. Collection de l'École française de Rome,* Vol. 419. Rome.

Volpe, R. 2012. "Republican villas in the suburbium of Rome." In Becker and Terrenato, 94–110.

Volpe, R. 2021. "Nuove mura per Roma repubblicana: questioni aperte e spunti di ricerca." In A. D'Alessio, C. Smith, and R. Volpe, eds., 235–53.

Volpe, R., V. Bartoloni, F. Pacetti, and S. Santucci. 2014. "Sepolcro degli Scipioni: Indagini nell'area archeologica 2008, 2010–2011." *Bullettino della Commissione archeologica comunale di Roma* 115: 175–91.

Von Fritz, K. 1950. "The reorganisation of the Roman government in 366 B.C. and the so-called Licinio-Sextian laws." *Historia* 1: 3–44.

Von Ungern-Sternberg, J. 2005 [1986]. "The formation of the 'annalistic tradition': The example of the Decemvirate." in Raaflaub, ed. 75–97.

Waagen, J. 2014. "Evaluating background noise: Assessing off-site data from field surveys around the Italic sanctuary of S. Giovanni in Galdo, Molise, Italy." *Journal of Field Archaeology* 39.4: 417–29.

Wales, N., J. Ramos-Madrigal, and M. T. P. Gilbert. 2017. "Ancient DNA analysis of vitis seeds from Cetamura del Chianti: Current results." In N. De Grummond, ed. *Wells of Wonders: New Discoveries at Cetamura del Chianti*, 294–302. Florence.

Ward-Perkins, B. 2006. *The Fall of Rome and the End of Civilization*. Oxford.

Warren, J. 1989. "The Kato Klitoria hoard." In G. Le Rider, ed. *Kraay-Mørkholm Essays: Numismatic Studies in Memory of C. M. Kraay and O. Mørkholm*, 291–300. Louvain-la-Neuve.

Watson, A. 1975. *Rome of the XII Tables: Persons and Property*. Princeton, NJ.

Weege, F. 1909. "Oskische Grabmalerei." *Jahrbuch des Kaiserlich Deutschen Archäologischen Instituts* 24: 99–162.

Welch, K. E. 2003. "A new view of the origins of the Basilica: The Atrium Regium, Graecostasis, and Roman diplomacy." *Journal of Roman Archaeology* 16: 5–34.

Welwei, K.-W. 2000. *Sub corona vendere: Quellenkritische Studien zu Kriegsgefangenschaft und Sklaverei in Rom bis zum Ende des Hannibalskrieges*. Stuttgart.

Werz, U. 2015. "Ein Aes grave aus Rheinau." *Archäologie Schweiz = Archéologie Suisse = Archeologia Svizzera* 38.4: 36-39.

White, K. D. 1970. *Roman Farming*. London.

White, R. 1991. *The Middle Ground: Indians, Empires, and Republics in the Great Lakes Region, 1650–1815*. Cambridge, UK.

Williams, J. H. C. 2001. *Beyond the Rubicon: Romans and Gauls in Republican Italy*. Oxford.

Williams-Thorpe, O., and R. S. Thorpe. 1990. "Millstone provenancing used in tracing the route of a fourth-century BC Greek merchant ship." *Archaeometry* 32.2: 115–37.

Wilson, A. 2012. "Saharan trade in the Roman period: Short-, medium- and long-distance trade networks." *Azania* 47: 409–49.

Winter, N. A. 2009. *Symbols of Wealth and Power: Architectural Terracotta Decoration in Etruria and Central Italy, 640–510 BC*. Ann Arbor, MI.

Wiseman, T. P. 1970. "The definition of 'Eques Romanus' in the Late Republic and Early Empire." *Historia* 19: 67–83.

Wiseman, T. P. 1971. *New Men in the Roman Senate, 139 BC–AD 14*. London.

Wiseman, T. P. 1979. *Clio's Cosmetics: Three Studies in Greco-Roman Literature*. Leicester.

Wiseman, T. P. 1981. "The temple of Victoria on the Palatine." *The Antiquaries Journal. The Journal of the Society of Antiquaries of London* 61: 35–52.

Wiseman, T. P. 1991. "Democracy and myth: The life and death of Remus." *Liverpool Classical Monthly* 16: 115–24.

Wiseman, T. P. 1994. *Historiography and Imagination: Eight Essays on Roman Culture*. Exeter.

Wiseman, T. P. 1995. *Remus: A Roman Myth*. Cambridge, UK.

Wiseman, T. P. 2018. "Writing Rome's past." In K. Sandberg and C. Smith, eds., *Omnium Annalium Monumenta: Historical Writing and Historical Evidence in Republican Rome*). *Histos* 12. Leiden.

Wiseman, T. P. 2008. *Unwritten Rome*. Exeter.

Witcher, R. 2016. "Agricultural production in Roman Italy." In A. E. Cooley, ed., *A Companion to Roman Italy*, 459–82. Chichester.

Woolf, G. 1998. *Becoming Roman: The Origins of Provincial Civilization in Gaul*. Cambridge, UK.

Woolf, G. 2011. *Tales of the Barbarians: Ethnography and Empire in the Roman West*. London.

Wright, J. 2007. *The Trans-Saharan Slave Trade*. London.

Yakobson, A. 2011. Untitled review of H. Flower. *Roman Republics. American Journal of Philology* 132.1: 153–6.

Yarrow, L. M. 2018. "Markers of identity for non-elite Romans: A prolegomenon to the study of glass paste intaglios." *Journal of Ancient History and Archeology* 5.3: 35–54.

Yarrow, L. M. 2021. *The Roman Republic to 49 BCE: Using Coins as Sources*. Cambridge, UK.

Zanin, M. 2021. "Autorappresentazione e onomastica: riflessioni sulla monetazione romano-repubblicana." In V. Varonesi and B. Callegher, eds., *Nuovi volti della ricerca archeologica, filologica e storica sul mondo antico II*, 209–38. Trieste.

Zehnacker, H. 1980. "Unciarium fenus (Tacitus, Annales VI.6.16)." In aa.vv. *Mélanges P. Wuilleumier*, 353–62. Paris.

Zerubavel, F. 2003. *Time Maps: Collective Memory and the Social Shape of the Past*. Chicago.

Zeuske, M. 2013. *Handbuch der Geschichte der Sklaverei: Eine Globalgeschichte von den Anfängen bis zur Gegenwart*. Berlin.

Zevi, F. 1976. "L'identificazione del tempio di Marte 'in circo' e altre osservazioni." In aa.vv. *Mélanges offerts à Jacques Heurgon*, 1047–60. Rome.

Zevi, F. 1996. "Un elemento architettonico dal tempio di via delle Botteghe oscure." *Bullettino dei Musei comunali di Roma*, new series 10: 39–62.

Ziolkowski, A. 1988. "Mummius' temple of Hercules Victor and the Round Temple on the Tiber." *Phoenix* 42: 309–33.

Ziolkowski, A. 1992. *The Temples of Mid-Republican Rome and Their Historical and Topographical Context.* Rome.

Ziolkowski, A. 2016. "The Servian enceinte: Should the debate continue?" *Palamedes* 11: 151–70.

Zuchtriegel, G. 2020. *Colonization and Subalternity in Classical Greece: Experience of the Nonelite Population.* Cambridge, UK.

Index

Adria, 31
aes formatum, 104
aes rude, 104
Africa, 80
ager gentilicius, 260
ager publicus, 259
agriculture, 165
   cereal culture, 173
   diversification, 171
Alba Fucens, 202
Alexander the Molossian, 209
Alfius, historian, 232
amphorae, 146
Anio Vetus, 194
Antium, 61, 137, 142
Appius Claudius Caecus, 6, 196, 210, 221, 253
Appius Herdonius, 31
Apulia, 236
Aqua Appia, 194, 220
Aquilonia, battle of, 233, 239
Ardea, 61, 199, 201, 205
Aricia, 201
Aristotle, 196
armor, Roman, 64
army, Roman, 64, 254
Artena, 205
Asculum, battle of, 75
Atellane farces, 233
Auditorium site, 134, 178

bioarchaeology, 11
Bourdieu, Pierre, 224
Bovianum, 242

C. Fabius Pictor, 235
C. Fabricius Luscinus, 34
C. Junius Bubulcus, 235, 242
C. Maenius, 196
Caere, 33, 180
calendar, Roman, 69
Campania, 1, 14, 32, 71, 230, 236

Capena, 137
Capua, 239, 245
Carthage, 84
Cato
   De Agri Cultura, 46
Cato the Elder, 24
Celtic. *See also* Gauls, *See* Gallic Sack
census, Roman, 56
centuriation, 135, 147, 156
Cerveteri, 176
Cetamura, 178
chronology, 46
Cincius Alimentus, 234
Circeii, 61
Cispadane Gaul, 183
citizens, 67
citizenship, 25, 38, 221
   civitas sine suffragio, 74, 240
Claudius Quadrigarius, 234
closing of the patriciate, 24
coinage, 10
   denominations, 111
   production technology, 128
   start of Roman coinage, 46
colonization, 61, 198, 202
   and architecture, 202
comitia centuriata, 258
commercium, 262
comparative history, 99
concrete, 197
Conflict of the Orders, 1, 24, 34, 132, 193. *See* Struggle of the Orders
consuls, 19
consulship, 26
Cora, 145, 200, 201, 205
Cosa, 202
Cumae, 238
Cures, 142
Cures Sabini, 148

D. Iunius Brutus Callaicus, 226
dan Fodio, Uthman, 90

Darius painter, the, 244
Daunia, 244
debt, 48, 55
    debt reform, 61
Decemvirate, 3
Decennovium, 151
demography, 157
    population, 67
    slave population, 80
dilectus, 53
Dionysius I, 84

Ennius, 233
Eretum, 137, 142
ethnicity, 25
Etruria, 32, 142
Etruscans, 31
exchange, 262

Fabius Pictor, 7, 231, 234, 242
Fabricius, 75
Falerii, 137, 142
farming. *See* agriculture
fasti, 40
    Fasti Triumphales, 69
Fasti Consulares. *See* consuls
Festus, 234
fetiales, 239
Finley, Moses, 80
First Punic War, 3
fiscality, 8
Foedus Cassianum, 209, 264
Forum Appii, 151
François tomb, 234
Fregellae, 202

Gabii, 180, 200, 205
Gallic Sack, 3, 197, 234, 255
Gauls, 3, 193
Ghiaccioforte, 105
Gortyn code, 259
Greek law, 259

Hellenization, 13, 236
Hermodorus of Salamis, 226
historical culture. *See* historiography
historiography, 231
    and historical culture, 235
    veracity of, 253
Hopkins, Keith, 81

intercolumniation, 216
Islam, 91

L. Cornelius Scipio Barbatus, 219
L. Fulvius Curvus, 32
L. Mamilius, 31
L. Postumius Megellus, 216
Labici, 61
labor, 165, 187, 215
    corvée, 215, 221
    cost, 151
landscape archaeology, 10
Lanuvium, 200, 205
    Temple of Iuno Sospita, 201
Largo Argentina, 216
Latin League, 209, 221
Latin War, 66
Latinization, 13, 199, 209
Latins, 53, 54
Latium, 1, 3, 5, 12, 32, 137, 144, 146, 198
Latium vetus. *See* Latium
Lavinium, 200, 201
leges Publiliae, 256
leges regiae, 267
lex Aquilia, 81
lex Hortensia, 210
lex Icilia, 260
lex Ogulnia, 33, 210
Licinian-Sextian Rogations. *See* Licinio-Sextian
    Laws
Licinio-Sextian Laws, 3, 6, 21, 34, 132, 161,
    210, 253
Licinius Macer, 234
linen legion, 239
loans, lending, 48

M.' Curius Dentatus, 24
M. Volteius, 227
magistrates, 20
Magna Graecia, 193, 202
malaria, 155
Maleventum, battle of, 65
mancipatio, 262
Mann, Michael, 259
manumission, 81, 83
marble, 225
marriage, 265
Mars, 242
meat consumption, 185
military pay. *See stipendium*
Minturnae, 151
mnemonic infrastructure, 244
mobility, 19, 24, 28
Mommsen, Theodor, 233
monosandalism, 239
Monte Bibele, 3

monumentum, 234
Münzer, Friedrich, 22

names, Roman, 20, 23
Naples, 146
Nemi, 106
Nepet, 61
nexum, 80
nobilitas, 6, 24, 210, 247
Nola, 245
Norba, 137, 142, 145, 200, 205

object agency, 211
olive cultivation, 171
Orvieto, 31
Oscans, 230
Ostia, 180

P. Cornelius Scapula, sarcophagus of, 219
P. Cornelius Sulla
Paestum, 202, 241, 245
    Andriuolo necropolis, 241
    Spinazzo necropolis, 245
painting, 231
Palatine, 177
periodization, 2, 136, 210, 256
Perusia, 33
Pietrabbondante, 181, 240
pig consumption, 185
pignoriscapio, 45
Plautus, 45
Pliny the Elder, 220
Po Valley, 3, 183
Podere Tartuchino, 178
Polybius, 3, 255
polygonal masonry, 201, 205
Pompeii, 177
Pontine, 11
populus, 258
Poseidonia. *See* Paestum
Praeneste, 32, 53, 105, 201, 205
Privernum, 32, 148
proletarii, 67
property, 259
Puglia, 178
Pyrgi, 106
Pyrrhus, 65, 209

Q. Caecilius Metellus, 226

ramo secco, 105
Reate, 148, 151
Regium, 75

Roman families
    Aemilii, 26, 30
    Atilii, 32
    Caecilii, 32
    Caedicii, 32
    Claudii, 29
    Cornelii, 26, 30
    Coruncanii, 32
    Fabii, 26, 30, 43
    Fabrici, 32
    Furii, 32
    gens Fabia, 235
    gens Mamilia, 31
    gens Sextia, 32
    Licinii, 31, 32
    Mamilii, 31
    Ogulnii, 32, 33
    Plautii, 32
    Postumii, 29
    Sulpicii, 26, 29
    Valerii, 26, 29, 43
    Volumnii, 32
Romanization, 13, 199
Rome
    suburbium, 136
Rome, city of, 13
    Ara Maxima, 228
    Aventine, 195, 213
    Campus Martius, 196, 213
    Circus Flaminius, 228
    Circus Maximus, 215
    Comitium, 196, 214
    Curia Hostilia, 214
    Forum, 213, 221
    Forum Boarium, 213
    Forum of Caesar, 224
    Graecostasis, 228
    Lapis Niger monument, 228
    Palatine, 195
    Pompey's Theater, 223
    Quirinal, 220
    Republican walls, 194
    Rostra, 215
    tabernae, 215
    temple building, 197, 215
    Temple of Apollo Medicus, 220
    Temple of Castor, 219
    Temple of Hercules Custos, 228
    Temple of Hercules Victor, 226
    Temple of Jupiter Optimus Maximus, 213, 227
    Temple of Jupiter Stator, 226
    Temple of Magna Mater, 219

Rome, city of (Cont.)
    Temple of Mars *in circo*, 226
    Temple of Portunus, 219
    Temple of Salus, 235, 242
    Temple of Saturn, 220
    Temple of Tellus, 193
    Temple of Victory, 216
    Tiber Island, 220
    Tomb of the Scipios, 220, 244
    Villa Publica, 214
Rome–Carthage Treaties, 209
Romulus and Remus, 33

Samnite Wars, 221, 235, 242
Samnium, 77
Santa Marinella, 126
Sardinia, 61
Satricum, 61, 144
Second Samnite War, 215
Servius Tullius, king, 228
Setia, 61, 145
Sicily, 111
Signia, 200, 201, 205
    Temple of Juno Moneta, 201
Sinuessa, 151
slave, 146
slavery, 8, 162
    Early Roman, 80
    in the Sudan, 88
    in the Twelve Tables, 81
    Saharan, 87
    slaves, 80
    Syracusan, 84
    war captives, 82, 97
società gentilizia, 25
Sokoto Caliphate, 9, 90
stipendium, 8, 38, 65, 71, 104,
    254
stock ranching, 182
Struggle of the Orders, 1, 24, 34, 132,
    193
suburbium, 195
Sudan, 88
Sulla. *See* P. Cornelius Sulla
survey archaeology, 134

Sutrium, 61
Syracuse, 84, 193, 209

Tarentum, 33
Tarquinia
    Tomb of the Shields, 247
Tarracina, 151
taxation, 38
taxes, 8
territory, Roman, 75
Third Samnite War, 81
Tiber Valley, 137
Tiberius Coruncanius, 35
Tibur, 199, 205
Timaeus, 230
Tomb of the Diver, 241
Transpadane Gaul, 184
tribuni aerarii, 38, 44, 254
    number of, 49
tributum, 8, 38, 39, 66, 104, 160, 254
Tullus Hostilius, king, 228
Tusculum, 31, 35, 202
Twelve Tables, 4, 103, 210, 257

urbanism
    terracing, 205
    urban planning, 12, 204
    urban sanctuaries, 201
    urban theory, 212
    zoning, 201

Valerius Antias, 234
Varro, 167, 221
Veii, 3, 81, 137, 142
Velitrae, 61
Via Appia, 151, 194, 201, 205, 220, 221, 222
Via Praenestina, 201, 222
Vicarello, 106
villas, 143, 162
Vitellia, 61
Vitruvius, 196, 213, 229
Volsinii, 193, *See* Orvieto

wine, 171
writing, 20

For EU product safety concerns, contact us at Calle de José Abascal, 56–1°, 28003 Madrid, Spain or eugpsr@cambridge.org.

www.ingramcontent.com/pod-product-compliance
Ingram Content Group UK Ltd.
Pitfield, Milton Keynes, MK11 3LW, UK
UKHW050108230326
469255UK00017B/244